The
Superpyramid
Eating Program

The
Superpyramid
Eating Program

INTRODUCING
THE REVOLUTIONARY
FIVE NEW FOOD GROUPS

▲

Dr. Gene Spiller

WITH RECIPES BY
Deborah Madison

▲

TIMES 𝕋 BOOKS

RANDOM HOUSE

Grateful acknowledgment is made to the following for permission to reprint previously published material:

   Gala Books Limited London: Excerpt from *The Sensual Body* by Lucy Liddell. Reprinted by permission.

   HRS Press, Inc.: Excerpt from *The Barm Bakers' Book* by Monica Spiller. Reprinted by permission of the author and the publisher, HRS Press, Inc.

   E. J. Kahn, Jr. and Roberta Pryor, Inc.: Excerpt from *The Staffs of Life* by E. J. Kahn, Jr., published by Little, Brown & Co. Copyright © 1985 by E. J. Kahn, Jr. Originally appeared in *The New Yorker*. Reprinted by permission of E. J. Kahn, Jr., and Roberta Pryor, Inc.

   National Academy Press: Excerpt from *Diet, Nutrition, and Cancer*, published by National Academy Press, Washington, D.C., 1982. Reprinted by permission.

   Alfred A. Knopf, Inc.: Excerpt from *Pomp and Sustenance* by Mary Jane Simeti. Copyright © 1989 by Mary Jane Simeti. Reprinted by permission of Alfred A. Knopf, Inc.

   W. W. Norton & Company: Excerpts from *The Last Puff* by John Farquhar, M.D., and Gene A. Spiller, Ph.D. Copyright © 1990 by John W. Farquhar and Gene A. Spiller. Reprinted by permission of the publisher, W. W. Norton & Company and the authors.

   St. Martin's Press, Inc.: Excerpt from *The Book of Coffee and Tea* by Joel Shapiro. Copyright © 1975 by Joel Shapiro. Reprinted by special permission of St. Martin's Press, Inc.

LIBRARY OF CONGRESS CATALOGING-IN-PUBLICATION DATA

Spiller, Gene A.
   The superpyramid program: introducing the revolutionary
five new food groups / Gene Spiller.
      p.   cm.
   ISBN 0-8129-2056-2
   1. Nutrition.   2. Diet.   3. High-fiber diet—Recipes.   4. Low-fat
diet—Recipes.   I. Title.
RA784.S657   1993
613.2—dc20   92-50497

Manufactured in the United States of America

9 8 7 6 5 4 3 2

First Edition

To Dr. Wenche Frølich of Oslo, Norway, who since 1984 —when this book and program were first conceived— has made invaluable contributions to various Superpyramid concepts and writings. This book has its roots in my work with Wenche. And to my wife, Monica, whose love and studies of ancient foods have deepened my understanding of the fascinating interactions of food and health throughout the ages.

Foreword

There is a strange notion that seems to be hovering over all of us, the notion that fitness, good health, and disease prevention equal asceticism, deprivation, and lack of joy of living. People want to avoid heart disease and cancer—who doesn't?—and want to look fit, but they feel that the price to pay is too high and awful words such as *sacrifice* come instantly to their minds. The truth is that none of this has to be true. We need to change some of our ways, but we can exchange one joy for an even greater joy. This new *joy of living* will be crowned by the deep-seated feeling that what we are doing is also good for us. If, after you have read this book, you can accept the fact that enjoyment of foods and life and maintenance of good health go together, you'll have taken a major step toward the prevention of chronic disease.

If you want to eat more healthfully, you need a method that is simple, free from complex calculations, free from extremes and impossible tasks. No one wants to make his or her kitchen into a laboratory or a hospital kitchen (what a grim thought!). Our kitchen should be a place full of flavors and aromas, our pantry and refrigerator full of real, fresh foods! And we should let our senses be satisfied and not deprived; we should feel the power of total well-being and fitness; we should experience new pleasures to replace old, less healthful ones. To make this possible, this book brings you the Superpyramid Program.

The Superpyramid—a concept that we began to develop in 1984 and later refined at the Health Research and Studies Center—is a program that can help everyone choose the best possible foods to help avoid some major chronic diseases, such as heart disease and some types of cancer, and to help prevent overweight and unfitness. As I've developed the Superpyramid concept, I've never forgotten that a *diet* based on ascetic, unenjoyable meals is not going to be kept up for very long by the majority of healthy people. The Superpyramid Program is not a diet in the sense the term *diet* is too often used today: It is based on the *enjoyment* of foods, of the wonderful, real foods of the land, the foods that our ancestors have enjoyed for centuries, foods that have been left as close to their natural, wonderfully flavorful taste and nutritional value as possible to please us, our hearts (literally!), and our minds.

Food pyramids became a topic of discussions and controversies in the United States in early 1991 when the United States Department of Agriculture announced the release of a new food pyramid, only to withhold it amid a flurry of newspaper articles and debates on this sudden change of policy. After more research and a large investment—close to a million dollars—on the pyramid concept, in the second part of 1991 and early 1992, the USDA decided that the pyramid design is a great tool to teach people how to eat right. The value of food pyramids as teaching tools had already been recognized in Norway, Sweden, Australia, and other countries for some years. These pyramids had been part of our early research work in 1984–1985 when the Superpyramid was born. The Superpyramid is *not* the USDA pyramid, even though it shares some basic features, such as making grains the foundation of the diet. The Superpyramid goes far beyond the USDA pyramid and its food groups.

Like other food pyramids, the Superpyramid divides foods into various tiers that tell us which foods we should eat freely as the foundation of our meals and which we should limit. But the Superpyramid does not, as the USDA does, put beans and meats together or relegate all fats to the smallest tier. And on the first tier we have true whole grains as well as some valuable protein foods such as beans, nonfat yogurts, and egg whites. These food groups or tiers are unique to the Superpyramid. Another example of a difference from *classical* food groups: In the Superpyramid, some foods, such as milk products, are found on different tiers to suggest that you may eat more freely those that are low in fat, while you should be more careful with others that you'll find on higher tiers. In other pyramids or food groups all dairy products are usually grouped together.

While saying all this, I do believe that the USDA pyramid is a great idea and a major step in the right direction. But the Superpyramid dares to go further, with more emphasis on whole unrefined foods, yogurts, beans, and truly fresh vegetables and fruits and even less emphasis on meats, high-fat dairy foods, and related products.

The joy of real food requires a closer contact with the foods of the land. We have gone too far in making fast foods, food substitutes, and prepared, prepackaged meals a *major* part of our daily life. These foods have an important place in the modern world for a change, in an emergency, when in a hurry, or—for some of these foods—in the treatment of disease. But if they become part of our daily routine day after day we can lose touch with fresh foods and their preparation so crucial in helping us develop the awareness of what food is and is not. We must find time to prepare our own foods at least a few times a week and limit the use of the prepared, precooked, ready-to-eat or fast foods that have too often moved from their proper occasional place in our daily life to a daily routine. In the Superpyramid you'll find only real foods as close to their natural state as possible. *This is a necessity for total pleasure.* Nothing can replace extra-virgin olive oil and Parmesan cheese on a plate of freshly cooked rice, pasta, or other grain or a good, freshly made oil-and-vinegar dressing on a salad of dark, flavorful greens and red tomatoes or the aroma of fresh sprigs of sage and oregano.

Needless to say, no miracles are possible: Each of us has a body with a lot of inherited strengths and weaknesses, which has been fed foods out of our control when we were very young, and has grown accustomed to other ways. But no matter where you are now, the Superpyramid Program should help you to make some major steps toward better health.

But food alone is not enough in our search for health, fitness, and disease prevention: Total health is impossible without adequate physical activity. And we must avoid as much as possible toxic substances, environmental pollutants, and tobacco smoke. Changing the foods you eat is but one part of more healthful living.

Show this book to your doctor; it's important to check with your doctor before beginning this or any other eating program. If you have a chronic disease, you may need to follow a very restricted diet, and the Superpyramid plan may not be right for you. I hope this book will help you create a stronger partnership with your doctor as you work together toward better health.

I've tried to relate stories of health and disease in a dramatic and creative way without ever compromising scientific truth. I've used anecdotes to brighten hard medical or nutritional facts as often as possible. I've limited scientific jargon to a very few occasions. Stories from around the world inspire ways that are new for us but are old for other populations. You can read this book like a detective story in which many of the mysteries of health and disease are solved.

To good food and good health!

Acknowledgments

A book such as this is the result of many years—1984–1992—of interactions with so many people that acknowledging them all is an impossible task. In my dedication I have already acknowledged Dr. Wenche Frølich of Oslo, Norway.

The studies and work of my wife, Monica, on ancient breads and whole-grain products have made possible the Superpyramid Bakery recipes. I am grateful to her for letting us use material from her *The Barm Bakers' Book* and her U.S. patents covering the commercial preparation of leavening barms.

Deborah Madison of Santa Fe, New Mexico, the founding chef of Greens at Fort Mason, the acclaimed vegetarian restaurant in San Francisco, developed and wrote many of the great recipes in the Superpyramid Kitchen. Her comments on many key ingredients will be invaluable to everyone preparing food the Superpyramid way. She is the inspiring author of two best-selling cookbooks: the award-winning *The Greens Cookbook* (New York: Bantam, 1986) and *The Savory Way* (New York: Bantam, 1990)—voted best cookbook of the year by The International Association of Culinary Professionals. Deborah's experience in Italy and other Mediterranean countries makes her contribution full of the great flavors and aromas of the cooking of these countries. Her recipes make the Superpyramid come to life for the most sophisticated cook as well as for anyone who wants to prepare a simple but savory meal.

Jody Main of Palo Alto, California, has added many recipes from Asia and other parts of the world to the Superpyramid Kitchen. She has contributed to other cookbooks, is a food consultant, and caters to high-technology companies in Silicon Valley that are looking for better and healthier foods. She divides her time between gardening and recipe development and is now working on a new cookbook.

Rowena Hubbard of Food Resources International in Sacramento, California, has brought to the Superpyramid Kitchen her expertise in recipes using nuts in sophisticated ways. She is the author of *International Dining with Spice Island, The Thatched Kitchen,* and *Hawaiian Kids Cook Book* and co-author of *California Cooks.* She has been a contributing editor to *Great Meals in Minutes,* from the Time-Life Books series, and others. She combines her background as a registered dietitian with her cooking talents to develop healthy recipes.

Hazel Gibson of Los Altos, California, has worked with me since 1985 —since the very first Superpyramid was drawn—to create all the artwork that is so essential to bringing a book to life. She has drawn many Superpyramids since that very first one as the concept evolved and was refined in the past seven years. Her talent and experience as an artist who has done both purely creative paintings of foods as well as graphic art have brought a fine creative touch to this book.

Margaret Denny has been a valuable editorial assistant for this final version of the Superpyramid Program, and Rebecca Carr has used her word-processing skills to make my work easier at crucial stages of manuscript development. Gail Minier and Cathy McGovern of Gibson Studios in Mountain View, California, have helped to polish many charts and graphics.

Some books deserve a special acknowledgment as an endless source of ideas and inspiration: *The Mediterranean Diets in Health and Disease,* with its many authors, Deborah Madison's *The Savory Way,* Kahn's *The Staff of Life,* Keys's *Seven Countries,* Simeti's *Pomp and Sustenance,* Tannahill's *Food in History,* Visser's *Much Depends On Dinner,* Cooper's *Health and Fitness Excellence,* and Lidell's *The Sensual Body.* These books, which make great reading for anyone interested in foods and its history or in exercise, are listed in the References (page 469). Not less important to me has been the influence of the many creative writers and editors I have been fortunate enough to work with over many years. Suggestions by Jean Carper and Raphael Sagalyn, both of Washington, D.C., were extremely helpful in the final stages of the publication process.

Of the many scientists, researchers, and physicians over the years who have helped me to understand what our way of life can do to prevent many diseases and often reverse them, I would like to acknowledge

David Jenkins, M.D., of the University of Toronto, John W. Farquhar, M.D., of the Stanford University Center for Disease Prevention, Gabriele Riccardi, M.D., of the University of Naples, Italy, and Ottavio Bosello, M.D., of the University of Verona.

And finally, a special place in my mind belongs to Elizabeth Rapoport of Times Books. Her suggestion that a section with recipes be added led to the Superpyramid Kitchen and Bakery, now a key part of this book. Other suggestions by Elizabeth helped me to write the final manuscript. Elizabeth instantly became a friend whom I sensed I could trust. And she became a major factor at Times Books in making the Superpyramid a major project. After working with her for six months I have grown to appreciate her talents and her editor's skills and intuition. This book as it is now would not have been possible without her.

Contents

In Search
of
Health and Fitness

Cherish the simple, ancient foods of the land; savor their fragrance; enjoy the flavor and aroma of herbs and spices; learn to appreciate real, whole foods as part of a joyful meal; make the path to better health satisfying and pleasant.

▲

CHAPTER

.1.

The Path to
Health and Fitness

et's look at the path to better health and fitness, disease prevention, and weight control. Must it be an arduous path, surrounded by stern and overrestrictive diets and a life deprived of
joy and pleasure? Or can it be a path that meanders through a pleasant
countryside, surrounded by the kinds of foods that certain people have
enjoyed for centuries, *real* foods full of flavor and beauty? Can you
follow the path to health and prevention of chronic disease and yet enjoy
your meals more than ever?

> *Such a path does indeed exist, and if you follow us we hope you'll find how
> joyful it can be.*

After reading this book, you should no longer be confused by conflict-
ing reports on what you should or shouldn't eat, and you'll no longer
need to search for new diet books or articles to see if you can avoid such
terrible things as heart disease or colon cancer without leading an ascetic
life. And you'll most likely discover that this healthful new way of life
can also help keep you from gaining weight and save you the continual
and costly search for new weight-loss diets.

Diseases of Western Societies

Somehow, in the past hundred years, people in affluent, industrialized Western societies strayed from the path to health and fitness. They became more sedentary and made some major changes in their eating patterns. For example, look at the food consumed in rural Wales in the 1870s and in the 1970s. The locals' consumption of animal fat rose from 25 to 42 percent of their energy intake, while their consumption of unsaturated fats from plants declined from 19 to 9 percent. Their carbohydrate intake from grains and potatoes declined from 60 to 30 percent, and their consumption of fiber went down from over two ounces per day to less than one ounce. A similar picture can be drawn for many other Western countries.

The dietary changes characteristic of the modern Western world seem to be linked with an increase in certain diseases, including some kinds of heart disease and cancer. In fact, Hugh Trowell and Dennis Burkitt, prominent British physicians who were medical missionaries in Uganda, were so struck by the lower incidence of such major chronic diseases among African natives, who ate diets low in animal fat and high in fiber, compared to the incidence among Europeans who ate typical Western diets, that they coined the term *Western diseases* to describe these illnesses.

Diseases and Obesity in the United States

More than 35 million people in the United States are obese, weighing 20 percent above their ideal weight, and many people have high blood cholesterol, a key indicator of heart trouble looming ahead. The higher the blood cholesterol in a population, the higher the risk of diseases of the coronary arteries, which bring blood to the heart muscle. In one study of 361,662 men, an increase in blood cholesterol from 200 to 300 was found to cause a fourfold increase in the risk of death from heart disease. And just as troublesome, the occurrence of colon cancer and other types of cancer, such as breast cancer, is dramatically higher in the United States than in less affluent countries.

Figure 1 shows U.S. death statistics for a typical year (1987). These deaths represent only a small portion of the tragic consequences of major chronic disease. Millions of Americans have battled heart disease or cancer and survived but must now endure very restricted lives loaded with unpleasant drugs and constrained by extremely limited food choices. Add to this group the large number of people who have adult-type diabetes and those who have aged prematurely, losing their fitness and healthy appearance far too early. This is the depressing picture of

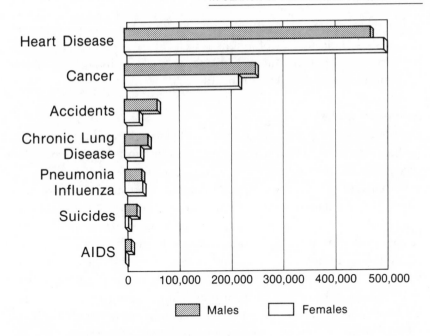

FIGURE 1. Death Statistics in the U.S. in 1987

the state of health and fitness in the U.S. and in many other Western industrialized societies.

Unfortunately, this sad picture is no longer confined to Western society. Less developed peasant societies whose traditional life-styles were quite different from those of the West used to have a lower incidence of many "Western diseases." But as these societies are increasingly influenced by Western technology, they are also slowly changing their long-standing habits of eating and living—often with tragic results, including increasing occurrence of heart disease and certain cancers.

These are some of the reasons that the Surgeon General of the United States and the National Research Council have issued major reports on diet and health, recommending changes in the American diet to prevent disease. Similarly, many governments and health organizations in countries around the world have also issued similar *dietary guidelines*.

A Common Cause

What's so fascinating for researchers on the causes of disease is that there is a common denominator in the patterns of eating that contributes to apparently unrelated chronic diseases such as heart disease and major types of cancer. And the ways of eating that help prevent these diseases also help to control weight as well. These common factors make life easier for all of us who want to choose the right foods for a lifetime of total fitness, good looks, and health.

Living on a Diet

Despite the tremendous amount of knowledge of health and disease that we have gathered in recent years, it seems that most people don't follow recommendations for better diets and ways of life. Why?

Perhaps it's because most people think that there are only two options: either a typical American diet, high in meats and saturated fats, or some restricted, ascetic, joyless way to eat. Or perhaps we think dieting means eating food substitutes that seldom rival the full flavor bounty of real, whole foods. In any case, most people don't follow guidelines to better health for long, unless they have already experienced a major crisis such as a heart attack. People often prefer taking a drug that lowers their cholesterol over sticking to a diet. They associate such diets with hospitals and really sick people, with cures rather than prevention.

People also don't stick to diets because they perceive them as too complicated, loaded with charts and hard-to-remember rules. No one wants to believe that we were meant to eat according to complex charts or that food must be horribly deprived of its most flavorful ingredients to be healthful.

Let's look into the lives of four quite different people. One, a man of fifty-five, is dieting for his life. Another, a young thirty-five-year-old woman, is dieting for her looks and for weight loss. And a young couple are trying to eat the ultimate diet for disease prevention.

For Don, diet became a matter of life and death. He had high blood cholesterol, the result of the typical American diet he'd eaten for most of his life, and was a veteran smoker. I interviewed him while writing a book about ex-smokers, *The Last Puff*. On a very warm Fourth of July, he began to feel terribly hot and tired. A little later that day he had some chest pain. By the late afternoon the pain had become so intense that his wife took him to the emergency clinic, where doctors diagnosed a heart attack.

Don was sent to a large hospital's intensive care unit, where emergency treatment saved his life. Later, a photograph of his coronary arteries (the vessels that bring blood to the heart) revealed partial blockage in two arteries, and Don had to have bypass surgery. Don had probably brought this upon himself with his smoking, fairly sedentary

life, and diet high in animal fats and low in whole grains, beans, vegetables, and fruits.

The cardiologists told him that the surgery wouldn't do him any good
in the long term if he went back to his old habits. Nearness to death is a
profound experience that often causes a person to make drastic changes.
Don stopped smoking and changed his diet. The high-fat beef he used
to love is gone; he is on an extremely restricted and not very appealing
diet. *It would have been much better if a more pleasant preventive diet had been
part of his previous way of life.* But Don didn't know that there was such a
thing as a great meal that wasn't loaded with the foods high in animal
fat that he used to like.

Joanne has a different problem. At thirty-five she is about twenty
pounds overweight and feels unfit, unhealthy, and unglamorous. Even
worse, her doctor just told her that her blood cholesterol is high—over
240—and that she should bring it down with proper diet and weight
loss. Joanne has gone on diets to lose weight so many times that she can
hardly remember them all. Often she was delighted with the results.
Unfortunately, each time she returned to her regular diet for a few
weeks, she not only gained her weight back but actually weighed a little
more than before she went on the diet.

Joanne now feels that dieting is hopeless and that she will just have to
put up with her excess weight for the rest of her life. Thoroughly dis-
couraged, she stopped at the supermarket on the way home from her
physical exam. Soon her basket was full of all kinds of foods, including
many she hadn't bought in years, foods that she knew weren't good for
her weight or her blood cholesterol. "No more diets for me," she
thought. "I might just as well enjoy my food the way I used to."

She knew the doctor was right, but she was convinced that nothing
worked for her: not the programs she'd read about in books and articles;
not the diet drinks she'd purchased at the supermarket and drugstore.

Joanne was a victim of what has become known as *yo-yo dieting*. Yo-yo
dieters go on a low-calorie diet for a few weeks, lose some weight, go
back to their old eating patterns, and gain back the weight they lost—
and even more. Many people repeat this cycle every few months, with
depressing results.

Medical scientists agree that what happened to Joanne is not unusual.
One possible explanation is that, by dieting, Joanne had unwittingly
trained her body to be more and more efficient at using the calories
from foods. This is a deep-rooted response built into our bodies by
nature to protect us from starvation. In times of famine in past centu-

ries, and today in developing countries, it has helped mankind survive on limited food intake.

Not every scientist accepts this theory. Some would say that Joanne was probably compensating for her reduced caloric intake by almost unconsciously decreasing her physical activity and saving calories that way. Or she might have been less careful in subsequent dieting periods, and when she returned to her normal menu, she might have unknowingly been making up for the calories she had deprived herself of for so many weeks. Whatever the reason—probably all of them contributed to the problem—the final results were very disheartening.

Researchers have found that yo-yo dieting can even have tragic consequences. A recent study, published in the prestigious New England Journal of Medicine *by Dr. Lauren Lissner and her associates, has established that people who repeatedly lose and gain weight are at greater risk for heart disease than people who never lost their excess weight.*

Unlike Don or Joanne, Janet and Ray were determined to change their habits before becoming heart-disease statistics. They were going to look after their health and weight the right way. Ray's physical motivated them to make a change: his cholesterol was in the 240 range. Both college graduates and career people in their thirties, they felt the time was right. They followed the advice of Ray's doctor on cutting down on this and that, bought a good book of recipes, and religiously followed a cholesterol-lowering diet for a few weeks.

Then, one Sunday morning, the book with recipes low in this and that was tossed into the fireplace and quickly turned into ashes. The book burning was a symbol of Janet and Ray's rebellion: They went to the nearest coffee shop for a high-fat, high-cholesterol brunch of sausage, white bread, eggs fried in butter, and potatoes fried in lard.

Deprivation or Enjoyment?

The Latin word *dieta*—the source for our word *diet*—meant primarily a way of living prescribed for medical reasons. A secondary Latin meaning for this ancient term was probably "way of eating" in general, whether good or bad. And even though modern dictionaries define *diet* as either "a prescription" or "a way of eating," most think of a diet as a restrictive regimen for weight loss or medical reasons. Today, when people say, "I am on a diet," they mean, "I am following with great effort a prescription for health or weight loss." There is little joy in that approach.

Consider the common problem Don, Joanne, Janet, and Ray faced. Diet regimens are too restricted, too remote from the joy of eating that is so deeply rooted in all of us. The foods in most of these diets have lost the delicate, natural flavors of traditional dishes people have loved for centuries.

It's difficult to modify the typical North American diet, based on meat and high in animal products, so that it is both healthful and satisfying. But there is an answer: the Superpyramid Program.

I have chosen not to use the word *diet* in relation to the Superpyramid Program. I want to avoid any implications of unpleasant restrictions. The Superpyramid Program relies on the traditional, regional, or ethnic dishes and cuisines found in certain parts of the world. Some of these dishes include the same foods that modern science has identified as the best to help prevent heart disease and other chronic disorders. These foods have withstood the test of time and are enjoyed by most people and are often served in sophisticated restaurants. They are the foods of southern Italy and the Middle East, sometimes called Mediterranean foods, and the foods of the Orient and of Latin America. People eating the local foods in these regions suffer much less from certain chronic diseases than those in industrialized Western societies.

The most recent findings about the benefits of certain foods, from unrefined whole-grain breads to fresh vegetables, from beans to olive oil, from yogurt to garlic, confirm the value of such time-tested diets.

Traditional menus from these regions have the proper balance required for good nutrition—large amounts of grains such as breads, pasta, and rice together with beans, vegetables, fruit, and the "good" fats, such as those found in olive oil and nuts and seeds. Meat or poultry is used only occasionally. Fish replaces meat quite often.

Returning to the Goodness and Taste of Real Foods

There is a tremendous array of beautiful, healthful food out there in our fields and orchards. These foods from plants, in their unrefined forms, are full of nutrients, protective factors, and, just as important, great taste. These are the *whole plant foods* that are the key to the Superpyramid Program. They are the foods that have kept humans alive for millennia. Add to these plant foods selected low-fat milk products and properly prepared eggs (without the yolk) and you'll have an admirable balance of taste and good nutrition.

Using these foods properly, you can create delicious meals that never taste restricted or prescribed, and you can bring the joy of foods back to your dinner table.

*S*uccessful prevention of chronic disease has to be based in part on the enjoyment of satisfying, flavorful whole foods. The joy of eating must not be defined by complex charts. We must not eat by numbers. A rigid, unyielding diet may help us treat disease, but most of us won't be able to stick with it for a lifetime.

The Superpyramid Program should never be misconstrued as a medical prescription for the treatment of disease, but rather seen as a plan to assist you as much as possible in preventing some of the major chronic diseases and in controlling weight.

*I*f after reading this book you tell your friends, "I am on the Superpyramid Diet," you won't have grasped the very essence of this beautiful plan. Say: "I am eating the Superpyramid way," or, "I am on the Superpyramid Program, and I never enjoyed food so much and felt so healthy!" There is no Superpyramid diet!

The Last Calorie

Another term that has degenerated in general usage is *calorie*. Scientifically, it is simply the unit by which we measure the energy contained in foods—the energy we require to sustain ourselves. We use calories to keep our hearts beating and our limbs moving. But the true meaning of the word has been overshadowed by the horrible thought that calories are things to be avoided, since they put weight on us.

We're going to forget the term *calorie* in this book. Instead, we'll think of foods as a source of much-needed energy. We certainly can take in energy in excess—as many people no doubt know—but energy is a basic necessity for life. In the Superpyramid Program we'll find another way to balance our food choices and the amount we eat without worrying about counting calories.

The Superpyramid Program

*A*bove all, the Superpyramid is a simple program. Its simplicity is its strength.

The Superpyramid Program uses the knowledge acquired from studying the foods used in regions around the world where there is a low occurrence of some of the major Western chronic diseases. It combines this knowledge of proven traditional foods with the discoveries of modern science, emphasizing the concept of *whole plant foods*. Because the food is truly enjoyable, the Superpyramid Program can succeed where other plans fail. Free from any artificial or single miracle food (though each food on the Superpyramid is in a way a miracle food, if used properly), this program will help you control your blood cholesterol and body weight and gives you the best possible food choices to build as much defense as possible against heart disease, some kinds of cancer, bone degeneration, and adult-type diabetes.

A New Way to Visualize the Foods You Eat

The Superpyramid Program uses a simple visual aid to help you make the right food choices. The Superpyramid makes it easy for you to select the foods that are most healthful and satisfying and to remember instantly which foods you can eat freely and which you should limit, and to what degree.

> *All this is accomplished by visualizing the five easy-to-remember tiers of the Superpyramid. You can choose a Superpyramid with fish and some poultry and meat or a vegetarian Superpyramid without any of these foods.*

Developing New Attitudes

Adopting a new way of eating will succeed only if, without hesitation, without wariness, we wholeheartedly love our way of eating. The ultimate measure of any eating plan's success is your ability to sit at the table and feel truly attracted to the right foods without craving less healthful foods. This process, unlike so many diet programs, should not be a series of conscious, unpleasant denials; rather, it must be sincere, impulsive, and joyful. It should feel as though there were absolutely no other way to eat. *This book will introduce you to just such foods and meals.*

But, no matter how good this new way of eating is, you must allow some time for adjustment. It may take you a few weeks, two or three months, or even longer, depending on how similar your present diet is to the Superpyramid Program. After this period of adaptation, you'll return home from your shopping trip to your food store or farmers' market with a bag full of beautiful, simple foods, untempered by manipulations that alter their flavor or nutritional bounty. You'll wonder how you ever could have bought anything but Superpyramid foods.

THE SUPERPYRAMID

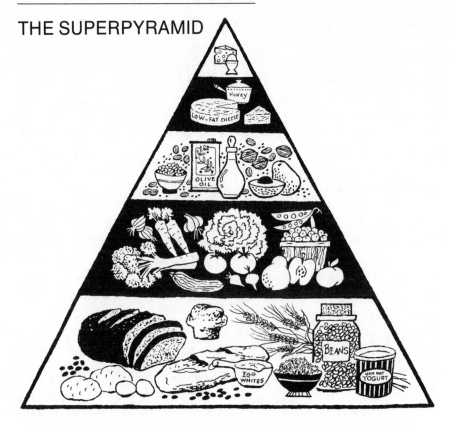

Learning the Superpyramid Program

In the first part of this book you'll learn which foods are most healthful and why. This is crucial before plunging into specific food choices or recipes, because you need to understand both the key relationships between disease and health and the basic principles of the Superpyramid structure.

You'll see that no matter how great a certain food may be, it must be used as but one part of a carefully planned food pattern to be most effective in helping prevent major chronic diseases and helping you to keep fit.

In part 2, "Exploring the Five Tiers of the Superpyramid," I'll focus in detail on the foods on each tier.

In part 3, "Beyond the Superpyramid," I'll cover flavorings such as herbs, salt, and vinegar and beverages such as water, wine, coffee, and tea. I'll explore the importance of the joy and beauty of real foods and then go beyond food, introducing the Exercise Pyramid and discussing physical activity, stress, and related topics, closing with some suggestions on how to protect yourself from toxic substances and contaminants in the environment.

Parts 4 and 5 are "The Superpyramid Kitchen" and "The Superpyramid Bakery," with exciting recipes and menus along with suggestions on how to adapt other cookbooks' recipes to the Superpyramid. All these recipes produce dishes that are as flavorful as anything you may decide to eliminate from your current meals.

Not Even the Superpyramid Is All-powerful

The condition of your health and body today is the sum of many factors, including your inherited genes, what happened in your mother's womb before you were born, the food you were fed as a child, possible toxic substances in your environment (such as tobacco smoke and unwanted chemicals in the water supply), and the amount and type of exercise you did or didn't do before reading this book. Previous injuries, surgery, or drug use can also have an effect for years to come.

The Superpyramid is a great plan for anyone now in good health who wants to do his or her best to try to prevent certain diseases and lead a healthy life. But the results will depend upon how the various factors in your background may have already affected you.

Before beginning this or any other food plan, check with your doctor. This is especially important if you suffer from a chronic disease, such as digestive diseases or allergies to certain foods. Your doctor can help you determine whether you need to modify the Superpyramid food choices for your particular situation. Let this book be an important step in improving your communication with your doctor, so you can both work together to keep you healthy and fit.

▲ KEY IDEAS

▲ The dietary changes characteristic of the Western world are linked with an increase in heart disease and certain cancers.

▲ More than a quarter of the U.S. population is seriously overweight.

▲ Too many people in affluent societies have high blood cholesterol.

▲ The higher the blood cholesterol in a population, the higher the risk of diseases of the coronary arteries of the heart.

▲ The incidence of colon cancer and other types of cancer is dramatically higher in the United States than in less affluent countries.

▲ As Western technology penetrates less developed peasant societies, there is an increase of typical Western diseases in those societies.

▲ There is a common denominator in the patterns of eating that contributes to chronic diseases such as heart disease and colon cancer.

▲ Yo-yo dieting can have serious adverse health consequences.

▲ People eating the local foods in certain regions—such as the Mediterranean—suffer much less from certain chronic diseases than people in industrialized Western societies.

▲ Meat or poultry is used only occasionally in many of the regions that boast low rates of heart disease and colon cancer.

▲ The Superpyramid uses a simple visual aid to help you learn healthful, time-proven eating patterns.

▲ The Superpyramid is a joyful, pleasant way of eating based on real, traditional foods, primarily whole foods from plants.

▲ 2 ▲

The Connection Between Food and Disease

THE AMAZING GEOGRAPHY OF HEART DISEASE AND CANCER

Studying the geography of health and disease is one of the best ways to learn how food and health are related. By investigating the patterns of major chronic diseases in various regions of the world, medical researchers can relate their high or low incidence to the traditional foods of the region.

Researchers can then test these observations in a controlled clinical setting to see if the biochemical and physiological changes that result from certain dietary modifications confirm the geographical evidence. This kind of controlled experiment proves or disproves the links between diet and health or disease and helps us pinpoint the foods that are beneficial or harmful.

Medical Detectives on the Track of Killers
Researchers who investigate world disease patterns are really medical detectives. And if you think that detectives like Sherlock Holmes, Miss Marple, or Jessica Fletcher have a lot of fun in finding the guilty person, just wait and see the kind of challenge it can be to find out why the peasants in Naples, in the south of Italy, have less heart disease than their counterparts in the industrial, affluent north of that country or the inhabitants of the Karelian region in Finland. And let's be unyielding: these suspects must be caught and eliminated. If you think of heart

disease and colon cancer as killers, it makes sense that we consider ourselves medical detectives on the track of vicious criminals.

There was a time, not too many years ago, when such medical detectives, known as epidemiologists, were mainly concerned with tracking
down the causes of infectious diseases. Often, with careful investigation,
epidemiologists might discover the culprit—perhaps a bad well supplying contaminated water to a neighborhood and causing cholera, or food
served in a particular restaurant the weekend before an outbreak of
salmonella poisoning.

Now that heart disease and cancer are so widespread in the industrialized Western world, more and more of these medical detectives have
turned their attention to tracking down these chronic killers.

The Tools of the Medical Detective

What tools do we need and what leads can we can follow in our detective
work? We need to do four things. First of all, we need to investigate
populations that have a very low occurrence of a given chronic disease,
say heart disease or colon cancer. Second, we need to study populations
with a high occurrence of the same disease and consider carefully the
differences in food choice and life-style between the two groups. Third,
to confirm that what we have found is not due to some inherited factor
in the people we have studied, we need to monitor individuals who move
from regions of low frequency of that disease to areas of high frequency
and see what happens as they change their life-styles and eating habits.
Are more of them falling prey to the disease as they change their way of
living? Finally, we need to watch what happens when habits change not
because people have immigrated to another country but because the
ways of other countries have infiltrated their society, a common happening these days as foods and machinery from affluent countries reach less
developed peasant populations.

HEART DISEASE

As heart disease is our number-one killer, let's investigate it first. Let's
look at its occurrence in four countries with different food patterns
(figure 2).

Now let's single out one type of heart disease that is a much-feared
major killer: *coronary heart disease,* or CHD, which affects the arteries that
supply blood to the heart. CHD has been researched very extensively
and is now quite well understood. It is the kind of heart disease caused

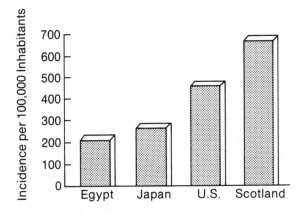

FIGURE 2. The Geography of Heart Disease

by abnormal levels of blood cholesterol, a topic frequently covered in the media.

In 1980, Dr. Ancel Keys published *Seven Countries*, one of the great books on the connection between disease and life-style. Full of complex statistical analyses, this highly scientific book brings to light the tremendous differences among various countries in the number of deaths caused by diseases of the coronary arteries. Let's see how many people die of coronary heart disease in various countries for each one hundred white men dying of this disease in the U.S.

The numbers are shocking. Three people in Crete died of this disease during the study, while in the same period 100 died in the U.S. and 171

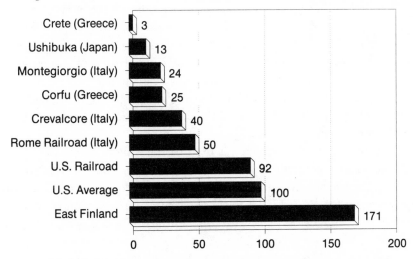

FIGURE 3. Some Heart Disease Statistics from the *Seven Countries* Study

in eastern Finland, just to pick a few numbers from the chart. Dr. Keys says in his book that "during the field work of this study it was not uncommon to see men [in Crete] of 80 to 100 years of age and more going off to work in the fields with a hoe."

Some general associations with the way people eat can be easily made from examining figures 2 and 3. The low consumption of animal fat and higher consumption of unrefined foods from plants in Crete, Egypt, and Japan relates well with the lower incidence of heart disease, and the higher consumption of animal food and saturated fat, and lower plant-food consumption in the U.S. (and even more so in Scotland and eastern Finland) with higher rates of heart disease. You don't need to be a sophisticated statistician to understand these two charts. Unfortunately, diets are changing in Crete and Japan as more Western-type, affluent habits take over, and the average level of blood cholesterol in those places is now rising.

From Naples to Northern Italy

These general associations need to be confirmed by controlled studies that focus on the typical pattern of eating in populations with high or low occurrence of coronary heart disease.

Two Italian physicians, Dr. Enrico Mancini and Dr. Gabriele Riccardi of the University of Naples School of Medicine, had been impressed by the healthy hearts of the peasants of the Naples region compared to the more affluent Neapolitans or the people from the affluent industrial regions of northern Italy.

The Neapolitan peasants shop for their foods in street markets where farmers and fishermen come early in the day to sell their products. The staples purchased in these street stands—and in some of the shops that open their doors onto the same streets in the old parts of Naples—are vegetables, fruits, breads from durum wheat (a special type of hard wheat used to make pasta and semolina products) pasta, beans, and fish. Other farmers sell spices and herbs like oregano. An occasional shop sells some cheese, used in moderate amounts.

In this region virgin olive oil is used freely, while butter is practically unknown as a condiment. *No butter plate is on the dinner table.* No one would dream of buttering bread; they pour olive oil on bread or the pizza called *focaccia,* which is flavored with tomatoes, oregano, and olive oil. Fatty sausages on pizzas are for the tourists or the rich, with their heart disease and excess weight.

The result is that these peasants in Naples, Italy, who eat pasta made from durum wheat, breads, pizzas, beans, fresh vegetables, garlic, and

olive oil, with some fish and very little meat, seldom develop atherosclerosis or coronary artery disease, the clogging of the arteries that bring blood to the heart.

Mancini, Riccardi, and their associates considered all this and decided to test the health effects of this way of eating. They fed the original peasant diet to more affluent people who had high levels of blood cholesterol. Even though their diets still included a reasonable amount of fat in the form of good local olive oil, the people's high cholesterol levels dropped.

This result is confirmed by the well-known fact that northern Italians, who use larger amounts of animal fats in their food preparation and who consume high-fat pork, have more heart disease. Another connection between diet and disease emerged from some related studies: they revealed more cases of colon cancer in northern than in southern Italy.

The Verona Experiment

Ottavio Bosello, Luciano Cominacini, and their associates at the University of Verona School of Medicine fed subjects in the affluent and industrialized north a diet similar to the Neapolitan peasant diet, high in pasta and other high-carbohydrate plant foods and low in meats, butter, and high-fat cheeses. The main source of fat was olive oil. They lowered the blood cholesterol in this group of people, whose initial cholesterol levels were considered too high. To make sure the results weren't a coincidence, the researchers had these patients return to their original meat and butter diet; their blood cholesterol readings went right back to the high levels recorded at the beginning of the study.

The Karelia-Cilento Investigation

A major step was taken toward confirming the value of southern Mediterranean diets when Dr. Christian Ehnolm and his collaborators studied a group of volunteers in North Karelia, Finland. These volunteers replaced their typical diet high in saturated fat with a southern Mediterranean diet. They used the ancient golden oil of the Mediterranean—olive oil—instead of animal fats. What happened? Exactly what a good medical detective would have foreseen: their blood cholesterol dropped dramatically. When these people returned to their former diets, high in saturated animal fats, their blood cholesterol went back up to the original higher values.

The time was right for researchers in southern Italy to verify this experiment. At the Istituto Nazionale della Nutrizione in Rome, Dr. Anna Ferro-Luzzi and her associates carried out the opposite study in Cilento in southern Italy. Subjects on a typical southern Italian diet changed to a northern European diet and their blood cholesterol went up; when they returned to their native diet, their blood cholesterol returned to normal again.

Searching for Clues in Japan

The death rate from heart disease in Japan is about half that of the U.S., as shown in figure 2. And only a few of these deaths are from coronary heart disease. The diet in Japan is low in saturated animal fat and high in vegetables, grains, and bean products. Fish is much more popular than beef. Coronary heart disease was so rare in Japan that when a Japanese physician came to Canada in the early 1980s for more training in cardiology, he saw his first case of this disease. He was amazed at how many critical cases of coronary heart disease were brought to his Canadian hospital each day.

The Common Denominator

It's our job as medical detectives to search out the common characteristics of the types of food that help to prevent (or favor) the development of heart disease in the populations we have studied.

We find that there is a common denominator in the diets of these disparate populations. In fact, southern Italy, Japan, and all the other places with little coronary heart disease—too many to discuss in detail in this book—consume foods that are very similar. Grains (rice, pasta, or bread, for example), which are high in complex carbohydrates, are the primary source of energy. Most of the time beans are also an intrinsic part of the meal. The Neapolitan *pasta e fagioli*—"pasta and beans"—

has its counterpart in the Orient in rice and soybeans or products made from soybeans, such as tofu or tempeh. Vegetables and fruits are next on the list of foods highly prized by these populations. And, just as important, these diets are low in animal fat and in saturated fat. All this adds up to fewer diseases of the coronary arteries and of other arteries.

In Japan, the olive oil of southern Italy is replaced by the oil in soybeans, one of the few common beans that contain meaningful levels of unsaturated fats (see chapter 4). As good medical detectives, we should not overlook this last point. There is a moderate amount of good vegetable oil in the diets of some Mediterranean regions as well as the diet of Japan.

The Next Step: Following Migrations

Let's now follow the migration of people from a region of low frequency of coronary heart disease to one of high frequency. A good example is the migration of Japanese people from Japan to Hawaii and to the U.S. mainland. Studying these people can tell us whether the low occurrence of coronary heart disease in Japan is due to inherited ethnic characteristics or to diet, as most of these Japanese immigrants quickly modified their traditional way of eating to the American way.

Diet did make the difference, as it had for the Italians in the north and south of Italy. The rate of coronary heart disease for Japanese people living in Hawaii was found to be much higher than for Japanese in Japan; the Japanese people living on the U.S. mainland who ate a typical Western diet high in saturated fat and low in plant food had an even higher occurrence of heart disease than those living in Hawaii. In fact, it was no different from the average occurrence of this disease in North America.

When Western Foods Move In

And if we needed more proof, the frequency of coronary artery disease is rapidly increasing in Japan as a more Western diet, higher in meats and fats and lower in vegetables, grains, and beans, has become popular in Japanese cities. The same is true in China, where some Western foods are replacing the simple original Chinese dishes. And as you'd expect with the consumption of increased levels of animal fats, blood cholesterol is slowly rising in these countries.

A great example of this Westernization is found in the Republic of Seychelles, a group of islands in the Indian Ocean. Tourism has become a major industry there since 1971, when an international airport was opened. As Western dietary habits have slowly reached these islands, heart disease and blood cholesterol levels have increased. Dr. P. Bover and his associates found typical blood cholesterol levels hovering around the 208 level, still not as high as is typical in more affluent countries, but rising rapidly from the pretourism days. The old diet was based on rice and fish, while the new diet uses a lot of hydrogenated fats. The consumption of meat is increasing, with fatty fast-food lunches becoming popular.

Many hundreds of miles from the Seychelles live the Tarahumara Indians of Mexico. Their traditional foods are high in fiber, low in animal fats, and moderate in total fat. Martha McMurry and her associates at the Oregon Health Sciences University in Portland, to confirm that the natives' normally low blood cholesterol could be easily affected by diet, fed thirteen subjects a diet typical of affluent societies. The subjects' blood cholesterol increased by 31 percent. These cases of the Tarahumara and of the Seychelles villagers are typical: many other studies have confirmed the problems with the Westernization of diets.

Blood Cholesterol and Heart Disease in the World

Can we draw a simple conclusion from the geography of coronary heart disease in the world? Seldom have all the medical detectives from different countries agreed about causes and clues for a major chronic disease as they have in this case.

The first clue is the level of blood cholesterol. The median blood cholesterol level in a population corresponds well to the occurrence of coronary heart disease. Just compare the very low cholesterol levels in Beijing, China—men, 157, and women, 161—to the values in industrialized areas with much higher occurrence of cardiovascular disease: California (men, 203, women, 200), Scotland (men, 238, women, 246), and Finland, (238 for both men and women).

The second clue is that food plays a major role in raising or lowering blood cholesterol, and the basic principles are simple and universal. You can look at the typical diet of a population and practically guess their blood cholesterol.

Solid fats—fats that are hard at room temperature—usually raise blood cholesterol. These are most often saturated fats present in animal products or vegetable fats that have been processed (hydrogenated) to make them hard. Oils from seeds, nuts, and the pulp of some fruits such as olives or avocados are unsaturated, and when they replace saturated fats in the diet, they usually lower blood cholesterol. One of the few exceptions among plant foods is coconut oil, which is saturated (you'll find out much more about oils from plants in chapter 6). Beans, fibers

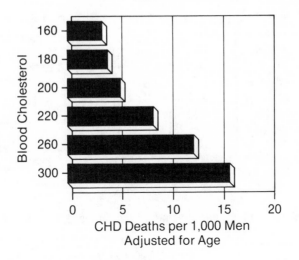

FIGURE 4. Blood Cholesterol and Mortality

from some grains, and other compounds in foods derived from plants also have a favorable effect on blood cholesterol.

When we look beyond the surface differences among the diets eaten by populations with little coronary heart disease, we find that their eating patterns are based on foods from plants. Their energy does not come from a large steak or piece of meat or fatty cheese; rather, such foods are used in small amounts for flavoring or variety and are usually of the low-fat type. Fish often replaces meats and poultry in these diets.

On the other hand, populations with high blood cholesterol and high rates of coronary heart disease obtain most of their energy from animal foods such as high-fat meats or high-fat milk products. Plant foods are not the main source of energy.

Figure 4 shows how blood cholesterol and deaths from heart disease are linked.

COLON AND OTHER MAJOR CANCERS
Major Cancers in Different Countries
If we set aside lung cancer—which we know is caused primarily by cigarette smoking or inhalation of other toxic substances—we'd find that many of the cancer killers in the U.S., especially colon and breast cancers, are related to diet. Figure 5 shows typical statistics for three major U.S. cancers.

Let's look at what happens in other countries. A chart prepared from data collected by the great British epidemiologist Sir Richard Doll (figure 6) confirms that people in affluent North American and Western

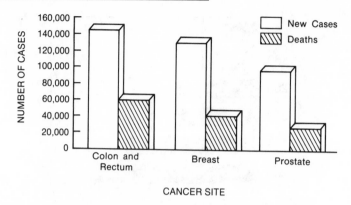

FIGURE 5. Colon, Breast, and Prostate Cancer in the U.S. (1987)

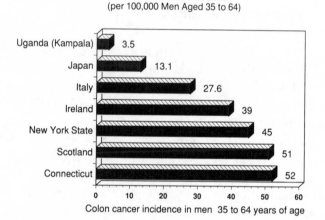

FIGURE 6. Geography of Colon Cancer

European societies, with their high-animal-fat diets and refined foods, have more colon cancer than people in countries where the diet includes much less fat and many more plant foods.

In 1983, Dr. Stephen Sidney and Dr. John Farquhar did some in-depth detective work that showed that when death from coronary heart disease is high in a country, so is death from colon cancer. When the death rate from one of these two killer diseases is low, the rate of the other one is low, too. As may be expected, countries where people eat large amounts of saturated fat, such as Denmark, Canada, Australia, Scotland, and the U.S., have higher rates of death for both diseases than such countries as Japan and Costa Rica.

For breast cancer in women, the difference among countries is also

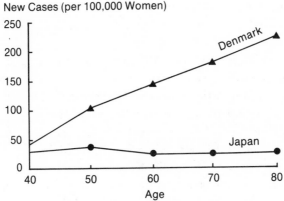

Source: Data from F. de Waard, *International Journal of Cancer*, 1969, vol. 4:577.

FIGURE 7. Breast Cancer in Denmark and Japan

impressive. Let's look at it from a slightly different perspective: its increase with age. In figure 7, breast cancer rates in Japan are low and do not change with age; breast cancer rates in Denmark and in other countries where people eat high-fat diets increase rapidly with age.

The Diet-Cancer Connection

As we continue our detective work on the connection between health and food in another part of the world, we find two British physicians, Dr. Dennis Burkitt and Dr. Hugh Trowell, in a hospital in Kampala, Uganda, in the days of British rule. Both of them were puzzled by something they observed. The natives, who ate a simple high-fiber, high-plant-food, low-animal-fat diet, practically never had colon cancer, while the affluent Western Europeans living in this region, who had brought their high-fat, high-meat diet with them from their native England and considered beans and dark breads foods for the peasants, had much higher rates of colon cancer and other colonic diseases.

Fortunately, these two physicians—great medical detectives indeed—were already highly respected in the medical world. So when they returned to England and proposed, in the late 1960s and 1970s, what they called the *fiber hypothesis* to account for the natives' lack of colon diseases, other scientists took them seriously and decided that the hypothesis was worth extensive clinical testing.

Things have come a long way since all this was happening. The relationship between diet and cancer is now well accepted. Public health researchers believe that if people changed their typical affluent Western diets and stopped smoking, a large number of cancer cases—probably close to 80 percent—could be prevented. It seems an easy choice: cancer prevention rather than the often painful, and sometimes unsuccessful, cancer treatments.

Now we could run into a problem. Suppose the diet that could help prevent colon cancer wasn't good for the heart or vice versa. Or is it possible that the same type of diet that kept the rate of heart disease low in Naples and in Japan could have other health benefits? It turns out that many of the foods that are good for the heart are also good for cancer prevention, and foods that are bad for the heart are often the ones that open the door to certain cancers. In countries where the risk of colon, breast, and prostate cancer is high, the diet is high in fat and meat, low in grains, beans, vegetables, fiber, and other plant foods. The parallel with heart disease is amazing. It should not be surprising that these diseases occur frequently in much of Western Europe and the U.S., where the typical diet is high in animal fat and too low in whole, unrefined carbohydrate foods such as grains and beans, and vegetable consumption is only moderate. Not so in Japan and other countries where plant foods, rather than meats, are the staple foods.

Let's Look at the Migrating Japanese Again

These cancer statistics raise the same questions as those concerning heart disease: is the difference due to race, environment, or diet? Scientists answered this question by doing studies similar to the one we talked about earlier on heart disease. They examined what happens when Japanese people move to Hawaii or to the continental U.S., and whether their rate of colon cancer was more like that of Japan or that of the U.S.

By now you can guess the answer. The rate of colon cancer for Japanese people living in Hawaii was found to be much higher than for Japanese in Japan, and those living in the U.S. who ate a Western diet high in animal foods and low in plant foods had an even higher rate. Food, not some special inherited trait, was indeed the link.

About 80 Percent of Cancers Can Be Prevented

We now know that, even by conservative estimates, about 80 percent of cancers could be prevented with some effort. The risk factors are clear: too much or too little of certain foods; smoking in relation to cancer; pollutants in air, water, and foods; many chemicals; excessive and careless exposure to the sun, especially for certain types of skin. That means that only about 20 percent of cancers are caused by heredity or other factors that we can't change or that medical science does not yet understand.

OBESITY, HEART DISEASE, AND ADULT DIABETES
Excessive Body Weight
Excessive body weight is a serious health concern, for it is associated with heart disease, adult diabetes, and possibly even certain types of cancer. When cholesterol or blood pressure is high, weight loss can often improve both conditions.

Whether these health problems occur because of excessive fat deposits in the body or because obese people eat too much of the wrong foods remains for the scientists to debate. What's certain is that obese people have a much higher risk of all those killer diseases. The fact that controlling your weight is not only good for appearance, fitness, and self-esteem but is also key in disease prevention should be a major stimulus in any weight-loss effort.

Obesity is such a serious problem in the U.S. that in 1985 the National Institutes of Health convened a conference and issued an official consensus document on obesity as a major health risk.

Adult Diabetes
Adult diabetes (called type-II diabetes), a condition that opens the door to heart disease and other disabilities, is so closely linked to obesity that weight loss in the adult type-II diabetic patient most often leads to great improvement, including lowered blood pressure and reduced need for drugs to control the abnormal blood sugar typical of this disease.

This link between obesity, diabetes, and heart disease underscores even more strongly the importance of weight control for good health.

It is difficult to control your weight if you consume high-saturated-fat animal foods as your main source of energy. When whole grains, beans, and other plant foods rich in fiber become the foundation of your meals and you use moderate amounts of plant oils or nuts, it's much more difficult for you to eat in excess of your energy needs.

DIET AND THE FIGHT AGAINST DISEASE
Bone Loss in Aging
The role that diet plays in bone loss in aging (osteoporosis) is more controversial than it is in heart disease, cancer, adult diabetes, or obesity. Experts agree that while hormones and exercise may be the most impor-

tant factors, people should consume more calcium and perhaps magnesium for strong bones. These nutrients are often deficient in adults' diets, as milk products are consumed less and less after adolescence and meat becomes the predominant source of protein. However, meat, the staple of the American diet, is practically calcium free, and some researchers believe that the phosphorus and the high protein content of high-meat diets may even increase calcium loss. This is probably more harmful to the bones when the diet is also low in calcium. While milk products are some of our best sources of calcium, there are some good plant sources of calcium. Studies have shown that osteoporosis is not a significant problem in countries such as China, where few dairy or meat products are consumed.

Focusing on More Foods from Plants

You can apply these findings about food and health to the way you eat by following the Superpyramid Program. The study of the connection between food and disease leads to several inescapable conclusions.

Our detectives have given us the evidence: we must eat more foods of plant origin. These foods are not just high in good carbohydrates; many of them also contain reasonable amounts of protein (nuts and many seeds, the germ of many grains, beans, etc.), and some of them contain very good oils (olives, nuts, some seeds, and many other plant foods).

The Superpyramid Program is based on these plant foods, balanced with low-fat or nonfat yogurt or milk products, egg whites, and some fish (optional). The Superpyramid plan gives you the further option of consuming some lean meat and poultry and limited amounts of certain cheeses and whole eggs.

Fiber and Health

Epidemiologists have also made important discoveries about the role of fiber in unrefined plant foods. Fiber is present in plant food and lacking in animal foods. Fibers from whole grains, beans, fruits, and vegetables help the large intestine (colon) function well, making normal elimination possible. Fiber helps to control the way sugars, fats, and cholesterol work in the body and in the blood. In addition, fiber may help eliminate toxic substances, such as those that cause cancer, from the body. Fiber even feeds microorganisms in the colon and helps produce substances that we are beginning to see as beneficial to the colonic environment. Some people believe this is one of the most important functions of fiber.

The fiber in food does something else that is often overlooked. Whole, high-fiber foods give us a sense of satiety we don't get from fiber-free

foods. Some scientists are reluctant to talk about this factor because it is so difficult to test for under the rigid methodologies of human clinical studies.

Foods containing fiber may help guard against overeating, because they are naturally high in bulk. The feeling of fullness caused by eating whole, high-fiber foods can help decrease food intake and thereby help control weight. You can also look at the fiber component of foods as making them less concentrated in energy value, while low-fiber foods are highly concentrated. Think of the number of apples needed to make one glass of juice. If you ate that many apples, you'd be very full indeed. You get a similar kind of appetite satisfaction from eating whole-grain bread instead of white bread. The Superpyramid Program is based on foods that are naturally high in fiber.

The Complexity of Additions and Subtractions

Before closing this introduction to the relationship of food to health and disease, we need to understand a key concept: *the addition-means-subtraction principle,* or *the plus-and-minus principle.* This is what happens when we start making serious changes in our eating patterns. You cannot simply add more good foods to a high-saturated-fat, low-fiber way of eating and expect the best health benefits. The idea is to create a new balance of foods. If you eat more whole-grain breads, rice, beans, and vegetables, you must also subtract something, perhaps meat or chicken. Soon, your dinner plate has a lot of rice, some beans, some tomatoes and olive oil, plenty of vegetables, and just a little piece of meat. You've not just removed some meat or added some rice: you've altered the entire balance of nutrients by making many additions and subtractions at the same time.

This crucial idea is so simple, yet its importance is often underestimated. The practical lesson is that you must do two things to stay

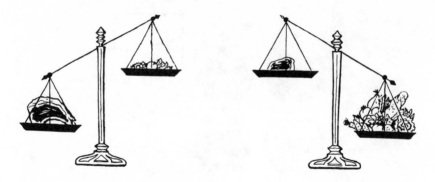

healthy: You must increase foods high in protective nutrients and decrease foods high in components that may promote some major chronic diseases. If you only add without subtracting—let's say if you add some good protective foods to your meals—you have made a step in the right direction, but it's not enough for total health and fitness. Take David . . .

David Goes to the Farmers' Market

David J. is a successful professional man in his early thirties who knows that his blood cholesterol is too high at 270 (it should be below 200). At one time he had participated in a clinical study in our research center to find out the effect of certain food fibers on blood cholesterol. One morning about a year after the study had ended, he was shopping at the local farmers' market, a great place for superfresh vegetables and fruits from nearby California farms. One of our researchers shopping there at the same time was amazed to see him buying all those healthful vegetables and fruits and said to him, "You must have changed your diet since our study; you're buying some great foods!" He replied, "Oh, I just buy these vegetables and fruits to make up for all the other food I'm not supposed to eat but I love! Well, I know it doesn't work that way, but . . ." Little did he realize that there are many other food choices that could be just as delightful as some of the foods he ought to leave out. Of course, David's method won't work for total health. It was good for him to eat those vegetables, but not as an excuse to eat other less healthful foods to excess.

▲ KEY IDEAS

▲ By studying the geography of health and disease, medical detectives can discover links between eating patterns and health.

▲ The high-animal-fat diet of industrialized Western societies promotes high blood cholesterol and coronary heart disease and may contribute to certain cancers.

▲ A high-plant-food diet helps protect against heart disease and colon cancer.

▲ Excess body weight contributes to heart disease, adult diabetes, and perhaps certain cancers.

▲ Fiber, present in unrefined plant foods, is essential for proper elimination and helps control sugars, fats, and cholesterol in the blood.

▲ The plus-and-minus principle is important when making dietary changes. Focus on adding beneficial plant foods while subtracting foods high in animal fat.

CHAPTER

▲ *3* ▲

From Dietary Guidelines to the Superpyramid

Deficiency Diseases and the RDAs

In the first part of the twentieth century, nutrition research had focused very successfully on the nutrient requirements to assure proper growth and development and to prevent the so-called *deficiency diseases*. Some of these diseases, such as scurvy (vitamin C deficiency) and pellagra (niacin deficiency), had been a scourge of humanity for centuries. The discovery of vitamins was one of the great achievements of that period of the history of nutrition.

As a result of all this research, the first recommended dietary allowances (RDAs) were published in the U.S. in 1943, and they have been updated every few years since then. Similar guidelines were published in many other countries. The primary purpose of the RDAs was—and still is—to recommend a desirable daily intake of nutrients, such as vitamins and minerals, to prevent deficiencies and ensure the proper growth and maintenance of the body. The RDAs turned out to be a milestone in good nutrition, but while chronic diseases were discussed in the RDA publications, they were and are not their major focus.

The Era of Guidelines
But even though deficiency diseases have become a thing of the past in affluent, industrialized Western countries, we still suffer from nutritional problems. Our main problem now is improper balance or excesses of major nutrients like saturated fat.

Inevitably, after a long period of apathy and indifference, the governments of many countries and other organizations interested in public health began to publish with great fervor recommendations for diets to prevent major chronic diseases such as heart disease and cancer. And so in the 1970s and 1980s, the era of dietary guidelines began.

Even though unrelated to nutrition, the fact that lung cancer, emphysema, and heart disease had in the 1960s been decisively linked to cigarette smoking galvanized many researchers to study environmental and food-related causes of chronic diseases.

From the U.S. Senate to the Surgeon General

In 1977, a key year for nutrition in the U.S., the Senate Select Committee on Nutrition and Human Needs of the Ninety-fifth Congress, chaired by Senator George McGovern, published a series of books, including the green books entitled *Diet Related to Killer Diseases*. These books were the result of extensive public hearings and of many submissions from scientists, physicians, and educators. In 1982 the National Research Council published its now-famous book *Nutrition and Cancer* and in 1989 its *Diet and Health: Implications for Reducing Chronic Disease Risk*. In 1988, Dr. C. Everett Koop, the surgeon general of the United States, published his *Report on Nutrition and Health*. Throughout the 1980s, the National Institutes of Health convened consensus conferences that led to position papers on cholesterol and heart disease, osteoporosis, and obesity, together with dietary recommendations. Nongovernmental organizations such as the American Heart Association and the American Cancer Society also came out with their own publications that amounted to guidelines for disease prevention.

Bringing Guidelines to the Public

Now the task was to bring all this knowledge to the general public in a simple, interesting way that did not require years of scientific and medical training to understand. Some of the books we've just mentioned are for professionals, and some of those major reports are over seven hundred pages long.

The concept of *food groups* was one simple way to teach people what to eat. Food groups had been used in nutrition education for quite a while, and they could be adapted to follow the newer guidelines. These groups were usually illustrated with pictures presenting the key foods of a group, say meat or bread, but you had to read the fine print to know how much or how little you should eat of a certain type of food. Food servings were used a lot in connection with food groups. The concept of a *serving* of a food is great in a community kitchen or a hospital with trained personnel but is not so appealing to the general public and the homemaker. People have a tough time grasping just what a serving is. When we do clinical studies with foods at our research center, explaining servings is something dietitians love to do, and most subjects hate.

Food groups have evolved over the years: in the U.S., the *basic seven* groups became the *basic four* plus a fifth group that included sweets, alcohol, and fats. The United States Department of Agriculture was usually responsible for making changes in the food groups.

Most of us in this country were raised on these four food groups: milk and dairy products; meat, chicken, and fish; grains and breads; and fruits and vegetables. The implication was that we needed to eat from all four categories every day to ensure optimal nutrition. Today we realize that two of those food groups—milk and dairy products and meat, chicken, and fish—include many less desirable, high-saturated-fat food choices.

Though food groups are good in principle, they are not powerful enough to visually convey the message of how much or how little to eat of a certain food. At times, seeing the various food groups illustrated with pictures of the same size could be downright confusing to the untrained.

The ultimate visual aid for making better food choices, so important for people living out in the real world and not sick in a hospital or afflicted by major illness, was not the food groups listed on a printed page, even with good illustrations. There had to be a better way to figure out instantly how much we should eat of a given food in relation to others. That's where pies and pyramids come into the picture.

From Pies to Pyramids

There are many possible ways to visualize the amount of food to eat. Two of the best are the *pie chart* and the *pyramid*. Both make possible an instant recall of what and how much to eat and are brilliant in their simplicity.

The pie has been used quite extensively in the U.S., while in Europe, Australia, and some other countries, the pyramid has been the preferred visualization method. Pyramids appeared in the U.S. in the 1980s in a small way, but it was not until a major controversy arose over a food pyramid developed by the U.S. Department of Agriculture and withdrawn just days before its formal release that the food pyramid became a news topic in early 1991. The USDA finally released its food pyramid in April of 1992.

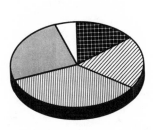 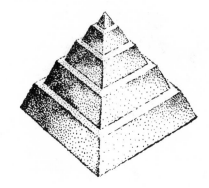

Why a Pyramid?

Structurally, the shape of a pyramid—large at the base and smaller and smaller toward the top—is ideal for describing the composition of a healthful diet. A large floor or tier—like the first and second tiers—is the place for foods like whole grains and vegetables that can be used freely as the foundation of a meal. As you move up to the higher tiers, you find foods like poultry and cheese that should be used in smaller and smaller amounts as the tiers narrow toward the top of the pyramid.

The USDA Pyramid

The USDA pyramid has four tiers. On the first tier we find grain products, on the second tier vegetables and fruits, and on the third tier on one side dairy products, all grouped together no matter how high or low in fat and on the other side meats, poultry, fish, dry beans, eggs, and nuts. The top tier has no pictures—not very visual for a food pyramid —and on this tier we find fats, oils, and sweets with the statement "use sparingly."

The USDA food pyramid is a good step in the right direction, certainly the result of much hard work. What is amazing is how much criticism it elicited from so many different people! The producers of milk, meats, and related foods felt that their products had been moved up too high on the pyramid, a directive to the public that they should use less of these foods. Other powerful groups, such as the grain millers and bakers, became very active in support of the USDA food pyramid.

Beyond the debate among trade groups that saw their commercial interests affected in either a positive or negative way, many scientists, physicians, and public health educators felt it did not go far enough in stressing plant foods as the foundation of the diet. Some thought that another flaw was the survival of the old food-groups concept, which

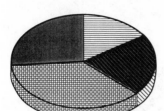

Food Group Pie

Food Pyramid

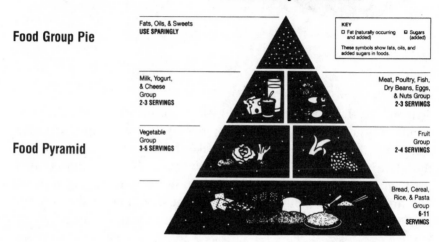

meant that beans, other legumes, and nuts were all clustered together on the third tier of the USDA pyramid with meats and poultry, just as low-fat or nonfat milk products were found together with milk products high in saturated fat. The survival of the old groups is found on tier three again, where fish is in the same group as hamburger, though these two foods have quite different types and amounts of fat.

Another problem arises when we reach tier four: all fats are found together on this tier. How can "good" oils, such as olive or other vegetable oils, be on the same tier as hard animal fats to be used with extreme restraint or, according to some public health educators, not as part of a regular diet? Some unsaturated fat is desirable to improve taste, texture, and nutritional properties of the diet. These good vegetable oils should be on a different tier than animal fats.

In summary, while the USDA pyramid is a vast improvement over the concept of the four basic food groups, it doesn't help people differentiate between more or less healthful foods on the same tier. And it still places on the same tier, for example, milk products that are high in saturated fats and that should be consumed with great moderation, alongside low-fat or nonfat milk products that can be consumed quite freely.

If a pyramid has to be a device that tells us how much or how little of a food we should eat, we need a drastic revision of the old concept of food groups, in which, for example, all dairy products were in the same group no matter how much or little fat they contained, and beans, nuts, and fish were together with meats and poultry. With this need for revision in mind, the Superpyramid was born.

Why the Superpyramid Is Superior

The Superpyramid Program goes far beyond the more conservative—even though very good—pyramids used in the past. The Superpyramid is designed to be the ultimate lifetime eating plan, combining ancient wisdom with the most recent scientific information about the benefits of various types of foods. And the Superpyramid goes further than most popular food pyramids by building on foods of plant origin and selected fermented milk products, while making meats, poultry, high-fat milk products, and fish a minor or optional part of the diet.

In a major departure from some other pyramids and classical food groups it places certain foods, such as milk products, on three different tiers according to their fat content. It places beans, nonfat, or very low-fat milk products and egg whites—all foods that can be eaten freely and are important sources of energy and proteins—on the first tier, creating a single food group. And it separates fish from meat and poultry. This approach appears revolutionary, but when you analyze it carefully you find that it fits the pyramid scheme much more than other pyramid designs that preserve the old food-groups concept. The choice of foods on various tiers in the Superpyramid is based not only on nutrient content but on geographical and clinical evidence to help us prevent deadly disease such as coronary heart disease and colon cancer.

The Superpyramid was first conceived in 1984 and 1985 and later developed and updated to become the present version. It uses only real, traditional foods full of flavor, which, when properly combined, will keep you from desiring the high-animal-fat foods you were eating before. Once you make the Superpyramid part of your life, it will enable you to cherish the simple, ancient foods of the land; savor their fragrance; enjoy the flavor and aroma of herbs and spices; learn to appreciate real, whole foods as part of a joyful meal; and make the path to better health satisfying and pleasant.

All of the foods on the Superpyramid tiers have some good nutritional properties. Even the foods on the top tier—to be used in extreme moderation—contain valuable nutrients. They have been put on the smallest tier because, in addition to their good nutrients, they may also include some components that should not be eaten in large amounts, such as cholesterol in egg yolks.

Other pyramids have placed on the top tier foods that do not appear at all in the Superpyramid. Isolated animal fats are one of them. We feel that you do not need such foods and should eat them only very occasionally.

How Foods Were Selected for the Superpyramid

Why would you want to follow a pyramid food plan that includes foods you should leave out of your regular eating pattern? The Superpyramid incorporates only foods that have intrinsically good properties when used in appropriate amounts. And why would you settle for a pyramid with refined foods, when the Superpyramid is full of whole, real foods, that, as much as possible, have been tested through generations of use in regions that have significantly lower rates of some of the killer diseases?

A few foods used as flavorings, such as vinegars, herbs, and salt, have been left out of the Superpyramid because they are naturally used in such small amounts that it is unnecessary to place them on a tier. Of course, these flavorings are an important part of cooking and will be discussed in a separate chapter. And we have left out wine, an ancient beverage that, in moderation, can be a valuable part of a meal. Wine and other beverages will be described in chapter 9.

Every food that is part of the Superpyramid has passed the rigorous tests we have just talked about. This is where the Superpyramid stands on its own.

There are two Superpyramids: one with meat, poultry, and fish and one without these products. These animal products will be discussed in detail in chapters 6 and 7, and you can decide which path you want to follow.

THE FIVE-TIER MEMORY SYSTEM

Both the regular Superpyramid and the vegetarian Superpyramid are divided into five different tiers.

The tiers quickly and clearly show how to eat to achieve a proper balance of different types of foods. You know instantly which foods to eat the most, and which foods to eat the least. It makes it simple to choose the best foods for better health, weight control, and disease prevention.

Tiers one and two of the Superpyramid are very spacious: the foods on these two levels are the basic foods for good health.

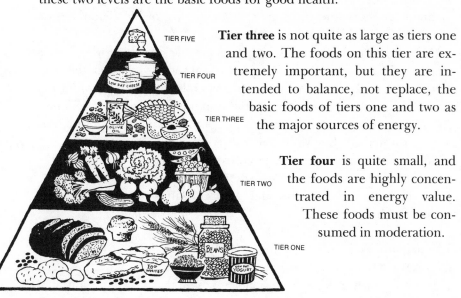

Tier three is not quite as large as tiers one and two. The foods on this tier are extremely important, but they are intended to balance, not replace, the basic foods of tiers one and two as the major sources of energy.

Tier four is quite small, and the foods are highly concentrated in energy value. These foods must be consumed in moderation.

Regular Superpyramid

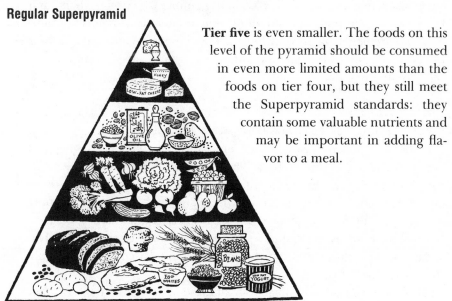

Tier five is even smaller. The foods on this level of the pyramid should be consumed in even more limited amounts than the foods on tier four, but they still meet the Superpyramid standards: they contain some valuable nutrients and may be important in adding flavor to a meal.

Vegetarian Superpyramid

THE FOODS OF EACH TIER

The First Tier
Whole Grains, Beans, Nonfat or Very Low-fat Yogurts and Milk Products,
and Egg Whites

This is the largest tier, which supports the entire structure of the Super-pyramid Program, and these are the basic foods for life. The foods on this tier must be the foundation of our meals.

Here we find whole grains and their products, such as whole-grain breads and pasta and brown rice. They supply energy, protein, the right kinds of fat and fiber, vitamins, and minerals. Beans help round out your carbohydrate, protein, fiber, and iron intake. Nonfat (or very low-fat) milk products contribute high-quality protein and calcium with little or no saturated fat. Egg whites provide additional protein.

All foods on this tier may be eaten freely and in sufficient amounts to meet your daily requirements for energy, protein, calcium, magnesium, other minerals and vitamins, and the right kinds of fat (from whole grains) and fiber.

The Second Tier
Vegetables and Fruits

This tier is nearly as large as tier one. Foods on this tier supply a host of superprotective factors such as vitamins, minerals, special fibers, and traces of other important compounds that are neither vitamins nor minerals but are beneficial to your health. These foods balance the nutrients of the foods found on tier one and are as vital to good health as the foods on the first tier.

The Third Tier
Nuts, Olives, Avocados, and Oil-Containing Seeds; Fish Optional

This tier is smaller than tiers one and two, showing that we need to begin to use some moderation. These foods should not be the main source of energy or protein in our meals, but rather supplement those energy sources found on tier one. The plant foods on this tier supply good oils to add to your foods in place of isolated animal fats. These are the oils from olives, nuts, and seeds such as sesame or sunflower. The same foods that give you these good oils can also be used whole to supply some good proteins, minerals, vitamins, and fiber. Lesser-known beneficial compounds are also present in all these foods and in the oils when they are not overrefined. Many of these foods, such as olives and almonds, have been dietary staples since ancient times.

Fish is the only animal food on this tier. Fish contains different fats—better fats—than do meat and poultry. It is because of these good fats that fish appears on tier three. And there are some fish, such as sole, that are quite tasty even though they are very low in fat.

The Fourth Tier
Low-fat Cheeses and Other Low-fat Milk Products; Honey and Other Natural Sweeteners; Low-fat Meats and Poultry Optional

The low-fat cheeses and other low-fat milk products on this tier supply excellent protein and calcium.

Natural sweeteners—honey, maple syrup, concentrated natural fruit sweeteners (such as concentrated grape juice), molasses, and dark brown sugar—are here to enhance food flavors. These sweeteners can be used regularly, but in small amounts, in recipes (such as breads) or as toppings for yogurt or other foods.

Very low-fat meats and poultry are included here but are not an essential part of the Superpyramid. Remember that meat and poultry should never be the foundation of the meal and the main source of energy. *The ultimate Superpyramid Program does not include these products.* The vegetarian Superpyramid or the Superpyramid with some fish are far better choices. Low-fat meats and poultry have been included here since they may be useful during the transition from a diet high in meat and poultry to the ultimate Superpyramid Program.

The Fifth Tier
Whole Eggs and Medium-fat Cheeses and Milk Products

This is the smallest of the tiers, and it's crucial for you to remember how small it really is. It includes whole eggs, medium-fat cheeses, and other medium-fat milk products. The medium-fat cheeses, such as Parmesan or cheddar, supply excellent flavor in small amounts and can enhance a dish without adding much saturated fat. Other foods on this tier, such as whole eggs, should be used in limited amounts. For example, one whole egg could be added to color an omelet or eaten when traveling or eating out.

One way to use tier-five foods such as cheddar cheese or whole eggs is to use them only a few times a week. Then your Superpyramid for the week will still be well balanced while making possible the use of four or five whole eggs each week or the enjoyment of a flavorful cheddar or Swiss cheese sandwich once or twice a week. *If you have high blood cholesterol, read chapter 12 on the use of cheeses and whole eggs.*

Foods Not on the Superpyramid

Some foods very high in saturated fat are not found on the Superpyramid. Meats, poultry, and cheeses that are very high in fat or cream, dairy butter, and cream-based ice creams are not part of the Superpyramid Program. These and other foods prepared with large amounts of saturated fat should not be part of your regular meals. They can, as any food not on the Superpyramid, be consumed occasionally with no harm, but *occasionally* is the key word here. It means a few times a month, not a few times a week. Similarly, candies and other sweets are not part of this program, but again, this should not preclude an occasional snack or dessert.

Before Going Any Further: Practice Visualization

Practice visualizing the Superpyramid tiers in your mind. Soon you'll be able to recall instantly which foods to eat the most of and which to eat the least of. Use this instant recall when you shop, when you plan and cook meals at home, and when you eat in a restaurant. Visualize typical foods and the optimal balance in each meal.

Even though you'll learn much more about the fine points of food selection and meal planning later in the book, you should be ready now to design an ideal meal and use the photographic part of your brain to recall the relative position of foods on the Superpyramid. You'll enjoy not worrying about exact measurements!

One final point: no matter how good any food is and no matter where it falls on the Superpyramid, anything can be eaten to excess. There is an inexorable law of nature that says if you consume excess energy it will be stored as fat. Superpyramid balanced meals are much better at preventing weight gain and overeating than regular high-meat, high-fat, low-fiber, low-plant-food meals, but if you naturally tend to overeat, remember that you can overeat almost anything.

And now let's start our journey. We'll spend some time on each tier in the four chapters that follow.

▲ KEY IDEAS

▲ Nutrition has evolved in the twentieth century from the prevention of deficiencies to the prevention of killer chronic diseases.

▲ Pyramids are one of the best ways to visualize food choice and plan meals. The Superpyramid goes beyond all other food pyramids.

▲ Whole plant foods complemented by low-fat or nonfat milk products, some egg whites, and foods containing good fat such as olives, nuts, and sesame and other seeds are the foundation of the Superpyramid.

▲ No food plan can be followed for a long time if the joy of food is not a major consideration. Foods with a long tradition of use and whole foods are ideally suited for a lifetime of great meals.

▲ Practice visualizing the tiers of the Superpyramid and use this visualization when shopping for food, planning a meal, or preparing a snack.

Exploring the Five Tiers of the Superpyramid

CHAPTER

▲ *4* ▲

The First Tier

The Foundation of All Healthy Meals

The foods on tier one are the foundation of your new, healthier approach to eating—and living—well. And the most important of these foods are *whole grains*. In their unrefined form, they supply ample complex carbohydrates as well as protein, fiber, vitamins and minerals, and precious oils. In the Superpyramid, whole grains are the major source of healthful, reliable energy.

The beautiful array of high-energy foods made from grains must be complemented by *yogurts* and related milk products that are very low in fat and high in protein and calcium, and by *beans*, the most unjustly neglected food in affluent, heart-disease-prone societies.

Getting to know and love this ultimate combination of grains, low-fat milk products, beans, and some egg whites is your first step toward eating for health, chronic disease prevention, fitness, and weight control.

47

THE FOODS OF THE *First Tier*

▲ Breads in all shapes and forms, *but made with whole-grain flour.* In addition to the familiar loaf, bread also includes other forms of baked or cooked doughs such as pancakes, pizzas, tortillas, chapatis, and pitas. For the greatest nutritional benefits, the bread should be *leavened with a live culture.*

▲ Cereals made from whole grains, including rice, porridges of various kinds, and dry cereals.

▲ Pastas made from whole-grain durum wheat or other special wheat varieties such as kamut or spelt, combined with other grains, if desired.

▲ Legumes of all kinds: beans and bean products such as tofu, tempeh, miso, and many others; lentils; and peas.

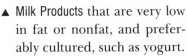

▲ Potatoes may occasionally replace grains in a meal as the basic source of energy.

▲ Milk Products that are very low in fat or nonfat, and preferably cultured, such as yogurt.

▲ Egg Whites

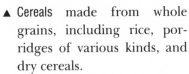

Where Has the Staff of Life Gone?

If you are accustomed to the meat-based meals typical of the U.S. and other affluent industrialized societies, it's hard to imagine that bread— and other grain-based foods such as rice, pasta, and tortillas—was once so central to human existence that it truly was the staff of life. It is only in the past eighty or ninety years that meat began to replace bread as the basic food in many Western societies.

In the Neolithic era, long before recorded history, man was already using wild wheat to make porridge or gruel. The ancient Egyptians made leavened wheat into a bread that was a major staple of their diet. In fact, the religious writings of all faiths have always reflected the importance of grains as basic sustenance. For example, the word *bread* appears 322 times in the Bible.

In ancient Greece, until the fifth century B.C., the basic foods were barley (used to make bread or gruel), olives, figs, some cheese, and occasionally some fish. As far back as 1000 B.C., the Greeks held barley in high esteem as a food that would give athletes great physical strength.

"For the Greeks," says Mary Taylor Simeti in *Pomp and Sustenance*, "the cultivation of grains and the baking of bread were the distinctive marks of civilized man: 'men who eat bread' is the conventional formula with which Homer distinguishes the Greeks and their likes from . . . barbaric races."

GRAINS AND BREADS

At the height of the Roman Empire bread was not considered supplemental to a meal, it was the meal.
—E. J. KAHN, JR.
The Staff of Life

Fiat panis—*Let there be bread.*
—*Motto of a publication of the Food and Agricultural Organization of the United Nations (FAO)*

Roman soldiers also relied on grains as their basic source of energy, and wheat was such a staple of Rome that the Roman Empire was known as a "wheat empire." A porridge called *puls* was the early Romans' national dish, although bread later became more important. Barley was fed to Roman gladiators. Millet was often used by the less affluent Romans to make porridge.

Throughout the Middle Ages in Europe, rye, wheat, and barley, most often in the form of bread, were an intrinsic part of the diet. Today, in less affluent countries, grains such as wheat, barley, rice, and corn still provide the largest percentage of the food energy consumed in the world, according to the United Nations Food and Agriculture Organization (FAO). More than a billion tons of grain are produced each year, supplying most of the energy and much of the protein for the world. About half of the world's population depends on rice, and the other half on wheat, especially bread. These grains stand between humanity and starvation.

The Superpyramid Program restores grains to their historical role as the staff of life, the superfoods of the human race, and our best hope for prevention of some of the most deadly common diseases.

Nutritional Value of Whole Grains
A grain is a seed that has three valuable parts, often encased in a rough inedible outer sheath (the chaff). The three parts are the germ, the most nutritionally rich portion; the endosperm, which is the core of the grain and provides good complex carbohydrates and proteins; and the bran, which supplies fiber, minerals, and vitamins. Let's look at these nutrients in detail.

Complex carbohydrates. Grains contain a plentiful supply of complex carbohydrates, probably the most healthful and reliable energy source for the human body. When you follow the Superpyramid Program, you'll be shifting your energy intake from high-protein foods such as meat to high-carbohydrate plant sources such as grains.

Proteins. The proteins supplied by the combination of the white flour (endosperm), germ, and bran of the grain are far superior to the protein of the white flour alone. Protein from whole grains should be present in large amounts in a Superpyramid meal and should be combined with the proteins of beans, very low-fat, preferably cultured, milk products, and nuts to provide the building blocks your body needs.

Unsaturated oils of superb nutritional quality are found in the germ of grains. Whole grains contain just the right kind of fat in the right amounts. When you combine these precious oils with the good oils from other plant sources such as almonds, olives, sesame seeds, and others, you are replacing saturated animal fats with a healthy balance of the best types of fats. (You'll learn more about the "good fats" in chapter 6.)

Unique oils. Some very special oils—unique compounds, in fact—are present in some parts of the grain. Some of these substances, tocotrienols, have been recently found to lower blood cholesterol. Many such oillike compounds, called lipids by biochemists, are found in various layers of different grains. Only whole grains or properly prepared food combinations will guarantee their presence. Researchers have not yet determined the health benefits of many of these oils, but like the cholesterol-lowering tocotrienols, they may yet prove to be valuable to human health.

Vitamins and minerals. The germ and bran of whole grains contain ample amounts of many vitamins and minerals. Wheat germ is one of the best sources for the B vitamins and vitamin E. The outer bran layers supply essential minerals, including iron, zinc, magnesium, and copper, which are lost in the refining process that produces white flour.

Fiber is a major contribution of whole grains to the diet. Grain or cereal fibers, such as wheat bran, are known for their ability to keep the digestive system functioning properly, and certain fibers (oats and possibly others) have been found to lower blood cholesterol. The fiber in whole-grain foods also makes you feel more satisfied than do low-fiber, refined products. This is of particular benefit if you're concerned about controlling your weight.

Not Refined

When we talk about all the great qualities of grains, you must always remember that we mean whole grains. This concept is particularly crucial when you use grain-based foods to replace meat, poultry, or fish as your main source of sustenance. A diet based on white flour and purified grains will not support good health the way whole grains do. Only by using whole-grain foods will you be assured of the presence of fiber, precious oils, vitamins and minerals, and good protein. (If you have especially high energy needs because of athletics or heavy physical work, for example, you may add some white-flour products to your diet.)

Choose whole-grain brown rice instead of white rice, true whole-grain cereals, such as old-fashioned oatmeal, and true 100% whole-wheat or other whole-grain flour for breads and pastas. There are so many varieties of breads that appear to be whole-grain but in reality are only partially whole-grain. If you bake bread at home you can choose the ultimate method, that is, to grind the grain yourself in one of the many household mills available, or you can buy real whole-grain flours. If you buy bread already baked, you may choose a specialty small bakery and ask for true whole-grain bread. If you buy prewrapped loaves you must read the label extremely carefully. Some bread labels have so many ingredients that they can be quite confusing. Be sure the label states something like "100% whole wheat [or rye or other grain] flour" as the first ingredient and that no white flour has been added, if you want the best for a Superpyramid meal. Small grains like millet, amaranth, quinoa, and teff are usually whole grains. Read the section on specific grains, page 57.

For humans, eating means much more than simply consuming the proper balance of nutrients. Learn the scientific reasons for the value of the special components of foods. Then go beyond that by choosing whole foods. Whole foods such as whole-grain breads combine nutritional values with rich aromas, flavors, and textures to nourish the senses as well as the body.

The Milling of Grains and Flour

It's ironic that, over the centuries, technological advances in food processing have led to a deterioration in the nutritional value of grains.

Early tools to grind grains date back to 8000 B.C. Slowly, the simple mortar and pestle evolved into stone mills, which became less primitive with passing centuries.

In Roman times, grain was ground and used before it had a chance to spoil. Visitors to ancient Roman ruins can see that ancient bakeries had a mill right on the premises. The reason was simple: you can store the whole grain, but the flour ground from it spoils quickly.

Later, water-powered stone mills became landmarks along streams and rivers in medieval Europe. Colonial settlers built European-style mills in America as soon as they could. These mills with their large paddle wheels were common in the United States through the mid-nineteenth century. Before the Civil War, most communities had their own mill and a miller to run it.

These old-fashioned milling methods retained all of the beneficial components of the whole grain. But in the nineteenth century, as more people moved away from rural communities to live in big cities, they left behind the traditional system of grain being grown, milled, and baked locally, before it could spoil. Now, more time elapsed between milling and baking, and the rich and healthful wheat germ oils went rancid with prolonged storage.

In the 1870s, steam-powered roller milling began to replace stone milling. This "modern" method of milling made it easier to remove the germ and bran and thus avoid the problem of spoilage. Additionally, it produced what was considered a beautifully white flour, which looked "cleaner" and more refined than the dark whole-grain flour. Unfortunately, most people didn't understand the nutritional consequences of this technological change.

Today, thanks to refrigeration, flour keeps longer. There is no longer any need to sift out the germ and bran, and no reason not to make the healthier whole grains and whole-grain flours the foundation of our diet. Many mills supply freshly ground flour, and there are even small household mills if you have enough time to grind your own grains.

Whole-grain flours are also available in many supermarkets or health food stores. It's best to buy these flours in stores that keep them refrigerated or in a cool place, but if that's not possible, choose the freshest packages available. At home, keep your flours in the refrigerator or other cold storage.

Other societies have found more nutritionally sensible ways to cope with the spoilage problem than the drastic and nutritionally unwise removal of the germ and bran. The Scandinavians bake their crisp flat breads once a year in autumn. The breads are made with a hole in the center and hung from the ceiling in the keeping room or pantry. These now-famous crisp breads keep well for the entire year.

Are Grain-Based Foods Coming Back?

No single food is sufficient for total health. But if bread and other grain-based foods again become the foundation of the diet in affluent societies, we will have taken a major step toward better health. Already some grain-based foods such as pastas are beginning to make inroads and are becoming more basic foods in North America. Still, the great pride of many restaurants—and many homemakers—is to present a large piece of meat, poultry, or fish flanked by an extremely small portion of vegetables that add little to the dinner except color.

The day should come when the pride of a good restaurant is not the great steak or slice of rare roast beef, but a unique bread, a properly prepared pasta or rice dish, a beautiful plate full of vegetables, beans, some kind of grain, and perhaps a small portion of meat, poultry, or fish.

Imagine making a bread bake the center of our backyard get-togethers. We could bake great breads to fit our taste with modern or old-fashioned ovens. These bread bakes could be just as popular as barbecues are today. As it bakes, that whole-grain loaf of bread would spread its aroma all around to remind us how delicious bread can be.

Breads, Grains, and Weight Control

A common misconception is that bread, pasta, grains, and potatoes are fattening. These foods themselves don't deserve that reputation; rather, it's the way they are prepared and served that can make them fattening. The problems? Adding saturated fats and removing the natural fibers.

Saturated and hydrogenated fats are frequently added to baked goods, either in cooking or at the table. Butter goes together with bread in typical American meals. Excess fats from meats or cheeses are loaded on the modern version of pizza. Too much dressing is poured over pasta in many restaurants, and these dressings often include cream. Potatoes are deep-fried or covered with butter or sour cream. It's these additives, not the whole-grain products themselves, that are fattening when consumed in excess of our needs. You can add fat judiciously, but choose good fats, such as olive oil, nut oil, or other vegetable oil.

Your Superpyramid Food Options

Now let's look at how to use—and choose—the many super grain options in the first tier of the Superpyramid.

The Superpyramid is based on the belief that bread (baked, leavened, or sprouted dough in whatever shape you may choose to eat it) must be one of the foundations of the diet.

The term *bread* as used here includes not only the typical loaves we are all familiar with, but also an almost endless number of flat breads (pitas, pocket breads, pizzas, Scandinavian-type crisp breads, and all types of crackers), muffins, pancakes, and many others.

Bringing Out the Best in Bread: Leavening and Sprouting

When bread assumes its fundamental place in your eating plan, the way it's leavened becomes more critical to health. Leavenings are the substances we add to foods made with flour, such as breads, to give them a light texture. All leavenings work by producing a gas that can be trapped in the bread dough, which in turn can expand sufficiently to hold the gas bubbles. The result is the sponginess that we associate with the light texture of breads and cakes.

When the leavening process is caused by microorganisms, it is a fermentation, or culturing, process. Bakers' yeast is the best-known product for leavening by fermentation.

Ancient breads must have been whole-grain breads, and their leavenings must have consisted of wild microorganisms, yeasts, and lactic bacteria. Growing readily in the bread dough, the microorganisms produced lots of carbon dioxide gas bubbles, which raised the bread. At the same time the dough became acidic, which gave the bread a different flavor from the plain grain and, most important, greater health benefits compared with unfermented breads and porridges. Leavening by fermentation also appears to increase the availability to the body of minerals from the whole-grain flours.

Bakers in ancient times could have started their leavening from sources such as the grain itself or grapes, beers, wines, or fermented milk, any of which can supply small starting amounts of yeasts and lactic bacteria. Once a successful leavening had been produced, it could be continued by saving a piece of already fermented dough to ferment subsequent batches. Breads made this way today are usually described as naturally leavened, and the saved piece of fermented dough is referred to as *barm* in English, *levain* in French, *biga* in Italian, *desem* in Flemish, and *Anstellgut* in German.

In the mid-1800s modern bakers' yeast was developed and has been widely used as leavening ever since, displacing the other natural leavenings from common use. Breads made with the several types of microbial leavenings can be quite varied in shapes, flavors, and textures, bringing variety and challenge to Superpyramid meals. Once you get to know some of the many great variations, you'll find that choosing a good bread can be compared to choosing a wine for the wine connoisseur.

Leavening with microorganisms, whichever type of microbial culture you choose, makes many of the precious minerals in the whole grain more easily absorbed from the digestive system. When whole grains become the foundation of an eating program, this greater availability of minerals is vital. And leavening makes breads more pleasant, flavorful, and easier to eat in a variety of ways. A loaf of bread does not taste right unless properly leavened, and on the Superpyramid Program we must make sure that our breads are thoroughly enjoyable so that they can become part of our daily life.

Sprouting and Malting

The sprouting and malting of grains are included here because, like the leavening process, they change the nutritional value, texture, and flavor of breads. Sprouts and malts are valuable additions to Superpyramid baked goods because, like leavening, they help unlock the minerals in whole grains, making them more easily absorbed by the human body. Several types of grains can be sprouted, including wheat, rye, and amaranth. The grains must be whole, with the germ intact, in order to sprout. In the Superpyramid Kitchen and Bakery (parts 4 and 5) you'll find much more about sprouts and naturally leavened breads.

Sprouts can be ground and added to bread dough before baking. Because fresh sprouts have high moisture content, when ground for use, their texture will be similar to the dough itself.

Malting takes the sprouting process a step further. The sprouts are first dried by a heat process and then ground into a flourlike substance called malt, which can be used as an ingredient in baked goods. In addition to providing the same nutritional value as sprouts, malt also sweetens the dough.

Baking Powders

Baking powders were invented early in the 1800s. They are mixtures of chemicals that produce gas (again carbon dioxide) in the flour product when the ingredients are first mixed together or during the cooking of a bread or cake. A typical mixture is baking soda (sodium bicarbonate) with other chemicals that are acidic enough to cause the sodium bicarbonate to give off carbon dioxide and water. Some of the chemicals used in baking powders are tartaric acid, cream of tartar, calcium acid phosphate, sodium acid phosphate, and sodium aluminum sulfate.

You must be aware, however, that baked goods prepared with baking powders do not provide the food values of those made with yeast-type leavenings. The popularity of baking powders is due to their instant leavening power, rather than their flavor or nutritional effects. Once the carbon dioxide has been released, the bread or cake becomes relatively alkaline, which may destroy some B vitamins. Baking powders also add sodium (see salt in chapter 8). It appears that minerals from baked products raised with baking powder are not as available to the body as minerals from products raised with yeast or other natural leavenings. So, as you can see, breads leavened through microbial action are your best choice when baked products become a major part of your diet. There is nothing wrong with occasionally eating baked goods made with baking powders, but the availability of minerals in baked products is vital to good health. Remember that the ultimate bread that must be consumed as a basic food in the Superpyramid is made with whole grains and leavened with either bakers' yeast or some other microbial agent.

Variety Is Vital: The Choice of Grains

Foods made from whole grains are the fundamental energy source in the Superpyramid. But when grains become the foundation of our meals, variety becomes essential. If boredom sets in, you might be tempted to eat less of these all-important foods and revert to unwise eating patterns. Fortunately, there are so many different types of grains and appealing ways to use them, you need never be bored.

You can achieve variety by using baked goods of different types and shapes, as well as grains prepared by other methods. And you have a wide range of whole-grain ingredients to choose from. Variety is important not just to avoid monotony but also to get the best possible balance of nutrients.

Let's take a look at some of the interesting grain options. Remember, this is just the beginning; there are so many that a whole book could be written about all the great grains of the world.

Wheat is the most fundamental and versatile of all the grains. As you know, it is the basic flour for bread, but it can also be prepared in a multitude of other ways, such as pastas, cereals, and pilafs.

Wheat has a particularly large germ that is full of vitamins, good oils, and the antioxidant vitamin E (the antioxidants are known to help prevent cancer and heart disease) and tocotrienols, proteins, and other nutrients. It has an outer layer we all known as bran, high in minerals and one of the best fibers for proper intestinal function. Constipation is unknown to a whole-grain eater who is otherwise in good health. Many clinical studies have been carried out with wheat bran, and they show that it is one of the best natural products to reduce the time it takes for food residues to move from the stomach to the large intestine and to be eventually eliminated.

Wheat

Hard red wheat yields the white or whole-wheat flours most commonly used by commercial bakeries in North America. Most bread recipes that you'll find in cookbooks use this type of wheat. It's a high-protein wheat, and the whole-grain loaves made from it are fairly dark because of the amount of bran present in relation to the white portion of the flour. This is due to the small size of the grain.

Soft white wheat is usually used in pastry, cakes, and other sweet items. This wheat is lower in protein and should not be used as the foundation of a Superpyramid meal.

Although *durum* means "hard" in Latin, *durum wheat* should not be confused with the common hard red wheat. Durum wheat is grown in arid regions and has become famous as the semolina used in making pasta. In some regions of Italy, durum wheat is also used to make a tasty whole-grain bread that is the basic sustenance of the hard-working local peasants. A whole-grain loaf made with durum wheat is high in protein and looks almost white, with a finer texture than hard wheat whole-grain bread.

Kamut and *spelt* are ancient forms of wheat that are now making a comeback in North America. Both make good pasta, and with proper leavening, they can produce loaf breads as well as pocket breads, pizzas, and other specialty breads. Kamut and spelt are slowly becoming available in specialty stores and in some of the better supermarkets.

Rice grows wild in India and other Asian countries. Wet-field cultivation of rice may date back to 5000 B.C. in India and China and it was known in Mediterranean countries as far back as 300 B.C. The famous ancient Apicius cookery book recommended rice for thickening sauces.

Together with wheat, rice provides basic sustenance for millions of people in the world today. In Superpyramid meals it should be consumed as *brown rice* rather than white, as the so-called rice polish (an outer layer of the seed) contains many valuable nutrients. The nutritional deficiency of polished rice (white rice) was dramatically demonstrated in the early twentieth century. Villagers in the Far East who used white rice as a staple food developed beriberi, a disease that affects the nervous and cardiovascular systems, resulting in wasting of muscles and, often, inability to walk. But a Dutch physician found that he could cure beriberi by feeding victims an extract of the rice polish. This observation led to the discovery of thiamine, or vitamin B_1, an essential nutrient lost in processing. This story underscores how important it is to use whole grains when you eat the Superpyramid way.

Wild rice is a close relative of cultivated rice. It's native to North America and has been an important food for native Americans. It is usually prepared in a way similar to regular rice and has a unique nutty flavor.

Rye is considered a northern grain, although even at the time of Pliny it was grown in limited quantities south of the Alps in northern Italy. Dark breads made from it were known in Roman times. Today, special rye breads such as German or Russian pumpernickels or Scandinavian crisp rye breads are common in northern Europe. When rye is used in loaf bread it is often blended with wheat for lighter texture.

Barley is a very ancient grain. Like wheat, it was used in Neolithic times either cooked as porridge or sprouted. It was often roasted before use. Barley contains fiber as well as special compounds called tocotrienols, which have been shown in some recent studies to control blood cholesterol (see chapter 6 on the good oils).

Hippocratic teachings in the fourth and fifth centuries B.C. recommended barley gruel as a healthful food and barley water (most likely a strained juice from cooked barley) for the sick. Fermented barley beer was used where grape wine was not available, as in northern countries, or where grapes did not grow well, as in Egypt.

Oats were probably brought to Europe from the Middle East between A.D. 1000 and 1300 by the Crusaders. When the Crusaders returned to their homes in Scotland, Ireland, England, Germany, Denmark, and France, oat cultivation began in Europe.

Oats

Oats contain good protein and, like barley, also have a soluble type of fiber that lowers blood cholesterol. This fiber has become so popular that many cereals with oat bran are now available.

The grain itself with the bran, when eaten in the form of oatmeal or so-called steel-cut oats or as a flour added to breads, combines the advantages of high fiber with the nutrition of the whole grain.

The fiber content in commercial oat brans can vary tremendously, so if you want to use oat bran, be careful to choose one that has a reasonable fiber content. In the Superpyramid we prefer the whole grain for its many added benefits.

Corn is known as the American grain. In the fifteenth century, it was found in the islands off the eastern shores of North America by early European explorers who introduced it to Europe. While corn is now second only to wheat as a world crop, a large amount of corn is used for the production of by-products such as corn syrup sweeteners. As a grain corn is not as widely used as wheat or rice in Western countries. The most common use where corn is a staple food is as a flour or coarse meal to make polenta in Mediterranean countries or tortillas and similar flat breads in Latin American countries. In the U.S. some people think of it as a vegetable when they eat it as corn on the cob, but corn is a grain and belongs on tier one no matter how you choose to eat it.

Corn kernels come in a multitude of colors, from yellow and white to the recently reintroduced blue corn. Corn is a wonderful grain, but it must be used properly. Eat your corn on the cob either plain with a little salt or with some flavorful extra-virgin olive oil, rather than with butter; eating fresh corn steamed in its own husk is a much better way of enjoying the nutritional benefits of this grain.

If you use corn as a major staple in your diet, some problems may arise because an essential vitamin—niacin—is not very available from corn unless it is treated. Pellagra, a serious skin and nervous system disease, was widespread in Mediterranean regions and in the southern

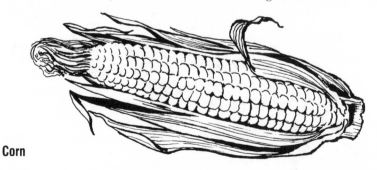

Corn

United States before the cause of the problem was identified. Why didn't the disease appear in Mexico, where corn and beans were staple foods? The Mexicans used lime (a calcium salt) to treat the corn before cooking, and this released the bound niacin. If you buy tortillas or similar products be sure they have been treated with lime, as most are. An occasional use of untreated corn within a good diet won't cause any problems. Combining beans with corn products, as the Mexicans do, is another way to help prevent this vitamin deficiency.

The kind of problem caused by using untreated corn as a major source of energy should remind us that when grains become our staple food, our perspective has to change. Facts that may be unimportant on a typical Western diet become critical when we make a major dietary change, so our way of thinking about foods must change, too.

The Small Grains

There is a group of ancient grains such as millet, amaranth, quinoa, and teff that are little known in North America. Some of them, such as quinoa and teff, have recently been brought into the United States by creative farmers who discovered them in their native lands. Now these fabulous grains are finding their way into stores in North America.

These small grains have a larger proportion of nutrient-rich outer layers to carbohydrate-rich inner portion than our staple grains. Combine them with some of the larger grains such as wheat for improved nutritional value and a pleasing change of texture and flavor. They work well in breads.

Millet was probably the staple food of north China before 4000 B.C. The Romans appreciated it because it could be sown in the spring if other crops had failed and it would ripen in a short time. It has a pleasant flavor of its own and it can be used successfully in place of rice or as an excellent porridge for breakfast.

Amaranth was an important food in the Americas during pre-Columbian times. It has been extensively studied in recent years by nutritionists because it is a good source of vegetable protein that when combined with wheat makes the wheat protein more valuable.

Quinoa was known as the "mother grain" by ancient South American Incas, and it has been cultivated in mountainous regions of the Andes since at least 3000 B.C. This grain is high in protein, calcium, and iron.

Teff is another ancient grain, long used by Ethiopian highlanders to make their staple bread. Today in Ethiopia over 50 percent of the farmland is devoted to teff. In North America it is grown in limited quantities in Idaho.

Variations on Bread

As you can see from the list above, many different types of grains—and combinations of them—can successfully be used in breads and other baked goods. Beyond that, you can add bean flours, yogurts, oils such as sesame or olive, honey, raisins or other dried fruits, and seeds or nuts.

You can also add some variety by choosing different types and shapes of breads and baked goods. Muffins, bagels, pizza, and pocket breads are a few examples of the bounty awaiting you. Just remember a few guidelines whether purchasing ready-made products or baking your own. Choose whole-grain ingredients, use "good" fats and sweeteners, and leaven the dough with yeast or culturing processes.

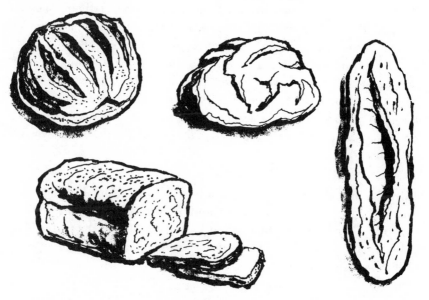

Muffins. Although muffins are often raised with baking powders, when you prepare them, remember to use natural leavening and, of course, whole-grain flours.

Muffins can be made with a variety of grains, and dried fruits and seeds like sesame seeds can be added for extra flavor and nutrition. Be careful when you buy muffins, as they may contain large amounts of saturated or hydrogenated fats. When you bake muffins at home, use only a good vegetable oil or nut butter.

Biscuits are different things to different people, but here we use the term in its original sense of "baked twice." Typically, this means a slice of sweet or regular bread baked gently until dry (not browned, as in toast). Biscuits are a good way to change the flavor and texture of baked products for variety. Any bread can be sliced and made into a biscuit. Biscuits are good for travel as they are dry and keep well for long periods.

Flat breads are the oldest form of bread. They look and taste different from typical loaves of bread and are ideal as the foundation of a creative meal.

Cultured (leavened) flat breads are common in many countries. With proper toppings or fillings they can make perfect Superpyramid meals full of flavor and variety. Remember that a Superpyramid flat bread is made with whole-grain flours. Flat breads made with white flours are acceptable when eating out but should never be your daily bread. For best nutrient availability, choose leavened flat breads.

The choice of fillings or toppings is very important. Be sure to choose mainly those foods found on the Superpyramid. Read carefully the following chapters on vegetables, fruits, oils and fats, cheeses, and meat products, because the benefits of the best type of flat bread can be sabotaged by the wrong additions.

In general, you should use plenty of fresh vegetables (tomatoes, peppers, dark lettuce leaves, onions, garlic, etc.), mushrooms, avocados, beans or bean products, some vegetable oil (see chapter 6), nonfat or low-fat yogurts, and limited amounts of low-fat cheeses. Naturally, choose the right item for the shape and type of flat bread you are preparing.

Pizza (fermented dough) was originally made in Naples from flour, tomatoes, olive oil, garlic, and oregano, without cheese. You need never use sausages or other high-fat meats to make delicious pizza. (See the recipes for healthful pizza on page 464.)

Pocket breads and pita breads (both fermented) probably originated in the Middle East. Pocket breads can be filled in many different ways for easy, complete meals.

Balady is a type of pocket bread produced in Egypt and other Arab countries. The dough undergoes repeated fermentation before baking.

Tortillas are a type of unleavened bread usually made from corn, but sometimes from wheat or other grains. They are a staple food of Mexico and Central America. They are usually prepared from cornmeal treated with lime and baked in small, flat cakes. As we have seen, the use of lime is a very important part of preparing tortillas, as it unlocks some bound nutrients in the cornmeal. Like other flat breads, tortillas can be served with beans, cheese, and vegetables.

In India, unrefined flours are hand ground at home. Indian flat-breads, such as *chapatis,* are made from whole wheat, barley, buckwheat, or millet. Round and chewy, they accompany meals of basmati rice flavored with curries and beans.

There are many—probably hundreds—of special flat breads in various countries. This is not the place to list all of them, but it's important to realize how much variety we can have in breads ranging from the ones we have briefly mentioned to *harsha,* an Algerian fermented flat bread made with durum wheat, to *injera,* a fermented flat bread made in Ethiopia from sorghum, teff, or corn. This bread can be a good way to use teff, which is high in many nutrients. The traditional process of fermentation of injera is said to take days.

Swedish crisp breads and other types of Scandinavian and Russian crisp breads are usually rye breads, though they are occasionally made from wheat. They were held in high esteem in medieval times as they kept for months, even years, without spoilage. Today, some of these breads are a major Swedish export.

Pancakes and waffles are often commercially made with baking powder. When making them at home, use a leavening that will cause fermentation whenever possible. Pancakes raised with natural leavening are delicious. Use egg whites instead of whole eggs. Pancakes in restaurants are usually based on white flour and should be relegated to occasional consumption.

Bagels are made with a simple bread dough that is leavened with yeast and then shaped into a ring. But unlike bread or other rolls, they are boiled before baking, which gives them a shiny, rather tough crust. Bagels have a dense, chewy texture. Although they are traditionally made with refined white wheat flour, bagels are now also available in whole wheat or rye and come topped with onions, garlic, or various types of seeds. Typical accompaniments for bagels are cream cheese and lox, but for use in the Superpyramid, choose a lower-fat soft cheese, such as a yogurt cheese or low-fat farmer's cheese.

Cookies, properly made, can be a great way to eat whole grains and to get quick energy from the added sweeteners. But be sure you follow the same guidelines for flours and baking methods as for breads. The cookies should be fermented as breads rather than prepared with baking powders. This becomes particularly important when grain products are the foundation of the diet. Of course, if you eat just an occasional cookie, the leavening doesn't make much difference.

But a greater problem than the baking powder is the fat in commercial cookies. Bakers prefer to use solid fats such as those found in pies and pastries, because they simplify cookie production. Such fats, solid at room temperature, are usually either animal fats or hydrogenated fats. Avoiding them is not easy even if you bake your own cookies—most recipes recommend them. However, you can adapt your own recipes with a vegetable oil or nut butter (read about the good fats in chapter 6) and try out various new recipes, or read labels in your market until you find the right fat.

If you bake your own, read chapter 6 on fats and chapter 7 on sweeteners.

Pastries. All of the cautions about cookies apply to pastry, pies, and cakes. Typically, these baked goods are made of white flour with fairly large amounts of sugar and fat. The fat is usually a solid fat, which means saturated or hydrogenated. Even made with whole-wheat flour, this kind of food supplies an excess of saturated fat and sugar and should not be a mainstay of your diet. Choose the right pastry, if you can find it, or bake your own following the same guidelines on fats and sweeteners as for cookies. Bake your own with a low-fat crust for pies and a different type of fat for pastry. Bakers are developing new ways to make good-tasting pastry with better fats, and these products should soon be more widely available.

This is just a sampling of many special breads and baked products made from different flours and preparation methods. Learn from the Superpyramid Bakery in part 5 or from other books on whole-grain breads how to make your own bread. It's a skill that will pay you back in better health many times over. A Superpyramid follower should develop a passion for discovering different breads and grains.

Robin's Diet Flaw

A highly trained nurse in the intensive care unit at a major northern California hospital, Robin was desperate. Her blood cholesterol was over 270, even though she thought she was doing everything right. Every morning she ran a few miles before work, and she avoided products high in animal fats such as high-fat cheeses, meats, and ice cream. Her only weakness was pastry, which she thought was all right. Nothing seemed to help lower her cholesterol. Looking at this beautiful, superfit young woman, you wouldn't believe that she could have such a problem.

In desperation and with little hope, she participated in a four-week study in our Health Research and Studies Center in California in which her food choices were limited and only good vegetable oils were allowed. Since her food choices were already great, she had to make only minor changes in her diet, but she did have to drop her pastry habit. At the end of the study, Robin was stunned to learn that her blood cholesterol had gone down by over 25 milligrams in just four weeks! The lesson is clear: avoid pastries that contain hidden animal or hydrogenated fats.

Other Ways to Eat Grains

In addition to eating different types of breads, you can add even more variety to your meals by preparing grains by other methods. Every region on earth has its own delicious and flavorful whole-grain dishes, such as pastas, risottos, and hot or cold cereals. Here is just a sampling to get you started. As you put the Superpyramid into practice in your own life, you'll undoubtedly discover countless new possibilities.

Pasta is found in both Oriental and Mediterranean cooking. Spaghetti, macaroni, and the like should be made from durum wheat (whole semolina) or one of its botanical relatives such as kamut or spelt. Quinoa, amaranth, or other small grains can be added for greater concentration of nutrients. Noodles, or *tagliatelle,* as the Italians call them, contain eggs as well. Whole-wheat pastas or those with some whole-grain flour are the best choices, of course, but regular semolina pastas are acceptable. Noodles are fairly easy to make at home using durum whole-wheat flour and egg whites—there's no need to use the yolk.

Ravioli, agnolotti, and tortellini offer interesting possibilities for preparing a self-contained Superpyramid meal. All of these little pasta pillows can be stuffed with low-fat cheeses, nonfat dairy products, bean products (such as tofu), or vegetables such as spinach or squash. Choose stuffed pastas made without meat or poultry.

The Italian minestrone is an example of a simple meal in a bowl based on pasta, rice, barley, or other grains together with plenty of vegetables and, for vegetarian Superpyramiders, a broth made without meat or poultry products.

Follow the Superpyramid Sauce Principle: Whether you're preparing pasta dishes at home or eating out, remember that in southern Italy, pastas are not covered with large amounts of fancy sauces or animal fats. Pasta dishes should be meatless. Use tomato sauce, plain olive oil, or one of the dressings given in the Superpyramid Kitchen. The same principles apply to related dishes such as risotto and polenta.

Cooking whole or cracked grains by boiling or steaming is one of the most ancient methods of food preparation, dating back to the Neolithic era. Ever since then, it has been widely used as a major part of meals in both Mediterranean and Oriental civilizations.

Perhaps the best known of these foods is rice, the staple of millions in Asia and other parts of the globe. Barley, steel-cut oats, millet, amaranth, wild rice, and other grains can be used in ways similar to brown rice. Cooked wheat also has many uses, such as bulgar or couscous.

Hot cereals, sometimes called porridges or gruels, are also prepared by cooking grains in water. Oatmeal, a staple food of the British Isles for generations, is made with steel-cut oats or old-fashioned, slow-cooking rolled oats and served with milk, honey, or brown sugar. Oats contain a special fiber called beta-glucan, found between the outside bran and the main part of the oat seed, that is good for blood cholesterol control. Many other grains, such as wheat and rice, make good hot cereals as well.

The Italians eat polenta, a cornmeal mush. In the Valle d'Aosta, near the glaciers of Monte Bianco, the highest peak in the Alps, the peasant restaurants called *trattorie* serve polenta with a small amount of fontina cheese (to be used sparingly, because of its fat content) or lean meat. Other restaurants in that region serve polenta with warm milk. You can make a good Superpyramid meal by slicing polenta after it has cooled and baking it with mushrooms and a little low-fat cheese.

Cold cereals such as Swiss-style muesli are served without cooking and make a fine quick breakfast. Oats, wheat, and other cereal flakes are mixed with raisins, dried apples, and shredded nuts, then served with milk, yogurt, and sometimes honey or brown sugar. Hotels in Switzerland and some other northern European countries offer a prepared muesli, which has been soaked in milk or yogurt to presoften it. Several types of muesli are commercially available in this country, or you can make your own (page 325).

Hundreds of types of prebaked, puffed, or extruded ready-to-eat cold cereals are available in the supermarkets. Be careful to avoid high-sugar, low-fiber products or products with hidden fats. Quite a few good varieties are available, so be sure to look for them.

▲ KEY IDEAS

▲ *Whole-grain products are the foundation of the Superpyramid. Whole grains should supply a large part of your energy needs.*

▲ *Whole grains provide not only fiber but also complex carbohydrate, protein, important oils, vitamins and minerals, and other nutrients.*

▲ *When grains become the major source of energy in the diet and less meat and poultry are consumed, the grains must supply a vast array of nutrients missing in refined products. Use whole-grain flours high in protein and nutrients.*

▲ *Variety is important when grains become the foundation of the way you eat. Vary the type of grains you eat and the way you prepare them.*

▲ *Avoid high-fat sauces based on animal or hydrogenated fats on your pasta, rice, or other dishes.*

▲ *Avoid solid animal fats in and on bread and other baked products.*

▲ *Potatoes and related roots can occasionally replace whole grains, but whole grains must remain your main source of energy.*

POTATOES

The potato is a basic energy source and belongs on the first tier of the Superpyramid along with other vegetables and fruits that are high in complex carbohydrates. These include sweet potatoes, yams, chestnuts, and water chestnuts, as well as certain vegetables such as taro, cassava, groundnut, and arrowroot, which are major sources of energy in other countries, though they are almost unknown in North America. Let's focus on the ones that are common in North America: potatoes, sweet potatoes, and yams.

Historically, the potato is a native American food. It was one of the first crops brought to Europe from the Americas by explorers. Some legends credit Sir Francis Drake and others Sir Walter Raleigh as being the first to present a potato plant to Queen Elizabeth I.

Potatoes, sweet potatoes, and yams deserve a more prominent place on our tables than most people give them. For many cultures, the potato has been an important source of energy, and during long hard winters in some northern countries potatoes have been the main source of vitamin C. But potatoes lack some of the key properties of whole grain, such as the grain fibers and the oils and vitamins of the germ of grains. Potatoes are also lower in protein than whole grains. This makes potatoes and related foods a good choice to introduce some variety into a meal, but they should not be the major source of energy on the Superpyramid plan.

Just like grains, potatoes shouldn't be covered with animal fats such as sour cream or butter, or deep-fried in some unknown fat, as are french fries. Instead, use some olive oil or one of the oils you'll find on the third tier (because these are tier-three foods, use them in moderation). If you want to fry potatoes use some olive oil or other vegetable oil. Yogurt makes a good low-fat dressing when mixed with some herbs such as parsley, sage, or basil and a trace of olive oil.

There are many gourmet ways to prepare potatoes, such as potato pancakes, popular in central Europe, and the Italian *gnocchi di patate* (see the recipes in part 4).

Orange or yellow sweet potatoes are a good source of beta-carotene, an antioxidant vitamin that we'll discuss in the next chapter. They need little or no dressing because of their sweetness and can be used as a change from white potatoes and other basic energy sources.

A note of caution: the vitamin C in potatoes vanishes when exposed to air for a sufficient length of time. Excessive heat can also destroy it. Avoid mashed potatoes that have been sitting in open hot trays for hours, as they do in many cafeterias.

LEGUMES OR PULSES

Legumes—a term derived from the botanical name of this family of foods (Leguminosae)—include beans, lentils, and peas. Legumes are usually consumed as seeds, such as beans, but sometimes the pod with unripened seeds inside is consumed, as with green beans and Chinese snow peas. The term *pulse,* from the Latin *puls,* is also used for beans, lentils, and peas.

In this chapter the terms *legumes* and *pulses* always refer to seeds, not pods. The seeds of legumes are a key part of the first tier of the Superpyramid and should be used with grains as part of our main meal.

The Seeds of Legumes, the Forgotten Treasure

While people living in affluent Western societies are slowly beginning to accept grain products as a desirable food, beans, lentils, and peas are still considered Cinderella foods.

In developing countries, replacing beans with meat or poultry is seen as a sign of prosperity. After all, that's what the rich people did. Take the peasants in a Brazilian village and their traditional *feijoada,* a dish that has fed many generations of Brazilians. It used to be prepared primarily from beans, with just a little meat flavoring, except among the wealthy, who used more meat and fewer beans. Now, more and more, it's becoming a meat dish flavored with beans.

Paintings by the European masters of the sixteenth and seventeenth centuries show the contrast between the overweight, meat-eating upper classes and the slender, wiry, bean- and grain-eating peasants. Perhaps eating meats became a sign of affluence because raising beef and other animals for food is so wasteful—it takes so much more water and land resources to provide the same amount of protein from meat as it does from beans, so much so that beans and other legumes have been often called the poor man's meat. This definition is interesting as it reflects the scientific fact that beans have good food value. Dry beans and lentils have a protein content of 20 to 25 percent.

Even today, legume consumption is much higher in the rural areas of Spain than in the cities. In Italy it's higher in the rural south than in the industrial north. In the Orient, as Western influences change the traditional eating patterns, meat, poultry, and related products begin to replace the venerable soybean products that have been, together with rice, the foundation of their diets for thousands of years.

> *It is the mature seeds of legumes, such as dry beans and lentils, that are a basic energy and protein food on tier one of the Superpyramid, balancing a meal based on grains. The pods, such as green beans, are vegetables, and belong on tier two. They should not be considered tier-one energy-protein foods.*

Legumes in History

We find dishes that combine beans with grains in many civilizations, often as the staple food. With a wisdom developed over thousands of years, the peasants of every continent discovered that a diet of grains mixed with beans enabled them to live and work in good health. Today, modern science has confirmed how right they were. Later on we'll see some of the benefits of bean proteins as ideal complements to grain proteins.

The history of beans and lentils as the mainstay of the diets of millions of people dates back at least seven thousand years. In ancient China, a nonpastoral society that did not have goats or sheep to provide milk, the people made a kind of milk from legumes and nuts. Foods such as tofu, a soybean cheese, have served as a major source of good protein for over two thousand years in China and probably for more than a thousand years in Japan. In these countries, soybean cultivation allowed people to produce much more protein per acre than raising beef cattle or similar animals. The soybean was so important to the Chinese that they called it "the great bean." In addition to tofu, other traditional Asian soybean products are tempeh, a fermented soy and grain patty that originated in Java and is a typical Indonesian food, and miso, based on another fermentation process of soybeans with or without grains. Miso, developed in China about twenty-five hundred years ago and brought to Japan by Buddhist priests in the seventh century, makes an excellent base for soups and adds an intriguing flavor to other cooked dishes.

In India the followers of the Vedic tradition consume a meatless diet. Beans and lentils—often referred to as *dals* when in the dry form—have played a key role for centuries as an essential part of this diet. *Dals* in India are combined with grains, cultured milks, and nuts. Vedic agriculturists have the reputation of cultivating some of the best and most digestible beans in the world.

In ancient Europe the legumes used were lentils, peas, chickpeas (garbanzo beans), and a few others. Chickpeas were known in Greece at the time of Homer in the eighth century B.C. Kidney, pinto, and soybeans were unknown.

In the Middle East beans were used as far back as 8000 B.C. A paste or dip called hummus, made of chickpeas with seasonings, has been a traditional dish for centuries. In Egyptian cookery, according to Claudia Roden, a dish called *ful midames*, made with dried beans and red lentils, is a national dish and a traditional breakfast. The use of beans in Egypt dates back to the time of the Pharaohs, and the Arabs say, "Beans have satisfied even the Pharaohs."

Lentils have a long history, too. Ancient Jews ate lentils: in fact, Esau renounced his birthright for a dish of lentils. Lentils were part of the diet during the Bronze Age, as shown by archaeological findings.

In South America, beans were known in 5000 B.C. The popular kidney bean—perhaps the first bean that comes to mind for many of us—originated in the Americas and was brought to Europe in the beginning of the sixteenth century and described by botanists in Europe in 1542.

The story of the hundreds of varieties of legumes is not for this book. This short historical overview is just to help you appreciate that, although beans have fallen from favor in the industrialized world, they have played a long, important role in the development of civilizations around the globe.

Nutritional Value of Pulses

Protein and iron. Why did legumes become such a major staple in so many different parts of the world? We now know from modern biochemical research that bean and lentil proteins complement grain proteins, and that the resulting mixture has a protein value that is higher than either grains or legumes alone. But long before modern science, ancient peoples learned by observation that the basic grain-legume combination kept them strong. Many dry legumes also provide valuable iron that is sometimes low in grains.

This ancient wisdom led to a long list of now-classic combinations. The Italians have their *pasta e fagioli* (pasta and beans), the Orientals have rice with tofu or tempeh or miso, the Middle Eastern people have their hummus (chickpea paste) with flat breads, the Mexicans and other Latin American people have their rice and beans and lime-treated corn tortillas or quinoa and beans, and East Indians combine rice with lentils.

These traditional dishes of legumes and grains are the reason civilizations survived with little or no meat. It is as though these two types of food were intended to go together, like interlocking pieces of a puzzle. We know now the scientific reason for all this. Some essential *amino acids* (the building blocks of proteins) that are low in grains are high in legumes and vice versa.

In making your own ultimate Superpyramid meal, you may want to add some cultured or other milk product to typical legume-grain dishes for extra protein and calcium, which is usually low in grains and beans. Sprinkling some cheese (preferably low-fat or in limited quantities) on pasta dishes is a typical example of such an addition.

Fats. Another advantage that beans have, especially over animal protein sources like meat, is that they are very low in fat (about 8 percent when dry), and this small amount of fat is unsaturated. The soybean is an exception to the rule, but even though it's 43 percent fat, that fat is highly unsaturated. Tofu, miso, tempeh, and soy milk—all soybean-based foods—are much lower in fat than the whole soybean. The protein and fat content of beans and bean products is shown in figure 8.

Carbohydrates. The carbohydrates found in beans are the type of complex carbohydrates we should use as our main source of energy.

Fiber. The soluble fiber in most beans is different from the insoluble fiber found in wheat or rice. The way it works is similar (even though different in chemical structure) to the special fibers found in oats and barley.

> *Even the fiber of legumes seems to have been made to complement the fiber of wheat and rice, the two most common staples of the human race. While the insoluble fiber of wheat and rice helps our digestive functions, the soluble fiber of beans has a beneficial effect on our blood cholesterol.*

Beans must be cooked or sprouted. There are some substances in raw beans that are easily inactivated by cooking (or sprouting) but that have some negative effects if beans are consumed raw. One of these substances inhibits an important digestive enzyme (trypsin), but cooking quickly destroys this substance.

Legumes, Blood Sugar, and Blood Cholesterol

Effect on blood sugar. Dr. David Jenkins, his wife, Alexandra, and their associates at the University of Toronto in Canada have spent years studying the effect of foods on blood sugar. This is important not only to people with diabetes, who have abnormal blood sugar levels, but also to anyone who wants a steady flow of energy. When blood sugar rises too high too fast, it usually drops too low a couple of hours later. The result is the kind of letdown we all feel after we eat or drink large amounts of sweets on an empty stomach. Dr. Jenkins and his research group found that lentils, beans, and other legumes cause a very minimal increase in blood sugar. This means you'll feel an even flow of energy after a meal of beans or lentils.

Effect on blood cholesterol. Beans lower blood cholesterol and help to keep it under control. In 1968, Dr. Mathur in India published an article in the prestigious *British Medical Journal* showing that people who eat diets high in beans have lower cholesterol than those who do not. More recent research on many fibers from beans has confirmed their cholesterol-lowering properties.

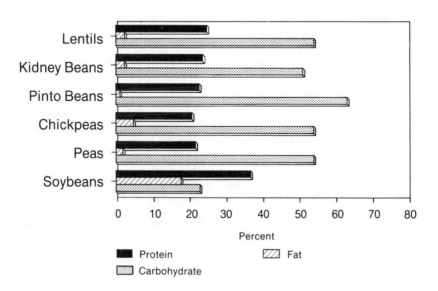

FIGURE 8. Nutritional Content of Legumes

The observed physiological effects of beans on blood sugar and blood cholesterol are most likely the result of the type of fiber that beans contain, but some of the effect on blood cholesterol may be due in part to bean eaters' consuming more vegetable protein and thus less animal food.

Beans and Gas

People who eat beans regularly don't usually have any more intestinal gas (flatulence) than people on typical Western diets. However, we must give our digestive systems a chance to adapt to new foods. The digestive microorganisms of the large intestine (colon) change with the type of food we eat. When we add a new food, the intestinal microorganisms are not adapted to it, and we may have some gas as a result. The *Laurel's Kitchen* cookbook recommends starting with lentils or split peas to let our bodies adjust to bean consumption. Soon we can add other kinds of beans with no problem. Some of the gas is most likely the result of the unique sugars present in beans, which aren't broken down by our digestive enzymes. These sugars reach the large intestine, and intestinal bacteria dine on them, producing gas.

Soaking beans overnight and changing the water before cooking usually helps by washing out some of the gas-producing compounds. This soaking also makes the dry beans softer, improves flavor, and probably makes them more digestible. You may use some hot water for a second soaking of about an hour, then change this water again before cooking, but if you do this you may lose some flavor and perhaps some nutrients. You can go further and let the bean sprout. To do this you soak them for twenty-four hours and then place the wet beans on a cloth for another day before cooking them. All these steps assume that you use *dry* beans and prepare them yourself. If you buy precooked frozen or canned beans, you don't know what the processing steps have been, or how many nutrients have been lost. You'll find more about cooking and sprouting beans in the Superpyramid Kitchen.

Making purees with beans without the skin can be a good choice for people who have problems with gas while their bodies are learning to adjust to a food plan higher in legumes. You may also find that different types of beans are easier for you to digest. Try adzuki or chickpeas or lentils instead of pinto or kidney beans. Because of their method of preparation, the soybean products tofu and tempeh should not cause gas and may be a good choice for you.

Betsy's New Diet

Betsy, a twenty-three-year-old college student, ate a typical American high-meat, low-fiber diet most of her life. Inspired by her husband, a longtime vegetarian, she decided to stop eating meats, poultry, and fish and to eat lots of legumes, whole grains, vegetables, and fruits. Betsy's case history for the first four weeks on her new diet was typical: she had a great deal of gas! Slowly things improved; without any additional change in her food choices the gas decreased dramatically each week. At the end of four weeks her digestive system was just about normal and the problems had almost disappeared. *Betsy made her drastic change of food overnight: you may choose to do it slowly or be more selective in the types of legumes you eat for the first few weeks.*

The Endless Varieties of Legumes

In ancient times each part of the world seemed to have its own typical beans. Now, nearly all beans are cultivated everywhere. For example, soybeans, once typical of the Orient, are now a major crop in North America as well.

It is unfortunate that so few medical researchers have studied the possible nutritional and physiological differences among the multitude of bean varieties, with the exception of the obvious differences between soybeans and other beans. In researching various topics for this book, I was amazed at how many publications, both scientific and popular, were available on grains and their products and how few on legumes, which were relegated to a lonesome supporting role.

Because of the limited knowledge we have of the possible differences among the legumes, you should simply choose the ones you like best and avoid monotony by trying new types and preparing them in different ways. The following is just a brief list of some key seeds of legumes.

Lentils. The lentil is a very digestible legume and cooks quickly and easily, a great advantage in the hurried modern world. A pot of lentils, even without soaking, can be cooked in twenty to thirty minutes, while unsoaked pinto beans may take up to two hours. Red lentils are the fastest-cooking variety; green and black lentils take somewhat longer.

Pinto, kidney, chili, and other red or pink beans. These beans are typical of North and Central America, and some of them are an intrinsic part of Mexican cuisine. They take longer to cook than lentils, but overnight soaking can shorten the cooking time (page 327). The exotic red-and-white anasazi (a Navajo word meaning "the ancient ones") beans cook in less time than other red beans, have a milder flavor, and are very tender, a combination that makes them great for the bean eater.

Adzuki (or azuki) beans. These small reddish brown beans, native to Japan and China, are now quite popular in India. Their flavor and texture are very different from typical red beans. In India they have a popular reputation for medicinal properties, which needs to be confirmed scientifically through controlled experiments. Adzuki beans are a delicious variation from the larger, more common red beans.

Black beans. These small beans are common in Caribbean countries and are sometimes called turtle beans. They release some of their color in the form of a thick black juice during cooking, which gives a unique tint to foods such as rice that may be mixed with these beans. They are quite mild in flavor.

Lima beans. There are large and small lima beans; they are best known for their use in a North American dish called succotash. Other white beans include *great northern beans* and *navy beans,* famous for making delicious soup.

Mung beans. These small green beans are best known in North America in the form of bean sprouts in Chinese food. But in addition to being sprouted, they are also easy to cook as whole beans. In India and other Asian countries, they are valued for their digestibility. Split mung beans with or without skins are part of many Indian soups. Removing the skins (by straining the cooked beans) adds variety and makes beans more digestible.

Chickpeas (garbanzo beans). In Mediterranean and Oriental countries chickpeas are much more popular than in North America. They can be used in a variety of ways and they have a unique flavor, which is an asset in achieving the variety that is so important to the Superpyramid food

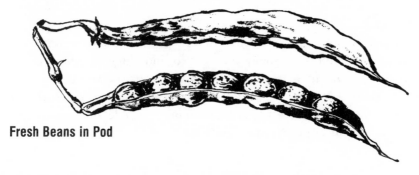

Fresh Beans in Pod

plan. Hummus, a Middle Eastern food made from these beans, makes a great spread for flat breads.

Fava (broad) beans. These are the only common bean that could cause favism, a specific illness that occurs in people with a hereditary predisposition. Favism is not a common problem, so it is difficult to say whether or not you should eat these beans. Fava beans are still very popular in Mediterranean countries. Broad bean seeds have been found in dwellings dating back to the Bronze Age. Ancient Greeks and Romans had a high regard for these beans.

Peas have long been part of classic dishes such as rice and peas. They can also be prepared as a separate dish just like any other legume. They were introduced in ancient times from India into China and were part of Greek and Roman cooking. Fresh peas, shelled at cooking time, or frozen peas add a special touch to any dish. Dry peas are widely available as split peas (green or yellow). Some restaurants pride themselves on their special recipes for split pea soup, reminding us how good such soups can be.

Lupines are not very popular today, but they are sometimes ground and used as a flour in some specialty products such as lupine pasta. In Mediterranean countries they were considered a food for the poor and, in fact, cooked lupines were given out free to the poor in ancient Rome. The Egyptians have used lupines since 2000 B.C.

Carob (or locust) bean and its pods. This unusual bean has found interesting uses in the food industry. Most likely you won't cook a pot of carob beans, but they have interesting properties. The bean itself is very high in a fiber that is effective at lowering blood cholesterol and is often found in some prepared foods. The pod is often roasted and used as a chocolate substitute. The carob is also known as St. John's bread, as legend has it that John the Baptist ate it in the desert.

Soybeans

Soybeans are in a group by themselves. Soybeans have a very high protein value but are usually not cooked and eaten as whole beans. Rather, they are used to prepare a multitude of special and valuable foods. These were once available only in Oriental or specialty stores but are now becoming more popular and more available and should be a key part of your Superpyramid food plan.

Soybean milk in liquid or powder form has become popular for people who cannot drink cow's milk (page 85). Many specialty stores carry soy milk, and pharmaceutical companies have developed infant formulas based on soy milk for infants who cannot tolerate cow's milk. The fact that soy milk is so valuable that it can be used in infant formula demonstrates the great body-building value of its proteins.

Tofu, a curded soy milk and the soy counterpart of cottage cheese, is the best known of the prepared soy products. It's high in protein and contains some good unsaturated fats (read more on fat in chapter 6). Tofu is made from cooked soybean milk that is coagulated with a calcium or magnesium salt. Many types and textures of tofu are used in Asia, and quite a few are now available in the United States.

Miso is a high-protein product made by fermenting, or culturing, soybeans and grains, usually rice or barley. It has a pasty consistency and is extremely aromatic. A soup made from it is as delicious as any you have ever tasted. Miso can also be used to make sauces, spreads, and other dishes. Some types of miso are fairly high in salt, so use only in moderation and in place of salt. Some pasteurized types of miso can be stored for months without refrigeration, while others require refrigeration. Read the label carefully.

Tempeh, another fermented soybean product, is popular in Indonesia. Tempeh comes in solid cakes that can be baked, broiled, or otherwise cooked as part of a main course. Often a grain such as rice or barley is cultured together with the soybeans.

Miso and tempeh transform the otherwise very mild soybean into highly flavorful products. There are entire books dedicated to recipes based on miso, tofu, tempeh, and related products.

Figure 9 shows the nutritional composition of tofu, tempeh, and miso.

The different flavors and texture of lentils, peas, chickpeas, red or white beans, and the various soybean products make meals exciting when legumes become an important part of your food plan. Each of these legumes makes possible the preparation of hundreds of diverse recipes. From now on do not think of legumes as just a pot of red beans but as an array of varied and appetizing dishes.

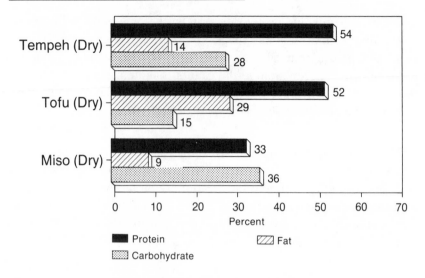

FIGURE 9. Nutritional Composition of Soybean Products

Don't Forget Variety

There are many ways to eat all these beans, lentils, and peas. They can be eaten whole, added to basic grain dishes such as pasta or rice, or prepared as soups and purees. Split pea and lentil soups have become famous in many regions, and hummus is a popular Mideastern chickpea puree. Look in the Superpyramid Kitchen (part 4) for more suggestions.

Flours made from legumes can be used in breads for variety and for extra protein value. Soybean proteins or whole soybeans are commonly used for this purpose.

In some European countries many beans are available in season as fresh beans in the pod. They are shelled fresh and cooked just like other legumes. No need for soaking, of course. Most commonly in North America beans are bought dry and make a very inexpensive food as a few ounces will supply many servings of cooked beans.

Beans as a Staple Superpyramid Food

It should now be clear why legumes and grains go together and are the cornerstones of the Superpyramid Plan. These two foods, with low-fat or nonfat milk products, preferably cultured, such as yogurt, must be your primary source of food energy, replacing some or all of the meat or poultry in your diet. If you choose not to eat any meat or fish at all, legumes become even more important, since they improve the protein value of grains and are a valuable source of iron.

Just as with grains, there are all kinds of legumes to suit all kinds of tastes. You can eat fresh or dry legumes, or you can choose the cultured beans, usually soybean products, that the Orient has given us.

A hearty *bean, lentil,* or *pea pot,* as described in the Superpyramid Kitchen, can be prepared every few days from many kinds of legumes. Each type has its own unique flavor. Experiment and find out which ones appeal to you. Add variety by alternating with dishes made with tofu or tempeh.

▲ KEY IDEAS

▲ *Legumes—beans, lentils, and peas—are one of the Superpyramid's cornerstones.*

▲ *Consume legumes or their products every day.*

▲ *The combination of legumes with whole grains is one key to a successful Super-pyramid Program.*

▲ *Combine beans and lentils with grains for good protein value.*

▲ *Red beans are a good source of iron.*

▲ *The fibers and proteins in legumes help control blood cholesterol.*

▲ *Most legumes are very low in fat. Soybeans and their products contain some fat, but it's good fat.*

NONFAT MILK PRODUCTS
A Treasure That Can Be Misused

Milk and its products are treasure troves of precious nutrients. But because they are sometimes high in saturated fat, they can be misused. *The milk products on tier one are either nonfat or so low in fat as to be practically fat-free.* These milk products are important to any healthy eating plan. They supply excellent proteins, calcium, and other important nutrients.

Milk is such a wonderful food that an endless number of products can be made—and indeed have been made—from it. They range from hundreds of yogurts and related cultured milks to cheeses and liquid milks.

Together with whole grains and beans, nonfat or very low-fat milk products should be the foundation of your meals.

Why Are Milk Products on Three Tiers?

Because the amount of fat in milk products ranges from nothing to quite high, you'll find milk products on three different tiers on the Superpyramid. Nonfat or practically nonfat (call them very low-fat if you wish) milk products are on tier one. Use them freely and as great sources of protein and calcium that balance grains and beans. From here we have to climb up all the way to tier four to find low-fat milk products. Tier four is small, and great moderation should be used with any food on this tier. On tier five, the smallest of the tiers, we find some medium-fat aged cheeses, such as Parmesan, which should be used only in small quantities as flavoring, or cheddar cheese, which should be used not more than once or twice a week in moderation in cooking or in sandwiches. And on tier five we find whole milk, to be used in tea or coffee or as a beverage in limited amounts. High-fat milk products such as butter, regular ice cream, cream cheese, half and half, and cream *are not on the Superpyramid,* which means they should not be part of your normal eating pattern. Like any food not on the Superpyramid, you can certainly use them for an occasional change of pace, say once or twice a month.

> **When** milk products are freed from most of their fat, they are the ultimate complement to the nutrients derived from plant foods. Keep this in mind whenever you plan a meal.

Nonfat Milk Products

How do you decide if a milk product belongs on tier one? If the label reads "nonfat" or if the nutritional analysis on the label shows fat as zero, you can buy that product with confidence and know that you can eat it freely. Skim (nonfat) milk and nonfat yogurt are two obvious choices.

But you do not have to be that strict. Even if a trace of fat is present the product can be very acceptable. *To understand how to judge this amount of fat, you must divide milk products into three groups.* The reason is that if a milk product is high in water—such as milk—the percentage of fat may appear to be very low, but if you removed that water, the percentage of fat would be quite high in relation to the other two major nutrients, protein and carbohydrates. If a product is labeled "95 percent fat-free," this is the same as saying that it is 5 percent fat *by weight.* In milk products with a high water content, most of the weight comes from the water— which is, of course, completely fat-free—but *all* of the fat comes from the milk solids. In other words, saying "this product has 3 percent fat, so it's practically fat-free" may be accurate for a fairly dry product such as mozzarella cheese but may not be correct for liquid milk, which has a large amount of fluid. There are ways to find out whether or not we have a very low-fat food without having to use a computer spreadsheet or go to a lab. The simplest way is to divide milk and its products— cheeses, yogurt, and so forth—according to the approximate amount of water present: high for whole milk and yogurts, medium for cottage cheese, and low for cheeses such as most aged cheese (cheddar, Swiss, etc.). Now we have a way to know if the product we want to use is truly so low in fat that it can be part of tier one as though it were nonfat or if this product belongs on tier four (low- and medium-low fat) or on tier five (medium fat).

▲ The first group—high in water—includes liquid milk, yogurts, and buttermilks. The percentage of water in these products is over 85 percent. Any of these products with less than *half a percent of fat*—in other words, the label might say something like "99.5 percent fat-free"—is so low in fat you should place it on the first tier as though for all practical purposes it was nonfat.

▲ The second group—medium water content, often about 70 to 75 percent—includes common cottage cheese. Any cottage cheese with 1 percent fat or less can be part of tier one. For all practical purposes you can consider these products nonfat. That trace of fat may in fact make the product much more acceptable to your taste buds than a totally nonfat cottage cheese.

▲ The third group—fairly low in water—is usually solid at room temperature. Aged cheeses belong in this third group, and their water content ranges from as little as 20 to 25 percent in dry grating cheeses to over 50 percent in softer cheeses. In this group the fat percent can be higher on the label—up to 3 percent—and still be a very acceptable and a true tier-one product. This is because there is so much less water that the amount of fat present *in relation to the total energy and nutrient intake* is just as low as for a product with half a percent fat but lots of water, such as fluid milk. However, you won't find too many aged cheeses that can be tier-one foods.

Another way to make sure that a milk product is nonfat or extremely low in fat is to make your own by skimming whole milk that has been pasteurized or boiled but not homogenized. Many dairies can supply this type of milk. The cream will float to the top, and after you remove it carefully you are left with real milk that has good flavor and is extremely low in fat. You can use this skim milk to make many products, such as yogurt or yogurt cheese. Another way is to buy the yogurt that some dairies make from this kind of nonhomogenized milk: you'll find a layer of fat on top. Remove this fat carefully, and the nonfat yogurt underneath is great.

Milk Products in History

In the eighth century B.C., the Greek poet Homer wrote:

> He sat down and milked the sheep and the bleating goat . . . he curdled half of the milk . . . the other part he put away in barrels to drink from.

Those were typical activities in ancient times in Mediterranean countries. Tools for grating cheese were described by other writers of that period. In those days hard cheese was used to flavor various foods. The Etruscans had pots to boil milk, and Roman writers give instructions on how to make and use milk products.

According to Persian tradition, Abraham owed his long life to yogurt. Yogurt was also given credit for curing Emperor Francis I of France of a debilitating illness.

In the history of milk products, liquid milk, as we are accustomed to drinking in North America, was the exception, not the rule. Milk was most often made into cheese or cultured into products that were the ancestors of yogurts. Why? Because before refrigeration, it was difficult to keep fresh milk. For this reason, milk as a beverage was uncommon except on the farms where it was produced or in local markets where farmers sold it the same day it was produced.

In those days, the best way to preserve milk was to culture it or to make it into cheese. Out of this need, yogurts, buttermilks, and cheeses became the most common way to consume the good things found in milk. These cultured foods and the various cheeses were found to be pleasant tasting and to keep much longer than fresh milk. You can still see how much longer cultured milk products keep by comparing the expiration date on a carton of milk to that on a container of yogurt. Some hard cheeses can keep for years in a reasonably cool place.

The nomadic peoples of the Middle East in past centuries used milk from goats, sheep, camels, and sometimes cows. Temperatures in the desert were high in the summer, and the risk of contamination or spoilage of fresh milk was high. As different microorganisms fermented milk in these harsh conditions, people soon discovered that the results were quite variable, and sometimes a nice-tasting product would result. This was due to the action of bacteria producing lactic acid (*lactic* from the Latin *lac* for "milk"). The resulting product was usually referred to as *sour milk*.

For these people, milk products had important practical implications. They discovered long ago that they could milk the same animals year after year, making it possible to enjoy food from an animal without killing it. And in doing so, they inadvertently got ample calcium and built strong bones as well. Meat, on the other hand, provides practically no calcium, and the animal can be eaten only once.

The process of making cultured milks in the Middle East evolved slowly, and eventually the raw milk was boiled over open fires and then fermented with a *culture* derived from a previous batch of the product in the same way we make yogurts today.

The Nutritional Treasures of Milk Products

Milk products have many valuable nutrients, but those that are the most vital in our food plan are proteins and calcium. A food plan totally devoid of milk proteins and milk calcium and based on grains and plant foods can indeed be successful—this is a *vegan* diet—but it is a very tough plan to execute properly.

Milk sugar and cultured milks. Cultured milks and cheeses have another advantage over liquid milk beyond better keeping qualities. Many people cannot digest milk sugar (lactose) well, which causes some digestive problems. However, in the process of making yogurt and related products, the milk sugar that was present in the fresh milk is converted to lactic acid. This lactic acid and other acids give yogurt its characteristic tangy flavor. In making cheeses, the lactose is drained off with the whey. (Whey is the liquid portion that is left after most cheeses are made.)

Lactose intolerance, as it's called, is found in many older people who have not drunk much milk in their adult life. The digestive enzyme, called lactase, that breaks down lactose has disappeared from their digestive tracts, probably from lack of use. Poor digestion of milk sugar also occurs in many Asian and other populations where milk is not a common food. Today some products are available that have been treated with lactase to make the milk lactose-free. But cultured milks and cheeses give us just as good a choice.

Proteins. The fact that milk proteins are great for building tissues was known long before twentieth-century biochemistry. Mammals, from humans to monkeys, from goats to dogs, give milk as the first food for their newborns. This superior source of protein combines well with grain and legume proteins, and such a mixture is one of the cornerstones of the Superpyramid plan.

Calcium. The milk proteins in natural foods are always associated with precious calcium, a mineral sorely lacking in meat, poultry, and fish. Meat-eating animals such as the dog always partake of the bones as well as the meat when they eat their prey. This adds calcium to the otherwise practically calcium-free muscle and organ meats. Humans have an easier choice: they can eat a calcium-rich, high-quality protein food in milk products.

The lack of calcium in meat may be one reason that osteoporosis (loss of bone) among the elderly is so widespread in North America. The high protein content of meat, poultry, and fish may in fact lead to increased calcium loss from the body.

Another problem is that meat, poultry, and fish (as well as some soft drinks) are high in phosphorus and practically calcium-free. The high-protein, high-phosphorus, and low-calcium intake typical of meat-based diets may well be a cause of bone degeneration.

A third factor contributing to bone loss in aging is lack of physical activity. Other factors such as hormones are involved, which is the reason postmenopausal women are at greater risk for osteoporosis than men or young women.

More About Calcium

Calcium is well known as a major component of bone. Most people think of bones as static structures like construction beams. Bones are, in fact, *alive,* and just like all other living tissues need nourishment and replenishment. Otherwise they disintegrate little by little, leaving what's left of the skeleton weak, brittle, and prone to fractures.

In 1983, the *British Medical Journal* carried an editorial by Dr. Allan St. J. Dixon entitled "Non-hormonal treatment of osteoporosis," and in the same year the National Institutes of Health called a major conference on degenerative bone diseases, which issued a consensus statement on the need for higher calcium intake in the American diet. In a short span of time, the problems of bone degeneration and fragile skeletons had become a major medical concern.

The reason for this is that calcium goes in and out of bones day after day to maintain the level of this mineral as constant as possible in blood and other body tissues. At the same time, bones have to retain enough calcium to stay strong. It is later in life that problems of weaker bones begin to show up, and at autopsy, the vertebrae of old people very often show the tremendous amount of bone loss that has taken place. Hip fractures and very painful fractures of the bones of the spinal column that lead to major forms of back pain can result from bone loss. This distressing condition should be enough to make anyone consider the need for more calcium from milk products and less protein from calcium-free meats.

Beyond Bone

But calcium does much more than build bones. A small but crucial part of the body's calcium supply remains in the bloodstream and plays a role in blood coagulation, hormone reactions, and nerve and muscle cell function. Even the heart needs calcium to do its job. In the 1980s two new functions of calcium in the body came to light: its role in preventing high blood pressure and possibly some forms of cancer.

High blood pressure. Dr. David McCarron and his associates at the Oregon Health Sciences University in Portland have determined that there is a connection between insufficient calcium intake and certain types of high blood pressure. They found that people with diets rich in calcium had a 50 percent lower risk of developing high blood pressure than people who did not consume enough calcium. Further experiments showed that under a physician's guidance, calcium could lower mildly elevated blood pressure.

Cancer. Dr. William R. Bruce, at the Ontario Cancer Institute in Toronto, and his colleagues have proposed an interesting theory regarding calcium's possible role in cancer prevention. We know that not all calcium we consume is absorbed; some winds up in the intestines waiting to be eliminated. This unabsorbed calcium may bind with toxic waste materials from our food and "escort" them from the body before they can do any harm. New research seems to support this hypothesis, though much more investigation of this calcium-cancer connection is needed. In the meantime, since reasonable levels of dietary calcium can do no harm and can help us in many ways, we should make sure that we get enough in our foods.

The Calcium-Phosphorus Connection

Let's look more closely at the calcium-phosphorus connection we mentioned earlier. Both calcium and phosphorus are essential to the body; no one can live without them. Like calcium, phosphorus plays key roles in bone formation and in hundreds of biochemical reactions in the body; it is also crucial in energy production. Biochemistry textbooks are full of phosphorus compounds.

But the problem is that most foods—not only meats but even our basic foods such as grains and beans—contain phosphorus but little calcium. For good health, phosphorus must be balanced with calcium and other minerals. While green vegetables and certain kinds of tofu contain some calcium, we may not consume enough of these foods to meet our calcium needs.

So if we wish to obtain our calcium from natural whole foods, the only practical solution is to consume it in the form of milk products. Yogurts and low-fat milk products also offer high-quality proteins that, together with grains and beans, complete the protein foundation of the Superpyramid plan.

It's important to remember that when fat is separated from milk, the calcium stays behind in the milk. That means butter and cream are not good sources of calcium. (Because of their high fat content you should avoid using them as a regular part of your meals anyway.)

Milk Products on the First Tier

The dairy products on the first tier include

1. nonfat (or very low-fat) yogurts and cultured milks such as kefir and buttermilk
2. nonfat (or very low-fat) cheeses
3. nonfat (or very low-fat) liquid milk

Yogurts and Other Cultured Milks

Yogurt and other cultured milks are some of your best dairy choices. Because of the predigested lactose, they can be tolerated by more people than regular liquid milk. In addition, the flavor and texture of a very low-fat sour milk product are often superior to a liquid milk deprived of its fat. There seems to be more substance to yogurt than to skim milk; yogurt gives us the sensation that we're eating something rich in flavor and good nutrients rather than just drinking a beverage too mild in taste to satisfy us.

Yogurt is a truly universal food. The word *yogurt*, which comes from the Turkish, is spelled differently in various languages—*yoghurt, yaort, yourt, yogur, yaghourt,* and so on. Yogurt also goes by some different names: in some regions of Italy it's *cieddu,* Greeks have *tiaourti,* in Nepal it's *shoshim,* and in Egypt it's *zabadi.* In fact, there are over fifty names for yogurt in languages around the world, and at least as many varieties of this product. Every civilization appears to have its yogurt-type foods.

Yogurts and many types of buttermilks are called *cultured,* meaning that they are made from the growth of living microorganisms in a nutrient base. Yogurts are produced by the action on milk of selected microorganisms such as *Lactobacillus acidophilus, Lactobacillus bulgaricus,* and others.

Yogurt has become so popular that you can buy it today in many forms, sweetened and unsweetened, with or without additives. Often gelatin, gums, or milk powders are added to make the yogurt firm. There are so many yogurts available that you need to read the labels very carefully. The best choice is an unsweetened nonfat plain yogurt. If it contains agents to make it more firm, choose a vegetable gum, such as guar or locust bean, or nonfat milk powder rather than gelatin. Sometimes yogurt without added thickeners is fairly liquid and is actually the traditional yogurt of many cultures. This kind of very plain yogurt gives you a versatile ingredient for many recipes. You can eat it straight from the container or add honey, brown sugar, or fruit. Or you can use it in salad dressings, sauces, or dips or as part of homemade breads and baked goods to provide extra protein and calcium. Yogurt can fit into Mexican, Italian, or Middle Eastern dishes very well.

As you make yogurt an important part of your meals, it's vital not only to choose the right type from a nutritional point of view, but to have variety in flavor as well. Different microorganisms are often used alone or together with the classic ones we've seen, resulting in different consistencies and flavors. An example is *bifidus,* which is becoming more popular both in the U.S. and in Europe. It is now sometimes added to commercially available yogurts. A milk cultured only with *bifidus* should be properly called *acidophilus milk.*

Presweetened yogurts, often with added fruit, are fine, but be careful as they often contain fairly large amounts of sugar. Commercial frozen yogurt is a good low-fat replacement for ice cream, but again, it's best not to overdo sweets. Unsweetened yogurt should be your first choice. You can then use it by itself, in savory dishes, with fresh or dry fruits, or blended with fruit juices for delicious drinks. You'll find recipes in the Superpyramid Kitchen, including ways to make yogurt and yogurt cheese at home. Enjoy the versatility of fresh, live yogurts!

Yogurt Consumption in the World

Yogurt consumption has increased dramatically in the U.S. and Canada in the past twenty years, but it's still much lower than in countries like France and Switzerland. It is in fact still extremely low, which means that few people are making yogurt a meaningful part of their meals. The average Frenchman consumed twenty-three pounds of yogurt a year in the early 1980s; in Switzerland during the same period the figure was about thirty-two pounds per person, some of it used in a muesli breakfast, which is quite common even in sophisticated hotels. In the U.S. and Canada, yogurt consumption has doubled in the last twenty years, but it was still only about two to three pounds per person per year in the 1980s, a negligible amount.

Other Milk Products

Buttermilk is the milk that remains after butter—which means the fat—has been removed. *Old-fashioned buttermilk is a nonfat or very low-fat product.* Some modern commercial buttermilks have been cultured and may or may not be the by-products of butter making. Always read the label carefully: buttermilk should have no fat—or at least less than half a percent—to belong to tier one. Higher-fat buttermilks should be used only in moderation and belong to the fourth or fifth tier of the Superpyramid, depending on the percentage of fat.

Kefir is somewhere between yogurt and buttermilk in flavor and is a pleasant change from either of these two products. Quite a few microorganisms contribute to the flavor of kefir; depending on the microorganisms present a variety of kefirs can be produced.

Acidophilus milk, as we have already seen, is usually cultured with the *bifidus* microorganism and is usually made from low-fat milk. It's popular in Russia, Romania, Greece, Turkey, and other countries in that region.

Sweet acidophilus milk is milk in which the lactose (milk sugar) has been predigested by splitting it into its two component sugars, galactose and glucose. It's for people who cannot tolerate lactose. The other choice for lactose-intolerant people, as we have seen, is a cultured yogurt.

Liquid whey is the by-product of cheesemaking. It's practically unknown in the U.S. If you make yogurt cheese at home, the liquid that remains after the cheese is separated is the *whey.* It contains excellent proteins (lactoalbumin) and calcium. When whey is made from a cultured milk product, the milk sugar is predigested because it has been changed to lactic acid, which gives the whey a delicious, thirst-quenching flavor. It's the ideal beverage on a hot summer day or after intense physical activity.

Nonfat Cheeses
Nonfat cheeses such as nonfat or very low-fat cottage cheese and related cheeses that have various local names are excellent sources of protein and calcium.

Yogurt cheese is another way to eat yogurt. It's uncommon in the U.S. but popular in other parts of the world. People in the Middle East used to place their yogurt in bags made of animal skins and then hang the bag so that the liquid would slowly seep out. The yogurt would become progressively firmer until it reached a cheeselike consistency, much more flavorful than nonfat cottage cheese (page 363).

Skim (Nonfat) Milk
Fresh nonfat milk (or milk with less than half a percent of fat) is a tier-one product. Sometimes commercial nonfat milk is thickened with nonfat dry milk powder, which is nutritionally acceptable but may not be quite as appealing if you plan to drink it regularly.

EGG WHITES
No discussion of high-quality protein would be complete without including egg whites. *In fact, egg white contains one of the best proteins available.* Its biological protein value, which measures how well a protein can build tissues such as muscles in the body, rates 100 percent on protein value scales and is used as a standard for judging other protein sources. Its protein value is higher than that of meat and fish. As an additional benefit, egg whites are fat-free and combine well with many dishes. They can act as a binder or increase fluffiness when used in baking.

Use egg whites freely in the Superpyramid plan. They are a basic tier-one food, supplying superior protein that goes well with grains and other plant foods.

See the section on eggs in the Superpyramid Kitchen for recipes and ideas on how to prepare great dishes with egg whites.

How It All Fits Together

We have now completed the foundation of our Superpyramid by combining milk products with grains, beans, potatoes, and egg whites. Together these foods give us energy, protein, essential fats, plus a long list of vitamins, minerals, and fibers. Nonfat or very low-fat milk products provide us with calcium, a precious and elusive element. Remember that calcium not only builds bones, but also controls many metabolic activities and may play a role in preventing some types of cancer and high blood pressure. The proteins in milk products and egg whites also complement the proteins in plant foods to provide our complete protein requirements.

▲ KEY IDEAS

- ▲ Nonfat (or very low-fat) milk products are the ultimate complements to grains and beans.
- ▲ Nonfat (or very low-fat) milk products provide precious calcium and high-quality protein. Combine them with grains and beans to enhance the plant proteins.
- ▲ Cultured milk products such as yogurt are easy to digest and very versatile.
- ▲ Egg whites supply excellent protein but no calcium.
- ▲ Keep in mind the cornerstones of the first tier:
    - ▲ whole grains
    - ▲ legumes
    - ▲ nonfat or very low-fat milk products complemented by egg whites
    - ▲ potatoes

CHAPTER

▲ *5* ▲

The Second Tier

Different Treasures

The foods on the second tier are vegetables and fruits. Remember, the foods on the first tier should be your main sources of energy and protein, while vegetables and fruits should be considered primarily as a source of *protective nutrients.* The only exceptions are fruits such as raisins and dates, which are high in fruit sugars, and some root vegetables, such as potatoes, which are high in complex carbohydrates. These are all significant sources of energy. In fact, potatoes provide so much energy that they are on tier one of the Superpyramid.

The key concept to remember is that the health-giving treasures found in the foods on the second tier are different from those found on the first tier.

The Protective Foods

Vegetables and fruits have long been called protective foods by scientists because of their high content of vitamin C, beta-carotene (a plant source of vitamin A), and other vitamins, minerals, and fiber. All these nutrients seem to have been specially made to complement the nutrients in grains, beans, and milk products found on the first tier of the Superpyramid.

THE FOODS OF THE *Second Tier*

▲ Vegetables of all kinds: green and red leaves, roots, stems, and non-sweet "fruits" such as tomatoes and peppers.

▲ Fruits of all kinds from peaches to oranges, from figs to grapes.

To obtain the protective benefits of vegetables and fruits, you must eat them in sufficient amounts every day. And the best way to eat them is fresh and raw. When these foods are cooked, prepared, or preserved, some precautions must be taken to prevent damage to the various nutrients.

One of the characteristics of the Mediterranean diet is the high consumption of fruits and vegetables compared to northern European countries. This is certainly one reason for the lower incidence of certain chronic diseases in the south.

Mysterious Protection Through the Ages

The endless variety of vegetables and fruits makes it difficult to tell a simple story of their history as human foods. They are so very different from one another that each has its own health-giving properties.

Vegetables, especially green leaves such as lettuce (the ancient lettuce had dark leaves, not pale, as some head lettuces—iceberg, for instance —have today), were at one time considered to have medicinal properties in the sense that we think of medicinal herbs today. Fruits too were considered medicinal, but because of their energy—fruit sugar—content, they were also considered energy-giving foods.

Our modern, science-oriented society should feel very humble that, thousands of years before the discovery of vitamins, minerals, and other protective factors in fruits and vegetables, people realized that the energy and protein foods—grains, beans, milk products, meats, and fishes —were not sufficient for good health. These foods needed to be balanced by others, which seemed to bring almost miraculous health benefits to a diet based on the traditional energy-protein foods.

Fruits and vegetables were miracle foods indeed. Picture a Chinese sailor of the fifth century. He carries pots to grow ginger on his ship. He knows that if he eats the ginger, his gums will not swell, his wounds will heal properly, he won't be debilitated or die by the end of a long sea journey. Why? We now know that ginger supplies vitamin C, which prevents a disease called scurvy, the cause of those problems. In the sixteenth century and later, the British navy used citrus fruit as the magic charm to ward off this dreadful disease. Vitamin C, an essential vitamin missing from cereals, beans, meat, poultry, fish, and milk products (unless the animal eats fresh grass), is present in most fresh fruits and vegetables.

Picture now a blind child in Central America. Here, children raised on corn and beans without the addition of fresh vegetables or fruits would sometimes lose their eyesight permanently. They had enough protein and enough energy but lacked a mysterious protective factor. It turned out to be beta-carotene, which is converted to vitamin A in the body and is essential to healthy eyes. This beta-carotene, as precious as vitamin C, is found in dark green and yellow vegetables and fruits.

Always think about fresh vegetables and fruits in terms of their protective action in the body. This protective action, known through the ages, has recently been found to be even greater than previously thought and to extend to such diseases as cancer and perhaps even heart disease.

It is tempting to write page after page of stories about how many different civilizations found ways to add the special properties of vegetables and fruits to their energy-supplying and body-building foods. The ancient Chinese, peasant or rich, were so aware of the health benefits of fresh vegetables that they developed special varieties to withstand the cold climate of northern China in the winter months and used straw mats to protect the plants as necessary. These measures made it possible for every Chinese to have fresh vegetables year round.

The Chinese also sprouted beans and bean sprouts are indeed a vegetable rather than a legume, like the beans on the first tier of the Superpyramid.

Once again, before modern science had identified and named the wonderful nutritional factors in vegetables, mankind had discovered how valuable these fresh vegetables were for good health, even though they did not supply much energy.

One family of vegetables had a special place in ancient history: the garlic and onion family. Garlic in particular was used as an antiseptic to treat wounds and was also used against intestinal parasites. This latter use has continued until recently and garlic is still used successfully for this purpose by dog breeders. (See page 110 for some of the beneficial compounds in garlic and onions.)

> **N**ot only did various ancient cultures realize the need for fruits and vegetables, but even meat-eating animals such as dogs in the wild normally eat grasses and other vegetation to supplement their high-meat diets.

Fruits in Ancient Mediterranean History

Many native fruits, including nuts, were an integral part of the diet in ancient Rome and Greece. The use of native Mediterranean fruits, including apples, pears, plums, grapes, figs, quinces, pomegranates, olives, and almonds, reaches back to prehistoric times.

Figs, pomegranates, grapes, olives, and almonds were held in high esteem by ancient Mediterranean people. In the Bible we find that the promise to Moses was to bring his people to "a land of vines [grapes], fig trees and pomegranates; a land of olive oil and honey." Just as milk was preserved by culturing, so grapes were preserved either by fermentation into wines (most likely quite low in alcohol) or vinegars or dried as raisins. Thus, many of the benefits of grapes could be preserved throughout the year. Grapes were so valued as a healthful food that ancient Italians used them to make a sweetening agent called *vino cotto*, which means "cooked wine." The name *wine* should not confuse you: there was no alcohol in this product. It was prepared by boiling down grape juice until quite condensed, with honey probably added to help preserve it. This long-forgotten sweetener could be a welcome addition to our modern tables.

Eating dried figs is an excellent way to get the benefit of this fruit. Figs were so important in the classical world that Athenaeus, an ancient writer on food and health, wrote about how various Mediterranean regions claimed to grow the best figs and how figs were recognized as one of the best foods to satisfy hunger quickly.

Later, other fruits were imported into Mediterranean countries and became part of the Mediterranean diet after the fall of the Roman Empire. Many of these came to the region from distant lands. The Seville orange—the bitter orange used to make orange marmalades—originated in India, came to the Arab countries, and entered Spain probably in the early Middle Ages. Although there were no sweet oranges in Europe until they were brought to Italy in the fifteenth century, lemons were known in ancient Greek and Roman times and were often called the Persian fruit. Some Roman writers attributed unique properties to lemons, using them for breath sweeteners and for medicinal purposes. The reputation of lemons was such that Dr. Thomas Braun, in *The Mediterranean Diets in Health and Disease* relates that criminals who had been condemned to die by snakebite in a public amphitheater believed they could be saved by eating lemons on their way to execution. (Certainly, an unproven use—don't try it!) Ancient Jews used lemons and possibly other citrus fruits in some major rituals.

Traditional Ways of Preserving Vegetables

Just as ancient peoples preserved fruits by various methods, they also felt the need to preserve the precious properties of vegetables for the cold winter months, especially in northern countries.

The methods available were curing with salt or honey (later sugar) and fermentation. In very cold Nordic regions, of course, the natural subfreezing weather provided ideal cold storage. Because salt was so crucial in preserving foods, wars were fought to gain access to areas where it could be obtained. It is ironic that, given our present concern about excessive use of salt, in many areas humanity has survived because sea salt helped preserve foods.

Sauerkraut, cabbage cultured with various microorganisms with some salt added, has been used for years in Germany, Switzerland, central Europe, and Russia as a wintertime source of vitamin C and fiber.

Kimchi, an essential dish in most Korean meals, is a mixture of fermented Oriental radish, Chinese cabbage and cucumber, and often other fruits and vegetables. Just as northern Europeans used sauerkraut, East Asians used kimchi as a source of vitamin C in winter.

The number of fermented fruits and vegetables that have been used through the centuries in the Orient, in the Middle East, and in nearly every region of the world is almost endless. With exotic names such as *chonggak-kimchi* or *nakamiso-zuké*, many of these products are deeply embedded in the traditional diet of each region.

These brief highlights of the history of some fruits and vegetables were chosen to reinforce their crucial protective role in the human body. They show how, long before modern science, humanity knew they had to have some fruits and vegetables throughout the year to stay well. No wonder fruits and vegetables became known as medicinal foods!

Why Fruits and Vegetables Are Protective

Let's look more closely at some of the key nutritional factors that make vegetables and fruits such essential additions to the energy foods of tier one. Only a few words need to be said about the classical function of vitamins and minerals in fruits and vegetables: They contain vitamin C and beta-carotene, which are practically absent from tier-one foods. Vitamin C is essential to wound healing, healthy gums, resistance to infection, and many other body functions. Beta-carotene can be converted by our body to vitamin A, which is critical to the health of the eyes, skin, and all the tissues of the body such as the lining of the lungs and digestive tract. Vitamin E, which we have seen in the germ of wheat and other grains, is also present in many foods of tier two. And vitamin K, critical to proper blood coagulation after injury, is found in green vegetables such as lettuce, broccoli, turnip greens, and asparagus.

Many minerals are also present in vegetables and fruits. They provide potassium, a key mineral in human cells, particularly important in controlling blood pressure. Oranges, bananas, tomatoes, and peppers are excellent sources in this regard, for they supply plentiful potassium with very little sodium. Edible green leaves always contain magnesium, because that mineral is an essential part of chlorophyll, the green pigment that colors leaves. Other good sources are avocados, Swiss chard, and other dark greens. Few people realize that some dark green leaves are also a reasonable source of calcium, though not as high in calcium as milk products.

These classical functions of vitamins and minerals have been described often and are well known. But in recent years a host of new functions has been discovered for some of these compounds in fruits and vegetables, and many other trace substances with special protective functions have been discovered, all making fruits and vegetables more important for disease prevention than ever before in the history of medicine and nutrition.

And in the past twenty years, the special fiber of fruits and vegetables has been found to be a valuable complement to the fibers of grains.

The Great Antioxidants

Let's start with the three great antioxidants in fruits and vegetables: vitamin C, beta-carotene, and vitamin E. Vitamin C is the body's water-soluble antioxidant, while vitamin E and beta-carotene are the oil-soluble antioxidants. The human body needs both kinds of protection, since it is made up of both types of materials, water inside and around cells, as well as cell membranes that have components more closely related to oils than to water.

Many of the vital reactions within the body involve oxygen. Unfortunately, these processes can create harmful by-products, including what biochemists call free radicals, which can attack the body's cells.

To protect us, we have vitamin C that works well as an antioxidant in the watery parts of the body. Considering that as much as 60 to 70 percent of our body weight is water, you can see what a key role vitamin C plays!

Vitamin C is also able to help protect our body from attack by *nitrosamines.* These cancer-causing compounds are formed when nitrites, a type of food preservative, react with amines present in all protein foods as amino acids. Nitrites and nitrates are typically used to preserve highly perishable meats such as bacon and ham as well as most luncheon meats (the label will usually say the product contains sodium nitrite and nitrate). High temperatures—when, for example, bacon is fried—can cause nitrites to form nitrosamines. But vitamin C seems to inhibit these reactions. If you eat bacon (not a Superpyramid food), be sure to drink some fresh citrus juice or eat some fresh fruit such as oranges or tomatoes with it.

Other parts of the body repel water just as oils do, but they accept oils and substances soluble in oils. These parts include our cell membranes, the delicate sheets that envelop our cells. The membranes keep in the water that's supposed to be inside the cell and keep out the water that's supposed to stay out. These membranes need oil-soluble factors to protect them, and vitamin E and beta-carotene can do just that.

Beta-carotene and other carotenes are the pigments that give color to green, yellow, and orange vegetables and fruits. Populations with low rates of certain cancers eat diets very rich in carotenes in the form of dark green leaves and many orange or yellow fruits and vegetables. Animal studies support this evidence from the geography of health and disease.

A fascinating new role for antioxidant vitamins has come to light recently, and we can truly say *come to light* as it refers to vision and the eye. It appears that antioxidants, particularly beta-carotene and vitamin E, may prevent the formation or the progress of cataracts in the eye. Both animal experiments and clinical studies support this protective effect. Over 20 million people in the world have cataracts or cataract-like changes in the eye. Cataracts cause the lens to become progressively more and more opaque until surgery is needed to treat it by extirpating it, a very drastic process. There appears to be a slowing-down of the progression of the opacity if antioxidants are given. Better yet, let's do our best to prevent the formation of cataracts by always keeping our intake of antioxidants high, in this case especially beta-carotene and vitamin E.

The Newer Protective Compounds

Plant sterols—found in many vegetables and seeds—have been known since the 1950s to lower blood cholesterol, which means they protect against heart disease. It's amazing that with so much talk about cholesterol these days, so little is said about the precious, beneficial sterols. Some animal studies seem to show that these compounds also offer some protection against certain types of cancer.

Phenols, flavonoids, phytates, sulfides, glucarates, indoles, isothiocynates, phtalides, lignans, mono- and di-terpenes, coumarins, salicilates, and others are found on the list of possible cancer-protective factors. The list of such compounds in fruits and vegetables keeps growing. For example, in 1992, a new sulfur compound in broccoli has been identified as protective.

Citric and malic acid are present in fruits and vegetables. These organic acids are used by the body for energy, and the final result—which puzzles the nonscientist—is that instead of making the body acid, they make it alkaline. Eat lots of fruits and your urine will be more alkaline. Why is this important? Because other foods contain substances that do the opposite, and the mixture of vegetables and fruits with grains, beans, or meat products results in a urine with the right acidity. This is important in preventing some types of kidney stones. This acid-alkaline balance was stressed much more in old physiological chemistry textbooks than it is now, but it is additional proof that fruits and vegetables go well with grains.

Mild laxatives that help proper bowel function are present in some fruits such as prunes and cherries.

More on Cancer Prevention

The importance of vegetables and fruits in cancer prevention led the National Academy of Sciences in 1992 to publish *Diet, Nutrition and Cancer*. In this book, a distinguished panel of medical and nutritional scientists concluded that "there is sufficient epidemiological evidence that consumption of certain vegetables, especially carotene-rich (dark green and deep yellow) vegetables and cruciferous vegetables (cabbage, broccoli, cauliflower, and Brussels sprouts) is associated with the reductions of cancer at several sites [organs] in humans."

Some of the compounds we have seen as protective against cancer were identified and studied because some medical detectives had earlier done their homework. In 1972, one of them, Dr. S. Graham, and his associates had found that people with stomach cancer ate fewer raw vegetables than the healthy "control" population. A 1976 study in Japan showed lower rates of stomach cancer among people who ate lettuce and celery. Studies in New York State and Israel showed that higher consumption of broccoli, cabbage, and Brussels sprouts was correlated with lower rates of cancer.

The American Cancer Society has in recent years run full-page ads in major magazines with the headline "A defense against cancer can be cooked up in your kitchen." They brightened up the ad with pictures of green and yellow vegetables and fruits. Among the plant foods they listed as part of this defense were all the dark green leafy vegetables (such as spinach, dark lettuce, and chicory), carrots, sweet potatoes, tomatoes, pumpkin, winter squash, citrus fruits, Brussels sprouts, cantaloupes, peaches, and broccoli.

The Special Fibers of Fruits and Vegetables

Pectin, a gellike water-soluble fiber, is abundant in fruits and vegetables but low in many grains such as wheat. Wheat and other grains, on the other hand, contain mostly insoluble fibers in their outer layers (the bran). There is no doubt that both types of fiber are beneficial and should be part of your daily food intake.

The cholesterol-lowering effect of pectins has been confirmed by many researchers, and recently the scientists at the Health Research Studies Center have shown that pectin mixed with other fibers in a pharmacological preparation helped lower blood cholesterol in people with high levels.

Antioxidants: Another Heart Disease Connection?

In the late 1980s and early 1990s something new has been emerging in the already complex picture of protection against heart disease. Damage by oxygen acting in an abnormal way—producing so-called free radicals —may make the effect of certain types of cholesterol on the arteries more harmful. It is possible that the oil-soluble antioxidant vitamins such as vitamins C, E, and beta-carotene may offer some protection and work together with a proper food plan.

Dr. Charles Hennekens and coworkers at Harvard University fed beta-carotene to a large number of volunteers and found less heart disease in the group taking beta-carotene than in a similar group not taking it. The researchers emphasize that these are preliminary results and should not be considered final, but these results make sense in light of the antioxidant protection beta-carotene may offer against the harmful kinds of cholesterol in the arteries.

Even though this research is in the very early stages and no definitive statements are possible, eating more fruits and vegetables rich in beta-carotene—as well as foods high in vitamins C and E—is a step that just may help. Another good reason to eat plenty of tier-two foods.

Omega-3 Oils in Green Leaves

Although vegetables are generally very low in fat, dark green leaves contain what may be important traces of some special oils. They are called omega-3 oils, and since they are similar to oils abundant in some fish, we will discuss them more extensively in chapter 6. These oils may also have a protective effect on the heart and blood circulation. They are used in the synthesis of *prostaglandins,* which are extremely important mediators of key biochemical reactions in the body. We'll see in chapter 6 some of the functions of these oils, which appear to protect against heart disease.

While all green leaves have some omega-3 oils, one weed has been found to be particularly rich in this oil. Drs. Artemis Simopoulos and Norman Salem at the National Institutes of Health found that a green leaf called *purslane (Portulaca oleracea),* widely used in Greece and other Mediterranean regions, is especially high in these omega-3 oils and is of course free from the cholesterol of high-fat fish, which are also a source of these oils. The researchers found this plant growing wild in fields around one of the buildings where their laboratory was located. It's interesting that in various parts of North America purslane is considered a weed.

A Weed in the Capay Valley

Between two small ranges of northern California mountains, isolated from the turbulent highways and byways of other parts of this region, rests the Capay Valley in quiet seclusion. It is the ideal fertile, peaceful place for the old-fashioned farming that Paul and Dru love to do. Here, together with vegetables, fruits, and nuts, the Mexican farmworkers also pick and eat what they call *verdolaga,* considered by most people a weed to remove and put in the compost pile. What was it? Nothing else but the omega-3-rich purslane we have just talked about. After learning about its value, Paul and Dru one day brought it along to the weekly farmers' market in Palo Alto, thus bringing back to the modern world a precious vegetable that had been forgotten.

Purslane

Omega-3 Oils in Seaweeds

Another source of omega-3 oils is sea plants such as seaweeds, and data are now being gathered about how much they may contain. These plants may also contain a particular type of omega-3 oil called EPA, which has special physiological qualities to be discussed in detail in chapter 6. Unless you are an expert on sea vegetation, do not harvest your own. Reputable brands use plants with a long history of safe use, which come from clean ocean waters, away from possible contamination.

Choose Whole Foods

What's important to keep in mind is that some research shows that eating fruits and vegetables high in vitamins, fiber, and other special substances may protect against some types of cancer and heart disease. However, it must be stressed that although this protective effect may be due in part to the nutrients we've discussed, it could also be due to lesser-known, or even undiscovered, compounds present in these foods. That's why *whole* foods should be the foundation of the meal.

Avoiding Nutrient Loss in Foods

Vitamin C and beta-carotene are highly sensitive to oxygen—that's what makes them such protective antioxidants. But that same sensitivity also makes them extremely vulnerable to damage when food is prepared. If you leave juices or cut fruits or vegetables exposed to the air longer than a few minutes, the vitamin C in them will be slowly destroyed by oxygen. By the time you consume the food, there may not be any vitamin C left. Make juices fresh and drink them right away, and if you cut your vegetables and fruits, do so just before using them. The same applies to such foods as mashed potatoes, french fries, or pureed vegetables: avoid them unless they are freshly prepared. Precooked foods, so popular in our fast-moving world, can lose a lot of their vitamin C when reheated.

Although beta-carotene is more resistant to degradation than vitamin C, you still need to be careful. In general, avoid reheating precooked foods. Preparing your own food fresh and investing some time in doing so will pay off in many ways!

Some cooks like to add baking soda to the water when cooking vegetables to keep them green (this method is often used with green beans). However, this addition causes B-vitamin losses and should be avoided. Adding vinegar, which is acidic, is a better way to preserve the bright green of vegetables while they cook.

The surest way to get all the benefits and goodness of fruits and vegetables is to consume them fresh, either raw or cooked just before use. Never discard the cooking water from vegetables—if you do, you're throwing away valuable water-soluble nutrients such as B vitamins! Drink that water as a broth, or use it as a base when you're making a soup. Microwaving or baking makes it possible to use little or no added water and thus minimize vitamin loss.

CHOICES OF VEGETABLES AND FRUITS

Is one vegetable or fruit better than another? It's like asking the parent of two wonderful, smart children who's the best. Any vegetable or fruit that you like and find in your area is probably a highly desirable part of a good food plan. However, in this chapter we'll focus on a few selected fruits and vegetables that are high in precious nutrients or that form a major part of the diet in regions with low rates of certain diseases. But remember, even though the vegetables mentioned in this book should be your leading choices, there are countless others—perhaps not so rich in nutrients—that you can also use in your meals for added variety, flavor, and color. And who knows? Some day some new protective factors may be found in these other vegetables.

VEGETABLES

Vegetables will be grouped into leaves, roots, stems, and the nonsweet fruits most people consider vegetables, such as peppers and tomatoes, even though botanically they are fruits.

Green Leaves

A green leaf is one of the most precious of all vegetables. One of the first choices is the kind of green leaves that can be eaten raw in a salad. As a general rule, dark-colored leaves are very high in carotenes, including beta-carotene (the same is true for roots and fruits). These high-carotene foods are a must in the daily menu. Eat some each day.

Leaves for Great Salads

Most of the leaves that can be used as the foundation for a salad are either one of the many *chicories* or *lettuces*. Cultivated chicories belong to the botanical genus *Cichorium*, while lettuces belong to the genus *Lactuca*.

Green leaf lettuces or chicories should be the predominant leaves in your salad. Lettuces mix well with chicories, as lettuce is quite mild while chicories have a more definite and pleasantly sharp flavor. Romaine, green leaf, and some butter lettuces are commonly available. Green chicories that are fairly common include endive and escarole. Their leaves are a mixture of green and white, but they are worth eating. It is

Romaine Lettuce

Endive

more difficult to find totally green chicories in the United States, though some of them, including *spadona di Mantova,* are common in many parts of Italy. If you have a garden, try growing one of these green chicories. You can cut them and new leaves will grow in a few weeks with no extra effort on your part.

There are over fifty varieties of lettuce, and probably just as many chicories. If you love gardening you can experiment with lettuces or chicories you've never seen in the supermarket. Even if you aren't a gardener, there are enough choices available to help you make your salad an exciting treat each time when you combine different lettuces and chicories with some of the flavorful leaves from other botanical groups.

Unfortunately, the commonly available *iceberg lettuce* and *Belgian endive* are pale and have much less food value than the darker varieties. Not only do they contain less carotene, but they also have a lower content of many minerals such as calcium and magnesium. Use them only if nothing else is available or for an occasional change.

Other Greens
In addition to lettuce and chicories, you can also choose other leaves to add flavor and nutrients to your salads. Some of these greens have an intense, deep green color, indicating extremely high carotene content. If you have a garden, grow them!

Dandelion is quite similar to chicory, and varieties of chicory are often sold as dandelion and vice versa. The dark green leaves can be tough, unless you grow them yourself and pick them very young. This makes them more palatable cooked than raw, though you can add a few fresh leaves to a salad.

Corn salad, also known as *lamb lettuce* or *valerianella,* is not botanically a lettuce at all. It has an intensely dark green leaf and a satisfying flavor.

Watercress, like other crucifers, is part of the mustard and cabbage family, and has a spicy flavor that brightens any salad. Watercress is often used to add sparkle to sandwiches. (More on the crucifers later.)

Arugula. One of the truly great dark leaves to add to a salad for both flavor and high nutrient content is *arugula,* often called *rocket, rugola,* or *rucola.* It is very flavorful and—just like watercress—should be added in small amounts to a salad.

Parsley comes in many forms with more or less curly leaves and can help to add variety to salads and other dishes. It was known in Roman times and in past centuries, like many other green leaves, was considered a medicinal herb with healing properties. It is particularly rich in iron and vitamin C. Three ounces of raw parsley supply about 100 milligrams of vitamin C—almost twice the RDA for adults.

Purslane is—as we have already seen—valuable for the omega-3 oils it contains. It's difficult to find but worth keeping in mind should it become more available.

Nongreen leaves. Of the nongreen leaves, *red chicories* add pleasant red color and subtle flavors to a salad. An excellent red leaf chicory that is becoming more available in North America is *radicchio* (pronounced ra-dee'-kee-o), which comes in many varieties. Radicchio is highly prized by sophisticated restaurants. It may be served cooked as well as raw.

Recipes, dressings, and ideas for salads and their place in a Superpyramid menu are given in the Superpyramid Kitchen.

Large salads based on green or other dark leaves with or without added tomatoes or other vegetables should be a key part of your daily food plan.

Cooking Greens

All the fresh greens we have discussed can be served cooked as well. Cooking has to be done with care, however, and should be the exception rather than the rule. It seems that a fresh, tender green leaf was made to be consumed raw. Less tender leaves can be used for cooking.

Some green leaves that can be used for salad but that seem particularly suitable for cooking include the popular *spinach, mustard greens, dandelion,* and *beet greens.*

The Green-Orange Law

In the Superpyramid Program, we like simple principles. We have avoided calculations, complex charts, or endless lists of rules that take the fun out of eating.

One simple and all-important principle that can be applied to all vegetables is what we call the *green-orange law:*

> **A** green or orange vegetable or fruit is usually a treasure chest of valuable nutrients such as beta-carotene, magnesium, calcium, and other precious factors. Eat some each day.

If two vegetables belong to the same group and one is white and the other has lots of green or orange or other dark colors, pick the dark-colored one. For example, in the cabbage family, the green or dark-colored broccoli and some purple-green cauliflowers are richer in nutrients than white cauliflower. Similarly, carrots, which are orange in color, have a greater abundance of carotenes than white root vegetables.

When you apply this guideline, be sure to base your choices on the color of the interior, or pulp, of the vegetable, not on the color of its skin or rind.

The Cabbage (Mustard) Family

The cabbage (mustard) family, botanically known as the Cruciferae, includes enough delightful vegetables to satisfy all tastes. Some may not even remind you of cabbage. Choices include cabbage (green, red, and Savoy), Brussels sprouts, broccoli, cauliflower, turnip, kale, kohlrabi, sea kale, mustard greens, and watercress. All of the cruciferous vegetables may be helpful in preventing cancer. Eat some of these vegetables at least two or three times a week.

As we have just seen, *broccoli* and the dark-colored varieties of *cauliflower* combine the advantages of the cabbage family with an excellent

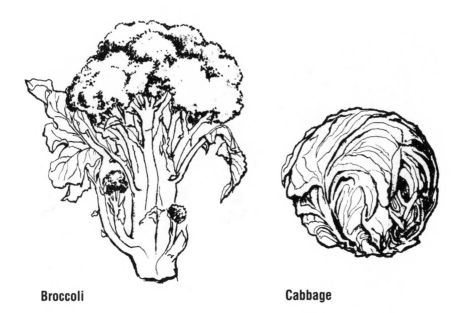

Broccoli   **Cabbage**

carotene content. In 1992, a new compound containing sulfur was discovered in broccoli that has been found to be protective against cancer in laboratory experiments. This is an additional reason that broccoli is a highly desirable food.

Red, curly-leaf savoy, the so-called *common cabbage,* and *Brussels sprouts* supply leaves rich in vitamin C. Brussels sprouts are a good source of folic acid, too. Cabbages can be eaten raw, cooked, or fermented as sauerkraut.

The leaves of another crucifer, the *horseradish,* are excellent for adding zip to a salad. If you have a garden, plant horseradish and pick some leaves as the plant develops; you can use the root later for spicy dips or spreads.

Roots, Tubers, and Other Underground Vegetables
Carrots and the tubers (the underground part) of the onion-garlic family should be frequent choices in your weekly menus. Make them your basic underground vegetables.

Carrots. The name *carotene* comes from carrots, which are abundant in this nutrient. For a long time, people have linked carrots to good eyesight, and that popular notion has a sound nutritional basis because of this vegetable's content of beta-carotene and other carotenes. Carrots are also a good source of vitamins C and E. With their slightly sweet

Carrots

fresh taste, carrots can be eaten raw or lightly cooked and are a standard ingredient for most soups and stews, including minestrone. If you like fresh juices, carrot is an excellent choice, but don't forget to eat enough whole carrots to take advantage of their fiber content.

In Roman times carrots grew wild and were considered medicinal. It was only in the sixteenth century that carrots began to be cultivated and many varieties were developed.

The Onion Family

Onions, garlic, shallots, and *leeks* all belong to the same botanical family (the lily family) and share some common compounds and flavors. They are so closely related that each of their Latin names begins with *allium*. They store well in cool, dry places and make good winter vegetables in cold climates.

> *As vegetables become a more important part of your meals, learn to enjoy and appreciate the subtle differences in taste and texture of these great underground vegetables.*

If garlic or onions are improperly prepared, their flavor may not be pleasing. Frying or cooking them at high temperatures in an oven brings out extremely pungent odors. Some people like this strong flavor, some don't. Boiling or sautéing with some water mixed with oil will result in a much milder flavor; it's your choice. If you don't eat these vegetables raw, you can cook them in soups or add them to a pot of rice as it boils for a delicate yet wonderful touch. Microwave whole onions or cook them with a little water as part of a stew; they'll be delicate and delightful. See the Superpyramid Kitchen for various options.

The flavor that cooking brings out—and the tears that cutting onions may bring to your eyes—are both the result of some important sulfur compounds found in the onion family. These compounds are most likely responsible for garlic's medicinal reputation. Garlic was used in ancient times as a powerful antibiotic for battlefield wounds; in veterinary medicine it has been used to eliminate intestinal parasites from dogs and cats; and in humans it appears to be helpful in preventing the formation of abnormal blood clots, a property that needs (and deserves) more study. Some studies on garlic's role in lowering blood cholesterol show promise as well.

Researchers have studied the consumption of vegetables from the garlic-onion family in two Hindu sects, both vegetarian, in India. One group consumed reasonable amounts of garlic and onions (an ounce and a half of garlic and over a pound of onions per week). The other consumed about one-third that amount or less. When these two groups were tested for the time it took their blood to clot, which is related to the risk of forming an internal clot or thrombus, the garlic and onion eaters took longer to form a clot. Of course, their blood coagulated as needed to plug up a wound or other injury to a blood vessel. The blood-clotting time was well within normal ranges, just slightly lower. But inside the body this can make a crucial difference.

Populations such as the southern Italians and other Mediterranean groups that use garlic and onions in their daily diet get less heart disease. But here, as in many other situations, it's the entire diet that counts. Southern Italians' low rates of heart disease probably stem not only from their consumption of garlic but also from their high intake of carbohydrate (mostly in the form of pasta) and low animal-fat and meat consumption, reasonable intake of olives and olive oil, and generous intake of fresh fruits and vegetables.

Onions and garlic are good sources of selenium, a mineral that has been associated with lower incidence of certain cancers. It is a good antioxidant that works together with vitamin E and beta-carotene in our cell membranes.

Some new research from China, where in some regions stomach cancer is a major killer disease, shows that garlic may be protective and may help to prevent this kind of cancer when added to a typical Chinese diet. But let's remember that nothing works in isolation, and garlic, as any other protective food we've already discussed, should be part of a wise disease prevention program.

The critical compounds in garlic and onions can slowly become biologically inactive after the skin that protects the edible portion has been removed or bruised or the cloves have been chopped or cut. This takes some time, so normal home preparation methods should not cause concern. As with other vegetables and fruits, use garlic and onions as fresh as possible, and if you chop them, do so just before using them.

All of these vegetables have the advantage of keeping well through the winter months and can be wonderful when fresh vegetables have disappeared in cold regions. So try to use at least one of the members of the onion family every day, all year round.

Onions come in enough colors (red, white, and yellow), flavors, sweetnesses, and sizes to please any eater. They have been called a "kitchen star" by some writers because they bring a savor to many dishes that could otherwise be dull. Can you imagine a good soup or stew without onions or one of their relatives? The fiber of onions is also a good complement to the fibers of wheat.

In southern Italy, the *fornaio* (baker) often places chopped onions on top of the local (and most likely, the original) pizza.

Garlic is probably the richest member of this family both in terms of sulfur compounds and folklore about its properties, some of which have been proven in laboratories.

The ancient Egyptians, Greeks, and Romans all held garlic in high esteem and used it for many purposes, some of which, though not yet confirmed or even studied, are most likely based on its true qualities. Ancient athletes were known to use it before competition, and Mohammed thought it helped after snakebite—an unproven use!

Shallots are probably derived from the onion, and their mild, delicate flavor makes them a pleasant substitute for garlic.

Leeks are considered by some to be a variety of Oriental garlic, and like shallots, are another flavorful option for using the onion family in your daily meals.

Other Roots
All edible roots can be used as part of a great Superpyramid meal, though not all of them have been studied for possible special properties.

While you should use the yellow and orange roots like carrots for their beta-carotene content, white roots should be part of the Superpyramid Program as well because variety is essential to success. All roots contain good fibers, including valuable pectin, that help control blood cholesterol and other fibers that help proper bowel function. Roots are usually good sources of minerals as well.

Radishes, in all shapes and degrees of sharpness, make nice crunchy snacks before a meal. Daikon, a type of radish used in the Orient, is considered an aid to digestion in Oriental folk medicine. Turnips and parsnips give soups and stews a special savory appeal. Celery root (celeriac) is a variety of the common celery that develops a large edible root that can be shredded and eaten raw or slightly cooked. Chicory roots can be cooked and make a delicious tangy dish; roasted they are used as a coffee substitute or additive. Less common but delightful roots that help to round out a vegetable plate are Jerusalem artichokes, jicama, and many other Oriental roots that can be found in Japanese, Chinese, and other ethnic stores.

Red beets probably originated on the west coast of Europe and North Africa. They are higher in sugars than other root vegetables (in fact, table sugar is derived from the sugar beet), and the sugar together with complex carbohydrates make the red beet a possible tier-one energy food. Beets are a reasonable source of minerals such as iron. Red beets can be cooked in a microwave, baked, or made into borscht, an Eastern European red beet stew.

Other common root vegetables like potatoes, sweet potatoes, and yams, all energy foods, are found on the first tier. You can read about them in chapter 4.

Stems

Many plants supply edible, flavorful stems or other parts that are neither leaf nor root; we'll list them together in this section for the sake of simplicity. Many of them have been used since antiquity, and there is a lot of folklore about them. It's worth repeating here that just because some of these vegetables have not been extensively studied by modern medicine doesn't mean they aren't valuable. They bring variety to the diet, they all supply potassium, other mineral salts, and nutrients, and the always beneficial fiber. However, stems are usually not a good source of carotenes.

Fennel belongs to the parsley family and its original name, *marathon*, should interest runners, since it comes from the same Greek word that named both the region and the footrace. This plant is mentioned in documents dating as far back as 1500 B.C. Pliny described fennel as a medicinal plant because of its soothing properties. With a flavor slightly reminiscent of licorice, fennel's bulbous stem can be used raw in salads or cooked. Its seeds and the seeds of the related *anise,* used as spices and in old pharmaceutical preparations, are better known than the plant itself.

Celery is a most valuable source of flavor and minerals. It was used in earlier days for its valuable diuretic properties and, like fennel, was considered useful for some gastrointestinal ailments. It makes a great addition to soups, stews, and salads. A recent study from China indicates that eating large quantities of celery may be helpful in lowering high blood pressure.

Artichokes, known in Europe since the second half of the sixteenth century, make an enjoyable change of pace from the more common vegetables. They have a valuable fiber content, which, though not directly studied by scientists for physiological effect, appears to make artichokes one of the best vegetables for proper intestinal functioning and elimination. Artichokes are a good way to boost the fiber content of a low-fiber meal. If you are forced to eat refined foods in restaurants, look for artichokes on the menu—you may find them more readily than whole-grain bread and beans. Artichokes can be used raw when tender and fresh (the white portion of the leaf is delicious dipped in olive oil) or they can be slightly cooked.

Artichokes

Other vegetables. Another diuretic vegetable (as you can test yourself!) is the *asparagus,* which with other white stems such as *Swiss chard, bok choy,* and many others, should never replace the richly nutritious dark green leaves, carrots, broccolis, and onions, but should accompany them for a complete and varied meal. *Cardoon* is a member of the artichoke family, with thick stems that must be cooked.

Sprouts

Young sprouts, grown from various seeds, are a good way to get some fresh vegetables in northern regions in the winter. They are also rich in many valuable nutrients and a good addition to any diet. You can easily sprout your own seeds, such as wheat or mung beans, or buy bean or alfalfa sprouts. (See more about sprouting seeds, pages 216–17.)

Nonsweet Fruits

Bell peppers, tomatoes, and yellow squashes should be on top of the list of highly prized nonsweet fruits. They all contain reasonable amounts of pectin, which, as we have seen, is a fiber that helps control blood cholesterol and probably other metabolic functions. When they are in season, eat fresh peppers or tomatoes daily. Eat squashes in the fall and winter months. You can use dried, canned, or otherwise preserved tomatoes in the winter, but do not expect the same food value you find in the fresh, raw fruit.

Sweet bell peppers belong to the genus *Capsicum.* Peppers probably originated in South America, most likely in Brazil. There are many types

and colors of sweet peppers, and few people realize that they are one of the best sources of vitamin C. Three ounces of raw peppers contain about 100 milligrams of C—about twice the RDA for adults. In earlier days, vitamin C was actually extracted from peppers. Yellow and red peppers are sweeter than green peppers and are great broiled, baked, or raw in salad.

In the *Capsicum* group, we also find many varieties of hot, spicy peppers such as *cayenne pepper* and *hot red peppers,* usually used as condiments. In open-air markets in warm countries, the varieties of hot peppers of all sizes—from very small to large—are almost endless.

Tomatoes, whenever available, should be part of a meal. There are many varieties, from red or yellow cherry tomatoes for snacks to large tomatoes (red, yellow, and yellow-green) for salads and sauces. The tomato appears to have originated in South America, probably Peru, and was sometimes called the Peruvian apple.

Tomatoes, olive oil, and a very moderate amount of cheese make a flavorful sauce for pasta or rice. The classic Italian pizzas and focaccias (see pages 463–65) are made with durum wheat flour and topped with tomatoes, olive oil, and oregano with onions. In fact, focaccias and pizzas are the ultimate combinations of vegetables, good oils, and grains. What a Superpyramid combination!

By now you should know that a fruit like the tomato is rich in carotenes, vitamin C, pectin fiber, and of course potassium. It's a *must* food, fresh or preserved, summer or winter.

Yellow squashes —that is, squashes with yellow pulp, come in so many varieties that entire cookbooks have been written just on how to prepare them. Some types have such superb flavor that they can simply be baked and enjoyed; others, with hardly any flavor of their own (American pumpkins and some squashes), are more commonly used as a base for fillings for pies and other dishes.

Yellow true squashes are preferable to pumpkins if you want great flavor without any addition of sweeteners or spices. Often, the squashes with a metallic gray or greenish rind and deep-yellow pulp are the sweetest and most flavorful, but there are so many varieties that you should experiment to find your favorites. Yellow squashes can be baked, stuffed, used as filling for ravioli or meatless pasta, and even eaten for dessert.

Both yellow squashes and pumpkins are excellent sources of beta-carotene and other carotenes.

White squashes, such as the many varieties of *zucchini* (Italian squash), supply good fiber but are not as rich in nutrients as the yellow varieties. If you garden or live close to a farm, try zucchini with their blossoms still on for a treat. The flower probably adds some food value to the fruit.

Squash

There are many other tasty white-pulp nonsweet fruits, from *eggplant*, known in India since ancient times, to *cucumbers*. They are good for a change of pace and as part of mixed vegetable dishes.

Okra has some very special fibers that make it unique. Mucilage, the viscous substance that is released when you cut cooked okra, is a type of fiber that may lower blood cholesterol. Similar fiber has been studied and found very effective. Unfortunately, to the best of our knowledge, no one has studied the fiber from okra, but its chemical composition is so similar to the other fibers that are known to lower blood cholesterol that some okra in the diet cannot hurt and could be beneficial.

SWEET FRUITS

"The police officers, secretaries, clerks and apprentices, hasten to their daily occupations, taking their breakfast on the road, which consists of some bread or biscuit and a little fresh fruits just gathered in the neighboring gardens and covered with a luxuriant bloom." This was written in 1798 by Bingham Richards (Letter from Sicily, quoted by Mary Taylor Simeti in *Pomp and Sustenance*) about life in Sicily.

What's more appealing than fresh, sweet fruit ready to eat just as the bush gives it to us? When we're walking in the woods of the American Northwest or in the Alps, wild berries seem to ask to be picked to give the weary traveler some quick energy and precious nutrients. Fruits are miraculous packages of goodness no man-made drink will ever surpass.

Think how sad it is for a child in a big city, where all the fruit-bearing trees have been replaced by hot asphalt, cement, and buildings. This child has never known what it means to pick an apple from a tree and eat it! A vending machine full of cans is a poor substitute.

Delicious and juicy, fruits are probably the ultimate, ready-to-eat, safe food. With their great fibers and all the trace nutrients, what a perfect food they make for a snack or to end a meal. In many Mediterranean countries, the meals end with fresh fruits. Any proper restaurant in Italy offers you a basket of fruits in season and a bowl of water to wash them in at the end of a meal.

There are so many sweet fruits that we won't attempt to describe the goodness of each one. The key here, even more so than in any other group of foods on the Superpyramid, is to enjoy a variety of fresh fruits in season as often as possible. Off season, choose dried fruits first.

Difficult Choices

Fresh and dried fruits are all so rich in good nutrients that I don't want to rank them as though one is better than another. They are all good and valuable; the key thing is to eat some fresh fruit every day. Below, I'll highlight the special properties of some selected fruits.

Grapes. There is probably no other food with the romance and history of grapes. Fresh, dried (raisins), fermented (wines), juiced, condensed as *vino cotto* (page 153), they have been part of the cuisine of many cultures. The number of varieties—red, purple, pink, white, and green —is almost endless, and winemakers have helped us become more aware of the subtle differences among grape varieties. Many civilizations have considered grapes a health-giving food. Even today in some European grape-growing regions, villages advertise their "grape cure" every fall. Raisins are a good source of minerals, including iron.

Grapes

Figs. There are purple and black varieties (sometimes called Mission figs in California) and white varieties. In North America, figs are best known in the dried form. Dried figs make great sources of energy year round, and because of their high content of natural sugars, they make a satisfying replacement for commercial snacks. Figs are also a great source of fiber and excellent for ensuring proper intestinal function and elimination. Together with other dried fruits (raisins, apricots, peaches, and many others) and nuts, they can be used as part of great high-energy mixes for travel and outdoor activities. Fig syrups can be used as sweeteners the same way as *vino cotto*.

Figs

*M*ake dried fruits, with or without nuts, your between-meal snack. Soak dried fruits for a great-tasting, nourishing dessert. Use concentrated fruit syrups as nutrient-rich sweeteners.

Berries grow in many climates and make it possible for you to have fresh fruits no matter where you live. All berries are rich in vitamin C and also contain beta-carotene and fiber. They are key sources of these nutrients and other trace minerals for Nordic peoples. In fact, the Norwegians have a special type of berry they call "cloud berry" that provides four times as much vitamin C per serving as oranges. Choose your favorite: *blueberries, raspberries, blackberries, gooseberries, boysenberries,* and the related *currants* and *cranberries*. While *strawberries* are easy to obtain,

Berries

they're not as nutritionally concentrated as other berries. Large commercial strawberries aren't as rich in nutrients as the smaller, wild type that's hard to find in supermarkets. Grow small strawberries and other berries if you have a garden—they adapt well to all climates. Berry jams and conserves supply good pectins in the winter months, but remember that much of the vitamin C is probably gone.

Citrus fruits—*oranges, tangerines, lemons, grapefruits*, and other less common varieties are the one year-round supply of fruit that enables people to have sufficient vitamin C intake in the winter. The peels of citrus fruits, discarded when we eat the fresh fruits but present in many orange marmalades, are high in pectin.

Lemon juice, squeezed just before using, is a tasty way to enrich salad dressing and other dressings with vitamin C.

For these high–vitamin C fruits, remember this key rule: once the peel is broken or bruised, the fruit begins to lose its vitamins.

Citrus Fruits

Juicing fruits, cooking them in an open pot, or cutting them up for a fruit salad immediately starts a process of vitamin C deterioration. Use the fruits as soon as possible after preparation, and do not overexpose them to air.

Apricots, nectarines, most melons, yellow peaches, cherries, persimmons, and other fruits that are yellow, orange, or red follow our green-orange law (page 108). If we call the berries and citrus fruits the vitamin C fruits, we should call this group the carotene fruits. Eat them often. And when they're not available fresh, dried apricots are still a good source of beta-carotene, which is not as sensitive to oxygen damage as vitamin C.

When it comes to melons, there are so many varieties that data on their carotene content are very incomplete. Still, the basic color guideline holds true for melons as well as all fruits: yellow, orange, and green usually mean carotene.

Cherries, many berries, plums, and, to a lesser degree, apples and other fruits contain a sugar—sorbitol—that has a mild laxative effect in sufficient quantities. Because this sugar is not fully digested when it reaches the large intestine, it feeds friendly microorganisms that multiply and favor proper elimination. For this reason, in years past the coming of cherries and berries in the spring was considered a way to clean out the body after the fruitless winter months.

Apples, pears, and quinces all contain a large amounts of pectin and other fibers, so much, in fact, that apples are used commercially to manufacture pectin for use in jams and jellies. Their versatility makes them delightful for apple butter, applesauce, or pie fillings. Properly stored in a cool, dry place, these fruits keep well in winter months for fresh fruits year round. Quinces need to be cooked—usually baked. In the Superpyramid plan, think of fresh apples and pears as an easy-to-eat snack in place of some other less desirable between-meal items.

Plums and dried prunes have long been known for their laxative effect, the result of some organic compounds they contain. Just as important, dried prunes are a valuable source of fruit fiber throughout the year and are delicious anytime as a convenient natural snack. Cooked dried prunes make great desserts mixed with unsweetened yogurts or kefirs.

Bananas are higher in complex carbohydrate than other fruits, are available all year, and are a good source of energy. They have a reputation as a high-potassium food (350 parts of potassium per 1 part sodium), but let's remember that most fruits are excellent sources of this mineral and very low in sodium.

When not completely ripe, bananas contain a special type of starch that isn't digested by humans (recently named *resistant starch*). This type of starch works in the intestine as fiber. It certainly appears to have some health benefits, though the research is still in progress, and not much can be reported yet.

Currants, red and black, most commonly used in North America in jam or jelly, are one of the fruits with the highest content of vitamin C (and a reasonable amount of beta-carotene for red currants). The *gooseberry,* a close botanical relative of currants, is not quite as rich as vitamin C, but it is still a great fruit, though it has lost its popularity in recent years.

Dates, like other dried fruits I have mentioned, are high-energy food. In their native Middle Eastern and North African countries, where dates are sometimes the only truly abundant food, they are a staple. Dates are also a reasonable source of iron and many other minerals in smaller amounts, but they do not contain vitamin C. The date palm tree that produces dates has been imported to southern California and other southwestern deserts of North America. There are soft, moist dates and dry dates to satisfy any taste. Date sugar makes a very flavorful addition to cereals, and dates, like other dried fruits, should be considered a way to add fruits to hot or cold cereals.

Other tier-two fruits. There are too many other great fruits in the world to begin to discuss them all here. For example, just think about *pomegranates* and the many great tropical and semitropical fruits such as *pineapples, papayas,* and *mangoes.* Other versatile fruits include *kiwis,* originally from China, now grown in New Zealand and California; *cherimoyas,* originally from the Peruvian Andes; and *prickly pears,* the fruit of a desert cactus found in many regions from Sicily to California, but originally from the Americas. Some of these fruits have not been extensively studied for their health benefits, but they all fit in a good food plan.

Avocados, olives, and nuts are very special fruits that we find on the third tier of the Superpyramid (chapter 6). They all supply large amounts of precious oils. Nuts supply protein as well and can be considered a supplemental source of energy. *Chestnuts*, high in complex carbohydrates and sugars, should be considered a source of energy rather than a typical tier-two food. They can be used in place of the high-carbohydrate foods on tier one for an occasional change of pace.

Edible Flowers

Many edible flowers can be added to salads and other dishes for color and flavor. Some are very mild, some quite spicy, like the onion flower. As no one seems interested in studying edible flowers from a nutritional point of view, little can be said about their food value. Until more research is available, let's use them as a flavorful and—not less important —colorful addition to our recipes. They will help prevent boredom just as much as culinary herbs and spices.

But be careful! Just as there are poisonous leaves and fruits, so there are poisonous or strongly medicinal flowers. Don't use just any flower, just as you wouldn't use any unknown leaf or fruits or root. Some of the prettiest flowers—lilies of the valley, for example—are actually poisonous. Never eat flowers from a flower shop: as they have not been grown as food, they may have been sprayed with pesticides more powerful than what would be considered safe for food use or otherwise treated to keep longer. For this reason, don't use rose petals from a flower shop.

If you are not familiar with the many edible flowers, do not venture into strange territory without advice. The safest option is to go to a farmers' market or specialty food store and buy your edible flowers there. Usually you'll find them as part of a mix of greens and flowers. Some seed companies sell packets of seeds of edible flowers you can grow yourself if you have a garden. (See "Sources," page 477.)

Zucchini and nasturtium flowers are widely used in some Mediterranean countries and add zest to many dishes. Orange, lemon, and rose flowers are delightfully fragrant and delicate. Rose water is used in many cuisines.

Zucchini and Their Flowers

Juices

Many of the protective factors of vegetables and fruits are present in juices, but the fiber is gone, and you need enough fiber from fruits and vegetables to balance the fiber from grain and legumes. By all means enjoy fresh juices—possibly freshly squeezed at home or commercial fresh raw juices—but always consume enough whole fruits and vegetables to meet your fiber requirements.

There is one advantage with juices from yellow and orange vegetables like carrots: their beta-carotene is absorbed from the intestine in a very efficient way and more beta-carotene can be consumed this way than by eating whole carrots, as you can drink the juice of five or six carrots in a small glass. If you drink this type of juice, use whole carrots as well for fiber.

▲ KEY IDEAS

▲ The foods on tier two of the Superpyramid are a source of essential protective nutrients, particularly vitamin C, beta-carotene, special types of fiber, and some important, though lesser-known, beneficial components.

▲ Though all vegetables deserve a place in your meals, dark green leaves, carrots, members of the onion-garlic family, and cruciferous vegetables are particularly valuable. Try to eat some of them every day.

▲ The color of the pulp of a vegetable or fruit is a good indicator of its beta-carotene content. Choose dark green, yellow, orange, or red over white or pale types.

▲ Certain nonsweet fruits (which most people think of as vegetables) are an important part of Superpyramid meals. Enjoy tomatoes, bell peppers, and yellow squashes as often as possible.

▲ Among the sweet fruits, the vitamin C group (berries and citrus fruits) and the carotene group (apricots, peaches, nectarines, yellow melons) are especially rich in protective nutrients.

▲ The nutrients in vegetables and fruits, particularly vitamin C, are easily damaged by peeling, bruising, or by improper preparation. Use these fruits and vegetables fresh, raw, and whole as much as possible.

▲ When you chop, juice, or cook fruits and vegetables, do so close to serving time and minimize their exposure to air.

.6.

The Third Tier

Rounding Out Tier One

All the plant foods on this tier—either the whole foods or the oils derived from them—are concentrated sources of energy. They complement the energy sources found on tier one with precious *unsaturated oils*. (I'll explain more about fats and oils in a moment.) Nuts and oil seeds also supply valuable proteins and contain important trace elements such as calcium, which is found in reasonable amounts in almonds and sesame seeds. No less important, the oils produced from the plant foods on this tier add flavor and texture to the foods of tiers one and two. What's a green salad without a good oil?

Fish—the only nonplant food on tier three—supplies excellent proteins, and fish fat is high in omega-3 oils (page 102). However, fish is an optional food on tier three. If you choose a vegetarian Superpyramid, you should be sure to eat plenty of egg whites, low-fat milk products, and beans from tier one to ensure adequate protein intake.

> *The foods on tier three round out the energy foods found on tier one.*

THE FOODS OF THE *Third Tier*

▲ FOODS FROM PLANTS

Olive oil and other products of the olive, such as olive paste.

Nuts such as almonds, hazelnuts, pistachios, cashews, walnuts, pecans, and other nuts consumed whole—preferably raw—or as nut butters or oils.

Oil seeds, such as sesame, sunflower, pumpkin, and other seeds high in oils. These seeds may be consumed whole or used for oil. Some also make good butters (such as sesame seeds for tahini). Additionally, this tier includes the oils of the germ of grains high in vitamin E (such as wheat germ). Soybeans, found on tier one, are also a source of oils.

Avocado and its oil.

▲ NONPLANT FOODS

Fish of various types contains different levels of fat. The Superpyramid food plan gives you a vegetarian option without fish.

Why Not Tier One?

Why are these foods on tier three and not on tier one? *Because they should not replace tier-one foods as basic sources of energy or protein.* Rather, they should help round out the nutrients supplied by the foods on tier one. There is another difference: the foods on tier one can be used liberally —that's why they are on tier one, the largest tier of the Superpyramid. But as we reach the smaller tier three, we must begin to use some moderation in the amount of these foods we eat.

When used properly, the precious oils supplied by tier-three foods meet the standard set for healthful eating by many national associations, such as the American Heart Association. However, throughout this chapter when I talk about the benefits of these oils, it is important for you to remember that I am discussing them in terms of the Superpyramid concept, as part of a food pattern high in plant foods and low in animal fat. These healthful foods and oils cannot be used so freely if poultry or high-fat meat and high-fat dairy products are the mainstay of your meals.

THE PLANT FOODS ON TIER THREE

Precious Oils and Fats

With today's emphasis on low-fat diets, can we say that the precious oils found in foods like olives, nuts, and oily seeds have a special place in your meals? Yes, we can. The biological role of different types of oils is very confusing for many people, and fat substitutes are becoming popular. Although these fat substitutes may be valuable in some situations, the best fats come from real foods or simple processing of real foods (such as pressing olive oil from olives or grinding grains). In the Superpyramid plan, preference is always given to foods with a long tradition of use.

But let's repeat a crucial point: because the Superpyramid is based on very low-fat foods (tiers one and two), the precious and safe oils on tier three are not only acceptable but desirable. Foods too low in fat are often not very tasty or satisfying, making it difficult to consume them day after day. And when fat intake is extremely low, some problems may arise. Some scientists, such as Dr. Scott Grundy at the University of Texas, are concerned that if the diet is too low in fat the good blood cholesterol—known as HDL cholesterol—may be lowered. Your HDL should be high while your total blood cholesterol should be low. Moreover, in extremely low-fat diets, the absorption of some of the oil-soluble vitamins, such as A, beta-carotene, and E, may be decreased.

Choosing the Right Fats and Oils

We can't go much further in understanding fats and oils without a quick summary of the key differences between saturated and unsaturated fats.

Saturated fats are usually solid at room temperature and have tight bonds in their molecular structure. Saturated fats are the predominant fats in animal products, except for fish. Most plant foods contain only minimal amounts of saturated fats, the chief exception being coconut and palm oils—sometimes called "tropical" oils. If you limit your intake of fatty foods of animal origin (except fish), you'll keep your saturated-fat intake within a desirable range.

Unsaturated fats. There are two types of unsaturated fats: the *monos* and the *polys*. *Mono* means "one," that is, one unsaturated link in the long chain of atoms in the molecule of the oil. *Poly* means "many," that is, more than one unsaturated link in the molecule. *Monounsaturated* fats are the predominant fats in olives, sesame seeds, pumpkin seeds, hazelnuts, almonds, pistachios, avocados, and some other foods. *Polyunsaturated* fats are also present in the foods I have just listed but are the predominant ones in other seeds and nuts, such as walnuts, some varieties of sunflower, and corn and soy oil. Both monos and polys play a key role in health and are a desirable part of the Superpyramid plan.

Hydrogenated fats. As you read food labels, you may find hydrogenated fats listed. These fats start out as liquid vegetable oils but are made solid by a chemical process that uses hydrogen. Some of the molecules become saturated—thus hard—but others turn into a special type of mono-unsaturated fat chemists call *trans*. These are not the desirable monos found in the oils we have talked about. Because of a strange switch in their molecular structure, trans fats do not lower blood cholesterol; in large quantities they may instead lower the good cholesterol (HDL). If you use foods that contain hydrogenated fat, do so in extreme moderation. They are not part of the Superpyramid. Read the labels of the foods you buy and watch out for words like "hydrogenated" or "partially hydrogenated."

The Polyunsaturated Oils

Oils are liquid fat—100 percent liquid fat. We must have a sufficient amount of polyunsaturated oils such as safflower or sunflower oil in our food because our bodies use them as raw material in synthesizing extremely important compounds in the body. Further, they lower blood cholesterol. Most people on typical Western diets would benefit by increasing their intake of these polyunsaturated oils. At the same time, these oils are powerful compounds and should not be consumed in excess. The bonds between atoms in the molecule of the polyunsaturated oil are very sensitive and enter into chemical reactions very easily. That's why they are important in health maintenance, and that's why at the same time they are so powerful that they should not be used in excess.

What kind of things can happen with excesses of polyunsaturated fats? First of all, they are very sensitive to oxidation, an energy-producing process that takes place constantly every day of our life. If these energy-yielding oxidations did not take place, we would soon die. Some of the by-products of these oxidations are compounds that are not very desirable. Antioxidant vitamins such as E help protect us against these by-products. That's why the germ of the wheat is such a safe food: it's very high in vitamin E. Its oil is one of the best sources of vitamin E as well as reasonable amounts of polyunsaturated oils. Many whole foods (for example, walnuts) high in polyunsaturated oils also contain enough protective agents such as vitamin E, which makes them a desirable part of a good food plan.

As far back as 1985, data from animal experiments presented at the Twelfth International Congress of Nutrition in Brighton, England, showed that excessive intake of polyunsaturated fat seems to favor the development of breast and colon cancer and possibly decreases immunity (resistance to infection). (I must emphasize that in these experiments the animals' intake of polyunsaturated fats was very high and the entire diet was high in fat.) These effects were later confirmed by other researchers.

The Monounsaturated Oils

In contrast the monounsaturated fats, abundant in olives, sesame seeds, almonds, and other seeds and nuts, seem to be the kind that we can use in reasonably larger amounts without problems, while consuming a balance of polyunsaturated fats as well. No harmful effects have been found when oils in which monounsaturated fat was the main component —such as olive oil—were fed to animals at the same high level as in the polyunsaturated-fat experiments. The good news is that when monounsaturated oils replace saturated fats, they lower blood cholesterol and keep it low.

Other Friendly Components

Some components of foods such as fiber seem to get a lot of publicity. Others like *plant sterols* do not. We find them in vegetables (chapter 5) but even more so in unrefined plant foods that contain reasonable amounts of oils, such as nuts, and of course in the oils after extraction if, again, the oil has not been overrefined. Although sterols sound like uncomfortably close cousins of cholesterol, the plant sterols are quite beneficial and have been studied for many years. They decrease the absorption of cholesterol and lately—as we have seen—there is some evidence from laboratory experiments that they may protect against the damage of cancer-producing chemicals in animals.

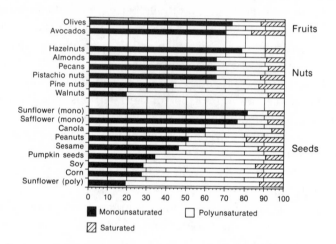

FIGURE 10: Composition of oils from fruits, nuts, and seeds

Choosing Oils and Foods High in Oils

> **Monounsaturated Oil** and foods high in this type of fat can be used more freely than any other type of fat.
>
> **Polyunsaturated Oils** are extremely valuable and essential, but avoid them in excess. Use them in foods high in antioxidant vitamins or as part of whole foods.

If you follow the recommended food choices on the Superpyramid, you'll get the right amount of polyunsaturated and monounsaturated oils with no fear of excesses or deficiencies.

Designing Meals with Tier-Three Whole Foods and Oils

Using this scientific information, you can now choose some great foods and oils that, when consumed regularly in place of animal or other solid fats, give you the right balance: little saturated fat, the right amount of polyunsaturated, and more liberal amounts of monounsaturated.

To accomplish this, first select foods and oils that have monounsaturated fat as their major constituent. Then add some foods and oils higher in polyunsaturated fats but not as the main or only sources of vegetable oils. And just as important, use a variety of these foods. Each will add its own special flavor and nutritional qualities to help avoid a monotonous diet.

Oils. Make an oil from the mono list your first choice to dress your salads, vegetables, pasta and rice, beans, breads, and other foods. Add some poly oils in moderation (or some poly whole foods; see below).

Whole nuts and seeds and their butters. Choose foods that are raw or have had only light, gentle roasting. Use some of the mono nuts or seeds, such as almonds or sesame seed butter (tahini), and add some poly nuts such as walnuts. Nuts and many oil seeds such as pumpkin or sunflower seeds make great snacks as well and are a fine source of extra energy for very active people.

Avocado. This versatile food can be consumed by itself, as an alternative to saturated spreads, or in salads and in dips.

Whole olives and olive paste. These products have the goodness of olive oil, but the processing needed to remove the bitter flavor of raw olives makes the finished product slightly salty (see details on olives and olive paste and salt on page 137). Use them as flavoring in place of salt.

Nut milks. Nuts, especially almonds, have been used for many years to make delicious milks or shakes (page 239).

There are many wonderful foods that could be described in detail in this chapter, but I'll focus on a few with a long history of use and a tradition as part of some ancient, delectable cuisine. These traditional foods will help you make the Superpyramid meals appealing and delicious. I'll discuss olives, sesame and some related seeds, almonds and some related nuts, avocados, walnuts, and their oils. And even though not an ancient oil, we'll add wheat germ oil because it's extremely rich in vitamin E.

▲

Food Sources for Good Oils

MONOUNSATURATED OILS

▲

Common Whole Foods

Nuts	**almonds, hazelnuts, pistachios, cashews, macadamia nuts, pecans**
Seeds	**sesame and monounsaturated sunflower seeds, peanuts**
Fruits	**olives and avocados**

▲

Common Butters or Pastes

Olive paste, almond and cashew butter, sesame butter, and other nut or seed butters such as roasted peanut butter all contain reasonable amounts of polyunsaturated fat, but it's never the predominant fat.

Common Oils

From Fruits olive, almond, hazelnut, and avocado oils

From Seeds sesame, monounsaturated sunflower oil, pumpkin seed oil, canola and peanut oils

▲

POLYUNSATURATED OILS

Common Whole Foods

Nuts and Other Fruits walnuts, Brazil nuts

Seeds polyunsaturated sunflowers

Germ of Grains wheat germ and the germ of other grains

▲

Common Oils

From Nuts walnut oil

From Seeds polyunsaturated sunflower, safflower, soybean oils

From the Germ of Grains wheat germ oil and corn germ oil (the common corn oil)

THE OLIVE AND ITS OIL
Six Thousand Years of Olive Oil

Some historians believe that the use of olives may go back as far as eight thousand years, while others think that six thousand years is a better estimate. Either way, the olive and its products are ancient, revered foods. In fact, few foods have been recognized by mankind as being so precious and health giving as the products of the olive tree. Diverse religious writings hold olive oil or the olive in high esteem. Olives are mentioned in the Koran and in the Old and New Testaments. The ancient Greeks believed it was their goddess Athena who created the first olive tree on the earth, and the ancient Egyptians gave the same credit to the goddess Isis.

The olive tree lives for centuries, and its deep roots find water in otherwise arid regions. In excavations of ancient Roman markets, a great deal of earthenware for transporting olive oil has been found, a sign of how important the olive oil trade was.

The olive tree itself assumed a mystic aura in antiquity. Its branches were used as symbols of peace and love in the earliest Greek and Roman art and literature. Olive oil was used not only for food but also as a lamp oil, a medicinal ointment, a cosmetic, an ingredient in soap, and—a sign of how it was revered—in religious ceremonies.

Olives

Olive Oil and Health

Olive oil is very high in the monounsaturated oils, which, as we have already seen, are the safest oils we can consume. Dr. Ancel Keys, in his famous medical book *Seven Countries*, showed how people on Mediterranean diets in which the main fat was olive oil had lower occurrence of heart disease.

It is common knowledge among Greek physicians that peasants on the island of Crete have a very low incidence of coronary heart disease. The chart on page 17 confirms that the deaths from this disease in the local villagers is one of the lowest in the world. These people grow olives and consume olive oil as their basic fat. Unfortunately, as Western diets move into Crete with increased tourism, things are beginning to change. As the olive and its oil are replaced in part by Western foods, health and disease patterns will inevitably change for the worse.

Olive Oils

The wonderful, delicate flavors of olive oil and the painstaking work needed to harvest olives—still picked by hand in most areas—make the choice of olive oil challenging and important when this oil becomes a staple in your diet.

Good olive oils are more expensive than some seed oils, which in the past has led to adulteration of olive oils. Some unscrupulous producers diluted olive oil with cheaper oils and sold it at the price of real olive oil. Now, strict controls and laws make adulteration difficult. In the U.S., most olive oils come either from the Mediterranean region (Spain, Italy, and Greece) or from California. The latter is still a small producer, as most California olives are used for canning.

Extra-virgin olive oil. This is the only oil to use if you want superior flavor. This oil is obtained from the fruit of the olive tree solely by mechanical means under conditions that do not cause deterioration of the oil. The oil is usually cold pressed or otherwise mechanically extracted so that no significant heat can damage the olives. Extra-virgin oil does not undergo any chemical treatment other than washing or filtration to eliminate the residue of the pressing. True extra-virgin olive oil is very low in acidity (less than 1 percent).

Extra-virgin oils can have different flavors. The age of the olives, the olive variety, the climate, the region and its soil, the finesse of the pressing technique, and even the way the olives are picked and handled all affect the flavor of the oil. (Nut and seed oils are not as sensitive.) As olive oil should be an important part of your meals, try a few brands to choose the one you like best.

Virgin olive oil. Though prepared just like the extra-virgin oil, the virgin olive oil has a less wonderful flavor and can have a higher acidity, ranging from 1 to 3 percent. The subtle differences between the virgin and extra-virgin oils are not the result of processing technique or less care. Most likely they are caused by the fact that olives are fresh fruits and not as uniform as seeds from year to year. Very little virgin olive oil is sold in North America.

Olive oil. Sometimes called "pure" or "100 percent pure olive oil," this third oil is usually a blend of refined olive oil and extra-virgin olive oil. It most often comes from a batch of olives that produced an oil with undesirable flavor and aroma, or it may have been extracted by mechanical or other means (solvents) and because of off-flavor or high acidity may have required refinement. This oil is usually mixed with extra-virgin oil to make it more flavorful and acceptable. This kind of oil is not the prize olive oil you should use for total enjoyment, but it is quite acceptable for sautéing if you can't afford virgin for everything. As the flavor of the olive oil on your food is such an important part of its use, try not to use anything less than the best.

> *F*or the finest flavor, there is only one choice: extra-virgin olive oil, which has been cold pressed and not refined. In Italy, France, Greece, Spain, or in Middle Eastern countries, this oil is the only true olive oil. No one would dress a salad with any other.

Now that you know which olive oil to buy—the extra-virgin type—go a step further. Become an olive oil connoisseur and savor the subtleties of olive oils just as wine connoisseurs enjoy the finesse of different fine wines.

Whole Olives

Olives were sold as a snack in the streets of ancient Rome, just one indication of their long-standing use. But raw olives contain a bitter substance called oleuropein that must be removed to make the olive palatable. When olive oil is pressed, the oleuropein simply floats away with the water layer produced by the pressing. Whole olives, however, require treatment, usually some kind of curing, to remove the bitterness.

Extracts of wood ash—a potassium salt—regular sea salt, sodium hydroxide, olive oil, and lactic acid (the acid from milk sugar) have all been used to cure olives. When salt or sodium hydroxide is used, the olives may contain significant levels of sodium. If you are concerned about salt intake, decrease the amount of salt in a recipe when using olives cured this way. For instance, salt your pizza dough less and place some olives on top instead. (More on salt in chapter 8.) The bitter substance may also be removed by prolonged soaking in water, but olives treated this way won't keep for long because they lack the salt that acts as a preservative. Properly cured olives have been found in Egyptian graves, reminding us how good a preservative salts of sodium or potassium are.

In most stores you'll find: olives processed with sodium hydroxide, quite mild and packed in a salt brine, then sold under various names usually derived from the spices added; Greek (or Italian) dry black olives, made by placing alternating layers of olives and sea salt in a barrel without any fluid, though they are sometimes rubbed with olive oil after curing and therefore called oil-cured; and Sicilian olives, cured in a salt brine that leaves much more flavor in the olive than does sodium hydroxide.

If you find olives cured with olive oil only, you can eat them freely without fear of excess sodium, and they should be your first choice. Unfortunately, they are not commonly available in North America. Some packers are now experimenting with a potassium salt similar to the one found in wood ash to cure olives for a low-sodium product.

Of the olives commonly available, a good choice is Greek (sometimes called Italian) dried or dry—that is, not packed in a jar or can with any fluid—black olives. These wrinkly black olives are the ones used to top focaccias in Italy and probably surpass all other types in flavor. Because of their intense flavor, you need only a few of them to give zest to a dish. Remember, you don't want to add excessive salt by adding too many olives. Soaking dry-cured olives in water will make them less salty.

As long as olives are high in salt, they should be used in moderation. For convenience I'm discussing them together with olive oil, but when salted they are not really a tier-three food. Rather, they're a condiment to be used like an herb or spice. Low-salt or potassium- or oil-cured olives would be a tier-three food.

Olive Paste

Olive paste is another delicious flavoring. It isn't well known in North America but makes a delicious spread or ingredient for various recipes. You can blend some olive paste into salad dressing in place of salt, or spread it on a sandwich instead of butter. Because olive paste is made by grinding olives that have most likely been treated with salt, it is usually high in salt and should be used sparingly. Fortunately, like the Italian-Greek dried olives, olive paste is so flavorful that you need only a very small amount to add zest to otherwise bland dishes.

SEEDS
Sesame Seeds
Just like the olive tree, sesame *(Sesamum indicum)* is a very ancient plant. It has been cultivated and its seeds used for food for thousands of years in India, the Middle East, Greece, and Egypt. The sesame plant is probably native to central Asia. The golden oil of sesame, the crushed seeds (sesame butters), or whole seeds have been important ingredients in the diet of people from these regions since the beginning of recorded history. The use and extraction of sesame oil in India parallels the history of olive oil in Mediterranean countries. There is a reverence toward sesame that reveals how important and healthful ancient people considered this seed and its oil. In some Indian temples, sesame seeds were used in religious ceremonies, another sign of the esteem in which they were held.

Sesame oil has an excellent balance of mono and poly oils, both being present in about the same amount, while the saturated fats are extremely low. Sesame oil has a mild but distinctive flavor that has made it a staple ingredient of certain cuisines: in India it is the preferred oil throughout the south and southwest and is known as *til-ka-tel.*

Use sesame oil by itself in any kind of dressing for salads, vegetables, pasta, or beans, or blend it with olive oil for a change of taste. Substituting sesame for olive oil and vice versa is a good way to add variety to a meal.

Sesame butters or *tahinis* are produced by crushing or grinding the hulled seeds. Their proteins, just like the proteins of beans, help to balance the proteins of grains, a fact that made these foods popular in tropical and semitropical countries long before we knew about protein composition. *Hummus,* a typical Middle Eastern food made from sesame butter and chickpeas (page 331), is a great dip or spread for grain-based foods. It gives you the benefits of two different proteins (chickpea and sesame) to balance your grain dishes. Some tahinis have added salt, but most of them are unsalted. Choose the unsalted type.

Halvah is a sweet Middle Eastern confection made with sesame seeds and honey. It comes as a candy bar and can be found in many specialty stores. You can also make an easy dessert by blending sesame butter and honey right at the table. These foods are very high in energy, as you would expect.

Whole sesame seeds are sometimes used on breads and other baked products.

Pumpkin Seeds

Pumpkin and squash seeds make delicious snacks either raw or gently roasted. They contain more polyunsaturated than monounsaturated fat, but they are still quite balanced and can expand your range of choices among seeds and nuts. *Pumpkin seed oil* is not very common but has quite a pleasant flavor and contains some omega-3 fats (see this kind of fat in the fish section of this chapter).

Soybeans and Soybean Oil

The oil of the soybean is also a source of omega-3 oils and as part of many soy foods like tofu it has been a component of healthful Oriental diets for a long time. The oil itself adds little flavor to foods as compared to olive or sesame oils. Perhaps the best way to take advantage of the soybean's omega-3 oils is to eat tofu and related products.

A Note of Caution

Deep frying. Olive, sesame, and other oils are at their best raw. When used in gentle cooking, as in some of the recipes in the Superpyramid Kitchen, they are still very acceptable. If mixed with other flavorings such as lemon or vinegar to marinate something that is then baked, we can assume that little or no harmful changes take place in the oil molecules. *But you should moderate your intake of deep-fried foods,* even if they are prepared with these vegetable oils instead of animal fat. If heated at high temperature and kept at that high temperature for prolonged periods, chemical changes can take place in these delicate oils from plants and they may lose some of their beneficial properties.

Hydrogenated fats and salt. Some seed butters or nut butters may have been partially hydrogenated or heavily salted. If you buy peanut butter, read the label carefully: sometimes hydrogenated fats are present to make the product more solid and to help it keep for longer periods. These are not the kind of nut or seed butters you want to use on a regular basis. The same applies to heavily salted nuts and seeds. Consider them an occasional snack but not a regular Superpyramid food. If you are worried about spoilage, you can buy smaller quantities of all-natural seed and nut butters in health food stores and some super-markets.

NUTS
A Handful of Nuts Each Day

Drs. Gary Frazer, Joan Sabaté, and their colleagues at Loma Linda University in California studied a large population that ate the equivalent of a handful of nuts every day for a long period of time. They compared this population to another group on a similar diet who did not consume nuts regularly. The incidence of heart disease was 50 percent lower in the group that ate nuts frequently.

Use a variety of nuts, preferably raw and unsalted. Gentle, light roasting probably does no damage to the oils, but we know little about the health effects of long roasting of nuts.

Which Nut Is Best?

Almonds, hazelnuts, pecans, pistachios, and *cashews* are all monounsaturated nuts. *Pine nuts* (pignolias) are somewhere between the mono and the poly nuts as they contain about 40 percent mono and 47 percent poly oils. *Walnuts* are the most popular polyunsaturated nut and contain some of the omega-3 oils that also occur in purslane and in a slightly different form in fish, as you'll see later in this chapter. (Peanuts, by the way, are considered legumes, not nuts.)

Choosing the best nut is practically impossible. All nuts are good and have a place in a good food plan. The monounsaturated nuts can be used more freely than nuts high in polyunsaturates, but they all have beneficial properties.

Almonds, like olives, have been used since antiquity. Their delicate flavor and their keeping qualities make them a very desirable nut. They have been grown since prehistoric times from Turkey to northern India. The Hebrews knew the almond well, and it's mentioned in the Book of Genesis. It was introduced to Greece during the third century B.C., where it became known as the Greek nut. Later, Greeks brought the plant to Italy, and it is now grown in many Mediterranean countries and in North and South America. In this century, California has become one

Almonds

of the principal growing regions for almonds in the world. The almond is a highly monounsaturated nut, and it also supplies valuable proteins and calcium, a mineral often in short supply in plant foods. The oil is very mild and is prized for cosmetic, as well as food, use.

The composition of almond oil is so similar to olive oil that some studies were undertaken in 1989 to see whether or not the consumption of a reasonable amount of almonds daily would help control or lower blood cholesterol. At our research center in California we fed raw almonds, both whole and ground, to subjects with high blood cholesterol in two different major studies. These subjects were compared to groups on similar diets who ate no almonds. The almonds were very effective in lowering blood cholesterol, confirming the efficacy of foods high in monounsaturated fat.

Pistachio Nuts, Hazelnuts, and Pecans. These nuts are very similar to almonds in fat composition, though no two nuts are exactly alike in this regard. Although I have no data from clinical studies on the effects of these nuts on blood cholesterol, I would expect them to have very desirable effects just like almonds.

Hazelnuts and *pistachios* are both ancient Mediterranean nuts, while *pecans* originated in the Americas. Fossil remains confirm the antiquity of hazelnut cultivation and use. The cultivation of pistachios originated in the Middle East and then spread east to India and other parts of Asia and west to Italy and later to North America, where in California's Central Valley it has become a prized crop.

Pecans are famous as the filling for the traditional American favorite, pecan pie. When raw, they make a good alternative to walnuts and have a similar flavor.

Tropical Nuts. *Cashew* and *macadamia* nuts are tropical nuts, the latter grown extensively in Hawaii. Macadamias have a very unusual composition; they contain large amounts not only of the common monounsat-urated fat (oleic acid) but also an unusually large amount of palmitoleic acid, another monounsaturated fat. Not much is known about the health effects of this unusual nut, but it has to be classified as a high-mono nut with an extremely low saturated fat content.

Walnuts. Is the walnut the oldest tree-grown food known to mankind? Or is it the olive or almond? This question may never be answered. With their justified love for their trees, walnut growers believe that the walnut is the most ancient (7000 B.C.), while olive and almond growers make the same claim for their trees.

> *As we approach the twenty-first century, as more and more people have lost touch with real, whole foods, let's look back and focus more on traditional foods. Let farmers be proud of their ancient crops and have some exciting debate as to whether the almond or the walnut or the olive has the longest history. It's refreshing and wholesome in an era when many people have never shelled a raw nut for themselves.*

The walnut is probably the queen of the polyunsaturated nuts. Be-cause it is so highly polyunsaturated, it turns rancid unless properly stored in a cool place. Use fresh walnuts in the fall, soon after picking. If kept in the shell, vacuum package or freeze them and they will keep longer. One of the special oils present in walnuts is of the omega-3 family we will discuss more on pages 144–45.

Drs. Gary Frazer and Joan Sabaté, who conducted the "handful of nuts" study already mentioned, successfully used walnuts to lower blood cholesterol in a group of volunteers in studies at Loma Linda University in 1991.

AVOCADOS
The Olive-Avocado Connection

Cut an avocado and an olive in half and you'll notice how similar they are. Both are typical fruits with a pulp surrounding a hard seed or stone. In both cases we eat, or press oil from, the pulp. The avocado can be considered the American counterpart of the European olive. It probably was originally widespread in Peru, Costa Rica, and Guatemala. Later, the avocado crossed the Atlantic to Europe, and the olive came to the Americas.

There is an intriguing similarity in the composition of fat in the avocado and the olive. Both are high in monounsaturated fats. Although we do not have the kind of geographical studies of disease in relation to avocado consumption that we have for olive oil, it makes sense that because they are so similar, avocados must also supply a safe type of fat. And Dr. David Colquhoun and his associates in Australia recently confirmed in a clinical study that when avocados with their good oils replaced saturated-fat foods, avocados do indeed lower blood cholesterol.

Perhaps the best use of avocados is sliced in salads or on sandwiches or as a superb foundation for great dips with various types of spices. Avocados turn black soon after they have been cut, so eat them quickly or prepare dips or other dishes that contain ingredients such as lemon juice that will prevent such blackening. Many good recipes, such as guacamole, from Mexico and other Latin American countries were developed with ingredients that prevent the color change for a reasonable length of time. Still, do not keep cut avocados around for too long.

WHEAT GERM OIL

Wheat germ oil has an unusually high vitamin E content, so it deserves special mention as a beneficial oil to add to your salad or other dressing. It's also a source of omega-3 fats like walnuts, soybeans, and pumpkin seeds. Use wheat germ oil sparingly. It has a fairly strong flavor, and large amounts may change the flavor of your food. A level teaspoon or even less in a large salad adds nutritional value without altering flavor.

FISH AND ITS OILS
The Fish Option

At this point we enter a new phase in the Superpyramid. For the first time we encounter an optional food—fish. Fish is a good food in many ways. As defined here it includes lean, white fishes such as sole, fatty fishes such as salmon, and shellfish and mollusks such as shrimp and oysters. Yet many people who have chosen a vegetarian diet do without fish quite successfully. If you follow a vegetarian plan, you must place greater emphasis on some of the superior proteins of yogurts and other low-fat milk products and egg whites. Among fish, poultry, and red meats, fish is the best choice and can supply excellent proteins. It differs in two major ways from both red meat and poultry as we know them today. First, you can find extremely low-fat fish such as sole that is delicious, while meat or poultry with a similar fat content would be dry and unpalatable. Second, fish contains a very special kind of fat, which in fact is a plant fat. These two points make fish the most desirable of the fish-meat-poultry triad and place it on tier three. But remember, as a tier-three food, it should never be your main source of energy. That role is reserved for the foods of tier one.

Fish and Its Unusual Fats

Although the Greenland Eskimos eat a high-fat diet, they have a low rate of heart disease. In the 1970s and 1980s, studies by the Scandinavian scientists Drs. Jorn Dyerberg and H. O. Bang revealed that the type of fat in the Eskimo diet seemed the key factor. These researchers suggested that it was the Eskimos' high consumption of cold-water ocean fish or of mammals that ate this type of fish that had a protective effect. Although many scientists were intrigued by these findings and started doing follow-up research, the general public did not learn about it until 1985, when newspapers and television news focused attention on a group of studies published that May by the prestigious *New England Journal of Medicine*. All the studies concluded that the consumption of cold-water fish is beneficial for the heart.

In another study, Dr. Daan Kromhout and associates at the University of Leiden in the Netherlands studied 852 middle-aged men in the town of Zutphen for twenty years. They found that eating as little as two fish meals per week helped prevent heart disease in this group. At the same time, Dr. William Connor of the University of Oregon School of Medicine confirmed that certain fish oils modify blood clotting in a favorable way, making blood less likely to form abnormal clots, or thrombi.

Japanese researchers at the University of Kyoto obtained similar results. They compared people living in a fishing village to people living in a farming village. In all cases, blood was slower to clot in people eating more fish or fish oils instead of other animal foods. By the late 1980s, fish oils had become the object of so many research projects that national meetings and chapters in medical books focused on this topic.

Why Is Fish Different?

What makes fish oils different from other animal fats? It is the kind of food ocean fish eat—saltwater algae and other sea vegetation. Fish do not make these oils themselves: rather, these special fats originate in plants. Larger fish obtain these fats indirectly by eating smaller fish, which, in turn, have been feeding on various types of marine plant life.

These beneficial fat components are called omega-3 fats. In fish and sea vegetation we find EPA (eicosapentaenoic acid) and DHA (docosa-hexaenoic acid). They are highly unsaturated and effective at preventing unwanted blood clot formation under experimental conditions. They may even be effective in lowering blood fat (not cholesterol) levels.

Some land plants contain a related oil, called linolenic acid, that can be changed to EPA in the body. If you choose not to eat fish, purslane (and green leaves in general) and some nuts and seeds (or their oils) such as walnuts, soybeans, and wheat germ are good choices. You can go a step further and use edible seaweed to get your omega-3 directly from sea plants just as fish do. Although seaweed is uncommon in the North American diet, people in Japan and other Asian countries bordering the ocean incorporate it into their meals. Many types of seaweed are now being analyzed to find out which are good sources of omega-3 oils.

Other Benefits of EPA and DHA

Recently, other possible benefits of EPA and DHA have been proposed, but they are not yet generally accepted by the scientific community. Some of these proposed effects include a role in enhanced brain function, increased sperm health, and proper function of the retina of the eye, which is crucial to good vision. Studies are in progress on potentially beneficial effects of omega-3 oils on some forms of arthritis, but again it is too early to draw conclusions. Meanwhile, eating some cold-water fish or plant sources of omega-3 oils cannot hurt and may help in disease prevention.

Choosing and Preparing Fish

Low-fat fish, sometimes called white fish, has a fat content that ranges from about 0.5 percent for whiting, haddock, or cod to 2.5 percent for halibut. Sole has about 1.5 percent fat, making it an almost ideal fish. These are truly low-fat foods!

Fatty fishes available in North America range in fat from 12 percent in Atlantic salmon to 16 to 18 percent in herring and mackerel. (These percentages for fat in fish are for the fish before cooking or other preparation.) It is easy to taste which fishes are low in fat: taste sole and then salmon; without any chemical test you'll know the sole is much, much lower in fat.

While white fish has practically no cholesterol, fatty fishes do. Salmon, for instance, has about seventy milligrams in three ounces, but the presnence of the omega-3 fats instead of the saturated fats of land animals make these fatty fishes, eaten in moderation, acceptable as tier-three foods. But remember that no tier-three food, including any type of fish, should be the foundation of your meals.

Shrimps and prawns have about 1.5 to 2.4 percent fat, crab about 5 percent. Scallops and other mollusks are also quite low in fat. In chapter 11 we'll see some cautions needed in the choice of shellfish and mollusks. Most shellfish and mollusks contain significant amounts of cholesterol: three ounces of shrimp contain about two hundred milligrams (very close to a large egg yolk) and crab about one hundred milligrams. For this reason choose white fish first, omega-3 fatty fishes next, and shellfish last.

In cooking fish be careful: preparation can add other fats. If you sauté, fry, or bake, use only the oils found on this tier. Baking with just a trace of olive oil in the pan is an excellent choice. So is boiling in water and flavoring the fish with some oil and vinegar. Do not use animal fats such as butter. If you eat out avoid batters: you don't know how they are made—they often contain whole eggs—and fish so prepared is often deep-fried in some unknown fat. Cooking without any fat added is a good option. See the fish section in the Superpyramid Kitchen (pages 374–76) for good low-fat recipes.

▲ KEY IDEAS

- ▲ Foods found on tier three should be used as complements to the energy foods of tier one. The tier-three foods have a high energy content and should be consumed in moderation.
- ▲ Use oils, nuts, and seeds, or nut and seed butters found on tier three in place of all solid animal fat or hydrogenated fats.
- ▲ Raw nuts, seeds, and the pulp of olives and avocados are all sources of good oils.
- ▲ Monounsaturated fats are some of the safest fats and are the highest in olives, almonds, sesame seeds, and avocados. Nonhydrogenated roasted peanut butter is another source.
- ▲ Omega-3 oils found in fish, soybeans, wheat germ, and other seeds have some unique health-giving properties.
- ▲ Do not deep-fry. Do not overheat oils in cooking.
- ▲ Solid animal fat and hydrogenated vegetable fats that are hard are not part of the Superpyramid.
- ▲ Fish is an optional food in the Superpyramid Program.

▲7▲

The Fourth and Fifth Tiers

MOVING UP TO TIERS FOUR AND FIVE

As you move up to the higher, smaller tiers, remember the basic concept of the Superpyramid: the smaller the tier, the less you should consume of the foods on that tier. Always visualize tiers four and five as small tiers.

CHEESES
In Search of Flavor

Two groups of foods on tier four—cheeses and sweeteners—are key in making a meal or a recipe more pleasant. Let's start with cheeses. Aged cheeses excel at adding a classic, wonderful flavor to a recipe, even in small quantities. The amount of fat in cheeses ranges from fairly low to quite high. Nonfat or very low-fat cheeses—for example, yogurt cheese made from nonfat or low-fat yogurt—belong on tier one. Low-fat cheeses belong on tier four, and medium-fat cheeses on tier five, to be eaten in correspondingly smaller amounts. There are some higher-fat cheeses that should be consumed only rarely for a change of pace, certainly not more than once or twice a month, and in limited amounts.

An important point: as you are searching for flavor in cheese, remember that a cheese marked "natural" is your best choice. Natural cheeses can have different amounts of fat, but they are made only from milk

THE FOODS OF THE *Fourth Tier*

▲ Low-fat Cheeses, with a very moderate fat content and always more protein than fat. Low-fat milk and low-fat yogurt (nonfat and extremely low-fat milk and yogurts are found on tier one).

▲ Sweeteners, such as honey, maple syrup, *vino cotto* and other fruit juice concentrates, and molasses, that are flavorful enough to be used in small amounts to enhance the flavor of foods such as low-fat yogurts.

▲ Low-fat Meat and Poultry products that are high in protein. These foods are optional and may be omitted for a vegetarian Superpyramid. For the ultimate Superpyramid, do not use these foods or use them only occasionally.

THE FOODS OF THE *Fifth Tier*

▲ Medium-fat Cheeses, which contain more fat than the cheeses of tier four but still have at least as much protein as fat. Whole milk and whole-milk yogurts.

▲ Whole Eggs —that is, eggs with the yolk. (Egg whites are found on tier one.)

with some salt, enzymes, and cultures. They are then aged for months or years in various ways to create the special flavors of the many regional cheeses of the world.

The Low-fat Cheeses of Tier Four

The term *low-fat* (some labels use the term *reduced-fat*) is vague. Take the low-fat yogurts we found on tier one. These are truly low in fat, and we can consume them freely. But many so-called low-fat cheeses actually have a much higher percentage of fat than a low-fat yogurt.

You can find many acceptable natural cheeses that are truly low in fat in your market, but you must read the labels carefully. *As a general rule, cheese with less than 15 percent fat and at least 30 percent protein is acceptable as a tier-four cheese in the context of the Superpyramid plan,* but try to stay with cheeses that are even lower in fat—for example, 10 percent fat and 30 percent protein. It just takes some getting used to reading labels. If the label does not give a percentage of fat, but rather fat and protein per serving, just make sure that there is about twice the amount of protein compared to the amount of fat by weight.

I'd like to stress this point: the Superpyramid plan up to this tier is so extremely low in saturated fat that when you add a moderate amount of a low-fat cheese to the foods of tiers one, two, and three, you are still within very acceptable limits of saturated-fat intake. The same rule would not apply to a person consuming a typical high-meat Western diet already high in saturated fat and low in unsaturated fat.

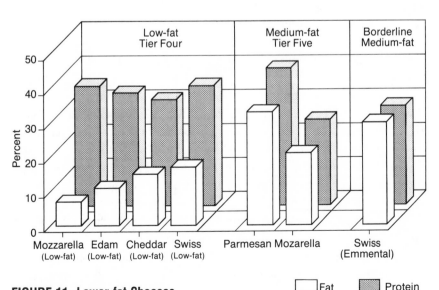

FIGURE 11. Lower-fat Cheeses

But as you see from figure 11, even low-fat cheeses have various levels of fat. The lower the fat, the freer you should feel to use the chosen cheese in your recipes. Many low-fat mozzarellas (excellent on pizzas and similar dishes) have as little as 7 percent fat and as much as 35 percent protein. An Edam cheese can be found with 11 percent fat and 33 percent protein. These two are true low-fat cheeses. But look at the low-fat Swiss on the same chart: it moves up to 17 percent fat, while the protein is still about 35 percent. Many other low-fat cheeses are coming on the market, many of them with excellent flavor, often better than their high-fat relatives. Use the principles we have described here for guidance in your shopping. But always remember you are on tier four, a fairly small tier.

Ricotta cheese. A special type of cheese is *ricotta cheese*. This cheese has some of the milk sugar left in (carbohydrate). We cannot use our protein to fat ratio to judge whether it belongs on tier four or five. The rule is simple: the skim ricotta belongs on tier four as it has about 16 percent protein and carbohydrate combined (11 percent protein and 5 percent carbohydrate) and about 7 percent fat. This means over twice as much carbohydrate plus protein as fat, which meets the requirements of a tier-four cheese.

The Medium-fat Cheeses of Tier Five

The two cheeses that follow on figure 10—Parmesan and regular mozzarella—are medium-fat cheeses and thus tier-five foods. You can see that the protein content still exceeds the fat. The next cheese on this chart is regular Swiss cheese, with about the same amount of protein and fat. Again, remember that the higher the fat, the more moderate you must be.

These tier-five cheeses should be used in very limited amounts to flavor foods, such as a tablespoon of grated Parmesan cheese on pasta, rice, or polenta, or a few pieces of mozzarella on pizza. One way to eat Swiss cheese or regular mozzarella is to have two or three slices on a sandwich not more than once or twice a week. The other way—which is the better way—is to use them sparingly as flavoring in such dishes as polenta or baked lasagnas.

Regular ricotta cheese has about 14 percent protein plus carbohydrate and 12 percent fat, which makes it a tier-five food.

What about cheeses that have slightly more fat than protein? Can we put cheddar cheese or blue cheese on tier five? Let's look at figure 12.

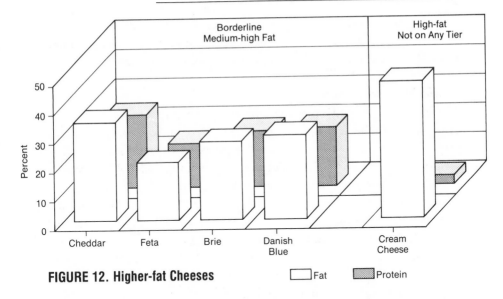

FIGURE 12. Higher-fat Cheeses ☐ Fat ▨ Protein

Here the protein bar is slightly lower than the fat bar, which means that the fat exceeds the protein. Should we eat cheddar and blue cheese? *Let's accept them as borderline tier-five foods,* that is, foods that we must use only occasionally in a way similar to Swiss cheese but with even greater moderation. We should now be even more cautious than with the other tier-five cheeses and not use cheddar or blue more than once a week. True high-fat cheeses such as cream cheese (35 percent fat and 8 percent protein) do not belong on the Superpyramid.

> *There are so many cheeses that the ones mentioned are intended just as examples. If you want to use a cheese not on the charts, read the label, find the relative amounts of fat and protein, and be sure the fat percentage is always lower than the protein percentage or, at the limit of a tier-five food, equal to it. If carbohydrate is present as in ricotta cheese, add the carbohydrate and protein together in your calculation.*

MILK AND YOGURTS
Low-fat Milk and Yogurts
While nonfat (or practically nonfat) milk and its products belong on tier one, low-fat milks and its products belong on tier four. Some moderation is needed; we cannot be as free as with the foods on tier one. The tier-

four products have "low-fat" on the label. Low-fat milk has about 2 percent fat, and a low-fat yogurt has about the same percentage, much higher than the milk products found on tier one.

Whole Milk and Yogurt

Whole milk is a tier-five product. Never use extra-rich milks or half and half, cream, or butter as regular foods. Whole milk is acceptable as a flavoring in tea or coffee or in similar beverages. There is no need to use artificial creamers that don't have the great taste of milk. Of course, low-fat milk is an even better choice. Use whole-milk yogurts in extreme moderation and only occasionally: there are so many low-fat or nonfat yogurts today that you don't need a whole-milk yogurt. Remember that one of the great advantages of the nonfat yogurts found on tier one is that their flavor is far superior to nonfat milk for most people. Use these higher-fat milk products when you have no choice and only very occasionally—for example, while traveling.

The diet and breed of the cow influence the amount of fat naturally present. Milk producers are aware of the need for naturally lower-fat milks, and changes in the diet of the cow can often make a difference.

Goat's milk is somewhat different from cow's milk. It is naturally homogenized; that is, the fat normally does not come to the top. You can use it as you would use whole cow's milk. A good whole goat's milk from goats free to graze in open pastures has about 35 percent less fat than cow's milk, so it could be a good choice if available. Goats grazing in an open pasture often have lower-fat milk—and perhaps the milk fat is somewhat different—than goats restricted to a barn. It's unfortunate that little research is available on the differences in fat composition between milks from goats (or cows) fed grass and goats fed grains. As we have seen, grass contains omega-3 oils, and these could affect the milk's composition.

Cheeses and Milk Products in a Meatless Diet

If you have chosen not to eat any red meats or poultry, your consumption of saturated fats will naturally be much lower, so you can increase somewhat your consumption of low-fat or medium-fat cheeses or low-fat milk or yogurt. Still, always be moderate with medium-fat cheeses and whole-milk products. In this case you can allow more medium-fat cheeses or whole milk than a person eating even a moderate amount of meat products.

SWEETENERS
Honey, **Vino Cotto,** *Maple Syrup, Brown Sugars, and Molasses*

Just as small amounts of an aged cheese can bring life to a recipe, so can a moderate use of sweeteners. Of course, all sweeteners should be used with a light touch. In a food plan based on traditional foods, honey, maple syrup, *vino cotto,* and similar products are our top choices, together with molasses and one of the various types of real brown sugars.

Honey is one of your best choices. It is sweeter than white sugar and, if unrefined, is more flavorful, so you need less to get the level of intensity you want. One of honey's great advantages is the almost endless range of flavors you can find; the taste and consistency of honey depend on the type of blossoms the bees have harvested for their pollen. Try different types of honey, from wild sage to tupelo and eucalyptus to wild mountain flowers. Become a honey connoisseur. For example, the difference in flavor between clover honey and wildflower honey is so great that people who do not like one may love the other. Using honey is much more fun and satisfying than using plain white sugar or corn syrup products, which taste the same all the time.

Is honey intrinsically healthier than white sugar? The answer is not clear, even though folklore abounds in stories about the benefits of honey. A recent laboratory study found that rats that consumed honey had more exercise endurance than rats that consumed sugar. But this kind of study needs to be confirmed in humans before we can consider it fact.

Maple syrup gives another option for variety. The delicious, full flavor of real maple syrup, even in limited amounts, can give you the sweet taste you may crave. Choose 100 percent real maple syrup. Because the real syrup is expensive, many imitation maple syrups on the market are made with less expensive sugars and flavored with either concentrated flavors or small amounts of real maple syrup. On the Superpyramid plan, always opt for the real thing!

Vino cotto (grape juice concentrate) or other liquid fruit concentrates are not well known in North America. Along with their fruit sugars, they bring numerous nutrients from the fruit and should be a regular part of a good Superpyramid plan. *Vino cotto* on low-fat yogurt is an unforgettable treat! Frozen fruit juice concentrates are also options.

Brown sugars and **molasses** contain minerals, from the sugar cane or other source, that are lost in the refining process used to make white sugar. Molasses is a particularly good source of iron. These products also give unique, often very intense, flavors to foods. Use brown sugar on your low-fat yogurt for a change of pace from honey or *vino cotto*.

Corn syrups—prepared by processing cornstarch and breaking it down into sugars—and regular *white sugar* are extremely bland and do not add the same zest to a recipe as the sweeteners I have mentioned above. White sugar probably has the better flavor of the two, but corn-syrup products have become very popular because of their lower cost. They are usually listed on labels as "corn syrup," "high fructose corn syrup," and "dark corn syrup."

Artificial sweeteners simply can't approach the flavor of honey or other truly natural sweeteners or foods made with them. It seems unnecessary for a healthy person to use artificial sweeteners. Artificial sweeteners do not help you learn the value of real food. *Physicians may advise people with certain diseases, such as diabetes, to use artificial sweeteners. Remember that the Superpyramid Program is intended for healthy people. If you have a disease, you should follow the nutritional guidelines of a health professional, who may in fact recommend this program.*

MEATS AND POULTRY

Lean red meats and poultry are optional tier-four foods. You may choose to eat them or not in the Superpyramid food plan. *If you do eat meat or poultry, remember to visualize the small size of tier four, where they belong.* Foods on this tier should never be substituted for foods on the lower tiers as foundations for your energy intake.

> *R*emember the key idea of the Superpyramid plan: if you eat meat or poultry, be sure it is not the major part of your meal. Meat and poultry portions should always be small and be accompanied by plenty of grains, beans, and vegetables complemented by very-low fat milk products and egg whites.

The Different Fats of Red Meats and Poultry

Most people concerned about heart disease feel free to eat chicken and turkey, compared to other kinds of meat. For example, studies carried out in our research center in California show that people with high blood cholesterol always have the impression that they can eat as much chicken or turkey as they wish. However, we should take a closer look at these assumptions.

There is no doubt that poultry in general has less saturated and more polyunsaturated fats than common red meat products such as beef, lamb, or pork.

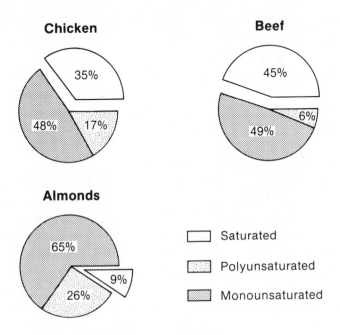

FIGURE 13. Fat Composition of Different Foods

You'll notice that the fats in beef and chicken are all about half mono-unsaturated but that chicken has less saturated and more polyunsaturated fats than beef. Still, all of these foods—including poultry—contain a lot of saturated fat. Compare them to any of the mono nuts or oily fruits such as olives. These too have large amounts of mono fats, but their saturated fat is minimal, usually around 10 percent. This is a key difference to remember.

No matter what kind of meat or poultry product you choose to eat, make sure it's extremely lean. Then make it even leaner by letting the fat drip off in cooking. If you choose beef, try to find a store that carries cuts from animals that were free to graze on open pastures, because their meat will most likely be leaner as a consequence and may contain healthier fats. Such beef is often called "range fed" or "free range."

Lamb and pork are sometimes very high in fat. Use them only if you find a reliable source of lean lamb or pork. Be sure to choose only lean chickens or turkeys, and always remove the skin when preparing poultry.

The meat and poultry industry is becoming aware of the demand for leaner products. It is up to consumers to encourage the industry to practice different feeding and raising methods. The producers want to sell their products, so vote for what you want by purchasing the right food. If you eat meats or poultry, buy them extra lean. Many markets already use well-designed labels to give you a good idea of the level of fat in red meats and poultry.

In cooking, avoid the kind of broiling or barbecuing that lets the fat burn after it has dripped onto hot charcoal, mesquite, or other fuel. This method produces fumes that contain cancer-causing substances. Putting foil under the meat may protect it from these fumes.

Preserved Meat and Poultry Products

Preserved meats such as bacon, ham, or cold cuts are often high in saturated fats and need preservatives to keep them safe without freezing. Nitrates and nitrites as well as salt are usually used for this purpose. Since nitrites and the amino acids in proteins combine to form possibly carcinogenic nitrosamines, if you eat these kinds of meats, do so in extreme moderation and always have them together with a vegetable or fruit that is rich in vitamin C, which appears to help prevent nitrosamine formation in the stomach. Orange juice, oranges, or tomatoes would be good choices with bacon, for example. If nothing else, protect yourself with a vitamin C supplement taken at the same time. Some prepared meats are now reaching the market without nitrites, but remember, they may still be high in fat.

The Meatless Option

The benefits of making whole grains the main source of energy are almost universally accepted. Raising animals for meat isn't very efficient. It requires much more land and water to produce protein and energy in the form of a meat animal than it does to produce the same amount of protein and energy in a plant food. We've already looked at the benefits of low- or no-meat (meaning both red meats and poultry) meals in the first part of this book. In fact, some researchers believe that the ultimate eating pattern should avoid all meat products, whether from fowl (chickens and turkeys) or mammals (pork, lamb, and beef). This trend is so strong that even some major fast food chains now offer low-meat or no-meat alternatives—unheard of just a few years ago.

Dr. Walter Willett of the Harvard University School of Public Health published a study in *The New England Journal of Medicine* in 1990 in which he showed that women who ate red meats had a much higher risk of colon cancer than women who did not. And remember (chapter 2) that populations with low rates of heart disease and colon cancer eat very little meat. Populations that eat meat freely—as we do in the U.S. —together with an abundance of other foods are more obese than populations that consume little meat. The Italians say—even though no study has been carried out to prove it—that "if you do not want to get fat, do not eat meat with your pasta."

If after reading this whole book you do just one thing—decrease your meat and poultry consumption so that meats are no longer your major source of energy—you'll have taken a major step toward better health.

Jon C. in the Wind Rivers Range

Many people think that it's going to be hard to eat only small amounts of meat or chicken or to eliminate them from their normal diet. It may not be so hard after all, as Jon C. found out.

"It all started in the summer of 1988. I had just finished my sophomore year in high school—I was about sixteen then—and went climbing in Wyoming with the National Outdoor Leadership School. We camped for thirty days in a mountain range called the Wind Rivers. As meat spoils easily and is just not practical for a long backpack trek, we didn't take any with us. We took along lots of pasta and other high-carbohydrate foods, so for thirty days I did not eat any meat. I did not know how I was going to survive, to be honest.

"Instead, when we came back I felt in great shape, probably in the best shape of my life. Still, my greatest desire was to eat a hamburger as soon as we reached the first village. When we came back from the wilderness, this desire for a hamburger was uppermost in my mind, so I went straight down to the local store and had one, but it really turned my stomach. I almost fell ill!

"At that point I decided never to eat meat again. For a while I did not eat any kind of meat or chicken or even fish. When I went to college on the East Coast in 1990, it became very difficult to avoid these foods while eating in a college dormitory or eating out all the time! There just wasn't very much to eat if you left these foods out. So I began to eat some light fish again, but I just can't eat any red meat or chicken anymore, even though I tried a couple of times. I guess that's the way it's going to be for me for a long time."

Calcium, Meat, Poultry, and Cheeses

Products derived from milk offer a great advantage over meat and poultry: they are much higher in precious calcium. Both meat and poultry are high in protein, high in phosphorus, and practically free of calcium. Dogs eat bones to make up for this deficiency, a habit typical of true meat-eating animals. High-protein, high-phosphorus diets may affect calcium balance in the body, as we have already seen. Weakened bone in aging brings about decreased physical activity, pain, and many other problems related to osteoporosis, a disease of epidemic proportion in North America. There is no doubt that milk products have a better balance of nutrients for bone maintenance than meats or poultry. As we have said so many times (but never too many times!) if you eat meat and poultry products, do so in very small amounts.

WHOLE EGGS

Whole eggs supply one of the best proteins we have and contain very little saturated fat—about 1.5 grams in a typical large egg—when not prepared with butter or bacon fat. The problem is all the cholesterol is in the egg yolk as is the fat. (As you remember, the white does not contain any cholesterol at all, and egg whites are a great tier-one food.) One typical large egg contains about 210 milligrams of cholesterol, which is close to what many researchers believe should be the maximum daily intake for normal people.

All this means that a few whole eggs a week are acceptable, but most often egg whites can be used just as well. Usually two whites can replace one whole egg in a recipe. Some public health groups recommend no more than three or four whole eggs a week. One good way to use whole eggs is to add one to an omelet made with egg whites. (See recipes in the Superpyramid Kitchen.)

> **On** the Superpyramid, whole eggs are optional and should be used only occasionally. Egg whites are a tier-one food and should be your first choice.

▲ KEY IDEAS

▲ Always visualize tiers four and five as small tiers. These foods should be eaten in much smaller amounts than those of tiers one, two, and three and should never substitute for the foods of the lower tiers.

▲ Learn about the fat and protein content of various cheeses. Choose the lower-fat options, and be sure protein content is always higher than fat content. All cheeses on tiers four and five should be used only in moderate amounts to add rich flavor dimensions to your recipes.

▲ Cheeses higher in fat (borderline tier-five cheeses) can be used for an occasional change in very small amounts when the rest of the meal is free from meats and poultry.

▲ Sweeteners such as honey, vino cotto, maple syrup, molasses, and brown sugar are more flavorful than white sugar, so they can be used in smaller amounts to satisfy your sweet tooth. Always use with a light touch!

▲ Lean meat and poultry are optional on the Superpyramid. Strive to reduce your overall meat consumption, choosing instead the plant foods of tier one as your main source of energy.

▲

PART

3

▲

Beyond
the
Superpyramid

▲

▲ *8* ▲

Vinegars, Herbs, Spices, and Salt

Not by Denial of the Senses

The joy of food is an essential ingredient in the success of a meal. Very often, the reason we enjoy certain foods is actually because of the herbs, spices, vinegar, or sweeteners used in preparing them. Some people consider the characteristic aroma of a delicious soup that pervades a kitchen is really the scent of the rosemary, sage, and other herbs used in its preparation.

Consider the importance of the sense of smell. Before food even reaches the stomach, a savory aroma stimulates secretions in the digestive tract, helping to prepare the stomach for the task of digestion. Recently, our research center tested the physiological response of ten- to twelve-year-old children to various beverages. Their first response was not to the flavor but to the smell of the drink before it ever touched their lips. One of the beverages didn't smell good, and one of the girls was able to drink it only after shutting off her sense of smell by holding her nose. That's how powerful our sense of smell is.

Enjoyment of aromas, appearance, and flavors is an integral part of eating and the key to lasting acceptance of any food. The harsh, austere denial of these senses cannot lead to success. It's both physiological and psychological. Just think how taste, sight, smell, and even touch play a role in our appreciation of food. Never deny yourself the joy of food. Beyond individual enjoyment, humanity has long known the shared pleasure of combining social interactions—whether between a man and woman, family members, or business associates—with fine meals.

Eating the Superpyramid way will be successful because you won't deny the extreme importance of the senses of smell, taste, touch, and sight.

We've already looked at the role of sweeteners. Now we'll see other ways of enhancing the flavors of foods with vinegars, herbs, spices, and salt.

Vinegars

Vinegar should be flavorful. Choose a natural, undistilled vinegar. *Wine vinegars* that have been properly aged and *apple cider vinegars*—if not refined—have some of the best flavors. Distilled vinegars have lost the natural aromas of the original fruits. Try other vinegars made from fruits such as berries, as long as the flavor of the original fruit is preserved. *Rice vinegar* is not a fruit vinegar and tends to be bland.

Good-tasting vinegars make excellent salad and vegetable dressings; the more flavorful they are, the less salt you'll need to use. When good vinegars are combined with a great extra-virgin olive oil, you have a taste treat that meets all the requirements of a Superpyramid salad. *Never forget that olive oil and vinegar make the classic salad dressing, practically the only one used in Mediterranean countries.*

Herbs

Rosemary, sage, basil, thyme, oregano (and *marjoram*, a variety of oregano), and *lovage* are the favorites of great cooks. You may also consider *arugula* (rocket or rucola), *parsley* (in one of its many varieties), *sorrel*, and of course *garlic*—all of which we have seen in chapter 5—herbs.

Some components of rosemary and sage seem to have antioxidant properties. Rosemary, for example, contains a rosemary diphenol that has been shown in the laboratory to act together with some of the antioxidant vitamins (chapter 5) to increase their effectiveness. While the extremely small amounts of these antioxidants found in herbs when used for flavoring may be of little importance in health, it reassures us that these are good foods. Some of these herbs were used in teas in earlier times; certain varieties of sage that grow wild in many regions, especially in dry parts of the Sierra Nevada and in the southern California deserts, were used by the native Americans as a tea to relieve upset stomachs. We have already seen that garlic contains possibly beneficial compounds, even though the amount used for flavoring could be too small for any meaningful biochemical effect.

Rosemary or oregano, sage or thyme, or other related herbs are almost a necessity when cooking beans, pasta, or rice. What's a pot of pinto beans without a good herb, maybe some aged vinegar, and a dash of salt?

Fresh, If Possible

For the fullest appreciation of herbs, consider growing them yourself. Nothing is better than a freshly picked herb. Even a small garden or yard has enough space for a few plants of sage, oregano, or rosemary. If you don't have a garden, try a pot or two on your windowsill.

There is something about the flavor and aroma of fresh or home-dried herbs that is unmatched. Dry your own in the summer, but don't make them into a powder or you'll lose much of the aroma. Look in a local farmer's market for bunches of freshly picked leaves you can dry yourself for the winter. If you must buy commercially dried herbs, choose whole leaves, not powders. Remember: using fresh or home-dried herbs is one of the ways of *being in touch with foods* (chapter 10).

Spices

Spices can add subtlety, variety, and zest to your dishes. Many are sharp and pungent. *Black pepper* is commonly used in Mediterranean countries as part of salad dressing (oil, vinegar, salt, and pepper). Buy whole peppercorns and grind them; they'll be more flavorful than powder. People in the Middle East and India use powerful spices in their cooking. *Cayenne pepper* in minute amounts can give zest to any Mexican or Middle Eastern dish, but do not overuse such strong spices or you'll forget what food tastes like. A recent study on cayenne pepper showed that it has some mild effect in controlling blood clotting inside the blood vessels, but this finding needs additional confirmation. Again, the amount used for flavoring is so small that we should not rely on these health effects.

Other good spices include mustard and horseradish. *Mustard* can be found in many good prepared forms, combined with vinegar, other spices, and some salt. It makes an excellent addition to vegetable and salad dressings and a wonderful nonfat, cholesterol-free spread for sandwiches. *Horseradish* can be purchased fresh in many areas, and it keeps for a very long time. You can also easily grow it yourself in a small vegetable garden. Horseradish, like mustard, is often sold prepared with vinegar and salt and can be used to add zest to some of the new foods you'll get acquainted with on the Superpyramid, such as tofu patties and bean dishes.

Ginger is an essential ingredient in many cuisines and it has been used since Roman times. Its pungent flavor makes it a favorite in many Eastern recipes. It has been shown to stimulate appetite and stomach secretions, and it seems beneficial in preventing some types of motion sickness and nausea. If you can, buy the whole root, which keeps well in a dry place. Many other great spices are available and you should dare to venture into this territory and try a variety of them. Sarah Garland's *The Complete Book of Herbs and Spices* (New York: The Viking Press) has wonderful stories and illustrations and it's a superb guide to growing your own.

Other Flavorings

For enhancing desserts, choose the natural kind of *vanilla* for richer, fuller flavor. *Lemon juice* can replace some of the vinegar on a salad or cooked vegetables. It is also excellent on fish or savory patties of various types, such as tofu patties.

Salt

Salt is a more difficult flavoring agent to talk about. Sea salt (or salts from deposits that are the residues of ancient seas) has been important to humans ever since ancient times. In earlier centuries, wars were fought to get control of territories that had sources of salt. The modern term *salary* is derived from *salt:* in Latin, *salarium* means "salt money," for people used to be paid their wages in salt. The importance of salt was not so much its use as a flavoring agent but rather as a preservative for food in the days before refrigeration.

Sodium and chloride, which make up salt, are absolutely essential to life and health. People tend to forget this when they read about health problems caused by *excess salt*. But sodium is naturally present in many foods, together with potassium. The problem is not sodium itself, it's how much we eat as well as the amount of sodium in relation to the amount of potassium in foods. In industrialized, meat-eating societies, we tend to consume too much sodium in general as well as in relation to our potassium intake. Too much sodium and a lack of balance between sodium and potassium intake can lead to high blood pressure (hypertension) and stroke in susceptible people. It's important to keep your potassium intake up and your sodium intake down. But let's not turn sodium —an essential mineral—into a villain.

While all foods—whether of animal or plant origin—contain both potassium and sodium, there is very often a major difference in the relative amounts of these two minerals. Plant foods, especially fruits and vegetables, contain very little sodium and meaningful amounts of potassium. In contrast, meat, poultry, or fish may have the same amount of potassium as fruits and vegetables, but their sodium content is much higher, even if no salt has been added during preparation. For example, one medium orange has 2 milligrams of sodium for each 300 milligrams of potassium—a ratio of 0.6 parts of sodium to 100 of potassium—while a typical beef cut *before any table salt is added* has about 50 milligrams of sodium for 250 milligrams of potassium, or a ratio of 20 parts of sodium to 100 of potassium.

Preserved meats, such as luncheon meats or bacon, not only have salt added but also sodium nitrites and nitrates, which contribute even more sodium; these types of food should not be part of your regular meal pattern. Two slices of a typical bacon have about 35 milligrams of potassium for every 100 of sodium—about three times more sodium than potassium. Aged cheeses can also be high in salt. If you use these cheeses, consider them as flavoring agents and avoid using salt on that dish. For example, if you use Parmesan cheese on pasta, salt the pasta cooking water less. Bread, such an important food on the Superpyramid, is often made with unnecessarily high levels of salt. A good loaf of true whole-grain bread needs just a little salt to give you the full flavor of the whole grain.

What happens when we eat the Superpyramid way? Here, plant foods are the foundation of the diet. Meats, poultry, and fish are not the basic foods. Cheeses are used in moderation. The result: we eat less sodium than people who base their diets on animal products. So if we need to add a little bit of salt to vegetables, a soup stock, or a salad, we can do so without fear of excess.

No matter what, use salt with great restraint. Try to replace some of the salt in your food with herbs or perhaps sea vegetation, which I'll discuss later. You may want to use some salt (sparingly) on vegetables, grains, and beans. These foods are naturally extremely low in sodium. There is already enough natural sodium in fish and meats that you do not need any salt if you spice them properly. If you choose to eat meat, never salt a meat dish!

Some people are more sensitive to sodium than others. It's an inherited trait. This sensitivity often leads to high blood pressure (hypertension). If your doctor tells you that you belong to this group, you must take extra precautions and follow the diet he or she recommends. But the general principles we have talked about apply to everyone.

Sea Plants: Low-sodium Salty Flavorings

Many sea plants such as dulse or kelp are high in potassium and low in sodium yet have that salty flavor many people crave. Sea vegetation is widely used not only in Japan and other Oriental countries bordering the sea but also in many other regions of the earth. In Scotland from Orkney to the Hebrides to the island of Barra, the leaves of sea plants were used in the past in various local dishes and their ashes used instead of salt to preserve cheese.

Granulated kelp and dulse, or leaves of these products, are available in many specialty and Oriental stores. Be sure the leaves have been washed of the seawater, which, of course, is a source of sodium salts. Sprinkle the granules on salads and vegetables, and use whole leaves in soups. You can find recipes for seaweed soups in Oriental cookbooks, and we have included a few in the Superpyramid kitchen. Remember that the flavor of sea plants is unique, and you may need time to adjust to it.

▲ KEY IDEAS

▲ The joy of food—the celebration of the senses of smell, taste, and sight—is an essential ingredient in the success of a meal.

▲ Enjoyment of aromas, appearance, and flavors is an integral part of eating and the key to lasting acceptance of any food.

▲ Use herbs, spices, vinegars, and other natural flavorings to enhance your foods.

▲ Vinegar should be flavorful. Choose a natural, undistilled vinegar.

▲ Herbs should be as fresh as possible. Grow or dry your own if you can.

▲ Although salt is essential to life, it's easy to overdo it. Using herbs, spices, and vinegars can help you cut back on excess salt.

▲ Try to keep your potassium consumption up and sodium consumption down.

CHAPTER

▲ *9* ▲

Water, Tea, Coffee, Wine, and Other Beverages

Water: Life-Giving, Precious Fluid

No food plan would be complete without a good understanding
of the place of fluids. Water is as essential as any nutrient we
have discussed. We drink it in many forms besides plain water:
as fruit and vegetable juices, coffee, tea, soft drinks, and wine and beer.
Water is also a major part of many foods such as milk, yogurt, fruits,
and vegetables. It's important to remember that some common beverages such as coffee, tea, cola drinks, and beer and wine are not only a
source of water but also have physiological and pharmacological effects
that should be understood.

There is no life as we know it without water. It has been known since
ancient times that people can survive for quite a few days without any
food at all but only for a very short time without water. The adult human
body is between 60 and 70 percent water. We lose water continuously
through sweat, urine, feces, breath, and in invisible evaporation processes that take place all the time. When we exhale under normal conditions, more water (as vapor) goes out than comes in. That's why you
can see your breath on a cold day. All these losses mean that we must
drink enough water every day to replace what we use.

Athletes know that dehydration is one of the first causes of fatigue.
Energy replacement—eating—can wait, but fluid replacement cannot.
Many athletes find their performance is better if they take small, fre-
quent drinks rather than wait until they feel thirsty and fatigued.

Even more important to your health is the direct effect of dehydration on our kidneys. When we do not take in enough water to compensate for our losses, the kidneys tend to produce more concentrated urine. High in waste matter, salts, and other normal excretory products, this concentrated urine can damage the delicate kidney tubes. Various types of kidney problems, some major, can develop if the dehydrated state continues for a long time.

Consume water often either plain or as part of a beverage or watery food such as fruits, vegetables, or milk.

Vegetable and Fruit Juices

Vegetable and fruit juices are good beverage choices—far superior to soft drinks because of their rich nutrient content. Raw and freshly squeezed juices should be your first choice. When freshly squeezed, juices retain both their vitamin C and their full flavor.

But don't completely replace fruits and vegetables with their juices. You need to eat whole fruits and vegetables to get the benefit of their special fibers. Also, remember that fruit juices contain a lot of sugar and energy. It's all too easy to drink more fruit juice than your activity level requires. When you eat a piece of whole raw fruit, chewing all that fiber slows you down. Just think of how fast you can drink a glass of apple juice compared to the time it would take you to eat the three or four apples needed to make that juice.

Soft Drinks

Sweetened soft drinks supply very little nutrition, except some pure sugar, and not even that if the drink is artificially sweetened. If a soft drink contains caffeine, remember to count it as part of your daily caffeine intake. Cola drinks may supply as much as 50 milligrams of caffeine per glass. Also, some soft drinks contain phosphates that may alter the body's calcium balance.

The better choice, and an increasingly popular one, is to drink sparkling mineral waters. These are available plain or with added fruit flavors or juices. A slice of lemon or lime in your sparkling water adds extra zest. Enjoy these satisfying beverages in place of caffeinated, sweetened, or artificially sweetened soft drinks.

Tea, the Ancient Beverage

Tea is optional on the Superpyramid Program. It is probably the most popular prepared beverage in the world, and people in many countries, from Japan to the United Kingdom, have developed rituals around tea drinking. Tea is consumed in many different ways: sweetened, unsweetened, with lemon or with milk.

Tea plants are probably native to the forested region of what is now Yunnan in southern China. The Chinese emperor Sh'en Nung, the Divine Cultivator, wrote about tea in 2737 B.C., extolling its medicinal properties and ability to gladden and cheer the heart. It was Kuo P'o in the year A.D. 350 who gave us what is probably the first authenticated description of tea. The first major work on tea growing and manufacturing was written in China in A.D. 780 by Lu Yu.

Tea connoisseurs find tremendous differences among teas growing in various regions and at different altitudes. Go to a tea shop and taste the difference between black and green teas, between Darjeelings and Assams and between Chinese and Indian leaves. Teas are cured in different ways to yield black teas, the most popular tea in the United States, Canada, and the United Kingdom, and green teas, more popular in the Orient. A process tea growers call *firing* makes the difference. This is a mild fermentation of the leaves, which is allowed to take place to different extents in green and black tea. Oolong tea falls between the black (long-firing) and green (short-firing) teas.

Teas contain a group of substances called *polyphenols* or *catechins*. Some recent research attributes various protective effects to these components. In laboratory experiments, these compounds extracted from tea have been shown to have antioxidant activity as well as to control blood coagulation and bacterial growth. Even though we do not know whether or not these tea polyphenols can prevent disease in people, they should be considered a positive component of tea.

Coffee: From Food to Beverage

Coffee is also an optional beverage on the Superpyramid. As a beverage, coffee is a newcomer compared to tea. The Arabs learned to boil coffee only recently, probably about A.D. 1000. Before that time, African tribes used to eat the coffee beans prepared in various forms; they often crushed them with stone mortars and blended them with animal fat, and the mixture was then consumed during war parties. The stimulating properties of coffee, which derive from its caffeine content, gave rise to early legends of the magical effects of the coffee bean. When people began to brew coffee, rituals evolved around this new drink as they had around the much more ancient tea.

Not all coffee beans are alike. The amount of caffeine present varies depending on the type and even the region where it is cultivated. There are two types of plants, the *arabica* and the *robusta*. Usually arabica beans have much less caffeine than the same weight of robusta beans. In a recent survey at Stanford university of various commercial, commonly used coffees in various facilities of the university, some coffees had three times the caffeine of others. These were most likely robusta coffees. Arabica beans are considered by many to be the more sophisticated, and many specialty coffee dealers sell only this type of bean. The roasting process also affects the character of the brew, ranging from the lower roasting temperatures of typical American coffees to the higher roasting temperatures that produce the dark Italian and French coffees. If you choose to drink coffee, use good arabica beans and do not exceed a couple of cups a day.

Even in the arabica varieties, various coffees have often dramatically different flavor and aromas. Colombian coffee, for example, is considered to have a medium body—to use the coffee connoisseur terminology—not sharp or weak or dull, while most African coffees like Kenya or Ethiopian have a sharp and acidic flavor and Sumatra is smooth and nutty, with a wonderful full body.

Caffeine in Tea and Coffee
Because caffeine is a powerful stimulant, it should be consumed in great moderation. If you exceed a certain limit in your coffee or tea drinking, a pharmacological effect takes place that can affect various hormones in your body. This threshold level varies with the individual and depends on how much coffee or tea he or she usually drinks. If you drink caffeinated beverages you know some of the pharmacological effects of caffeine well. The most important is the effect of caffeine on the brain, which is the reason for the popularity of tea, coffee, and cola drinks. This stimulation of the brain is so great that heavy caffeine drinkers have withdrawal headaches for a few days if they stop drinking beverages with caffeine. Caffeine in large amounts affects the heart and has a diuretic effect. Let's realize that these are powerful actions and if we choose to drink beverages with caffeine, we should be very moderate. It is probably not wise to drink more than approximately 100 milligrams of caffeine at one time, possibly less. That's about one to one and a half cups of strong coffee or two or three cups of tea-bag-type tea. If you brew the beverage from loose tea leaves, the limit is one or two rounded teaspoons of leaves. Whatever your choice, wait at least three hours before drinking your next cup. By then, part of the caffeine in your blood from your last dose has been inactivated or excreted through your urine.

Since caffeine stimulates the brain and the nervous system, it makes little sense to drink it before attempting to go to sleep. In the morning, do not shock your system with caffeine when it's still half asleep. Let your body wake up naturally while you take your shower and dress.

The caffeine content of a cup of tea from a tea bag is approximately 20 milligrams (after brewing one minute) to 40 milligrams (after brewing five minutes) according to the data presented by Dr. Harold Graham in a recent book on coffee and tea, *The Methylxanthine Beverages and Foods.* As the caffeine content of Assam tea leaves is about 3.5 percent, a rounded teaspoon would yield about 70 milligrams of caffeine if left steeping in the teapot for a long time. A typical cup of American coffee probably contains about 70 to 80 milligrams of caffeine, but published data show that some stronger brews contains as much as 100 milligrams of caffeine per cup. Many Americans consume about 200 milligrams per day from coffee and tea. This is close to what one should consider the upper limit. Caffeinated soft drinks, which often contain about 50 milligrams of caffeine in a serving, often push the intake over this limit without most people realizing it.

Coffee, even when decaffeinated, retains factors such as caffeinic acid that stimulate stomach secretions. Tea does not seem to have the same effect. That is probably why many people find tea easier to drink than coffee.

What role do coffee and tea play in disease? Let's take coffee first. There are many contradictions in the medical literature on the relationship of coffee to chronic diseases. In Norway, Dr. Olav Helge Forde and other researchers carried out a famous study, called the Tromso study, published in *The New England Journal of Medicine* in March 1983. The study showed a strong correlation between levels of coffee (but not tea) consumption and high levels of blood cholesterol. This correlation was for high amounts such as five cups per day. Also, Norwegians prepare coffee in a way that extracts many more substances from the coffee bean than the common American methods of brewing.

In a 1985 issue of the *British Medical Journal,* Dr. J. D. Kark, a Jerusalem physician, published a study of 1007 men and 589 women aged thirty-five to sixty-four years. He found effects on blood cholesterol similar to the Tromso study when coffee consumption was high, *but tea drinking failed to show any change that would cause concern.* Dr. Paul Williams and other scientists at the Stanford University Center for Research in Disease Prevention found no cholesterol increase with up to two cups of coffee a day, but when intake went higher, so did cholesterol. They published their results in the *Journal of the American Medical Association* in March 1985 and concluded that "heavy coffee drinkers have blood lipid profiles suggestive of increased cardiovascular disease risk." The same group at Stanford carried out another study in the late 1980s with carefully controlled intakes of a given type of coffee and found no increased blood cholesterol for moderate coffee drinkers.

In Italy, a country where strong espresso coffee is commonly drunk, Dr. Antonio Salvaggio and his associates investigated blood cholesterol and coffee consumption between 1986 and 1989 in about nine thousand people. In this study with coffees that were usually prepared with steam from dark-roasted beans, the investigators found a definite increase in blood cholesterol as the number of cups per day increased from none to five.

In view of the confusing evidence, the best choice is to limit coffee consumption to no more than one or two cups daily of a filtered coffee and to use a good arabica coffee. Or, better yet, choose tea.

An intriguing point in some of the studies is that tea drinking does not seem to cause the kind of biochemical changes that may contribute to heart disease. It seems likely that there are components in tea that make it less harmful than coffee. The findings may also reflect the fact that the average cup of coffee supplies much more caffeine than the average cup of tea.

If you choose tea as your beverage, make tea drinking a satisfying experience. Unfortunately, in many homes and restaurants in North America, tea means a tea bag poorly brewed in lukewarm water. For tea, brewing is everything. A poorly made cup of tea is a bad-tasting cup of tea. Your best choice is loose tea. The leaves have been carefully selected; there can be no powdered, inferior leaves such as you may find in a poor tea bag, and you can truly brew a cup of tea in a time-honored manner. If you use tea bags, buy them from a specialty shop or find a quality brand in a grocery store. Tea goes well with some milk and honey or milk alone. For tea, regular whole milk is preferable to low-fat milk for the flavor it can add to the cup of tea. The amount of milk is so small that the fat content is minimal. If you go to a restaurant and they give you half and half, ask for whole milk instead. Milk is the traditional complement to tea for the United Kingdom, not cream or half and half! Make your tea drinking not just a casual habit but a relaxing ritual.

Think of the Japanese tea ceremony. Here a cup of tea is not so much a quick caffeine lift for the brain as it is a simple serene refreshment for the soul. In this ceremony, a series of carefully executed steps culminates in the drinking of the tea itself. As far back as the sixteenth century, tea masters such as Rikyu "emphasized simplicity, purity, harmony, love of nature, proper frame of mind, politeness, and the esthetic aspects of the experience," as it is so well described by Joel, David, and Karl Schapira in *The Book of Coffee and Tea*.

Similar rituals are still common today. We often go to a coffee- or teahouse to seek much more than the physical effect of the beverages. We go for a restful break or for social reasons. These are rituals. Rituals involving food and beverage are somehow an ingrained need of all people.

Herb Teas

One way to avoid excessive caffeine is to choose from the many leaves, roots, and flowers that make delicious herb teas when brewed in hot water. Try flavoring them with lemon and honey. There are so many wonderful prepared herb teas on the market these days that even restaurants now offer them as an alternative to black teas and coffees. Some good-tasting herbs include various mints such as peppermint, spearmint, and verbena (leaves), hibiscus and chamomile (blossoms), and rose hips (fruit with seeds). Try a few to find your favorites.

Ginseng is popular in China, Korea, Japan, and other Asian countries. It has a history of safety as a tea that goes back over three thousand years, and Chinese folk medicine attributes to it uplifting and tonic properties. It's considered by some to help in endurance exercises, but more good studies are needed to confirm these properties.

If you buy herbs for use in teas, remember that many plants have powerful medicinal properties and are in fact part of common medications. For example, senna leaves are a stimulant laxative, and foxglove substances are used in heart medications. The list of medicinal herbs is much too long to be given here, so if you are at all unsure, you should consult a reference in this subject. Just remember that many herbs have a medicinal effect and are in a different category from peppermint or hibiscus teas.

Chocolate and Carob

The use of cacao originated in Mexico; the cacao tree probably came from the Amazon region and was considered sacred. It was introduced in Europe in the early 1600s and found to be mildly stimulating, which helped make it popular in Europe, and especially in Germany. In children, before the advent of modern cola beverages, chocolate was probably the main source of caffeine, although its caffeine content is much less than that of coffees and teas.

Chocolate contains reasonable amounts of a close relative of caffeine called *theobromine* that has less effect on the brain and the nervous system in general than caffeine but has diuretic properties. Depending on the origin of the cacao beans, chocolate may contain two to five times more theobromine than caffeine.

Not much long-term research is available on chocolate and health, and just like any beverage containing active pharmacological agents, it should be used in moderation. As cacao beans are bitter, commercially prepared chocolate bars or beverage powders are usually high in sugar, and you should consider this when you consume these products. Often sugar is the first ingredient listed on the label of chocolate products, telling us that it's the one present in the largest amount.

Carob in powder or candy bar form can be used in place of chocolate as it has a pleasant chocolate-like flavor. It does not contain the caffeine and theobromine of cacao. It's made by roasting the pod of the carob bean, also known as locust bean. It's a native plant of Asia, now grown in North America and Mediterranean countries as well, and it's often called St. John's bread, as it was probably the locust bean eaten by St. John the Baptist.

Be Careful with Hot *Beverages*

Never drink these or any other beverages scalding hot. Drinking very hot beverages may damage your upper digestive system, including your mouth and esophagus. There appears to be some relationship between regular use of very hot beverages and cancer of the esophagus. The same consideration applies to other hot foods such as soups and broths.

ALCOHOLIC BEVERAGES

The damage caused by excessive alcohol consumption is so well known that it needs no detailed description here. The pancreas, liver, and other organs suffer in a way that often cannot be reversed. Alcohol itself is a toxic substance when it has the chance to bypass the liver. The safe approach is not to exceed the equivalent of one or two glasses of wine per day.

Considering the way alcohol is handled by the body teaches us how to drink it. Alcohol is absorbed into the bloodstream very quickly because it needs no digestion. It is carried to the liver, where it is changed into harmless compounds that are then used for energy. But the liver needs time to do its job. If we flood the liver with alcohol, some will bypass it and come in contact with many important tissues and organs, including the brain. Excessive consumption damages the liver and the result is a fatty liver. If excessive consumption takes place only occasionally, the damage can be reversed, but if excessive consumption is habitual, the liver will not have a chance to regenerate, and it will suffer serious, irreversible damage.

When alcohol is consumed in moderation with meals, it is absorbed slowly into the blood from the digestive system, because the stomach contains food. Under these conditions, the alcohol reaches the liver slowly and in limited amounts. Little or no damage follows. In practical terms, this means that one or two glasses of wine with a meal once a day may not be harmful, if you are healthy. Wine and beer have an advantage over distilled liquors such as vodka or whiskey, since they are naturally diluted and contain trace amounts of some nutrients, such as minerals, in addition to the alcohol. There is some evidence that very moderate wine or beer drinking may raise the good blood cholesterol (HDL).

There is no reason to drink hard liquors of any kind as part of a normal meal and a healthy way of life. If you really have to, limit yourself to one drink on rare occasions. But most healthy people who are not addicted to alcohol and who do not drink hard liquor for a while usually lose their desire for these beverages completely.

Wine, the Divine Beverage of Antiquity

The Mediterranean people considered wine a divine gift. Even today in some churches, wine is part of the holy rituals. In the painting *The Last Supper* by Leonardo da Vinci, we find the two fermented foods so deeply rooted in the Mediterranean culture: bread and wine. The goblet most likely contained a very light natural wine, low in alcohol. Fermenting grapes was a way to preserve fruit for the winter months. Homer, the ancient Greek poet, said, "Bread and wine give strength and courage." The ancient Greeks had a wine god, Dionysus.

There are hundreds of different natural wines, which have individual characteristics that depend on the region where the grapes are grown, the variety of grape, its ripeness at the time of picking, and the wine-making methods. The amount of rainfall during the season, the temperature during the summer, and the type of soil all affect the finished wine. What's interesting is that wines with similar amounts of alcohol—the alcohol in natural wines does not vary much—may taste more or less alcoholic and have pleasant or unpleasant aftereffects based on the complexity and the balance of the wine. The best way to choose is to taste the wine yourself.

Some people are sensitive to the *sulfites* present in most wine. That's why, in California, the law requires the label to state if the wine contains sulfites. A few brands are available that are low in or free from sulfites. For many people, the sulfite is probably harmless.

If you choose to drink wine, choose natural wines, that is, wines containing only the alcohol produced by the fermentation process under natural conditions. Most common wines—"table wines"—belong to this category, with 10 to 13 percent alcohol. These low-alcohol wines are preferable to higher-alcohol wines such as port and sherry.

I feel strongly that success in the Superpyramid Program is intertwined with the joy of food and peaceful meals. Of all alcoholic beverages, natural wine is best suited to complement and enhance our major meals. Evening is, of course, the ideal time for wine—its relaxing properties are perfect for the end of the day. But moderation is essential.

An important exception: Pregnant women should not drink any alcohol. The fetus is extremely sensitive to alcohol and fetal damage is possible. In this situation the best rule is to avoid alcoholic beverages completely.

▲ KEY IDEAS

- ▲ Dehydration leads to fatigue and causes kidney damage. Be sure to get plenty of water or other fluids every day. Water is as essential as any nutrient we have discussed.
- ▲ Although fruit juices can be a source of water and nutrients, don't let them replace fruits entirely.
- ▲ The best soft drink is plain or lightly flavored sparkling water.
- ▲ If you drink coffee, do not exceed two cups of coffee per day.
- ▲ Make tea and coffee from good leaves and beans.
- ▲ If you drink alcoholic beverages, choose wine or beer in moderation.

CHAPTER

.*10*.

The Joy and Beauty
of Real Food

Ascetic or Joyful Path?

Now that we've learned all about the Superpyramid tiers and how to design great meals, we need to go back to some of the ideas we talked about in chapter 1 on the failure of diets and the assumption that healthy food is necessarily austere, devoid of any pleasure. Too many diets are indeed this way, so let's never make the Superpyramid plan a *diet*.

Although people may decide to go on a diet, it can seem as dreary as a medical prescription. Dietitians, physicians, and other health professionals do in fact have to prescribe diets for many diseases, where it may be a question of life or death. But healthy people usually do not have the incentive of the chronically ill to change their eating habits. To succeed in their quest for healthier eating, they must be able to enjoy their food and life. Otherwise, these healthy people will suffer from a sense of deprivation and look with a sorrowful eye at the foods they used to eat. Depending on their willpower and earlier health or weight problems, they may stay—more or less faithfully—on this diet for months or years. But without the joy of eating, they slowly slip back to their old ways, until the so-called diet has failed.

Some people think of a healthy diet as insipid. This word is derived from the Latin *insipidus*, which means "without zest, unpalatable, dull." Insipid, flavorless, or monotonous foods without variety of color and aromas were never meant for us.

The Superpyramid Program is far from being one of those monotonous, unappealing diets. In fact, if you follow it carefully, after a few weeks or months, depending on how different your eating habits were before, you'll enjoy it so much that you'll never want to eat any other way again.

Have We Lost the Sense for Real Foods?

The troublesome fact is that even people not on special diets have lost the feel for the beauty of real food and their sense of a meal as a peaceful ritual. The Superpyramid or any other food plan cannot succeed unless we can.

Walk into an herb garden; smell the rosemary and sage. Look at the array of colors of fresh vegetables and fruits at your local farmers' market. Taste a salad made with an aromatic vinegar and extra-virgin olive oil. Savor the taste of a true whole-grain bread. Delight yourself with a blend of yogurt and wildflower honey. Have we lost this feeling for beauty and real aromas? Have we become so dependent on ready-to-eat food that most of us have forgotten what real food looks and tastes like in its natural or close-to-natural state?

There's a story about a teacher in Sweden: When she asked some children to draw a picture of a fish, they drew a square. They were so used to frozen, precut fish that they thought of fish as a geometric, headless, tailless block.

A Pyramid of Joy and Beauty

We must bring back joy. The Superpyramid food plan is not about deprivation!

> We must cherish the simple, ancient foods of the land; savor their fragrance; enjoy the flavor and aroma of herbs and spices; learn to appreciate real, whole foods as part of a joyful meal; make the path to better health satisfying and pleasant.

The Hindus believe that food prepared with love tastes better. This makes sense, since the ritual of preparing food with love helps us get more joy from eating it. Yet many of us have removed these joyous rituals from our lives.

Imagine yourself preparing dinner on a cold winter evening in a warm kitchen. A pot of pinto beans and another of brown rice are boiling on the stove. The aroma of the rosemary, oregano, and aged wine vinegar that you've used to flavor the beans pervades the kitchen. The profusion of fresh vegetables on the cutting board looks like a classical still-life painting. It is all here for a painter or photographer sensitive to the hues of nature to capture: the reddish oranges of the carrots and tomatoes, the rich greens of the romaine lettuce and broccoli, and the pearly white of the garlic and onions. In this family, some have chosen a vegetarian Superpyramid, so they will eat some low-fat cheese. Others enjoy some fish, so a lean white fish—fillet of sole—with a simple dressing of olive oil, fresh sage leaves, and lemon juice is ready for the oven in a baking pan. A bowl of fresh almonds waits to be served for dessert with yogurt and wildflower honey and fresh berries. When this family eats dinner, there is no hurry, no pressure. The meal is not just the consumption of some food, it's a feast, and beyond that, a ritual. A few in this family have chosen to drink some wine for an additional touch of pleasure. This evening meal has become a quiet celebration of life.

Imagine yourself baking some fresh, naturally leavened breads for a gathering of friends in your garden on a warm summer day. The new garden brick oven you have just built—where your old barbecue pit used to be—is hot and the bread goes in as your guests begin to arrive. The aroma of the baking whole-grain bread pervades the air. You are tossing a large salad of green leaves and tomatoes, flavored with arugula and accented with pieces of red bell pepper. The extra-virgin olive oil and aromatic vinegar in antique bottles are ready. A wood board with a low-fat mozzarella and some yogurt cheese you have just made is waiting. A bowl of homemade low-fat yogurt, a large jar of wildflower natural honey, and another bowl full of colorful fresh fruit completes the picture. No one will leave this gathering with the heavy feeling of overeating. *This is the new way and the ancient way; this is the Superpyramid way.*

Preparing all these great foods is a feast for the senses, just as much as the actual eating. For this sensual joy in food to come through to you, choose foods so fresh and bright with a variety of colors that you could photograph them. Learn to love these simple whole foods for their natural full beauty and flavor. Work with this beautiful food by preparing it with sensitivity and care.

Deborah Madison uses the word *savory* in the introduction to her cookbook, *The Savory Way:* "The word savory . . . to me suggests the place where flavor and fragrance meet, in foods with deep full taste that are exciting to the palate." She describes these as "nourishing foods, set forth in a climate of happy anticipation." This is the spirit of the Super-pyramid, and the only spirit that will allow you to eat the right foods not in a climate of fear of disease or unfitness, but rather of joy and excitement.

Not an Engineered Meal

People who have read earlier drafts of this book have occasionally asked why there are no exact amounts or measures, no hard data on serving sizes, no dicta on how much of this and how much of that one should or should not eat, and so forth. The answer is simple: *exact measures are not the Superpyramid Program.*

If a meal becomes a sequence of carefully weighed and measured portions, or something in which an extra serving of one basic food is going to cause problems, then that meal is not worth eating for very long.

All you really need to know is that the foods on tiers four and five have to be consumed in limited amounts. It just takes some common sense to see how balanced or unbalanced your plate is. That's what the Superpyramid is all about.

The Narrow Staircase to Tiers Four and Five

If you really want an additional device to help you balance your meals, there is a way that is much more fun than worrying about the hard measures of serving sizes and diet scales. *Let's introduce an advanced Superpyramid technique: a staircase between tiers.* Visualize yourself living on the first tier of the Superpyramid and taking an occasional climb to the higher tiers. The staircases between the first three tiers are quite wide and easy to climb. You can easily bring foods from these tiers to your kitchen. The staircase that leaves tier three and moves up to tiers four and five is narrow and allows you to carry out only small amounts of foods from these two higher tiers into your kitchen.

Bring Back That Earthy Feeling

Today we have indeed moved away from the good earthy feeling of real food. We hurry so much that what is meant to be useful in an emergency —fast or convenience food—has become our daily fare. But how is it that we find time to treat the illnesses improper diet may bring about and time to attend meetings on losing the pounds our eating habits add but have no time to prevent at least some, if not all, of these problems? Learning to work with, touch, and love real food from plants is the answer to this dilemma, and no scientist or book can do it for you.

Although convenience foods and fast foods have their place, they should not regularly replace our own home cooking or snacks such as fruits or fresh nuts, no matter how busy we are. Otherwise, we indeed lose touch with what food really is. Are we so busy that when we go home from work, be it from an office or factory or farm, we must have an instant dinner? Of course not. It's just a habit. To break it, we must take back control of our meals. Touch food more. Prepare it yourself. There is an incredible awareness process that goes on when we prepare food. As we chop vegetables or measure grains, we are forging a link to countless generations of humanity and, at the same time, to our own bodies. We feel the complex processes that have taken place as the plant developed from seed, and we sense the marvels of life itself.

You can and must find time to cook with fresh foods. Have other members of your family or a close friend share in the act of food preparation. Procuring, preparing, and sharing food were once all rituals that helped families and friends become close. Perhaps that's part of what's missing in today's fast-food world. Prepare food with people you love or for people you love or just for yourself. Make it a ritual that's part of your life, and you will understand how wonderful food really is. Make cooking dinner a high point of the day, a chance for family and friends to relax together in a warm, nurturing environment.

At a time when medical, drug, and hospital costs have skyrocketed and we worry about health insurance, we should consider that the best and cheapest insurance we can buy is that small fraction of time we give to proper eating (and physical activity, as we'll see later).

Variety Is a Key Part of Good Nutrition

Going beyond the Superpyramid's basic concepts, we can't forget the importance of variety. Nature gives us foods of all colors, flavors, and fragrances. Before the advent of sophisticated twentieth-century nutritional science, people instinctively balanced their diets because they craved variety. If you are eating natural foods, this means that certain foods go nicely with other foods. For example, a high-protein food goes well with a high-carbohydrate food, as in the classic combinations of fish and rice or cheese and bread. Variety is important, for without it we can get bored and be tempted to consume less-desirable foods.

▲ *KEY IDEAS*

▲ *Make the Superpyramid a joyful path.*

▲ *Choose real, whole foods.*

▲ *Prepare your own fresh foods as often as possible.*

▲ *Learn to enjoy the simple rituals of food preparation.*

▲ *Make your meals peaceful, joyous experiences.*

▲ *Place fast foods and snacks in proper perspective.*

▲ *Variety is important to good nutrition.*

CHAPTER

▲ *11* ▲

In Search of Total Health and Fitness

Beyond Food

Now that we have learned about the easy way to choose the right foods, we need to move ahead by considering all the other crucial factors that are part of better health and fitness. There are things to be added to our lives and things to be abandoned. The result of this addition-subtraction process is not only better health and a major step in the prevention of some serious diseases, but also improved quality of life, fitness, proper weight, appearance, alertness, and joy of living. Any attempt to isolate one facet of a better way of living—such as food—from our total way of life is bound to fail. As John Muir said, "When we try to pick out something by itself, we find it hitched to everything else in the universe."

Although this book is primarily concerned with food choices, in this chapter we'll touch on what we need to do *beyond food*, looking at how we can best . . .

▲ Increase exercise and physical activity. We'll introduce the *Exercise Pyramid* to rank various types of physical activity—aerobic, stretching, and weight lifting—for promoting fitness, strength, and healthy good looks.
▲ Develop greater body awareness to enhance physical fitness.
▲ Prevent stress while opening the door to relaxation and rest, and use exercise to prevent or overcome stress.

185

And finally, we'll consider toxic substances and their often deadly effects. Such substances as tobacco smoke and certain chemicals in the environment or in foods can counteract many of the benefits of proper eating.

The New Exercise Awareness

People's awareness of the need for exercise has come a long way in just a hundred years. In the 1890s, people rarely exercised for exercise's sake, and excess weight was almost a status symbol.

Sir Arthur Conan Doyle, whose Sherlock Holmes stories presented a vivid portrait of life in the late nineteenth century, describes in "The Copper Beeches" a successful man as "a prodigiously stout man . . . with a heavy chin which rolled down in fold upon fold over his throat." And in "The Beryl Coronet" he describes an affluent, middle-aged London banker who had come to him after a long, fast walk as "a weary man who is little accustomed to set any tax upon his legs . . . puffing and blowing."

Lost Muscles, Lost Bones, Lost Fitness

Let's focus on just a few points that underscore the essential part that physical activity plays in health and fitness. When the body is deprived of regular and intense physical activity for long periods, unused muscles become weak and later degenerate or shrink. Shrinkage of muscles is what medical people call *atrophy*. This is the result of years of lack of use of a muscle or group of muscles. Inactivity also plays a key role in bone loss over the years.

Not only do leg and arm muscles atrophy, but the muscles of the chest, the back, and the abdomen do, too. As the muscles of the stomach weaken, the waist expands and a paunch appears. A larger waistline is caused partly by overeating and partly by weakening muscles. Just as bad, the chest and back muscles that control posture become weak, and poor posture slowly becomes a chronic curvature of the spine. Just look around as you walk down any city street. See a frail old man or woman with a spine so bowed that any resemblance to good posture has disappeared, trying to take a walk and moving so slowly that it looks as though each step is painful. This sad condition is often a combination of muscle and bone degeneration caused by inactivity. The brighter side of this picture is that muscles and bones can be kept stronger by physical activity.

Learning from the Extremes of Inactivity

We can better understand this process of bone and muscle loss by looking at some extreme cases. It has been known for years that total prolonged bedrest, restriction to a wheelchair, and similar situations lead to negative balances of some key nutrients such as protein and calcium. In cases of such extreme inactivity, more calcium and by-products of protein metabolism go out than come in, independent of the amount taken in from food. The result is loss of bone and muscle. Just as with our bank accounts, if we always spend more than we put in, we are bound for trouble. Our reserve—whether money or muscle or bone—may delay a disaster, but disaster is inevitable. In contrast, physical activity helps maintain a proper balance between the protein and calcium going in and that going out in various products of the body's biochemical reactions.

The Heart as a Muscle

We need to remember that the heart is a muscle, pumping blood twenty-four hours a day until it dies. Like any other muscle, it is a major target of the effects of lack of intense exercise. The coronary arteries that feed the heart suffer from inactivity; when aggravated by improper eating habits and smoking, this can result in clogged blood vessels and later deadly or at least debilitating heart attacks. And remember: heart disease is still the number-one killer in North America and many Western European countries.

This is a good place for a note of caution, however. Because the heart is so involved in physical activity, if you have any kind of heart disease or other chronic ailment and you have not exercised for a long time, you should consult a health professional before beginning an exercise program.

Food, Exercise, and Body Weight

No less important than prevention of disease is prevention of overweight. Weight maintenance is extremely difficult without exercise. An active person can worry less about minor variations in the amount of food he or she consumes than an inactive one, especially when following the Superpyramid plan, where whole grains, vegetables, and fruits are such important parts of the meal.

> *Ultimate fitness cannot be achieved by either exercise or food alone. The right food and sufficient physical activity must go together.*

Types of Exercise and the Exercise Pyramid

There are three basic types of physical activity, and all three play a role in health and fitness: *aerobic, resistance (weight lifting),* and *stretching (flexibility) exercises.* A fourth type could be added, the *balancing exercises.* Because many good books are available on different types of exercise (a few are suggested in the references section), I'll just focus on some key principles. As we have learned to use a food pyramid, let's create an exercise pyramid. There are only three tiers on this pyramid.

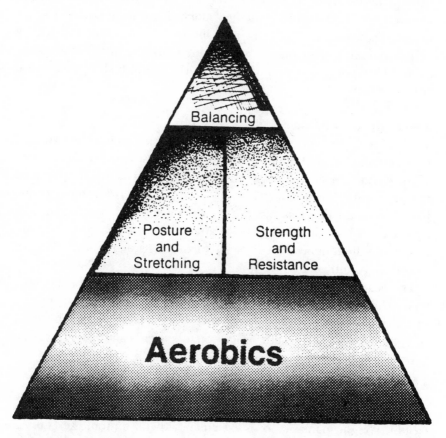

The Exercise Pyramid

The first tier. On the first tier are *aerobic activities,* which should be the most basic part of your exercise plan. When done at a reasonable intensity, these activities increase the rate of your pulse, or heart rate. If you like electronic devices and they help you understand your body better, you can buy one of the many wrist or other devices that measure your pulse rate. Examples of aerobic activities are jogging, bicycling, swimming, or hiking in the mountains. Walking and climbing stairs are examples of low-intensity aerobic activities that we do as part of everyday life. But aerobic activities need to be complemented with other types of exercise for true fitness.

The second tier. The second tier is divided into two rooms. *Stretching, flexibility, and posture exercises* are in one room. These are exercises in which a group of muscles is stretched and often kept in that stretched condition for a brief time. Many yoga exercises belong in this room of the exercise pyramid.

In the other room of tier two are the *resistance* or *strength exercises.* They include lifting a weight such as a barbell or dumbbell or lifting all or part of your own body, such as in push-ups, chin-ups, or rock climbing.

The third tier. On the third tier are *balance exercises.* These activities are often overlooked, and even though not as essential as the others, they help to develop body awareness and enable you to perform the exercises of the other two tiers better. The effects of this kind of exercise are more difficult to measure by modern scientific techniques. As a consequence they are not talked about so much by scientists studying exercise physiology.

> *Aerobics, stretching, and strength exercises are all needed for total fitness. Together with balance and coordination exercises, these activities help to develop greater body awareness and to release stress.*

Aerobic Activities

Aerobic exercises use oxygen to produce energy in a very balanced way. They are usually exercises in which the legs play a major role, even though in swimming and cross-country skiing there is a role for both legs and arms, and rowing is mostly an arm exercise. The large muscles of the legs and arms make the heart pump a large amount of blood, and the work of the heart is not concentrated in a short spurt of extremely intense work as in lifting a heavy weight.

You should do aerobic activity as often as possible, ideally once a day for about twenty to thirty minutes. Work hard enough to make your heart beat faster than normal. Even if some days you have little time to exercise, try to do something, even if it seems too short for any benefit. Buy a good exercise book that will help you determine your resting and target heart rates, the type of aerobic exercise that is best for you, and more. Ask your health professional to recommend a good program for you.

Some aerobic activities are what you may consider *pure,* that is, without any objective but the exercise itself. There is no goal but the joy of that activity and the sensation that your body is doing something wonderful. There is no game or competition involved. *Consider at least one and possibly more of these pure aerobic exercises as part of your exercise plan.* Some of the most common pure aerobic activities are cross-country skiing, jogging and running, bicycling, swimming, hiking uphill or taking long treks on mountainous terrain, rowing, aerobic dancing, water aerobics, ice and roller skating, and jumping rope. Downhill skiing has some components of both aerobic and strength exercise, but is not sufficient by itself since chair lifts have removed one of the traditional aerobic features of the sport—walking uphill. If you love downhill skiing, do enough uphill climbing with your skis to make it aerobic to some extent.

Why do we need some pure aerobics? A great advantage of pure aerobics is that they are not competitive, so you can fully relax as you do them. When competition is added, as in a road race or a tennis match, other factors come into play. There is nothing wrong with racing or playing tennis if you like competition and if that is a stimulus to regular physical activity. But remember that if you play aerobic games or run in races, the stress and tension intrinsic in such competition may not be what you need to add to your life, unless you are a professional athlete. So do these sports in a relaxed fashion. Try to do them well, but don't make winning such an overwhelming necessity that mental tension and stress become a major part of your game.

And don't forget something else: as in choosing, preparing, and eating food, it is important to instill beauty and joy into your activity. Mind and body must work together. Perhaps the ultimate combination of beauty and exercise is a long trek on a beautiful mountain trail, culminating in a breathtaking view of distant mountain chains.

One more point about games. Some of them, like golf, result in very little activity for the heart, leg, or arm muscles. It's even worse when instead of walking on the golf course you use a motorized cart. Don't consider this kind of activity a major contributor to fitness. Don't drop it —there is some good in it—but be sure to add proper intense aerobics.

Not to be overlooked, and good for rounding out your formal aerobic exercises, are activities that are part of everyday life and that should be emphasized more. Walk or bicycle instead of using a car; take the stairs instead of the elevator as often as possible. These are but a few examples of ways to add to your exercise. If you work in an office, walk during a break or try going up and down a flight of stairs rapidly.

Stretching and Posture Activities

Stretching and related activities give you flexibility and strength. Athletes in sports such as running and tennis use all kinds of stretching exercises to help them perform better at their aerobic activities. Stretching before an intense aerobic session is important to prevent damage to muscles, but it does much more than just prepare you for your aerobic workout. There is a great beauty in a stretching exercise properly executed.

This kind of exercise is very easy to perform anywhere. Whether you are at home or in a hotel, you must do some stretching with your legs and feet, arms and hands, abdomen, torso and shoulders, back, and neck each day. Stretching exercises are important, as they make you feel good and relaxed and are a key component of looking physically fit. Proper posture is beneficial not only for health but also for good looks.

Many yoga positions are good examples of stretching that also helps to develop inner peace and harmony. Again, find a class or a good book on the subject that will keep you interested and involved. Perhaps a health professional has some recommendations.

Resistance and Weight-Lifting Exercises

Lifting weights belongs to the group that exercise experts call *resistance exercises*. You can lift the weight of your own body, free weights, or weights attached to an apparatus typically found in health clubs. But you don't have to belong to a health club to benefit from this type of activity. At home you can easily do push-ups, use a set of barbells or dumbbells with changeable weights, or, if you really want to be modern, buy a machine to help you. Some of us need the stimulus of exercising with other people, and for that purpose, classes or gyms are great. Or you may want to listen to a tape or record or watch a video. Create the best possible conditions for yourself.

Dumbbells and barbells are excellent, for you can choose more or less weight to lift as you develop more strength, and you can work a wide range of muscles. Don't overdo it; you shouldn't be trying to show off. Injuries are very possible if you lift weights incorrectly or in excess of your strength. Reasonable weights—and this is relative to your previous training and muscle development—are all you need. You can have fun with some dumbbells or other inexpensive apparatus. A good professional store should be able to advise you and suggest a good, clear instruction manual. Be sure to learn the basics to avoid injuries while lifting.

Balancing Exercises

Balancing exercises should round out your daily exercise routine. They are not as essential as the exercises on tiers one and two of the exercise pyramid, but they help you build confidence, poise, and coolness and to perform other physical activities more efficiently and safely. Sometimes they help to relieve stress. The harmony of a well-executed balancing exercise is important in our busy and often noisy world.

Examples of this type of exercise are walking on a balance beam close to the ground, standing on one leg for a minute or two (then on the other leg), perhaps while doing some stretching exercises. Bicycling at very low speed or standing almost still on a bicycle is another example of this kind of exercise. Some yoga exercises are also good balancing exercises. Or just invent your own and have fun.

Prevent Injuries

Every exercise carries the risk of injury. Because exercise is so important and we want to be active throughout our lives into very advanced age, an injury can be a major setback. This is one of the risks of games in which competition becomes the major goal. We have all heard of super-athletes hurt and sidelined for months, of bad knees, shoulders, and other problems, especially in people who focus on one type of activity to an extreme and do it competitively. Don't try to be a hero on a ski slope by coming down an expert descent on icy snow; you could end up with a major knee or ankle injury that could be a lifelong problem. Be wise; simple common sense should tell you not to push yourself into situations where the risk of injury is high.

Seek Beauty and Joy Through Physical Activity

To keep up our activities on a regular basis, we must not only think of them as something that's good for us, we must also enjoy them. Use your love for the mountains, the sea, primitive lakes and rivers, or wide-open plains to add natural seasonal beauty to your exercise sessions. Hike into the mountains when the spring flowers are blooming, walk through a meadow in summer, or ski cross-country through the same meadow in winter. Choose an activity you like and combine it with a search for a beautiful scene or a joyful outing. If you like photography, use it as a reason for long outdoor treks in beautiful areas. By seeking beauty, you'll add a dimension that's difficult to measure in a clinical setting but of extreme importance to your happiness and well-being.

Body Awareness

One of the frequently overlooked benefits of physical activity is the way it helps us develop a better awareness of our bodies and helps to release stress. Just as in choosing better ways to eat, we must develop better awareness of the beauty of foods—their aroma, their colors, their taste, and the rituals of proper meals—so in exercising we need to feel a sense of joy in our bodies during the activity itself and during the rest that follows it. If not, we will reap only part of the tremendous benefits of physical activity. We should not feel like machines jogging around the park with no other sensation but the thought "This is good for me . . . this is good for me . . . I must do it!"

Watching your muscles as they work—when possible—is a simple way to greater body awareness. This is easier if you wear clothing like shorts or leotards. Look at the muscles directly, or look in a mirror as you exercise to see your total self (this is easy during stretching and weight lifting). Touching the muscles that are involved in the exercise—such as your leg muscle in a stretching activity—adds a new dimension. Walking barefoot, especially in the sand, over grass, or just about anywhere you can touch the earth is another good way to develop body awareness. Another great body-awareness activity is massage, an ancient art that in addition to helping us relax and soothing our sore muscles will help us develop greater body consciousness.

In *The Sensual Body,* Lucy Lidell says, "When you are fully aware of your body, you exist as one being, rejoicing in a feeling of harmony and integration . . . Body awareness rewakens your senses."

Finding Ourselves: The Search for Solitude

For ultimate well-being, we must strive to find enough time to be alone, let our minds wander, think freely, and search for our innermost selves. Great thinkers and writers have always needed to remove themselves occasionally from people—even the most loved ones—and find some time to be alone in a peaceful place. This is the search for solitude, and we must find some time for it in our busy lives. It has a great healing effect and a few minutes of being alone—more, if possible—each day or at least each week will give you great benefits.

Stress

Many books have been written about stress and how to relieve it. For our purpose, I'll repeat that physical activity and an increased awareness of our bodies are excellent ways to prevent or treat excessive stress. Massage can be added to this list. After coming home from the office after a long drive on the freeway or just a busy day of work, nothing is better than some intense physical activity followed by the ritual of a great Superpyramid dinner.

Noise. We should also consider that *noise pollution* in the modern world, especially in the cities, is another cause of stress even though we may grow so accustomed to it that we forget it's there. Search for silence frequently. As it is often almost impossible to get away from the din of a major highway or roadway, railroad track, or airport, consider what you can do to insulate yourself from the noise and to get away whenever possible to a quiet, peaceful place.

Sleep. The ultimate relief from stress, the ultimate regenerator of a tired mind and muscles, is proper sleep. To sleep well, you must allow enough time to sleep. Learn to sleep naturally; avoid the use of medication unless it is prescribed because of pain or illness. Avoid stimulants like caffeine late in the day and—even worse—in the evening after dinner. Clear your mind of the problems that may have arisen during the day; many will be resolved after a good night's rest.

Music. The right kind of music can be a good way to relieve stress, just as some types of music tend to excite. To counteract stress, choose peaceful music. You might even want to learn to play a musical instrument yourself.

Toxic Substances

Toxic substances can have tragic consequences if left uncontrolled in the environment, no matter how well we eat, exercise, and otherwise take care of ourselves. No one needs to be told that we should avoid them, but sometimes they are beyond our control. Just think of smog, fumes from factories in our neighborhoods or where we work, toxins in dumps close to our homes or leaking into our water supplies, or improper use of pesticides on foods.

Addicting substances. There are some toxic substances we have the power to choose whether or not to inhale, drink, or eat. We can control smoking, excessive alcohol intake, and the use of illegal drugs. All these can lead to many diseases, and often early death.

Addicting substances, legal or illegal, have a powerful grip on us. Let's take one of the most common addictions: cigarette smoking. The stories of people who have earnestly tried to quit and failed time after time are endless. And if they were true addicts, when they finally quit, they can't smoke even one cigarette without again falling prey to their addiction.

While writing the book *The Last Puff,* my coauthor John Farquhar and I interviewed many ex-smokers. Nearly all of them, after they had been off smoking for a while, thought, I can have a cigarette today . . . I am not addicted anymore. The result: they were right back where they had been before, soon smoking a pack or two a day. Some of them were later able to quit again, and they succeeded in remaining nonsmokers because they knew there is no such thing as a cigarette or a cigar once in a while for an addict. One ex-smoker (A.S.) said, "In the early seventies I quit for one year. Then I began to believe that I could indulge myself with an occasional cigar after dinner . . . I often traveled for business, and I remember walking up to my hotel room and looking across from my bed and seeing a large number of empty cigar five-pack boxes. I realized I was smoking cigars the way I was smoking cigarettes." A.S. has learned his lesson and is now a nonsmoker.

Or take Dick, who quit in 1966. In 1980, his wife suddenly died when still quite young. He remembers what happened the day after her death: "I had a cigarette within twenty-four hours after she died. Somebody offered me one and I have wanted to cuss him out ever since." More than ten years later, Dick still wants to quit but can't.

No food or exercise can prevent the higher risk for cancer, heart disease, or emphysema that is the common consequence of regular heavy smoking. And if we are interested in healthy looks, we should be aware that many lifelong smokers develop what has been called the *smoker's face,* riddled with excessive wrinkles far beyond the normal aging of the skin. You can recognize lifelong smokers, as they always look older than they are. If they are still alive.

Drugs used as medicines. People seem to forget that medicinal drugs are powerful substances and should be used with great care, and only when needed. We are overwhelmed each day by ads for various drugs promising to relieve stress, cure our headaches, mitigate the effects of overeating the wrong foods, treat our constipation, or help us fall asleep instantly. We are not referring to drugs prescribed to you by a health professional for a disease or an emergency, but the so-called over-the-counter medications you can buy freely at the drugstore. Many of these widely available drugs and medicines have become part of everyday life for some people. Remember that many effective drugs have some other, often undesirable, effects, and if they are potent enough to treat your symptoms, they probably alter some biochemical reactions in your body. As such, these medicines should never become a part of daily life. Probably most adult Americans take some medication every day.

How much of this is really necessary? For example, sales of over-the-counter laxatives in the U.S. amount to billions of dollars a year. But apart from clinical cases that should be handled by a physician, in most instances proper diet and sufficient exercise make laxatives unnecessary. Many headaches can be prevented or cured by proper relaxation, exercise, eating, and sleeping. *Remember, any drug you take is a powerful substance, not to be used carelessly!*

Contaminants in water. Because good flavors and aromas are so important in the Superpyramid, always use good, pure water for cooking. Most city water doesn't taste very good and won't help the flavor of your cooking. If the water evaporates, you may eliminate such substances as chlorine, but you may also concentrate some of the bad flavors and any possible toxins. If you are satisfied with the taste of your tap water and know where your water comes from and how it is treated, of course go ahead and use it. Otherwise, it may be wise to use filtered or bottled water for cooking and the last washing of vegetables and fruits. Often, taste is the deciding factor in considering whether to use filtered or bottled water.

Contaminants in fish. In extreme cases of toxic spills into rivers or lakes or in uncontrolled release of sewage into ocean bays, fish die. This is terrible, but at least those fish will never reach our tables. But more subtle and elusive is the presence of smaller quantities of toxic substances in ocean, lake, and stream fishes. Inorganic substances such as mercury, organic toxins such as pesticides, other highly toxic chemical discharges from chemical plants, and radioactive material slowly accumulate in a fish's body. If we consume fish occasionally, we probably won't suffer. But if we eat fish regularly, we must be more careful. Fish from the open ocean or away from coastlines near densely inhabited or industrial areas are probably safer. Lakes and streams are easy for you to check out. Certainly a stream flowing through a high mountain meadow is probably as safe as anything you can find. Shellfish gathered in bays and near the coast in areas where no chemicals or sewage are dumped are probably free from toxic substances, but they can be quite high in harmful substances if gathered in waters close to industrial discharges. Stay alert for reports of fish contamination and avoid those fish on the "toxic" list.

Be careful in choosing your fish, and if you have doubts, leave the fish alone. This is unfortunate, as fish can be an important Superpyramid food and, as we have seen, has some of the safest fats found in animal products. Another way to approach this problem is to remember that some toxic substances, such as pesticides, tend to accumulate in the fat of the animal, so a lean fish is probably safer than a fatty fish from a contaminated area. In spite of all this, fish is a good food for the non-vegetarian as long as you exercise some caution.

Pesticides. It's unfortunate that some pesticides banned in the U.S. are used in other countries—sometimes even sold by U.S. companies—quite freely. Often the farmworker who applies it cannot read the English instructions and cautions. And some of these users may think that if a little bit is good, more is even better. This means that we must be extra careful with produce and even animal products (which may have consumed contaminated feeds) that come from other countries, especially developing countries. It is a sad situation, as many of these countries need these food exports. Things are getting better, but more controls are needed.

Even in the U.S. there have been cases in which excessive levels of pesticides have been applied to foods. A few years ago some California watermelons reached the market and caused outright sickness: too much pesticide had been applied in error. Even though in the hands of experts some pesticides are considered safe—and indeed they may be—we have to realize that they are very powerful substances and may sometimes not be applied with care during the busy everyday life of a large farm.

We need to learn more about the long-term effect of pesticides, as some of them are needed at times. But we may have gone too far in their widespread use. Buying produce at farmers' markets allows you to talk to the growers themselves. Some companies now test produce for pesticide residues and label the foods properly. Government agencies do their best, but their manpower and analytical resources are often too limited for widespread testing, Some people prefer produce not sprayed with chemical pesticides, and there are some state laws that control such produce, such as the California law on *organic foods.* Some gourmet chefs, such as Deborah Madison, prefer organic produce, as it is grown more naturally and often has better flavor. Whatever your choice, as you make vegetables, fruits, and grains a major part of your meals, be wise and find the best possible.

It is important to say that some scientists feel that produce carefully sprayed with chemical pesticides should have such a small amount of residue (or no residue) as to be quite safe. But remember that the key phrase here is *carefully sprayed!*

The Intertwined Paths to Health and Fitness

> *The currents that lead to health, well-being, fitness, and happiness or to chronic illness, premature aging, and unfitness are intertwined in a complex crisscrossing of physical and mental paths. Always think of your body as a whole.*

Never expect to do just one thing well—for example, eating the right foods—and achieve the ultimate state of health. In a nutshell, this is the basic message I have been trying to convey to you in this chapter. On the other hand, don't be a fanatic: if the human body could not withstand a certain amount of stressful inputs, the human race would be extinct. In food choices, this means that occasionally eating a food not on the Superpyramid or eating too much of a food on one of the top two tiers will most likely cause you no harm.

If you are not overweight or do not have high cholesterol, you can skip the next chapter. Go right to the exciting recipes and meal plans in parts 4 and 5. You'll find simple, basic recipes for the Superpyramid beginner and more complex dishes that will please any taste.

> *In this chapter I have talked about what you need to do beyond following the Superpyramid food plan to try to achieve and maintain health. You cannot change some inherited tendencies, such as high blood cholesterol, and what was fed to you as a child or how you lived when very young. But you can do your best to stay as healthy and fit as possible, to enjoy life, and to be productive in your chosen path if you follow the concepts expressed in this book.*

▲ KEY IDEAS

▲ Exercise is crucial in preventing overweight.

▲ Disease prevention requires physical activity.

▲ Bones stay stronger with exercise.

▲ Muscles atrophy—become smaller and weaker—without activity.

▲ Do some intense aerobic, some stretching, and some resistance exercise each day, even if very limited.

▲ Make your activity enjoyable; search for beauty or fun.

▲ If you need competition, play active games, but do some pure aerobics as well.

▲ Find some time in your life for solitude and stress-reducing activities such as massage and music.

▲ Good-tasting food or drink should be prepared with pure, good-tasting water.

▲ Avoid foods such as fish from waters that may contain toxic substances.

▲ Avoid foods that may have been improperly treated with pesticides. Pesticide-free foods are always a good option.

▲ *12* ▲

Superpyramids for Weight Loss and Lowering Cholesterol

WEIGHT LOSS: IS IT SO DIFFICULT?

Remember poor Joanne and her eternal cycles of dieting and weight gain, chronicled in chapter 1? If you are moderately overweight, you can shed more excess pounds by following the simple, fun food guidelines below and increasing your physical activity. If you are extremely overweight or outright obese, you should consult a health professional for your weight loss program. In such cases you may have *adult-type diabetes* and should be under a physician's care.

Remember, if you look a little out of shape, it may be the result of unexercised, weak muscles. A combination of the exercises you have read about in chapter 11 and some extra care in following the Superpyramid may be all you need. Again, check with your doctor.

Simple In-and-Out Body Bookkeeping

To lose weight you must use up the excessive fat deposits you build up under your skin. In the bookkeeeping of the human body your choices are to increase what goes out, decrease what goes in, or do both. The most effective way to lose weight is to do both. Decreasing what goes in means eating fewer high-energy foods; increasing what goes out means being more active, especially doing prolonged aerobic activities on a regular basis. If you are overweight, you also need to do some stretching and weight lifting exercises to help you look and feel fit.

Now, let's assume that you have increased your physical activity to a reasonable level. Let's see what you can do about reducing your food intake without having to learn another complicated new system. The solution is simple.

Living on the First Three Tiers of the Superpyramid

Remember the narrow staircase that leads to tiers four and five where we find meats, poultry, and cheeses (except for the very low-fat cheeses)? Let's take a quick trip to tier four and bring down to tier three our favorite sweetener—for example, honey. Not much, just a small jar. Then let's go back up to tier five—wow, is it a small tier!—and bring down a couple of eggs. Having made this trip, say once a week, let's lock the door that leads from tier three to tiers four and five.

With the door locked between tier three and tiers four and five, we have made tier three the top available tier of the Superpyramid. You, as a consummate pyramid expert, know what this means: you must consume the foods on this new top tier in smaller amounts. That means a little less oil and not as many nuts or avocados. Why, you may ask, not eliminate these energy foods completely? This may be necessary in extreme cases of overweight—cases we are not dealing with here. If you are moderately overweight, such excessive restriction will make your food less palatable, and this will usually lead you to abandon your weight loss plan no matter how great the concept behind it may be. Nuts and oil give you a feel of satiety a diet too low in fat does not give. Overrestriction may be necessary for sick people, and often very crucial for them indeed, but it is seldom conducive to lasting compliance in healthy people. Let's make one small change on tier three: while you're trying to reach your weight loss goal, eliminate all fishes except the very lean ones such as sole.

Something else happened after we locked the door to tiers four and five. Tiers one and two assumed greater importance than on a normal Superpyramid. You already know what this means: you must put greater emphasis on whole grains, egg whites, nonfat yogurts and related products, and vegetables and fruits. Simple enough, isn't it? If you need extra help during your weight loss period, you may replace one or two meals with a good powdered or liquid formula diet product made by a reputable manufacturer. But be sure your other meal or meals are Superpyramid meals.

Go a step further. More than ever, avoid refined flour products or grains, baked goods high in added fats, and fruit juices (replacing them with whole fruits). And avoid any kind of fried chips.

If you have a lot of weight to lose, you may use smaller portions of tier-one foods. Remember, your goal here is to cut back, not starve yourself or restrict your calories drastically. Extreme deprivation is not the sensible route to weight loss. This is all there is to it. Once your weight is normal, go back to a regular Superpyramid plan but keep in mind the relative size of the tiers! If you really have a tendency to gain weight, follow the rules you have just learned, only relax them a little bit more. Weight maintenance should become part of your life-style, which should be filled with the right amount of physical activity, the right food choices, and the right ratio of foods on the various tiers and should be freed from toxic substances such as tobacco smoke.

LOWERING BLOOD CHOLESTEROL

No need to repeat the value of keeping blood cholesterol low. If your blood cholesterol is over 220 milligrams (the scientific way to express this is to say 220 milligrams per deciliter)—some researchers believe even 200—you should try to reduce it. If your cholesterol is extremely high—usually an inherited condition—you might need to take cholesterol-lowering drugs and your physician should guide you in that direction. No matter what you do, changing your food habits can have profound effects.

The normal Superpyramid is already designed to help you control your blood cholesterol. If you are in the normal range—below 200 milligrams—the normal Superpyramid is just great. There is a good chance that if you switch to the Superpyramid from a typical Western diet, your blood cholesterol will go down. If your cholesterol is much higher than 200, you may need a more drastic plan to lower it. Check with your physician.

Here is where the Superpyramid design is so great: to lower your cholesterol, you need only make the same changes in the Superpyramid design as indicated for weight loss. The only difference—assuming your weight is normal—is that you can eat full portions of your foods.

The Locked Door

Again, once a week you should take a trip up to tier four and bring back with you some honey or other sweeteners. You can use these a little more freely than if you're trying to lose weight. Bring down a little bit of your favorite poultry product, such as turkey or chicken, if you feel you need some meat, but you don't have to. Even though many recommendations for lowering cholesterol include some poultry, it does have plenty of saturated fat.

Having brought these items down to tier three, lock the door behind you until next week. What have you accomplished? You have practically eliminated all saturated animal fats! While most people can adapt to eating less meat or poultry, cutting out cheeses—even the medium-fat cheeses of tier four—removes a lot of the great flavors from your meals. This is a fact you have to accept. Only a blood cholesterol test will tell you how drastic you must be in eliminating certain foods from the top tiers.

Remember that if your blood cholesterol is below 200, the normal Superpyramid is ideal. If you go too far in restricting foods from tiers four and five, you risk abandoning the plan altogether.

Oils and Nuts
The somewhat restricted plan you are now following still has a sufficient amount of mono- and polyunsaturated oils from olives, nuts, and seeds to give you flavor and pleasure. These will help you create meals very low in saturated fat and cholesterol and reasonably but not too low in total fat.

Exercise
Again, exercise plays a role in determining your blood cholesterol. While exercising does not really lower total cholesterol directly, it often helps to raise the good blood cholesterol, or HDL—the high-density lipoprotein. And exercise can help relieve stress, which can also help to lower your cholesterol level.

Whole Foods, Always Whole Foods!
All the things I've said in this book have been said in the context of a plan that uses whole foods, high-fiber foods, beans, and whole grains, golden vegetable oils, and raw nuts. If refined foods become a common part of your regular meals or snacks, remember that you have left the Superpyramid with its beauty and simplicity.

It is the ultimate enjoyment of a proper meal that will make it possible for you to eat right for the rest of your life. This chapter ends the first part of the book. Now we have the key to unlock the Superpyramid

Kitchen, filled with the great recipes, meal plans, and other practical hints. To do this, let's move along to part 4.

▲ KEY IDEAS

▲ Check with your doctor before starting any weight-loss or cholesterol-lowering plan.

▲ To lose weight you must increase what goes out (energy in exercise) and decrease what goes in (energy from food).

▲ Shrink the top three tiers of the Superpyramid both in width and height for weight loss.

▲ Tiers one and two must assume greater importance for weight loss than on a normal Superpyramid.

▲ To help reduce high blood cholesterol, live on the first three tiers of the Superpyramid—except for some of the sweeteners from tier four.

▲ If your blood cholesterol is over 220 milligrams, you should try to reduce it. Food can be a key component of a cholesterol-lowering program.

▲ Exercise can play a role in helping you raise your good blood cholesterol (HDL).

▲ If refined or fried or other non-Superpyramid foods become a common part of your meals or snacks, remember that you have left the Superpyramid with its beauty and simplicity.

The Superpyramid Kitchen

▲

The Wonderful World of the Superpyramid Kitchen

L et's now enter the wonderful world of the Superpyramid Kitchen. Let it be a kitchen of joy, full of colorful foods, delicious aromas, fragrant oils, and subtle taste treats, a kitchen of real foods, whole foods, fresh foods. Touch the dark green leaves of the lettuce; inhale the aroma of the bean pot cooking with rosemary, vinegar, and wine; let the scent of the baking squash make you anxious to taste its sweet orange pulp . . .

We'll touch briefly upon some of the key ingredients in these recipes as they relate to the tiers of the Superpyramid as we go along in this section. This way you'll have the information you need to make your choices right near the recipes.

Many of the recipes are inspired by the cultures we have read so much about and have been adapted to the whole-food concepts of the Superpyramid. You'll find the name of the contributor after each recipe. The recipes range from very simple to very sophisticated. Some Superpyramid menus follow the recipes.

Fat Analyses of Recipes

The Superpyramid Program is designed to be well balanced just by following the *tier* concept. For readers who want more precision, fat analyses are given at the end of those recipes containing reasonable amounts of fat. The analyses indicate both saturated and unsaturated fat. Remember: try to keep your unsaturated fat intake higher than your saturated fat intake. Many recipes include options to decrease the amount of saturated animal fat. Remember that the oils, nuts, avocados, and related foods used in the Superpyramid Kitchen are high in unsaturated fats and extremely low in saturated fats.

The fat analyses are valuable for recipes that use cheeses from tiers four and five and meats or poultry from tier four. Some of these recipes —very few—contain more saturated than unsaturated fat; balance them with other foods so that your saturated animal fat intake remains low. You may, for example, eat a large salad dressed with olive oil and vinegar along with a recipe that is lower in unsaturated than saturated fat.

Go back and reread chapter 6 to remind yourself of the good sources of fat such as olive and sesame oil, nuts and seeds, and—of the animal foods—fish. Olive oil, sesame, almonds, walnuts, and avocados are all over 80 percent unsaturated. It's crucial to remember that fats are an important part of your meals and perhaps a little more olive oil or a few extra nuts might be all it takes to make a good dish an excellent one.

Variability in Fat Content

Make the same recipe ten times with oils or nuts or cheeses from different sources and you'll find variations in fat content or in percentages of types of fat. The composition of olive oil varies depending on where the olives were grown—how warm or cold the winters in that region are, for example—and other factors. Available food analysis tables have been prepared with great care, but the variability of natural foods is great. In our research center we have analyzed almonds and oils and found that no two batches really matched. The fat in sprouted seeds is another variable and just a difference of a few hours in sprouting time can change its content.

It's important therefore to use the fat analyses that follow the recipes as general guidance only, as probably five different analyses of the same prepared foods with ingredients from different farms would yield different results. Equally so, different computer programs can produce different results.

> *In the Superpyramid Program, let the pyramid tiers, not fat analyses, guide you.*

Simple or Elaborate: You Make the Choice

You can eat very simple foods or prepare elaborate gourmet recipes as you follow the Superpyramid path. The choice is yours. The recipes that follow range from very simple to very sophisticated. Many of the recipes by Deborah Madison have been inspired by the Mediterranean way of cooking. Jody Main brings in her talent for Asian cooking, and Rowena Hubbard for recipes using almonds and other nuts. A special section is dedicated to breadmaking and we urge you to take time and read this section carefully: Bread should be a major part of your meals. In this section, rather than repeating what you may find in many other good books on bread, we have chosen to show you the way to make breads and related bread products using natural leavening, and Monica Spiller will take us on an interesting journey through a natural breadmaking Superpyramid kitchen. Other general recipes complete this part of the book, together with a list of cookbooks with recipes that can easily be adapted to the Superpyramid way.

The Key to Success

The key to success is to find a true, wholehearted joy in your new way of cooking and eating. A day will come—sooner or later depending on your previous eating habits—when the old foods and the old ways will be totally unappealing to you. That will be one of the great days in your life. That will be a day you'll look back at over the years and be thankful for. This part of the book will help you reach that day very soon.

MEDITERRANEAN INGREDIENTS AND EQUIPMENT
Some Suggestions by Deborah Madison

Many of the recipes in the Superpyramid kitchen are inspired by Mediterranean cooking. The countries of the Mediterranean are all those which border the great sea—Southern France, Italy, Greece, Turkey, Syria, Lebanon, Israel, Egypt, Libya, Tunisia, Algeria, Morocco, and Spain. There are great differences among these countries in their histories, religions, ways of living, and even ways of eating, but they all share the coast of this sea and with it, the moderate Mediterranean climate. Since climate determines the life of plants and ultimately agriculture, these countries also share, to a great extent, a common larder. Olive oil, almonds, beans and other legumes, a rich bounty of fruits and vegetables, fish, garlic, herbs, cheese and yogurt made from sheep's milk, goat's milk (and to a lesser extent, cow's milk), olives, honey—these are principal foods of the Mediterranean. How they are put together varies from area to area, but one can see at a glance that these staple foods fit comfortably with the emphasis of the Superpyramid. They are clearly the ingredients of good health as we understand it today.

The recipes assembled here represent but an introduction to this vast and colorful cuisine, drawing on the classic dishes of several countries but by no means covering them all. Many of the dishes chosen are ones with which we are already somewhat familiar while others are undoubtedly less so. Some aren't truly Mediterranean at all but are broad interpretations, drawing on the ingredients and adapting them to fit the Superpyramid more closely. We've chosen recipes that are for the most part easy to make with ingredients that aren't hard to find. These recipes also work well together, which makes them particularly useful for the home cook. Legumes are cooked throughout the Mediterranean, very deliciously and effectively. For many this is a difficult and mysterious area so we have included quite a few recipes for pulses—bean-based dishes. Since these foods are so important in the Superpyramid and in other diets as well, we wanted to give plenty of examples to show how easy they are to cook and how many ways they can be used.

Cooking foods of the Mediterranean doesn't require hard-to-find ingredients or special equipment. What is important is to use the best ingredients possible—the freshest vegetables and fruits, the most fragrant, flavorful oils, the best-quality cheeses. The better the quality of the materials you start with, the easier it is to cook well and be happy with your results. For these recipes there are a few ingredients that deserve special mention.

Grains. Grains, along with beans, make up a good part of the Superpyramid. It is usually possible to buy them in bulk in natural or specialty food stores. Keep them stored in a dark, cool place. Whole-wheat, buckwheat, and spinach noodles are good alternatives to white flour for making pasta.

Grains are remarkably versatile foods. They vary enormously in taste and their ability to absorb moisture. Usually they're relegated to the side of a main dish. Throughout this collection of recipes we've tried to show how grains can be used as salads and in soups and main dishes. We're also viewing pasta as a *grain*, and giving recipe examples of whole-wheat, buckwheat, spinach pasta, and others.

The richest source of grain recipes, especially those intended to be main dishes, can be found in vegetarian cookbooks, where grains are often used to take the place of meat dishes.

Polenta. Polenta, or coarse cornmeal, can easily become a staple in this diet for those who love corn. When buying the cornmeal, try to use coarse cornmeal that has not been degerminated—in other words, whole corn with the germ. It may not be available in bulk, but it is usually available in one-pound packages. These should clearly indicate that the milling process has retained the germ.

Herbs and spices. Herbs and spices give life and dimension to all foods, even the plainest. Fortunately, the availability of fresh herbs has increased dramatically in just the past few years. Whenever possible, cook with fresh herbs. Their wonderful perfumes are an advantage for both the food and the cook who has the pleasure of handling them. Sage, rosemary, thyme, and some other herbs can be easily dried at home by hanging a bunch in a dry place in your kitchen or pantry. Soon they will be dry and keep for a few months or longer.

If using dried herbs, make sure they are still flavorful. Time diminishes flavor, so pinch a few dry leaves between your fingers and take a sniff to make sure they are still fragrant before using them. Dried herbs should be replaced at least once a year, more frequently if possible.

Generally the rule of thumb is three parts fresh to one part dried herb, but that will depend on the quality of your dried herbs.

Spices as well as herbs are used in the cuisines of North Africa and the Middle East. Cumin, cardamom, saffron, ginger, pepper, coriander, and cinnamon are used frequently. Buy them whole if possible and grind them in a little coffee grinder as you need them. They will yield much more flavor than spices bought already powdered, and they will last longer too.

Olive oil. Olive oil is the principal oil of the Mediterranean diet. A lot has been written about the different kinds of olive oil as it has become better known and used by more people. Remember that there are several types of olive oil on the market (see page 135): The highest grade, called *extra-virgin*, is the oil that comes from the first pressing. But to be called extra-virgin, it must contain less than 1 percent acidity. First-pressing oils that contain less than 4 percent acidity are called virgin olive oils. Both extra-virgin and virgin are rich and fruity, with a soft, full flavor that becomes one of the major elements of taste whenever it's used. The color is deep green or golden green. Nowadays it's easy to find plenty of inexpensive oils labeled extra-virgin and virgin, but one should be suspicious of the contents, for acidity can be lowered chemically. They probably aren't the genuine article, but they may, however, be just the oil you want to use for cooking—rich and flavorful though not quite as refined as the real thing.

After the first cold pressing, further pressings are made and the extraction of oil may be aided with the use of heat and chemicals. These oils are frequently harsh and can vary greatly in flavor. If they haven't been blended with other oils, they are labeled "pure olive oil." When blended, they might still be called "olive oil," and the flavor and color are extremely light, if not neutral.

Olive oil is produced throughout the Mediterranean—in Spain, Portugal, Turkey, Greece, Italy, France, Lebanon. Different varieties of olives and different styles of production result in many kinds of oils. There is also a great deal of buying and selling between countries and subsequent blending of oils, which makes it even more difficult to offer a single description of different olive oils. Like wine, olive oil varies from place to place and year to year. The true virgin olive oils do differ in style from one country to another, but for the most part, you simply have to try different kinds and decide for yourself what's best. Italian and Middle Eastern markets and specialty stores generally offer the widest variety and range of prices.

Yogurt. Yogurt is used a great deal in the Superpyramid plan, in sauces, dressings, drinks, and as a cheese. When selecting yogurt, either make your own (see page 361) or use those brands that have not been stabilized with guars, gums, and gelatins or flavored with sugars and fruits. They will have a looser texture and the taste will be more delicate and fresh.

Fruits and vegetables. When choosing fruits and vegetables, freshness is essential and organic produce is preferable. Try to go as close to the source as you can. For gardeners, it's home, but for the rest of us, it may be the local farmer's markets, farms that allow you to pick your own fruits and vegetables, and other nearby sources of produce. Truly fresh produce has a quality that is far superior to supermarket food, not just its taste, but in texture and perfume as well. Real produce is inspiring to work with because it is alive. It also tastes better. If you can find good, fresh produce, you have won at least half the cooking battle. With food that tastes good from the start, only a minimum effort is needed to prepare it, whereas lackluster fruits and vegetables need a lot of work (not to mention salt, sugar, and fat) to make them taste good.

Garlic. Along with olive oil, garlic is probably the most frequently used ingredient in Mediterranean cooking. When raw, it is lively and sharp; when cooked it becomes mellow and sweet. In some recipes it is the main ingredient (garlic mayonnaise or whole baked heads of garlic), and in nearly all recipes it's used as a seasoning.

Always use fresh garlic: never dried, powdered garlic or garlic salt. They are quite different from each other. Powdered garlic does not have the nuance and sweetness of the fresh vegetable: it tends to be harsh and a little acrid.

When choosing garlic, look for heads with firm cloves. If it is long past the garlic season you'll notice that many of the cloves have sprouted inside. Slice the cloves in half, then remove the green sprouts with the tip of a knife, for the sprouts have a rather bitter flavor. If the cloves have brown spots on them, cut them away completely. The off flavor can penetrate the rest of the clove, so trim generously.

There are different kinds of garlic, some stronger, some sweeter or milder than others. The large elephant cloves don't have as much character or flavor as the small red Mexican garlic, for example. The first garlic of the season (midsummer) is delicate and sweet, with pure milky-white cloves. Immature heads are often sold with the greens as *green garlic,* and they make wonderful soups. The new garlic is the one to roast and eat whole. As it gets older it becomes less sweet.

Many of the Mediterranean recipes begin with garlic that has been pounded to a paste in a mortar. I personally prefer pounding the garlic to squeezing it through a garlic press (to me it seems to have a sweeter flavor), but you may prefer the press. Whole heads of garlic can also be stewed or baked with olive oil and thyme until soft, then put through a food mill to separate the skins from the puree within. This makes a very good seasoning for soups and sauces.

Garlic is a great food, but sautéed garlic has a fairly strong aroma. By boiling the garlic instead of sautéing you have a much milder flavor but still a delightful dish. The pasta dish on page 321 provides an example of the use of cooked garlic. Instead of sautéing the garlic in olive oil, bring a large pot of water to a boil, add salt to taste, then the pasta. *Add the garlic so it will flavor the pasta as it cooks.* Give it a stir then cook until it is *al dente.* While the pasta is cooking, prepare the greens. Otherwise, follow all the other instructions in the recipe.

Parmesan cheese. In the Superpyramid motif, medium-fat cheeses play a small part. But Parmesan cheese, which is a medium-fat cheese (tier five), is the most important cheese you'll use for it does a great deal in small amounts to complete a dish, by rounding out its flavor and adding the tangy accent that makes a plate of pasta or warm polenta come alive. For this reason, it's important to use cheese of excellent quality. *Parmesan Reggiano* is the best of the Parmesans and the only true Parmesan. It is also the most expensive. It is from Parma, made strictly according to the old ways, and properly aged. It has a beautiful golden straw color and a marvelous full flavor. Other similar cheeses are referred to as *grana.* They are made in the same style but are not true Parmesan. Many of them are very good and others are so-so. The only so-called Parmesan cheese to avoid is the kind that is preground and comes in a box. It has no flavor and will do nothing for your food. You are far better off choosing the best Parmesan or grana you can afford and shaving or grating it as you need it. Other medium-fat hard cheeses are Asiago, dry Jack, and Pecorino Romano. Romano is often used in combination with Parmesan as it is quite strong. All add a clear note to whatever you're cooking.

Mortar and pestle. This is probably the only piece of equipment that doesn't commonly exist in the American kitchen, but which is ubiquitous to the cultures of the Mediterranean and others. The mortar and pestle are used for pounding nuts, herbs, and spices and in this book for pounding garlic into a paste, which is a frequent first step for making many sauces. When pounded into a puree the garlic tastes sweet and is not altered by contact with metal. A food processor or garlic press does not get quite the same result. The mortar and pestle are ancient, primitive tools; they work extremely well and are a pleasure to handle and easy to clean. With familiarity, you may find yourself using them all the time.

In selecting a mortar, start with a small one. It can be made of marble, stone, wood, or porcelain. Unless it's made of wood, it's better if the bottom of the bowl is roughly textured for it helps the garlic (or whatever is being pounded) to adhere and not go flying off. If you have a mortar with a smooth surface, adding a little coarse salt to the garlic makes it easier to handle and helps it to break down more rapidly.

ASIAN BEAN FOODS

Some Suggestions by Jody Main

Tofu, also referred to as *bean cake* or *bean curd,* is made from soybeans, water, and a coagulant that separates the soy milk into curds and whey, much the way cheese is made from dairy milk. The traditional coagulant, nigari, a magnesium-rich solution, is preferred by many. Calcium sulfate is another popular coagulant used and it increases tofu's calcium content.

Firm, medium, and soft-style tofu are distinguished by the water content. Firm and medium tofu are best for sandwiches, stir-frys, and cutlets. Soft tofu is smooth and creamy and suited for soups and desserts.

Tofu needs to be kept refrigerated and will keep for about a week. Rinse the tofu and place in fresh water daily to ensure freshness. Check the date on the container before purchasing. Tofu is located in the refrigerated deli section, dairy section, or produce section in grocery or specialty stores.

Tempeh. Tempeh (tem'-pay) is a traditional Indonesian whole soy food sold in cakes near the tofu section in food stores. It is as versatile as tofu and very adaptable to Western cuisine.

Tempeh is made by splitting soybeans and inoculating them with a tempeh starter and incubating them. Rice, quinoa, and other grains are added for different flavors. Tempeh is rich and hearty.

Miso. Miso (mee'-so) is a savory high-protein seasoning. Soybeans are mixed with rice or other grains, salt, and a starter and allowed to ferment for one month to several years. Miso is a traditional Japanese food that ranges in color, texture, and flavor from salty, dark, and rich to sweet, light, and mellow. Miso is a good substitute for salt, butter, or oil. It can be added to any vegetable stock (½ cup miso to 1 quart stock) to make a rich soup. A cup of miso can be made by mixing in 1 tablespoon of miso to 1 cup hot water. Miso may also be used as a condiment with grains, vegetables, and tofu. For a full miso flavor choose a red traditional miso. For milder flavor choose white misos.

HOW TO SPROUT SEEDS
by Jody Main

Sprouting grains, beans, almonds, and other seeds is a much overlooked way to use these basic foods. You'll find ways to use sprouts in various recipes in this section. You may also use them in place of green leaves in the winter. As a sandwich filling sprouts give body and flavor. The following instructions and table will show you how simple it is to prepare sprouts. Use dry beans, whole hulled sunflower and similar seeds, and shelled, unblanched almonds.

Soak seeds in water overnight in a mason jar. Next morning, drain off the water and rinse the seeds until the water runs clear. Drain well. Place a stainless steel screen in a metal ring or cheesecloth with a rubber band over the jar opening to hold in the seeds. (Think of this as an ideal mini-greenhouse, especially valuable in cold climates.) Larger seeds may be grown and rinsed in a colander.

Set the jar on its side, and rinse the seeds two to three times a day for one to four days. Refrigerate the sprouts when they are ready (see Seed Sprouting Chart).

▲

Seed Sprouting Chart

VARIETY	NUMBER OF DAYS	AMOUNT OF SEEDS PER QUART JAR	SERVING SUGGESTIONS
Alfalfa	3–4	1½ Tbs.	**Raw in salads, sandwiches, or chopped in baked goods**
Almonds	1	1 cup	**Raw or roasted; snacks, salads, hors d'oeuvres**

VARIETY	NUMBER OF DAYS	AMOUNT OF SEEDS PER QUART JAR	SERVING SUGGESTIONS
Adzuki beans	2–3	1 cup	Cook until tender and use in bean salad or chili.
Black beans	1–3	1 cup	Cook and serve on tortillas or other flat breads. Use in bean soup.
Garbanzo beans	1–2	1 cup	Cook until tender and use to make hummus or toss in salad or soup.
Lentils	1–3	1 cup	For lentil soup and cooked for lentil salad
Mung beans (the common Chinese sprouts)	2–3	1 cup	In Chinese recipes, salads, or in a miso soup.
Radishes	3–4	2 Tbs.	To add spice to any salad or sandwich
Soybeans	2–4	1 cup	Cook until tender, add to salads, mash for sandwich spread
Sunflowers	1–2	1 cup	Toasted or raw for snacks, tabbouleh, fruit salads
Wheat berries	see bread section		

Sauces, Salad Dressings, and Spreads

S auces, dressings, and spreads enliven everything they touch and
are a cornerstone of the Superpyramid Kitchen. Spreads are wonderful on a slice of bread, pita, or other flat breads and crackers.
Using spreads instead of solid fats such as butter is an easy way to enjoy
a Superpyramid meal. A good salad dressing is basic to the salads that
are a key part of a Superpyramid meal.

Mediterranean cuisine. The cuisines of the Mediterranean abound with
richly flavored sauces that are naturally healthful and simply made.
Butter and cream are not indigenous to this part of the world; *olive oil* is
used instead. This collection of sauces, dressings, and spreads gives only
glimpses of the great realm of delicious condiments, but they are chosen
because they are easy to make. There are many, many more and those
who wish to discover them will find them in the cookbooks listed at the
end of this section as well as other cookbooks on Mediterranean countries.

Oriental, Mexican, and other cuisines. Other countries have great sauces
and spreads too. Some of the recipes you'll find have been inspired by
Oriental and other cuisines.

FAT ANALYSES IN SAUCES AND SPREADS

Fat analyses for sauces, spreads, and dressings are very approximate and are given by the tablespoon. Usually a tablespoon of good extra-virgin olive oil weighs about 8 to 10 grams (some tables give the weight of a tablespoon of olive oil as 13.5 grams, but in practical terms it's hard to fill a measuring tablespoon to that level). Our values are based on extra-virgin olive oils from California and Italy. The figures given after the recipes are for a tablespoon weighing about 8 or 9 grams, which is the average weight in everyday measurements in a typical kitchen. This amount of olive oil contains about 1 to 1.5 grams of saturated fat and the rest—about 7–8 grams—is unsaturated. This unsaturated fat is about 90 percent monounsaturated (remember chapter 6). The changes in fat composition caused by climate, age of the olive, and other factors have only minor implications from a practical point of view, but they should be remembered as you may read other values in other books.

All these recipes are carefully designed with good oils, nuts, or seeds and whenever medium-fat cheeses or a trace of egg yolk (in just one recipe) are used, their amount is very small and meets all the Superpyramid principles.

Pesto

by Deborah Madison

*T*his sauce is intensely flavored and rich with olive oil, cheese, and nuts. But because it is so flavorful, it is very useful as a seasoning for all kinds of dishes— soups, pasta, vegetables, rice, potatoes, eggs—and it is one of the best-known sauces of the Mediterranean. Even a teaspoonful will go far to wake up a dull soup and make it shine.

Herbs taste best when freshly prepared. Although this pesto can be made and held for a week or more, it's so quick to prepare with a food processor that you can just whip it up as you need it. Conversely, it can also be made and frozen for later use.

MAKES ABOUT 1 CUP

3–4 cloves garlic, peeled
¼ teaspoon salt
⅓ cup pine nuts
1½ cups fresh basil leaves, separated from the stems and washed
5 tablespoons freshly grated Parmesan Reggiano cheese or a mixture of Reggiano and Romano cheeses
⅓ to ½ cup olive oil

1. Pound the garlic and salt together in a mortar, then transfer to a food processor. Add the pine nuts and puree with the garlic, then add the basil leaves and the cheese. Work until well chopped, then, with the machine running, gradually pour in the olive oil.
2. Work just until a fairly homogenous mixture is formed, then stop. Taste and season with salt, if needed. Keep in the refrigerator until ready to use.

FAT PER TABLESPOON: Saturated 0.5–1 gram; unsaturated 5–6 grams

Greek Garlic Sauce (Skordalia)

by Deborah Madison

Skordalia is a garlic mayonnaise thickened with bread crumbs or mashed potatoes and ground almonds rather than egg yolks. It is traditionally served with fish, especially salt cod (as is aioli), but is also delicious with vegetables, especially vegetable fritters, fried eggplants and zucchini, boiled green beans, baked beets, etc.

A survey of Greek recipes will reveal different emphases on the amounts of thickeners and garlic. Like most of these recipes there isn't just one way to prepare it. Each cook has her own way, and you undoubtedly will too.

For olive oil, use one that has good flavor but that isn't your most expensive extra-virgin. Or use a light olive oil for most of the quantity, and a few tablespoons of stronger-tasting oil or extra-virgin at the end, for flavor.

MAKES ABOUT 1½ CUPS

¼ cup bread crumbs or cooked potato
1 cup almonds
4–6 cloves garlic
½ teaspoon salt
¾ cup olive oil
red wine vinegar, to taste

1. If using bread crumbs, soak them in water for a half-minute or so, then squeeze out any excess moisture.
2. To blanch the almonds, bring a few cups of water to a boil, remove the pot from the heat, add the almonds, and let stand for a minute. Try slipping the skin from a few almonds and if they come off easily, drain them and peel the rest. Dry them out in the oven for a few minutes, then grind in a food processor or hand grinder as finely as possible.
3. Crush the garlic with the salt in a mortar, add the bread crumbs or potato, then gradually work in the almonds, pounding constantly with the pestle. When the mixture is smooth and homogenous, add the oil a drop at a time at first, then in a slow, steady stream. This process can be done in a food processor, once the garlic has been pounded.
4. When the oil is completely incorporated, season the sauce with vinegar and more salt, as needed.

FAT PER TABLESPOON: Saturated 0.6–1 gram; unsaturated 5–6 grams

Olive Paste (Tapenade)

by Deborah Madison

*O*live paste, a Provençal and Italian condiment, keeps well and is easy to make, although it can also be bought ready-made in small jars. Use it spread over toasted or grilled bread for an appetizer, or as a zesty element in a tomato and mozzarella cheese sandwich. If you love olives you'll have no trouble finding many uses for this delicious spread.

Recipes for tapenade vary widely in the amounts of capers called for in proportion to olives, naturally reflecting the taste of the cook. Your own taste might also dictate quite a different balance than the recipe below suggests, but it is generally agreed that the small Niçoise olives make the best olive paste. However, if they're not available, other olives can be used in their place. Kalamata and other brine-cured olives need to be rinsed briefly to wash away some of the saltiness. You can also experiment using different kinds of olives mixed together. A few green cracked olives will give a little sharpness to the paste.

MAKES ABOUT 1 CUP

1 cup Niçoise or Kalamata olives
1 tablespoon capers
1 large garlic clove, finely minced
¼ cup extra-virgin olive oil, or more, as needed
   lemon juice or vinegar, to taste

1. Press on the olives with the heel of your hand to open them up, then remove the pits and discard.
2. Put the olives in a food processor with the capers, garlic, and olive oil. Process until everything is broken down into a coarse puree. It may be necessary to add more oil as you work.
3. Remove the paste to a bowl, taste, and season with lemon juice or vinegar.
4. Store in a covered jar in the refrigerator.

VARIATIONS

1. Include herbs such as thyme, savory, fresh parsley, a pinch of herbes de Provence, or basil.
2. Departing from tradition altogether, use some finely diced sun-dried tomatoes with the olives. If they're hard, sauté them first with finely

minced onion in a little oil and water. Season with herbs. This makes a richly flavored spread for sandwiches and grilled bread brushed with olive oil and garlic (crostini).

3. For the original, nonvegetarian, tapenade, add 6–8 chopped anchovy filets.

FAT PER TABLESPOON: Saturated 0.5–1 gram; unsaturated 5–6 grams

Yogurt Dressing

by Deborah Madison

*T*his lemony yogurt dressing can be served with greens of all kinds, both cooked and uncooked, with raw vegetables, as a spread for sandwiches in place of mayonnaise, a sauce for fish or beans, a dressing for cucumber and other vegetable salads, and so on. Brought to room temperature, it can also be stirred into soups—it's especially good with bean, lentil, and pea soups. Not only is this dressing versatile in its use, the yogurt lends itself readily to a wide range of flavors depending on the herbs and spices you choose to season it with.

This dressing will keep for days, but if you've seasoned it heavily, taste it before serving as the flavors will develop with time. You might wish to adjust it, adding a little more yogurt. If you're planning to make enough to last a week, use just a little garlic and add more each time you use it—it tastes better fresh.

MAKES 1 CUP

1 cup nonfat (or low-fat) yogurt
1 clove garlic (or to taste), finely minced
1 tablespoon olive oil
  zest of lemon
1 teaspoon lemon juice, or more, to taste
  pinch of salt
  freshly ground pepper
  fresh herbs and spices, to taste (choose from dill, parsley, cilantro, mint
    leaves, chives, cumin, cayenne, and paprika, used alone or in combina-
    tion with one another)

1. Combine the yogurt with the garlic, olive oil, and lemon zest. Stir together and add the lemon juice, to taste, a pinch of salt, and the pepper.

2. Leave as is or stir in fresh herbs or dried spices, as suggested above. Use a tablespoon (or more) of the fresh herbs and try them in different combinations. All would be delicious together, or just one or two. The flavors will develop as the dressing sits, so if you're not sure if the herbs and spices are strong enough, wait an hour and taste it again. This is especially true with cayenne or any kind of chili.

FAT PER TABLESPOON: Only traces of fat—practically fat-free

Yogurt Dressing with Lemon and Tahini

by Deborah Madison

The addition of tahini (sesame paste) to yogurt makes a richer dressing with more body, an alternative to a plain yogurt dressing. It can be used in a variety of ways but it's especially good with white beans, whether warm or in a salad, and grilled or roasted eggplant.

Tahini can be purchased already made in Middle Eastern stores and many specialty food stores. If the oil has floated to the top, simply stir it back in until you have a homogenous mixture.

MAKES 1 CUP

2 small cloves garlic
  pinch of salt
1 cup nonfat (low-fat) yogurt
1 tablespoon tahini, or more, to taste
  lemon juice, to taste
  freshly ground pepper

1. Mince the garlic very finely with the salt, or pound in a mortar to make a smooth paste. Stir into the yogurt.
2. If the tahini is very pasty and thick, gradually loosen it by working the yogurt into it by spoonfuls until it is diluted. If it is thin and runny, simply stir it into the yogurt. Season to taste with a squeeze of fresh lemon and freshly ground pepper.
3. Let stand at least fifteen minutes for the flavors to merge.

FAT PER TABLESPOON: Saturated trace; unsaturated 0.5–1 gram

Lebanese Tarator Sauce

by Deborah Madison

*B*ased *on almonds and bread crumbs, this sauce is thick and creamy. It is delicious served with cooked or raw vegetables and is particularly good with grilled eggplant and fennel. It can also be served with fish, falafel, as a sauce in pita sandwiches, and as a dressing for cooked beans.*

MAKES ABOUT 1 CUP

2 slices strong textured bread
1 cup almonds
1 clove garlic
½ cup olive oil
   juice of 1 or 2 lemons or white wine vinegar to taste
   salt

1. Remove the crusts from the bread, dip it briefly in water, then squeeze dry. (If the bread is rather soft, not a strong bread, make the bread into crumbs and don't soak it. It will merely turn to mush.)
2. Put the nuts, bread, and garlic in the work bowl of a food processor and work until everything is finely ground. If you've used bread crumbs without soaking, add a little hot water to loosen things up. With the machine running, gradually add the oil until all is incorporated.
3. Add the lemon juice or vinegar and salt to taste.

VARIATIONS

1. Season the sauce with ¼ teaspoon fennel seeds or cumin seeds, freshly ground or pounded in a mortar.
2. Increase the amount of garlic for a strong garlicky sauce, if you don't mind overwhelming the delicate taste of the almonds.
3. To make the sauce thinner and a little more tart, season with yogurt to taste.

FAT PER TABLESPOON: Saturated 0.5–1 gram; unsaturated 5–8 grams

Fresh Tomato Sauce

by Deborah Madison

A tomato sauce need not be simmered a long time to be good. In fact, quickly cooked sauces are far lighter and have a bright tomato flavor, providing you've begun with good-tasting tomatoes. I find them preferable to long-simmered sauces and they are versatile. They can be seasoned variously, with garlic, a small branch of rosemary or marjoram, a leaf of basil, or nothing at all. The sauce itself can be used with pasta, polenta, rice, and vegetables or used as an ingredient in a soup.

Romas always make a good sauce because they are so meaty, but other tomatoes often have better flavor. The important thing is to use tomatoes with great flavor whether they be beefsteaks, cherry tomatoes, Romas, yellow tomatoes, or whatever. If they are juicy, the sauce will need to cook a little longer for it to reduce.

MAKES 1 CUP OR A LITTLE MORE

1 pound ripe tomatoes
1 tablespoon olive oil (use one with good flavor)
1 large shallot, finely diced
1 small garlic clove, thinly sliced
    optional: a small piece of rosemary, marjoram, or thyme, parsley or a few
      basil leaves
    salt

1. Chop the tomatoes into pieces about ½ inch square. If you're using a food mill later, it isn't necessary to peel and seed the tomatoes. If not, peel the tomatoes first (scald them 10 seconds in boiling water), squeeze out the seeds, then chop finely.
2. Warm the olive oil with the shallot and garlic and cook gently until you can smell the garlic. Don't let either the garlic or shallots brown, though.
3. Add the tomatoes and herb, if using. Salt lightly. Raise the heat and cook everything together, stirring frequently, until the tomatoes have broken down and the shallots are soft, about 8 minutes.
4. Pass the tomatoes through a food mill using an attachment with large holes. The sauce should have a little texture; it should not be a puree.
5. If a great deal of water separates out from the sauce, return it to the heat and cook until reduced.

FAT PER TABLESPOON: Only traces—practically fat-free

Tomatillo Salsa

by Deborah Madison

This is not a Mediterranean sauce, since tomatillos are a New World food. How-ever, this is a good sauce—very light and versatile. It gives sparkle to rice, eggs, avocados, and potatoes and can be used as a dip for chips or anywhere you use a salsa. It keeps, refrigerated, about a week.

Tomatillos, also called Mexican green tomatoes, look like small green tomatoes covered with a papery husk. They can be found in more and more groceries since Mexican and New Mexican foods have become better known. Although they aren't tomatoes, they can be used to some extent like green tomatoes where a tart, crisp effect is wanted.

MAKES ABOUT 1 CUP

8 bright green tomatillos, husks removed
1 white or yellow onion, thickly sliced
1 or 2 serrano or jalapeño peppers, halved and seeds removed
4 garlic cloves, peeled
1 large bunch cilantro
    lime juice, to taste
    salt
    optional: 2 teaspoons light olive or sesame oil

1. Bring several cups of water to a boil, add the tomatillos, half the onion, peppers, and garlic, and simmer gently just until the tomatillos have turned a dull shade of green, about 10 minutes.
2. Transfer the vegetables to a food processor or blender. Add the remaining onion, peppers, and garlic and the cilantro, then process until well blended. If the sauce is too thick, add a little of the cooking water until you have the consistency you want.
3. Season with lime juice and salt, to taste, and stir in the oil, if using. Allow to cool before serving.

VARIATION

For a richer, creamier salsa, puree the sauce with a medium-sized avo-cado. Use as a dip or as a dressing for boiled potatoes or rice. This ver-sion should be used soon after it is made as the avocado doesn't keep well.

FAT PER TABLESPOON: Without oil: no fat. With the oil added: saturated trace; unsaturated 1–2 grams

Roasted Eggplant Spread

by Deborah Madison

Variations of this dish are found throughout the countries of the Middle East. Eggplants are famous for their ability to absorb oil, especially when fried, but when roasted first they don't require much at all.

This spread is good with crackers, warmed triangles of pita bread, or on a slice of any good whole-grain bread. Its flavor can be varied by including yogurt or sesame paste (tahini) in the mixture, or a bit of Tunisian Hot Pepper Sauce.

MAKES ABOUT 1½ CUPS

> 1 large, firm eggplant weighing about 1½ pounds
> 1 large clove garlic, thinly sliced
> 1 clove garlic, minced
> 3–4 tablespoons lemon juice
> ⅓ cup olive oil
>> salt and pepper, to taste
>> freshly chopped parsley
>> extra-virgin olive oil
>> optional garnish: Tunisian Hot Pepper Sauce (Harissa) (p. 234)

1. Preheat the oven to 375° F.
2. Wipe the eggplant, make several small incisions, and insert a slice of garlic into each one.
3. Bake the eggplant in a pan or wrapped in foil until it is completely soft, about an hour, depending on the size.
4. When done, set the eggplant in a colander over a bowl and let any bitter juices drain out while it cools. Then scrape out the flesh and discard the skins.
5. Mash with a fork or in a food processor to make a coarse puree, then stir in the minced garlic, lemon juice as needed, and olive oil. Season to taste with salt and pepper.
6. Serve piled in a bowl, garnished with freshly chopped parsley and extra-virgin olive oil dribbled over the top. If you like, garnish with black olives and wedges of ripe tomatoes.

VARIATIONS
1. Stir low-fat yogurt into the puree, to taste.
2. Add a tablespoon or more, to taste, of tahini.

3. For a more piquant dip, stir a little Harissa into the eggplant, or season with cumin seeds and fresh coriander (cilantro), finely chopped.

FAT PER TABLESPOON: Saturated 0.5–1 gram; unsaturated 2–3 grams

Green Herb Sauce (Salsa Verde)

by Deborah Madison

A green herb sauce is a versatile condiment that lends itself to herbal variations as befits the season and one's taste.

Parsley is usually the main herb, used alone or with additions of tarragon, thyme, capers, shallots, and garlic. Italian, or flat-leafed, parsley is preferable to the curly-leafed variety because it has more flavor, but if it isn't available, don't let its lack deter you; use the curly variety instead.

Like many of these flavorful sauces, a green herb sauce goes with virtually everything. Stirred into soups just before serving, it makes a lively, fresh garnish. It can be tossed with pasta or rice, added to omelets, drizzled over ripe tomatoes, cucumbers, artichokes, and beets or over grilled vegetables, and it's delicious with fish whether poached, broiled, or grilled. It makes a richly flavored dressing for warm beans, both green and dried.

Salsa verde will stay green and keep for several days if you wait to add the lemon juice until just before using. Thus you can make a large quantity and season it as you use it.

MAKES ABOUT 1 CUP

   1 cup parsley leaves, finely chopped
   2 small garlic cloves, minced
1–2 tablespoons capers, rinsed and chopped
   1 shallot, finely diced
  ¾ cup olive oil (use some extra-virgin for flavor)
     salt, to taste
     the juice of 1 large lemon, to taste

Combine everything but the lemon juice in a bowl. Just before using, add lemon juice, to taste.

VARIATIONS
1. In addition to the parsley, use one or more of the following herbs: chives, chervil, salad burnet, lovage, arugula leaves, tarragon, basil, thyme, marjoram, summer savory.
2. Include a little lemon or orange zest.
3. Season the sauce with vinegar rather than lemon juice.
4. Add a small amount of minced green chili.
5. If you like cilantro, use it in place of the parsley, or in combination with the parsley according to your taste. If you are serving this with something like grilled fennel, replace half the parsley with the fennel greens, finely chopped.

FAT PER TABLESPOON: Saturated 0.5–1 gram; unsaturated 4–7 grams

Garlic Mayonnaise (Aioli)

by Deborah Madison

*T*he famous aioli of Provence enhances everything it touches with the perfume of garlic. It's wonderful with all kinds of raw and cooked vegetables, stirred into soup, tossed with pasta, eaten with fish, shellfish, and all kinds of beans, spread on grilled toast, and in many other ways. It is usually made like a mayonnaise, with egg yolks as the binder, but it can also be made without eggs. Both versions are given here.

Chopping garlic and adding it to mayonnaise does not make an aioli, although it will jazz up a jar of mayonnaise. The garlic needs to be pounded to bring out its best flavor and to create a consistency that will spread the flavor evenly throughout the sauce. The mortar and pestle are essential tools, and pounding garlic takes less time than cleaning a garlic press.

Classic recipes for aioli will vary quite a bit as to how much garlic to use. And of course its effectiveness depends on the type of garlic, how fresh it is, and how big the cloves are. The "right amount" of garlic depends ultimately on you. You may find your capacity for garlic grows greatly with experience.

MAKES ABOUT 1 CUP

    5 medium-sized garlic cloves, peeled and roughly chopped
    ½ teaspoon salt
    1 egg yolk
    ½ cup plus 2 tablespoons olive oil
2–4 tablespoons extra-virgin olive oil
        lemon juice, to taste

1. Pound the garlic in a mortar with the salt until it is well broken up into a paste. The salt helps this process. Then stir in the egg yolk with the mortar.
2. Using the pestle or a whisk, gradually add the oil, as for making a mayonnaise, slowly at first then in a steady stream. Add the extra-virgin oil last, to taste.
3. Season with lemon juice to taste. Cover and refrigerate until ready to use.

FAT PER TABLESPOON: Saturated 1 gram; unsaturated 6–7 grams; cholesterol 14 milligrams

Notice how little cholesterol is present even with egg yolk, as long as you use this aioli in moderation.

Garlic Mayonnaise Without Eggs

by Deborah Madison

*T*he addition of bread crumbs or a little boiled potato to the garlic helps bind the oil into an emulsion.

MAKES ABOUT 1 CUP

¼ cup bread crumbs (or boiled potato)
5 medium-sized cloves garlic
½ teaspoon salt
¾ cup olive oil plus 2–4 tablespoons extra-virgin olive oil
    lemon juice, to taste

1. If using bread crumbs, cover them with enough water to moisten, let stand for a minute, then squeeze them dry.
2. Pound the garlic with the salt in a mortar until it is well broken up into a smooth paste, then work in the soaked bread crumbs or potato.
3. While whisking continually, add the oil drop by drop until you have a thick mayonnaise. Whisk in lemon juice, to taste.

FAT PER TABLESPOON: Saturated 1 gram; unsaturated 5–6 grams; no cholesterol

Tunisian Hot Pepper Sauce (Harissa)
by Deborah Madison

T his spicy sauce, which is closer to a paste, is one of those useful condiments that can find its way into all kinds of foods. Try it with couscous or rice, add it to dishes made with lentils, chick-peas, and white beans, or stir it into soups and stews. Harissa can be made easily with a mortar or pestle or in a mini food processor, and it will keep more or less indefinitely if refrigerated.

This version includes roasted bell peppers, which soften the heat with their natural sweetness and which make the harissa more like sauce, less like paste. More heat can be induced by using more chili flakes. Or, in place of chili flakes, use a pure New Mexican chili powder.

MAKES ABOUT ½ CUP

⅓ cup red pepper flakes or New Mexican ground chili
1 teaspoon caraway seeds
1 teaspoon ground cumin, or cumin seeds
2 large cloves garlic, peeled and roughly chopped
2 red bell peppers, roasted and chopped (page 342)
1 tablespoon olive oil
  salt

1. Work the pepper flakes, caraway, and cumin seeds in a mortar or small food processor until they are well pulverized.
2. Add the rest of the ingredients and continue working until you have a well-amalgamated paste. Season with salt. Place in a jar, cover with additional oil, and store in the refrigerator.

FAT PER TABLESPOON: Saturated trace; unsaturated 1–2 grams

Fresh Garden Salsa

by Rowena Hubbard

A perfect dip for chips, pita triangles, or crisp vegetables.

MAKES ABOUT ⅔ CUP

⅓ cup slivered almonds, toasted
2 medium tomatoes, chopped
2 tablespoons chopped green onion
1 tablespoon chopped cilantro
¼ teaspoon salt
¼ teaspoon hot pepper sauce, or season to taste

Combine all ingredients in a small bowl. Cover and chill until ready to use.

FAT PER TABLESPOON: Saturated trace; unsaturated 2–3 grams

Cumin Parmesan Salad Dressing

by Jody Main

This is great on green salad for a change from the classic Italian oil and vinegar dressing

MAKES 1½ CUPS

1 cup extra-virgin olive oil
2 tablespoons balsamic vinegar
  juice of ½ fresh lemon
1 teaspoon cumin
2 cloves garlic, crushed
1 tablespoon minced fresh onion
1 tablespoon fresh parsley, minced
1 tablespoon fresh oregano, minced
1 tablespoon Parmesan cheese, grated
  fresh coarsely ground pepper to taste

Whirl in a blender until smooth, and refrigerate.

FAT PER TABLESPOON: Saturated 0.5 gram; unsaturated 5–6 grams

Chili Lime Dressing

by Rowena Hubbard

MAKES ABOUT ⅓ CUP

¼ cup extra-virgin olive oil
3 tablespoons lime juice
1 teaspoon grated lime peel
1 teaspoon Dijon-style mustard
¼ teaspoon ground cumin
¼ teaspoon chili powder

Combine all ingredients in a small bowl. Whisk until thoroughly mixed.

FAT PER TABLESPOON: Saturated 0.5 gram; unsaturated 5–6 grams

Mustard-Lemon Dressing

by Rowena Hubbard

MAKES ABOUT ¾ CUP

½ cup lemon juice
¼ cup olive oil
2 tablespoons chopped fresh mint
1 clove garlic, minced
1 teaspoon Dijon-style mustard
½ teaspoon thyme
½ teaspoon grated lemon peel

Whip all ingredients together until blended.

FAT PER TABLESPOON: Saturated 0.5 gram; unsaturated 3–4 grams

Miso Sauce

by Jody Main

*T*his classic recipe is great over steamed vegetables or used as a delicious dipping sauce.

MAKES 1 CUP

½ cup red miso
3 tablespoons mirin (Japanese cooking wine)
½ cup spring water, or more
¼ teaspoon sesame oil
1 clove garlic, crushed
   a few grates of fresh ginger

Blend ingredients with a whisk while simmering a few minutes until creamy smooth.

FAT PER TABLESPOON: Traces only

Almond Milk

by Rowena Hubbard

*A*lmond milk is an example of milk prepared from nuts. Other nuts such as hazel-nuts can replace the almonds. All nut milks are refreshing and can be used alone with some sweetening as a beverage or as part of a recipe in place of cow's or goat's milk. Nut milks can be used by people who cannot tolerate the milk sugar in noncultured cow's and goat's milks. Use ground almond pulp to thicken soups or stews, add to fruit or vegetables as a flavorful topping, to stir into breakfast yogurt, or to add to Top Ten Cereal (page 325). Other seeds such as soybeans can be used to prepare milks, but more work is needed as the soybeans must be cooked.

MAKES ABOUT 1 CUP

1 cup whole almonds, natural or blanched
3 or 4 ice cubes
  cold water

1. Place almonds in bowl of food processor with metal blade in place. Place ice cubes in a 2-cup measure and add cold water to make 1¼ cups. Add to almonds; process until almonds are finely crushed and ice cubes disintegrated.
2. Place double thickness of cheesecloth in a 2-cup strainer. Pour mixture into cheesecloth and allow to drip through. Pull ends of cheesecloth together and squeeze mixture until all moisture has drained out. Store in refrigerator for up to a week and a half.

FAT PER ½ CUP: Saturated 2–3 grams; unsaturated 15–20 grams

(Very approximate values only, as fat depends on processing and how much pulp is left).

Salads

GREEN SALADS
by Deborah Madison

Salads are enormously versatile. They can be made of greens, grains, fruits, vegetables, and beans, and they can be eaten warm, tepid, or cold. For this section we've chosen many different types of salads to demonstrate the wide number of possibilities that exist for this food. Regardless of the type of salad you make, it can't be better than the ingredients you start with. Really fresh, flavorful produce always makes the most delicious and therefore satisfying dishes.

For many, salad may frequently constitute the body of a meal, while others don't see themselves as "salad" eaters at all—maybe because they are unfamiliar with the range of what salads can be. Grains and legumes are often more appealing when perked up with a vinaigrette and tossed with other ingredients, so we've given several examples of those possibilities based on wheat, wild rice, quinoa, lentils, and butter beans. Vegetables, both fresh and cooked, make delicious salads and there are several examples of those. And lastly we have fruit as a salad, but it's not just "fruit salad."

There are probably an infinite number of wonderful salads. We've selected only a few, but these particular recipes have been chosen not only because they are good in themselves, but because they can be taken in various directions and transformed into whole new dishes with a few changes of seasonings or choice of condiments. Use them as they are, or use them as a springboard for your own ideas.

240

Choice of Greens

There are now many more lettuces available to us than there were a few years ago. Old and new varieties have been introduced to many parts of the country. The shapes and colors of their leaves are often quite gorgeous and they make beautiful as well as delicious salads. When picked small, the leaves can be used whole, but the heads need not be young to be good. If you're growing your own lettuces, let them mature a bit so that the leaves are about 5 inches long. If you're using standard commercial lettuces, cut off the base, open up the heads and pull out the small leaves at the heart. Leave them whole and cut or tear the remaining leaves.

In addition to lettuces, other greens can be included in a green salad: spinach, tender napa cabbage, arugula (rucola), Belgian endive, curly endive, radicchio, mache, and even wild greens. Fresh herbs and their blossoms are delicious tossed right along with the other greens. (Buy these blossoms at stores or farmers' markets; many flowers are inedible —even poisonous—so leave the selection to the experts.) A green salad can be an ever-changing dish on the table, always reflecting the garden, the market, the season. Those lucky people who garden, even a small plot, can easily grow their own salads. The look and taste of really fresh lettuce forever spoils us. Fortunately, salad greens and herbs are the easiest vegetables to grow.

Preparing a Green Salad

Nothing is more basic than a green salad, but it seldom lives up to its possibilities. The greens are often not treated well, the dressing is weak or acidic, and more frequently than not, salads aren't even tossed so that there are big pools of dressing along with whole areas of undressed leaves. Making a great salad is not so difficult. There are just a few things to keep in mind:

1. Choose whatever greens appeal to you, but discard any that are badly bruised, yellowed, or very tough. (The outer leaves of lettuce make good soup stock and can be cooked as well and eaten as a vegetable.) Wash them well and make sure they are *dry* so that the dressing will stay on the leaves and not mix with the water in the bottom of the bowl. Well-dried lettuce can be stored for days in a perforated plastic bag— wet lettuce will rot.

2. For a dressing, use good oils (extra-virgin olive oil or a mixture of olive oil and sesame or one of the oils described in chapter 6) and vinegars or freshly squeezed lemon. If you mix them together, don't just rely on the 3:1 rule of vinegar to oil—rely on your own taste. Some

vinegars are very strong, others are weaker. Instead of making a dressing, try tossing the greens with a little oil right out of the bottle, then adding lemon juice or vinegar to taste. With a little practice, you'll get the hang of how much is enough and you won't ever avoid making salad because you don't have a dressing.

Fat Analyses for Salads

The amount and type of dressing used is a major factor in the fat content of the finished salad. All analyses given here are approximate and you should read the analyses for the dressing you have chosen in this or the preceding section of the Superpyramid Kitchen. As we have said earlier, these analyses are to be used only for general guidance.

Basic Green Salad

by Deborah Madison

The following recipe serves 4, but if you develop a taste for salads it may serve only 2!

6 handfuls greens, washed and dried thoroughly
   optional: fresh herbs, plucked from the branches or chopped if large
1 shallot, finely diced
4 teaspoons vinegar (Champagne, white wine, tarragon, or a mild red wine
   vinegar)
   several pinches salt
   approximately 4 tablespoons extra-virgin olive oil
   freshly ground pepper
   herb blossoms or edible flowers (optional)

1. Put the greens in a spacious bowl or platter and toss them with the herbs, if using. Refrigerate, covered with a damp towel, until ready to serve.
2. Combine the shallot, vinegar, and salt in a small bowl and stir together. Let stand a few minutes to dissolve the salt, then whisk in olive oil, to taste. Make it as tart or smooth as you like.
3. When ready to serve, pour the dressing over the greens and toss them gently but thoroughly so that all the leaves are lightly coated. Season with pepper and garnish, if you wish, with herb blossoms or edible flowers.

VARIATIONS

1. Include a little minced garlic in the dressing. Rub warm whole-grain croutons with garlic and serve them along with the salad.
2. Use a mustard vinaigrette made with a strong sherry vinegar for strong greens, hearty lettuces, spinach, and the more bitter winter greens such as radicchio.
3. Use walnut oil either alone or mixed with olive oil, for a change of flavor. This oil is particularly good with the slightly bitter chicories, but is delicious with lettuce too. It can take a strong vinegar or lighter ones.

FAT PER SERVING (BASED ON 4 SERVINGS): Saturated 1–1.5 grams; unsaturated 7–8 grams

Salad of Mixed Tomatoes with Olive Oil, Herbs, and Capers

by *Deborah Madison*

*C*aprese is a classic Italian salad, a plate of sliced tomatoes alternating with layers of sliced mozzarella—the kind that's fresh and comes floating in water. This cheese is tender and delicate, balanced with the acid of the tomatoes. It hasn't the rubbery texture of most processed mozzarellas, but it's usually made with whole milk, so enjoy it occasionally and the rest of the time make a tomato salad like this one.

As with all simple foods, it's essential to have impeccable ingredients—tomatoes that are full of flavor and the sweetest, most aromatic olive oil. As for kinds of tomatoes, choose whatever pleases you from what's available. My favorite kind of salad is one that combines all different kinds and colors of tomatoes on one plate, some cut in rounds, others quartered or halved, depending on their size. Use anything from the tiniest currant tomatoes to big beefsteaks.

For herbs, try using a single herb to really appreciate its particular essence. Basil is always paired with tomatoes, but marjoram is very good too. Other herbs you might include are dill, lovage (but only half as much), Italian parsley, and oregano.

SERVES 2 TO 4

> an assortment of delicious tomatoes, about a pound
> extra-virgin olive oil
> 1 tablespoon capers, tiny ones or giants, rinsed briefly in cold water
> 2–3 tablespoons chopped marjoram or basil
> sliced low-fat mozzarella cheese (or goat mozzarella)
> salt
> freshly ground pepper

Slice the tomatoes however you wish and arrange them on a plate. Drizzle the oil over the tomatoes, then scatter the capers and herbs over all. Add pieces or dices of mozzarella cheese. Season with a light sprinkling of salt and freshly ground pepper and serve right away.

VARIATIONS

1. Include a few Niçoise olives on the platter as well. Or serve the salad with a crouton spread with Olive Paste (page 222).
2. Build this into a fuller summer salad plate, including some sliced or quartered cucumbers and blanched green beans on the plate as well, a crouton on the side.

3. For a sparkling presentation, garnish the plate with blossoms, such as bright blue borage flowers, tiny Mexican marigolds, or more subtle arugula flowers, along with some of their leaves.

FAT PER SERVING: (per tablespoon of olive oil)
Saturated 1–1.5 grams; unsaturated 7–8 grams

Orange Salad with Pomegranates and Olives

by Deborah Madison

Oranges are often used in Mediterranean salads and they in fact make a very refreshing winter accompaniment to the heavier foods of the cold weather. Moroccan orange salads are often flavored with perfumed orange blossom water, lemon juice, and a hint of cinnamon, making a wonderful aromatic sweet salad. There is a wonderful Sicilian salad of oranges and lemons, onion and mint. We have our own classic winter salad of grapefruit and avocados, the mild acid of the grapefruit sparking the creamy avocado.

An orange salad can be as simple as a plate of overlapping rounds of oranges left unadorned save for a garnish of watercress and a splash of olive oil, or a combination of different kinds of citrus (navels, blood oranges, sweet Meyer lemons, ruby grapefruit) or by including other ingredients, such as fennel, parsley, cilantro, pine nuts, and almonds. Many things go well with citrus and there is room for a great deal of improvisation.

SERVES 4

4 navel oranges
2 blood oranges (if available)
12 bright green pistachio nuts, peeled and chopped
12 black Moroccan olives
    approximately 2 tablespoon pomegranate seeds*
2 teaspoons extra-virgin olive oil
    juice from the pomegranate and blood oranges, to taste
    optional: watercress or other peppery green, such as arugula

Slice off pieces from both ends of each orange. Set each orange on the counter and using a sharp knife and a downward, sawing motion, slice away the peel and the pith, working your way around the orange. Make sure all the white part is removed. Slice the oranges into rounds, about ¼ inch thick, and lay them on a platter. Scatter the pistachio nuts, olives, and pomegranate seeds over all. Whisk the oil with a bit of juice to sharpen it, to taste, and drizzle over the fruit. Garnish with the watercress or arugula leaves, if using, and serve.

FAT PER SERVING: Saturated 0.5–1 gram; unsaturated 6–8 grams

---

* To remove the seeds from a pomegranate, first cut it into quarters with a sharp knife, then pull back the skin and separate the seeds. The main thing to watch for is the juice, which stains. The rest of the pomegranate can be squeezed to extract the juice, which is pleasantly tart and rich tasting. It makes a wonderful cold beverage or can be used in place of vinegar to give a little tartness to a salad.

Cucumber Salad with Yogurt Dressing

by Deborah Madison

Simple, summery, and refreshing, this salad lends itself well to improvisation and variation. For example, it can be made with several varieties of cucumbers such as lemon and Armenian cucumbers as well as the standard varieties. It it's a good time for tomatoes, add slices or wedges of tomatoes to the plate as well. Beets are also delicious with cucumbers and yogurt, so your plate might include them as well. Watercress and arugula leaves make a simple garnish with a spicy flavor of their own. Cucumber Salad with Yogurt Dressing or Lebanese Tarator Sauce (page 226) would make a good filling for a pita sandwich too.

Make the dressing first so the flavors can develop.

SERVES 4 OR MORE

THE YOGURT DRESSING

Make half of the Yogurt Dressing on page 223, and stir in ¼–½ teaspoon ground cumin, a dash of cayenne, some finely chopped mint and parsley leaves, and a little minced scallion or onion.

THE CUCUMBER SALAD

1½ pounds cucumbers, mixed varieties, hothouse, garden, or whatever is available and appealing
    handful of unblemished arugula leaves or watercress
    olives, preferably Moroccan, Niçoise, or Greek
½ cup Yogurt Dressing
    a few mint leaves, finely chopped

If the cucumbers are waxed, they should be peeled. Slice the cucumbers in whatever fashion you like—in rounds, in wedges, etc. It's not necessary to remove the seeds. If you're using several varieties, you might cut them in different shapes. Lay the greens on a serving plate or individual plates. Set a few aside for garnish. Arrange the cucumbers however you like, scatter the olives here and there, add additional vegetables if using, and place the reserved greens around the edge of the plate. Drizzle the yogurt dressing over the whole plate, but don't cover it entirely with dressing. Garnish with chopped mint leaves and serve right away.

FAT PER SERVING: approximate for 2–3 olives. Saturated trace; unsaturated 1.5 grams

Summer Vegetable Antipasto
by Deborah Madison

A plate of vegetable salads makes one of the most pleasing appetizers or light meals possible. This salad is but a suggestion, reflecting the summer season. It will change as the season progresses and the parade of vegetables and herbs passes. Midsummer brings salads of green beans, tomatoes, cucumbers, sweet bell peppers, and steamed new potatoes. Later you might prefer the smokiness of roasted peppers and roasted potatoes, leeks vinaigrette, raw fennel or fennel à la Grècque, roasted or pickled onions, beets with lemon dressing . . . Seasonal combinations will virtually never fail. If you can, have something that's cooked along with something completely fresh to provide an interesting range of tastes and textures. While any one vegetable could serve as a salad alone, bringing several together on a single plate makes a dramatic and colorful statement that will bring pleasure to all taking part. Take advantage of your farmers' market to find the freshest produce and, often, the most interesting varieties.

SERVES 6 OR MORE

  1 pound green or yellow beans (haricots verts, blue lakes, Kentucky won-
     ders, Romano beans, or yellow wax beans)
  1 shallot, finely diced
     extra-virgin olive oil
     salt
     fresh herbs (such as tarragon, marjoram, basil, parsley)
½ pound small, new potatoes, quartered
  1 pound ripe tomatoes (different colors and shapes, if available)
  1 or 2 sweet bell peppers, roasted (page 342) or sliced raw
  1 cucumber, peeled if waxed, and sliced, or 2 lemon cucumbers, sliced in
     wedges
  6 radishes
12 small carrots
     basil, chopped
     ground pepper
     Niçoise olives
     Olive Paste (page 222) or Garlic Mayonnaise (page 232)
     wedge of lemon

1. Tip the beans and boil them in a large quantity of salted water until they are tender but still a little firm, about 8 minutes, depending on the beans. If using different varieties, cook each separately. When done, drain them, shake off the excess water, then put them in a bowl and toss with the shallot and enough olive oil to coat lightly. Season with salt. Toss with some finely chopped green herbs, either a mixture or a single herb. Set aside.

2. Steam the potatoes.

3. Wash and slice the rest of the vegetables.

4. Arrange the vegetables attractively in a large platter. Drizzle a little olive oil over the tomatoes along with some chopped basil, a pinch of salt, and some pepper. Season the potatoes. Scatter olives here and there and place a mound of olive paste and/or garlic mayonnaise. People can help themselves to a selection and spread the sauces on their potatoes or eat it with the beans.

FAT PER SERVING: approximate, depending on choice and amount of olive paste or garlic mayonnaise and amount of olive oil used. Saturated 1.5 grams; unsaturated 11 grams

Salad of Greens and Herbs

by Deborah Madison

This is a very rustic salad of greens and herbs that tastes wonderful in pita pocket bread. The nuttiness of the wheat is a good balance to the intensity of the greens. The measurements are approximate. Feel free to adjust them to your own taste and to what is available.

FOR 2 SANDWICHES

   a large handful of tender spinach, stems removed
½ bunch cilantro
10 large parsley branches
10 dill branches
2–4 scallions, finely diced
   extra-virgin olive oil or sesame oil, to moisten
   salt, to taste
 2 whole wheat pita breads, halved
½ cup nonfat Yogurt Cheese (page 363)
 4 lemon wedges

Make sure all the greens and herbs are clean and dried. Chop them together, roughly, then toss with a little salt and enough oil to moisten. Line the pita breads with the yogurt cheese. Stuff in the greens and serve with lemon wedges on the side to squeeze into the sandwich.

VARIATIONS
Instead of Yogurt Cheese, toss the greens with the Lebanese Tarator Sauce (page 226) or the Yogurt Dressing with Lemon and Tahini (page 225). This pungent mixture of greens would also be nicely complimented with Hummus (page 331).

FAT PER SERVING: Saturated trace to 0.5 grams, unsaturated 3–4 grams (depending on amount of oil)

Wild Rice Salad with Almonds and Lemon Vinaigrette

by Deborah Madison

*W*ild rice makes a wonderful winter salad mixed with toasted nuts, currants, celery, and apples. The wild rice can be mixed with other kinds of rice. If you don't have wild rice, use brown rice, preferably a long-grain variety, and boil it as you would pasta rather than steaming it. This method insures that it will be properly cooked and not mushy.

While the rice is cooking, prepare the rest of the ingredients and the vinaigrette.

SERVES 4 TO 6

¾ cup wild rice
½ teaspoon salt
½ cup almonds
¼ cup currants
   zest and juice of one orange
1 stalk celery
1 crisp apple
   lemon vinaigrette (page 241)
4 scallions, white part only, minced, or 1 large shallot, diced
1 tablespoon chives, cut in narrow rounds
2 tablespoons celery leaves, finely chopped
2 tablespoons parsley, finely chopped
   freshly ground pepper
   parsley and celery leaves for garnish, chopped or left whole

1. Rinse the wild rice, soak it in water for ½ hour, then drain. Put it in a pot with 4 cups water and the salt, and bring to a boil. Lower the heat and simmer until the grains are swollen and tender, but still chewy, about 30 minutes. Taste to be sure, then drain.

2. Blanch the almonds: Let them stand in a pot of water that has come to a boil for one minute, then drain. Slip off the skins, then put the almonds on a baking sheet and bake in a 350° F. oven until they smell toasty, about 7–10 minutes. Remove and roughly chop.

3. Rinse the currants with warm water to soften them, squeeze them dry, then put them in a cup with the orange juice (reserve the orange zest) and let them soak.

4. Peel the celery if it's stringy, then cut into a fine dice. If the apple is organic, leave the skin on, remove the core, and cut into small pieces.
5. Make a lemon vinaigrette, adding to it the grated orange zest, scallions or shallot, chives, celery and celery leaves, and parsley leaves.
6. Put the rice in a bowl, add the currants, celery, apples, and almonds. Toss with the vinaigrette and season to taste with salt and pepper. Serve garnished with the additional parsley and celery leaves.

VARIATIONS

Use pine nuts, hazelnuts, or walnuts in place of the almonds, or raisins instead of currants. Fennel could replace the celery, giving the same texture but a more anise-like flavor, which is very good with apples.

FAT PER SERVING: Saturated 2 grams; unsaturated 11 grams

Cracked-Wheat Salad (Tabbouleh)

by Deborah Madison

Tabbouleh is well enough known now to be found in delicatessens and supermarkets, but it's one of those dishes that tastes far better when it is freshly made and the herbs are vibrant. With regard to the herbs my own preference is to use plenty of them so that the salad ends up green, moist, and intensely flavorful.

Tabbouleh can be served by itself with a garnish of lettuce leaves or shredded cabbage; it can be tucked inside a large tomato, or eaten with pita bread, Hummus (page 331), and Lebanese Tarator Sauce (page 226). It is beautiful heaped into a pyramid on a plate and garnished with olives, wedges of tomatoes, spears of peppers, and cucumbers. Diced cucumbers and tomatoes are often added to the tabbouleh, but not until the cucumbers have been salted and their excess water allowed to drain.

Tabbouleh is a natural to serve as part of an assortment of dishes, along with Yogurt Cheese (page 363), olives, Roasted Eggplant Spread (page 229), vegetable or bean salads. Such a platter can be offered as an appetizer or comprise a light meal.

For the cracked wheat, or bulgur, use the smallest size you can find. It is usually available in Greek or Lebanese stores and in natural food stores.

MAKES ENOUGH FOR 4

    1 cup finely ground cracked wheat
    4 scallions (with some of the greens), finely chopped
¼–½ cup mint leaves, finely chopped
    1 cup parsley, finely chopped
    ¼ cup olive oil
2–4 tablespoons lemon juice
    salt and freshly ground pepper
    garnishes: Kalamata or Moroccan olives, wedges of tomatoes, slices of
        bell peppers, wedges of cucumbers, branches of Italian parsley

1. Cover the cracked wheat with plenty of water and set it aside to soak for at least 30 minutes or until most of the water is absorbed and the grains are tender. Pour it into a fine-meshed sieve and let the excess water drip out. Press or squeeze it with your hands to get it as dry as possible, then spread it on a tea towel to dry further while you chop the herbs.
2. Mix the cracked wheat in a bowl with the scallions, mint, parsley, olive oil, and lemon juice. Season to taste. There should be plenty of lemon. Serve with any of garnishes suggested above.

FAT PER SERVING: Saturated 1.5–2 grams; unsaturated 10–12 grams

Quinoa with Pistachios, Dried Apricots, and Cumin Vinaigrette

by Deborah Madison

This fruity, spicy salad would also be very good made with rice, cracked wheat, or couscous. Leftover grains are fine to use, but when warm, the flavors of the herbs and spices come out much more. Quinoa is a high-protein grain native to the Andes (page 61). It can usually be found in natural food stores. The grain is very delicate so this dish looks most appealing if everything is cut as finely as possible.

SERVES 4

SALAD

1 cup quinoa
2 cups water
  salt, to taste
4 dried apricots, finely diced
2 tablespoons snipped chives
2 tablespoons currants, soaked in hot water then drained
¼ cup finely diced bell peppers, green, red, or yellow
2 tablespoons unsalted pistachio nuts, peeled and finely chopped
1 tablespoon almonds, toasted and finely chopped

1. Rinse the quinoa very well in cold water, then pour through a fine-meshed strainer. This rinsing is important for it removes a natural bitter coating on the seeds.
2. Bring water to a boil, add salt, then the quinoa. Lower the heat, cover, and cook until the grain tastes done, about 15–18 minutes. You will see a little white spiral in each grain and it should taste cooked but still a little crunchy. Drain, but save the liquid to use in soups.
3. Toss the cooked quinoa while still warm with the dressing, below, and the fruits, vegetables, almonds, and most of the pistachios. Mound in a bowl and garnish with the remaining pistachios.

DRESSING

grated zest of 1 large lime
2 tablespoons lime juice
2 teaspoons finely chopped cilantro, parsley, or dill
¼ teaspoon sweet paprika
½ teaspoon ground cumin
¼ teaspoon ground coriander
¼ teaspoon salt
4 tablespoons olive oil

Combine the zest, juice, spices, herbs, and salt together in a bowl, then whisk in the oil. Adjust the balance of flavors, adding more juice or oil to taste.

FAT PER SERVING: Saturated 3 grams; unsaturated 13 grams

Lentil Salad with Roasted Peppers and Mint

by Deborah Madison

*L*entil salads can take different turns depending on the dressing, but one usually begins by cooking lentils with aromatics until they are just done, that is firm, not mushy. The lentils are then tossed, while warm, with a zesty dressing. All of the dressings in this book—the lemon, mustard, and yogurt dressings, would be great with lentils. Feta cheese makes a wonderful sharp contrast in flavor and is an excellent addition crumbled over the salad.

The little slate-green lentils from Le Puy, France, are the best, for they always hold their shape and have a rich, delicious flavor. They can be found in specialty food stores. If they're not available, use the brown lentils, but watch them carefully so that they don't overcook.

SERVES 4 TO 6

1½ cups green or brown lentils
 1 medium carrot, peeled and cut in tiny, even squares
 ½ small onion, finely diced
 1 bay leaf
 1 large clove garlic, sliced
 ½ teaspoon salt
 2 Roasted Peppers (page 342), or 1 cup raw peppers, finely diced
    mustard or lemon vinaigrette (page 241)
 2 teaspoons fresh mint leaves, chopped
 3 tablespoons chopped parsley
    freshly ground pepper
 2 ounces feta cheese, crumbled

1. Rinse the lentils, cover them generously with water, and bring to a boil. Skim off any foam that rises to the top, then add the carrot, onion, bay leaf, garlic, and salt. Lower the heat and simmer until the lentils are tender but still firm, about 25 minutes. Drain (reserve the liquid for soup) and pull out the bay leaf. Set the lentils aside in a colander for a few minutes to finish draining.

2. Dice roasted or raw bell peppers. Red, yellow, or green peppers can be used, or a combination of the three.

3. Place the lentils in a bowl and toss with the peppers and enough vinaigrette to generously coat, the mint, and half the parsley. Taste and season with salt and pepper. Garnish with the remaining parsley and serve. The flavors are most aromatic when the salad is warm, but it does keep for several days and is very good later, served at room temperature.

FAT PER SERVING: Saturated traces; unsaturated 1–2 grams (depends on choice of dressing)

Oriental Broiled Tofu Salad

by Jody Main

This whole-meal salad keeps for several days because it is made with cabbage instead of lettuce. The flavors are those of a traditional Chinese salad.

SERVES 4 TO 8

1 broiled tofu, chilled
1 small head cabbage, shredded
2 cups cooked whole-grain rice spaghetti or whole-wheat pasta (page 315) (about 6 ounces dry)
1 bunch cilantro, chopped
1 scallion, chopped
2 tablespoons sesame seeds
1 tablespoon extra-virgin olive oil or sesame oil
1 tablespoon brown-rice vinegar
1 tablespoon red miso
1 teaspoon honey
2 tablespoons spring water
  dash white pepper

1. To broil tofu: If the cake is very thick, split in half. Drizzle with olive or sesame oil and vinegar or soy sauce. Broil about 5 minutes on each side, or until lightly browned.
2. Slice the tofu into attractive strips and combine with cabbage, noodles (spaghetti), cilantro, scallion, and sesame seeds.
3. Blend together the oil, vinegar, miso, honey, water, and pepper.
4. Toss with cabbage mixture and refrigerate 1–2 hours before serving.

FAT PER SERVING: Saturated 2 grams; unsaturated 11 grams

Upside-down Tofu Salad

by Jody Main

*T*his is a layered salad, good to take along for a picnic or lunch away from home. The vegetables on the bottom marinate in the dressing, while the leafy greens on top remain crisp until lunchtime. Tofu makes this salad very satisfying as a complete meal, when combined with some whole-grain bread.

SERVES 1

(1 container with a tight-fitting lid)
½ cake regular or firm tofu
½ sliced avocado
½ sliced tomato
½ bunch spinach, washed and gently torn
1 tablespoon vinegar
   juice of ½ fresh lemon
1 tablespoon natural soy sauce or tamari
   drizzle of sesame oil
   sprinkle of ginger, garlic powder, cayenne

Cut the tofu into small cubes and layer in the bottom of the container with the avocado and tomato. Blend together vinegar, lemon juice, soy sauce, sesame oil, ginger, garlic, and cayenne pepper and pour over tofu, tomato, and avocado. Cover with fresh spinach and seal container. Toss just before eating.

FAT PER SERVING: Saturated 3–4 grams; unsaturated 13–16 grams

Quinoa Salad

by Jody Main

*T*his is a very refreshing salad with a nourishing grain. It's a salad that travels well and is great for picnics.

SERVES 4

3 cups cooked quinoa (prepared from 1 cup dry quinoa; see page 304)
1 stalk celery, chopped fine
½ cucumber, chopped fine
1 carrot, grated
½ cup dried Greek-style olives, chopped
¼ cup fresh basil, chopped fine
½ cup sweet red pepper, chopped fine

Combine ingredients and toss with 4–6 tablespoons of your favorite dressing. The Cumin Parmesan Salad Dressing (page 236) is great on this salad.

FAT PER SERVING: Saturated approximately 2 grams; unsaturated 15 grams (depends on dressing)

Tempeh Salad

by Jody Main

A delightful salad in place of chicken or tuna salad, this dish can also be used as a sandwich spread, filling for a scooped tomato, or served on a bed of lettuce. Tempeh salad is also delicious on crackers or celery sticks for snacks or hors d'oeuvres.

SERVES 4

1 package tempeh (8 ounces)
¼ cup chopped celery
1 tablespoon minced parsley
2 teaspoons minced fresh herb (dill, basil, etc.)
½ teaspoon minced onion
1 teaspoon pickle relish
½ teaspoon prepared mustard
2 tablespoons natural soy sauce
¼ cup nonfat yogurt

Slice tempeh cake lengthwise to create two thin, flat cakes. Steam for 5–10 minutes. Cut into very small cubes and blend with remaining ingredients. Refrigerate for several hours for the flavors to marry.

FAT PER SERVING: Saturated 1–1.5 grams; unsaturated 7–8 grams

Lentil Salad

by Rowena Hubbard

*T*his chilled salad presents a dazzling variety of colors and textures.

SERVES 8

1 cup lentils
½ cup long-grain brown rice
⅔ cup vegetable stock or miso broth
1 cup water
   Mustard-Lemon Dressing (page 237)
½ cup diced red bell peppers
½ cup diced zucchini
½ cup sliced radishes
½ cup blanched slivered almonds, toasted
½ cup chopped parsley

Combine lentils, rice, vegetable stock or broth, and water in medium saucepan. Bring to a boil; cover and simmer 20 minutes. Remove from heat. Spoon hot lentil mixture into a large bowl and toss with Mustard-Lemon Dressing. Stir in red bell peppers, zucchini, and radishes. Cover and cool, tossing occasionally, to distribute dressing. Chill 2–4 hours. Just before serving, toss in almonds and parsley.

FAT PER SERVING: Saturated 1–2 grams; unsaturated 10–14 grams

Curried Couscous Salad

by Rowena Hubbard

SERVES 6

1½ cups miso (page 295) or vegetable broth or stock (page 267)
⅓ cup currants
1 teaspoon curry powder
¾ teaspoon ground cumin
1 cup uncooked couscous
½ cup thinly sliced green onions
½ cup whole natural almonds, toasted
¼ teaspoon grated lemon peel
2 tablespoons lemon juice
½ cup extra-virgin olive oil
¼ cup chopped parsley
    romaine lettuce leaves
2 tomatoes, cut into ¼-inch thick rounds

Combine broth, currants, curry powder, and cumin in medium sauce-pan; bring to a boil. Remove from heat; stir in couscous and green onions. Cover and let sit 5 minutes. Fluff couscous with a fork; cool. Grind 2 tablespoons almonds in blender. Add lemon peel, lemon juice, and olive oil; blend until thoroughly mixed. Toss cooled couscous with dressing, remaining almonds, and parsley. Line serving platter with lettuce leaves. Arrange tomato rounds to sides of platter and mound couscous in center to serve.

FAT PER SERVING: Saturated 2–3 grams; unsaturated 12–15 grams

Acapulco Salad

by Rowena Hubbard

SERVES 6

2 cups peeled jicama strips
   Chili Lime Dressing (page 237)
1 head lettuce leaves, rinsed and crisped
2 oranges, peeled and cut into rounds
1 tomato, cut into rounds
1 red bell pepper, cut into strips
8 ounces cooked kidney beans (page 327), drained
⅓ cup whole natural almonds, toasted
¼ cup thinly sliced green onions
2 tablespoons chopped cilantro
1 avocado

Toss jicama with Chili Lime Dressing in large bowl; let stand 20 minutes. Line serving platter with lettuce leaves. Toss remaining ingredients, except avocado, with jicama and dressing; arrange in center of serving platter. Peel, pit, and cut avocado into quarters; fan quarters and place on salad to serve.

FAT PER SERVING: Saturated 2–3 grams; unsaturated 13–16 grams

Pasta Salad Piquant

by Rowena Hubbard

SERVES 6

    2 medium tomatoes, diced
    2 tablespoons balsamic vinegar
    ¼ cup chopped fresh basil
    ¼ cup olive oil
    1 clove garlic, minced
1½ cups fresh whole-grain bread crumbs
    8 ounces bowtie, rotini, or similar pasta
    2 cups fresh chopped spinach
    ½ cup blanched slivered almonds, toasted

Toss together tomatoes, vinegar, and basil; set aside. Stir together olive oil and garlic in skillet over medium heat; cook until garlic is lightly browned. Stir in bread crumbs; cook, stirring constantly, until crumbs are golden brown. Remove from heat. Cook pasta in large pot of boiling water; stir in chopped spinach during last minute of cooking. Drain. Toss pasta with tomato mixture. Toss with bread crumb mixture and almonds. Serve at once.

FAT PER SERVING: Saturated 2–3 grams; unsaturated 12–16 grams

Zucchini Vinaigrette
by Rowena Hubbard

*T*his is a wonderful vegetable dish that is only lightly cooked.

SERVES 4

1 cup slivered almonds, toasted
⅓ cup almond or olive oil
¼ cup tarragon-flavored wine vinegar
1 tablespoon Dijon mustard
1 teaspoon seasoned salt
1 clove garlic, minced
½ teaspoon onion powder
½ teaspoon tarragon, crumbled
2 cups zucchini sticks
1 cup red bell pepper slivers
3 large oranges
1 head lettuce

Grind ½ cup almonds in food processor or with Mouli grater until fine. Combine ground almonds with oil, vinegar, mustard, salt, garlic, onion powder, and tarragon; mix well. Pour boiling water over zucchini; let stand 2 minutes or until slightly tender; drain. Toss zucchini with red peppers and dressing. Refrigerate several hours for flavors to blend. Peel oranges; slice thinly. Line serving plates with lettuce leaves. Arrange orange slices on lettuce; spoon zucchini mixture next to orange slices and top each plate with remaining ½ cup slivered almonds.

FAT PER SERVING: Saturated 2–3 grams; unsaturated 15–20 grams

Soups

AN INTRODUCTION TO SOUPS
by Deborah Madison

Soup is probably the most simple, easy, economical, and healthy food one can make. Whether thick or thin, made with one or two vegetables or a garden harvest, creamy or chunky, the basic method for soup making is quite similar from soup to soup. The technique goes more or less like this: Begin with a base of leeks or onions gently stewed in a little olive oil until they are soft. Bay leaf, thyme, garlic, and other herbs or spices are added to the onions while they are stewing, then after 10 or 15 minutes the main vegetable and the water or stock are added. When many vegetables are used, they may be added at different points as their cooking times vary. Potatoes are often included for body. Beans in soups are wonderful and their broth always makes a good, strong ingredient.

Garnishes for soups can be as simple as chopped parsley or an herb sauce such as pesto or salsa verde, a little freshly grated Parmesan cheese, croutons, or a spoonful of fragrant olive oil.

Soups often taste even better a day or two after they're made, which usually works in the cook's favor as it's easy to reheat soup after a day at work and have a more or less instant meal. Soup generally freezes well, so if you're cooking in quantity but don't want to eat the same soup all week, set some aside in the freezer for another time.

The soups chosen for this chapter are intended to give the reader a range of styles that harmonize with the Superpyramid, drawing heavily from the bottom tier. We begin with a basic Leek and Potato Soup and several variations, showing how you can expand upon the basic method of soup making. There are two vegetable stews, thicker and more hearty than soups and intended to be eaten with couscous or rice, and several soups that make use of legumes, showing their surprising versatility. Recipes are very easy to come by, for soup is a basic food in all cultures. Almost all cookbooks have a chapter devoted to soup. The Italians especially are great soup eaters and soup makers and they make great use of beans. Even if you are unfamiliar with soup making, once you try a few you will see all kinds of possibilities to explore.

VEGETABLE STOCKS FOR SOUP
by Deborah Madison

For many—even most—soups, no stock of any kind is necessary. If the soup is a simple vegetable soup, such as a carrot or fennel soup, a rich and complex stock gets in the way of the vegetables' own fine flavors. When the soup is one with many ingredients, such as a minestrone, or one with many spices, such as a curried soup, a stock isn't necessary because the ingredients themselves provide a great deal of rich flavor. Soups that do benefit from having a stock are broths and very thin soups, the kind that are usually dependent on a rich chicken broth. In such a case, the stock must be made with great care for it is, essentially, the soup and it has to be able to stand alone.

Frequently a simple stock suggests itself from the soup vegetables themselves. For example, mushroom stems, leek greens, and potato skins (the trimmings for a leek, mushroom, and potato soup) can be simmered for 25 minutes while the vegetables are being cut, then strained, the liquid used for the soup. In such a case the stock will taste thin by itself, but it echoes the flavors of the soup ingredients and thereby enhances the soup. When you cook your own beans, the resulting broth always makes an excellent, nutritious stock. The flavor isn't overly strong and the broth lends "body" wherever it is used. Always reserve the liquid in which legumes have been cooked. If garlic and herbs have been used with the beans, so much the better for the broth.

Recipes for vegetable stocks are usually not very well thought out. A good vegetable stock is not just a matter of a carrot, onion, and piece of celery. There are many surprising sources of flavor in the foods we use, not all of them obvious, while some of the more available items don't necessarily make a good stock. Cabbage trimmings, for example, do not go well in most stocks, onion skins are bitter, many greens and herbs can also turn bitter if cooked too long or allowed to steep. The subject of vegetable stock has been treated quite thoroughly in *The Greens Cookbook,* and several stock recipes are given there as well as a detailed list of ingredients and how they work if you wish to know more about vegetable stocks. The few recipes for stocks included here, however, are for soups that don't require a specially made broth for their success. Included are two stocks, one for summer and one for winter. Both stocks add flavor to soups.

A Good Basic Winter Vegetable Stock

By Deborah Madison

*T*his is a full-bodied stock that lends a good supporting role to delicate soups, such as the Potato-Leek Soup on page 271. Browning the vegetables first draws out their sugars, which then caramelize, ultimately contributing more flavor and body to the stock. If you don't have some ingredients, such as celery root trimmings, just omit them.

MAKES 7 CUPS

1½ tablespoons olive oil
  1 large onion, diced in ½-inch squares
  3 medium carrots, peeled and diced
  4 celery stalks plus leaves, diced
  ¼ teaspoon or several branches thyme
  3 bay leaves
  3 sage leaves
12 branches parsley, roughly chopped
  1 cup or more chopped winter squash, or the seeds and skins
  2 teaspoons nutritional yeast (optional)
  2 cups chard stems, cut in 1-inch lengths
  3 cups chopped leek greens
  1 medium potato or 1 cup thick potato parings
  ½ cup celery root or 1 cup parings
  ¼ cup lentils
  6 cloves garlic, unpeeled
1½ teaspoons salt
10 cups water

Warm the oil in a large soup pot and add the onion, carrots, celery, herbs, squash, and nutritional yeast. Sauté over a medium-high heat, stirring frequently, until the onions are a rich, golden brown, about 12 minutes. Add the rest of the ingredients, pour in the water, and bring to a boil. Lower the heat, simmer 40 minutes. Pour the stock through a sieve and press out as much of the liquid as possible.

FAT PER CUP: Saturated trace; unsaturated about 1–2 grams

A Good Basic Summer Vegetable Stock

By Deborah Madison

*T*his stock is naturally sweet and aromatic. If you have a garden, include some borage leaves or leek thinnings. The initial sautéing in oil helps develop flavor, but if a fat-free stock is desired, combine all ingredients, bring to a boil, then simmer.

MAKES ABOUT 7 CUPS

1 tablespoon olive oil
1 large onion, chopped in ½-inch squares
3 carrots, peeled and diced
3 celery stalks, chopped
8 branches parsley, chopped
2 bay leaves
   several large basil leaves or 1 teaspoon dried
   several branches marjoram or 1 teaspoon dried
2 teaspoons nutritional yeast
8 cloves garlic, unpeeled
1 potato, diced
4 ripe tomatoes, coarsely chopped
4 summer squash, diced
   handful green beans
2 cups chard leaves
1 cup chard stems
1 Asian eggplant, chopped
2–4 ounces mushrooms or mushroom stems
1 teaspoon salt
9 cups water

Heat the oil in a large soup pot and add the onion, carrots, celery, herbs, and yeast. Sauté, stirring frequently, until the onions are lightly browned, about 12 minutes, then add the remaining ingredients. Bring to a boil, then lower the heat and simmer for 40 minutes. Strain immediately.

FAT PER CUP: Saturated traces; unsaturated 1–2 grams

Potato-Leek Soup

by Deborah Madison

A peasant soup of leeks and potatoes boiled in water, the original may be a little bland for our tastes. Using a vegetable stock helps to develop more flavor. Use one of the basic stocks (either Winter or Summer) on pages 269–70, fortified with the leek roots, an extra potato or two, and a few cups of the leek greens. Although the ingredients are humble and the preparation simple, the resulting soup never fails to satisfy. Use plenty of leeks in proportion to potatoes.

This classic soup stands well alone, and it can also be used as a springboard for several other good soups made by basically the same method.

SERVES 4 TO 6

6 to 8 cups vegetable stock
5 medium-sized leeks (about 1¼ pounds)
1 pound red potatoes
2 tablespoons olive oil
1 teaspoon or less salt or to taste
   freshly ground pepper
   parsley or chervil, finely chopped

1. Make the soup stock first, as described on pages 269–70, using the leek trimmings and a few extra potatoes. While the stock is cooking, chop the leeks finely and rinse them well, and scrub the potatoes, cut them in quarters, and slice thinly.
2. Heat the oil in a soup pot, then add the leeks and potatoes. Stir quickly to coat them well, season with salt, and cook about 5 minutes, stirring frequently.
3. Pour in the stock, bring to a boil, then simmer until the potatoes are soft, about 35 minutes. Crush them against the side of the pot with the back of a spoon to break a portion of them up and thereby thicken the soup.
4. Taste the soup and season with additional salt, if needed. Serve with the freshly ground pepper and the chopped herbs.

FAT PER CUP: Saturated traces; unsaturated 1.5–2.5 grams

Leek, Mushroom, and Potato Soup

by Deborah Madison

*M*ushrooms make the Potato-Leek soup (page 271) richer with their woodsy flavor. The stems can be added to the stock ingredients, and a few dried wild mushrooms, soaked then sliced and added to the fresh mushrooms, would make a great addition. Be sure to use the soaking liquid in the soup.

To the list of ingredients for the Potato-Leek Soup add ½ pound (or more) sliced mushrooms and ¼ teaspoon each dried thyme and marjoram, and 1 clove minced garlic. Sauté the mushrooms, herbs, and garlic with the leeks and potatoes, then proceed according to the rest of the recipe. Serve the soup garnished with fresh herbs—parsley or chervil.

FAT PER CUP: Saturated traces; unsaturated 1.5–2.5 grams

Potato-Sorrel Soup

by Deborah Madison

*S*orrel is a tart green herb that looks much like spinach. Even large amounts cook to almost nothing, but its lemony acidic flavor goes far. It's best to have your own plant (an easy perennial) or a garden/market source. The little packages in the supermarket are better suited for adding to salads, as they are quite expensive to buy in sufficient quantity for a soup. Sorrel is a lively herb, and once cooked it is wonderful with potatoes and with eggs.

To the Potato-Leek Soup on page 271, add several handfuls of sorrel to the leeks, the stems first removed and the leaves coarsely shredded. If you have just a little sorrel, fine—use it! But you can use up to about 8 cups of leaves. Once it has wilted, after several minutes, add the potatoes, then the stock or water, and cook according to the directions. Serve the soup with freshly ground pepper and minced chives or fresh sorrel leaves, finely sliced in strips. The soup is good both hot and chilled. If serving it cold, stir in a spoonful of yogurt before serving.

Another good soup can be made by using chopped kale, the leaves first removed from the stems, in place of sorrel, or most any green. Using fewer potatoes will allow the chosen green to become the main character of the soup, but some potato is always helpful for both flavor and background texture.

FAT PER CUP: Saturated traces; unsaturated 1.5–2.5 grams

Potato-Fennel Soup

by Deborah Madison

B ulb fennel, or anise, makes a very refreshing soup. In this variation on the Potato-Leek Soup, page 271, replace half or more of the potatoes with thinly sliced fennel bulb. Reserve some of the greens for a garnish and use the stalks and trimmings in the soup stock. Proceed according to the directions for the Potato-Leek Soup. If you prefer a creamy-textured soup, puree the soup, then pass it through a sieve. Garnish with freshly ground pepper and scatter the fennel greens, finely chopped, over the top.

Another good winter soup can be made by replacing the potatoes with celery root. Fennel and celery root are very good together and the celery root provides the starch in this combination. If leeks aren't available, replace them with onions. Also consider using turnips or rutabagas along with potatoes—they sweeten the soup and give it subtle character.

FAT PER CUP: Saturated traces; unsaturated 1.5–2.5 grams

Lentil Soup with Spinach

by Deborah Madison

The pairing of greens with legumes occurs over and over again in recipes through-out the world. Lentils with spinach, white beans with kale, chickpeas with chard —there are endless variations on this theme. This is a beneficial pairing, for the greens brighten legumes and make them come alive, while the softer flavor of beans and lentils neutralizes the strength of some of the stronger, more bitter greens. This soup is but one example of this combination. Lentils are also particularly delicious with chard and sorrel, or a combination of greens.

For a special soup, make this, or any lentil dish, with the little green lentils from France. They are usually available in specialty stores. They are more expensive, but they have a richer flavor than brown lentils and they keep their shape and beautiful dark color.

SERVES 6

1½ cups lentils
3 tablespoons olive oil
1 bay leaf
1 onion, finely chopped
2 large cloves garlic, minced
2 stalks celery, finely diced
1 carrot, finely diced
1 tablespoon chopped fresh marjoram (in summer) or rosemary (in winter)
¼ cup chopped parsley
1 pound ripe or canned tomatoes, peeled, seeded, and chopped, juice reserved
1 teaspoon salt
7 cups water
1 bunch spinach, stems removed and leaves well washed
Parmesan cheese
freshly ground pepper

1. First go through the lentils, remove any stones, then wash them well. Cover with water, bring to a boil, and boil vigorously for 5 minutes. Remove any foam that rises to the surface, drain, and rinse.

2. Warm half the olive oil with the bay leaf, then add the bay leaf, onion, half the garlic, the celery, carrot, and herbs. Sauté over medium heat until the onions have softened, about 10 minutes.

3. In a soup pot, combine the lentils with the onion mixture, the tomatoes and their juice, and the water. Add salt. Bring to a boil, then lower the heat and simmer, partially covered, until the lentils are done. Taste and season, if needed, with more salt.

4. Just before serving, heat the remaining olive oil in a skillet and add the spinach leaves with the remaining garlic. Cook them briefly until they are just wilted and still bright green. (Or simply wilt them in a pan with the water that clings to their leaves.) Once cooked, cut into large pieces and stir the spinach into the soup. Serve with freshly grated Parmesan cheese and plenty of black pepper.

FAT PER SERVING: Saturated 0.5 gram; unsaturated 4–5 grams

Split-Pea Soup with Yogurt

by Deborah Madison

*T*ry *seasoning a pea soup with spiced yogurt instead of the usual smoky, salty ham bone. The ginger and cumin, along with the tart yogurt, greatly enliven dried legumes of all kinds, including peas. The same soup is also good made with yellow peas or red lentils. Although smaller than beans, dried peas need to be soaked before cooking, preferably overnight. Make the yogurt mixture first so the flavors have a chance to develop.*

SERVES 4–6

SPICED YOGURT

½ cup plain low-fat or nonfat yogurt
½ teaspoon each turmeric and paprika
¼ teaspoon each cayenne and cumin, or more to taste
    pinch of salt

Combine the yogurt and spices and stir together.

THE SOUP

2 cups split peas, soaked overnight
1 large onion, finely diced
2 cloves garlic, minced
1- inch piece fresh gingerroot, peeled and minced
1 bay leaf
2 tablespoons olive or sesame oil
½ teaspoon ground cumin
2 whole cloves or pinch of ground cloves
    salt to taste
2 branches celery, finely diced
2 carrots, peeled and finely diced
7 cups water or vegetable stock
    chopped cilantro

1. Drain the peas and set them aside.
2. Fry the onion, garlic, ginger, and bay leaf in the oil along with the cumin and cloves in a soup pot. When the onion is soft, after about 10 minutes, season with salt.

3. Add the peas, celery, carrots, and water or stock. Bring to a boil, then lower the heat and simmer, partially covered, until the peas are completely soft, about an hour.

4. Pass the soup through a food mill or puree in a blender, then return to the stove. Add more water or stock to achieve the consistency you like, and season to taste with salt. Serve with a spoonful of the spiced yogurt swirled in and a garnish of chopped cilantro.

FAT PER SERVING: Saturated 0.5–1 gram; unsaturated 4–5 grams (depends on kind of yogurt used)

Buttermilk Soup with Barley and Cucumbers

by Deborah Madison

Yogurt soups are found in the hot countries of the Mediterranean, the North African side, where the tartness of yogurt is welcome and refreshing. I prefer to use buttermilk instead of yogurt—it seems less sour and more consistent in its taste, but if you do use yogurt, use one that has not been stabilized with gelatin or other additives.

The barley gives a good chewy texture to the soup and sets off the buttermilk with its nutty flavor. You could also use cooked whole kernels of wheat, cracked wheat, or wild or brown rice to the same effect. A Bulgarian yogurt soup called tarator *uses crushed walnuts to give the soup body and texture.*

Additional variations can be made by using herbs other than those suggested below. Try different herbs—basil, lovage, marjoram, and thyme—as well as the dill-parsley-cilantro combination suggested, or something entirely different such as peppery watercress or arugula. This is a soup that lends itself easily to all kinds of variations and once the grain is cooked, it is quick to put together, requiring time only to chill.

SERVES 4

½ cup uncooked barley, rinsed
1 quart water
   salt to taste
1 quart low-fat buttermilk
½ cup finely chopped parsley, dill, and cilantro, mixed to taste
1 bunch scallions, finely chopped
1 large cucumber, peeled and coarsely grated
   grated zest and juice of 1 lemon
   freshly ground pepper
   herb blossoms for garnish, if available, or some of the chopped herbs, above

1. Combine the barley, water, and salt in a saucepan, bring to a boil, then lower the heat to a simmer. Cook until the barley is tender, about 40 minutes. When tender, drain, but reserve the liquid. Let stand until cool.

2. Put the cooled barley in a soup bowl with the rest of the ingredients, except the lemon juice and garnish. Stir gently to combine. Season with salt, pepper, and lemon juice to taste. If you wish a thinner soup, stir in the cooking liquid from the barley until you get the consistency you want.

3. Cover and refrigerate until chilled. Serve garnished with herb blossoms, or the parsley, chives, and dill. This is excellent with black bread, crackers, or a sturdy whole-wheat bread.

FAT PER SERVING: Saturated approximately 1–2 grams; unsaturated traces (depends on buttermilk used; you can raise the unsaturated fat by adding some olive or other vegetable oil)

Black Bean Chili

by Deborah Madison

*B*lack beans are common to Mexico and the Caribbean. They are especially popular for soups. The Black Bean Chili recipe from Greens has been on the menu for more than ten years! This is a simpler version than the one in The Greens Cookbook but it has a lot of flavor from the smoky-tasting chipotle chili (available canned, in adobo sauce, or dried). The chili is hot, so start with a little and taste as you go. A little grated cheese stirred in at the end is offered as an optional garnish. Some nonfat yogurt could also be used, or nothing at all.

SERVES 4 TO 6

2 cups black beans, soaked overnight
1 tablespoon olive or sesame oil
1 onion, finely diced
2 garlic cloves, minced
1 teaspoon ground cumin
½ teaspoon oregano
1 teaspoon paprika
1 16-ounce can tomatoes, chopped, with juice reserved
½ bunch cilantro, chopped
1 teaspoon or more minced chipotle chili, to taste
  cilantro leaves for garnish
  optional: 1 tablespoon grated muenster, Monterey Jack, or low-fat
    mozzarella cheese, per serving

1. Parboil the beans (see page 327), then put them in a pot with enough fresh water to cover by several inches. Bring to a boil, then lower the heat to a simmer.
2. While the beans are cooking, heat the oil in a skillet and add the onion, garlic, cumin, oregano, and paprika. Sauté until the onion has started to soften, about 10 minutes, then add to the beans along with the tomatoes and cilantro. As the beans cook, check the water liquid and make sure the beans are as thick or soupy as you want. Add more water if needed.
3. Add the minced chipotle in gradual amounts, tasting as you go.
4. Simmer the beans until they are fairly soft, about an hour, then season with salt and continue cooking until they are tender. Serve with

the grated cheese, if using, and a garnish of fresh cilantro leaves. Like most bean soups, this will taste better if it has a chance to sit even an hour, and best overnight.

FAT PER SERVING: Without cheese, traces only
With 1 tablespoon grated low-fat mozzarella per serving: saturated 1–1.5 grams; (you can raise the unsaturated fat by adding some more olive oil or other vegetable oil)

Minestrone

by Deborah Madison

*E*veryone knows some form of minestrone. This is a key recipe in the Superpyramid plan. It is a well-loved soup that is nourishing, comforting, and delicious. It is also an ideal soup as it draws completely from the lower two levels of the pyramid, combining vegetables and beans in one dish.

There are many styles of minestrone. Some include rice, pasta, or potatoes—or even two or three of these starches. Some, like the famous Pistou of Southern France, use largely summer vegetables, while others rely more heavily upon winter vegetables, particularly greens like chard and kale. In the fall you can make beautiful minestrone soups using pumpkins and squash along with the last good tomatoes and the first winter greens. Pasta e fagioli is yet another style of minestrone. There are enough versions to reflect a very wide range of seasonal ingredients and personal tastes.

Minestrone is a satisfying soup to make as well as to eat for there is nothing about it that's fussy or complicated. Although the list of ingredients appears long, the vegetables are easily prepared, mostly coarsely chopped and diced. A glance at Italian cookbooks will give you some more specific recipes to branch out from. Here's one to *start that features large white cannellini beans and lots of greens—a good fall or winter soup. Feel free about adding other available greens or other preferred vegetables.*

This is the kind of soup that improves with time. It's always better the second day, and well after that—a great convenience to the cook.

SERVES 6 TO 8

10 ounces cannellini or other white beans, soaked overnight
2½ quarts water
½ teaspoon dried sage or 3–4 sage leaves
   salt to taste
¼ cup olive oil
1 large onion, chopped in ½-inch squares
   two leeks, white parts only, chopped and rinsed well
2 small celery branches, diced
2 carrots, peeled and diced
3 garlic cloves, chopped
1 bay leaf
   approximately ½ cup chopped Italian parsley
8 ounces cabbage, preferably savoy, shredded or diced
1 bunch kale, the leaves removed from the stems and coarsely chopped
1 bunch green chard, the leaves removed from the stems and chopped
1 15-ounce can tomatoes, coarsely chopped
3 red potatoes, scrubbed and diced
   freshly ground pepper
   grated Parmesan Reggiano cheese

1. Rinse the beans and cook them according to the instructions on page 327. Remove any scum that forms, then add the sage, lower the heat, and simmer partially covered until the beans are tender, about an hour. When soft, add salt to taste. Drain the beans but reserve the broth. Puree half of them, or pass them through a food mill.
2. Heat the oil in a wide, ample soup pot and add the onion, leeks, celery, carrots, garlic, bay leaf, and parsley. Stir together to coat with the oil, then cook, stirring occasionally, for about 15 minutes or until the vegetables are lightly colored. Season with salt.
3. Next add the cabbage, kale, chard, tomatoes, and potatoes. Pour in a few cups of the bean broth, then cover and simmer for 15 minutes.
4. Now add the pureed beans and enough of the broth to make the soup the thickness you like. Continue to simmer until the potatoes and

kale are tender and the flavors have had a chance to marry, about another 20 minutes. Taste and season with salt, as needed.

5. When everything is cooked, stir in the rest of the beans and cook until they are warmed through. (At this point the soup can be served or it can be allowed to stand for a while. The flavors will develop as it stands.) Season with pepper, drizzle a little extra-virgin olive oil over the top, and serve with a piece of Parmesan Reggiano and a grater for people to grate into their own soup.

FAT PER SERVING: With about 1 teaspoon Parmesan Reggiano cheese per serving: saturated 1–2 grams; unsaturated 6–7 grams

Summer Minestrone with Fresh Tomatoes and Salsa Verde

by Deborah Madison

*B*eans need not be relegated to cold-weather menus if they are treated in a fashion that is light and fresh. In this soup nearly all the beans are left whole so that the consistency is thin rather than thick, and the sauce of wonderful and green herbs lends a fresh, vibrant note. This would be a good soup for the end of the summer when tomatoes are really flavorful and fall is finally on the horizon. If allowed to sit a day before serving, the flavors will soften and build.

SERVES 4

1 cup dry navy, cannellini, or other white beans, soaked 6 hours or
   overnight
3 quarts (12 cups) water
10 sage leaves or 1 teaspoon dried sage
6 cloves garlic, peeled
2 bay leaves
   several thyme branches or two pinches dried thyme
3 tablespoons fruity olive oil
   salt to taste
1 onion, finely diced
1 pound ripe tomatoes, peeled, seeded, and chopped
½ pound green or yellow beans, cut in ½-inch lengths
   freshly ground pepper
   Salsa Verde (page 230)
   grated Parmesan cheese (optional)

1. Precook the beans (page 327), then put them in the soup pot with the 3 quarts fresh water, half the sage, half the garlic, the bay leaves, thyme, and a tablespoon of the oil. Bring to a boil, then lower the heat and simmer slowly, partially covered, until the beans are tender but still have some texture, about an hour. Season to taste with salt, then drain in a colander, reserving the cooking liquid.
2. Warm the remaining oil in the soup pot with the rest of the sage, the garlic, thinly sliced, and the onion. Cook until the onion is soft, stirring frequently, about 10 minutes. Once it's tender, add the tomatoes, most of the broth, and the green beans. Taste and season with salt, if needed. Simmer 10 minutes or until the green beans are cooked.

3. Puree ½ cup of the white beans in a blender or food processor with a cup of the remaining broth. Add it to the soup along with the rest of the beans.

4. Serve the soup with freshly ground pepper and a spoonful of the Salsa Verde stirred in at the last minute. If you like, add a little freshly grated Parmesan. A toasted piece of bread brushed with olive oil and rubbed with a garlic clove would be fine served alongside or right in the bowl of soup.

FAT PER SERVING: With 1 teaspoon Parmesan cheese per serving: saturated 1 gram; unsaturated 6–8 grams

White Bean and Pasta Soup with Sage (Pasta e Fagioli)

by Deborah Madison

Pasta e fagioli *is the most basic, simple, and satisfying soup. Here is a bare-bones recipe that needs nothing else, but could become a more complex soup with the addition of other vegetables or garnishes of herb sauces, or a somewhat different soup with the use of red beans rather than white. An excellent olive oil is a most important ingredient, added at the end. In Italy it would be on the table, in a cruet, for you to add as you wish.*

Like most soups with beans, this one will gain in flavor if allowed to sit several hours or even overnight before serving. If you plan to do this, wait until just before serving to add the pasta so it will keep its texture.

SERVES 6 OR MORE

    2 cups cannellini beans or other white bean, soaked overnight
   10 cups water
    1 large onion, finely diced
    4 cloves garlic, peeled and sliced
    6 sage leaves or 2 teaspoons dried sage
2–3 tablespoons olive oil
      salt and pepper to taste
    1 pound tomatoes, peeled, seeded, and chopped
   ½ cup dried pasta shapes, cooked and rinsed
      chopped parsley
      freshly ground pepper
      extra-virgin olive oil
      grated Parmesan cheese (optional)

1. Cover the beans with fresh water, bring to a boil for 5 minutes, then drain and rinse. Return the beans to a soup pot and add water, the onion, half the garlic, the sage leaves, and a tablespoon of olive oil. Bring to a boil, then lower the heat and simmer the beans, partially covered, until they are tender. Season to taste with salt.

2. Remove a cup of the beans and puree in a blender with some of the broth, then return the puree to the pot. This will give the soup a rich background texture.

3. Warm the remaining oil in a pan with the remaining garlic. When you can smell the garlic, add the chopped tomatoes, season with salt and pepper, and stew for about five minutes. Break up the tomatoes with a spoon, as they cook, so that they form a kind of rough sauce, then add them to the beans. Or, if you prefer a smoother, more uniform soup, puree them first.

4. Bring the soup up to temperature, then stir in the cooked pasta just before serving.

5. Ladle into bowls and add a little parsley, plenty of pepper, and a spoonful of extra-virgin olive oil to each bowl. If you like, freshly grated Parmesan cheese can be served as well, but the soup should have ample flavor without it. If you have an abundance of fresh sage leaves, fry them in a little olive oil until they are crisp and dark, shiny green. Crumble them into the soup just before serving, or float a single whole leaf in each bowl. Sage with white beans is a classic combination, but rosemary is also wonderful with beans. These are both strong herbs which are not always easy to use, but both work well here.

FAT PER SERVING: Saturated 1–2 grams; unsaturated 6–7 grams

Vegetable Soup with Pesto (*Soupe au Pistou*)

by Deborah Madison

*T*his famous Provençal soup is a minestrone type of soup for early summer when vegetables are abundant, sweet, and tender. Let your market or garden determine the soup and use what looks the freshest. Peas, summer squash, new leeks and onions, bell peppers, tender young turnips, and green beans might all be among your chosen vegetables. The finishing sauce, the pistou (or pesto) is well known as a sauce for pasta. This version for Soupe au Pistou, however, includes tomato.

The amounts given are suggested guidelines. You'll need about 8 cups chopped vegetables in all, including onion, but they need not be these exact vegetables, or in these exact proportions.

SERVES 8

½ cup dried navy beans, soaked overnight
10 cups water
3 cloves garlic, peeled
4 branches parsley
 pinch of thyme
2 bay leaves
 salt
2 tablespoons olive oil
1 medium onion, finely chopped
2 leeks, white part only, diced and rinsed
4 carrots, peeled and chopped
4 medium-sized new potatoes, scrubbed and cubed
¼ cup chopped parsley
1 branch thyme leaves, or several pinches dried thyme
3 medium-sized turnips, diced
1 pound tender green beans, cut in ½-inch pieces
1 pound peas, shelled, or 1 cup frozen
2 medium-sized zucchini, diced in cubes
½ cup spinach pasta (shapes or broken spaghetti), boiled in salted water,
 then drained and rinsed under cold water
 freshly ground pepper
 Pistou (see below)

1. Blanch the beans according to the instructions on page 327, then rinse and cover with water. Add the garlic, parsley, thyme, and one bay leaf, bring to a boil, then simmer until the beans are tender. Season with salt. Drain, but reserve the liquid. Remove the bay leaf and parsley.

2. Heat the oil in a spacious soup pot and add the onion, leeks, carrots, and potatoes. Stir everything together, season with salt, and add the second batch of parsley, bay leaf, and thyme. Pour in the reserved liquid from the beans, bring to a boil, then simmer until the vegetables are tender but firm, about 25 minutes.

3. Add the turnips, green beans, peas, and zucchini. Simmer 10 minutes more or until tender. Then add the cooked beans and the pasta and heat through. If the soup is too thick, thin with water as needed. Taste for salt and season with pepper. Serve the soup with a spoonful of the sauce stirred into each bowl.

THE PISTOU

*F*or the tomato paste, the kind that comes in a tube is excellent. For a puree, a fresh tomato puree would be preferable to a canned one.

    4 cloves garlic
    salt
2–3 tablespoons tomato paste or 3–4 tablespoons tomato puree
    approximately ⅓ cup fresh basil leaves, finely chopped
    ⅓ cup freshly grated Parmesan cheese
    ¼ cup or more, as needed, extra-virgin olive oil

Using a mortar and pestle, pound the garlic cloves with a pinch of salt until they are well broken up, then work in the tomato paste or puree, making a smooth paste. Next add the basil and the cheese and stir in enough olive oil to make a thick sauce.

FAT PER SERVING: Saturated 1.5–3 grams; unsaturated 6–8 grams

Split-Pea Soup with Wild Rice

by Jody Main

This is an easy-to-make, flavorful soup much enjoyed on a cold night with a dollop of nonfat yogurt or crunchy sunflower seeds.

SERVES 8–12

2 cups split peas
10 cups water
¼ cup wild rice
¼ cup long-grain brown rice
3 large cloves garlic, crushed
3 tablespoons natural soy sauce

Bring ingredients to a boil, turn down heat, cover and simmer gently for 1½ hours or until creamy but not too thick. Stir frequently toward the end of cooking.

FAT PER CUP: Traces only

Hearty Broccoli-Potato-Almond Soup

by Rowena Hubbard

A good combination of potatoes, a dark green vegetable (broccoli), and almond (a good tier-three food).

MAKES ABOUT 7 CUPS

> 3 medium potatoes (about 1 pound)
> 4 cups plain miso broth (page 295)
> 2 green onions, sliced
> ½ cup ground almonds, toasted
> 1½ cups chopped broccoli
> 1 teaspoon garlic salt
> dash of pepper
> 1 cup nonfat plain yogurt
> blanched slivered almonds, toasted
> chopped parsley

Peel and dice potatoes. Put in saucepan with broth and onions. Bring to boil; then simmer, covered, 10 minutes, or until tender. Add ground almonds and broccoli; cook 3 minutes. Pour into food processor or blender jar. Cover and process until smooth. Stir in seasonings and yogurt; garnish with slivered almonds and parsley to serve. Soup may be chilled and served cold.

FAT PER CUP: Saturated 0.5 gram; unsaturated 5–7 grams

Lentil-Pumpkin Soup Amandine

by Rowena Hubbard

*T*his is an easy microwave oven recipe that can be modified to stovetop cooking if you prefer.

SERVES 4

½ cup blanched slivered almonds
2 tablespoons olive oil
1 cup chopped onions
½ cup chopped celery
1 teaspoon curry powder
1 can (16 ounce) solid pack pumpkin
1 cup vegetable stock (page 267) or miso broth (page 295)
2 cups water
½ cup dry lentils
1 tablespoon lemon juice
1 cup low-fat milk
1 tablespoon honey
½ cup nonfat plain yogurt

IN MICROWAVE

1. Spread almonds in single layer on microwave-safe plate. Microwave on high power for 3 minutes, stirring halfway through. Cool. Remove ⅓ cup toasted almonds; chop finely in food processor or electric blender. Set aside.

2. Add olive oil to large microwave-safe bowl. Stir in onions, celery, and curry powder. Cover bowl with waxed paper; microwave at high power 5 minutes. Remove from microwave; stir in pumpkin, vegetable stock or broth, water, lentils, and lemon juice. Cover bowl with waxed paper or lid; microwave on high power 20 minutes, stirring mixture every 5 minutes.

3. Remove soup from microwave; stir in reserved chopped almonds, milk, and honey. Ladle soup into serving bowls. Just before serving, dollop each bowl with 2 tablespoons yogurt and sprinkle with reserved almonds.

OVEN/STOVETOP

To toast almonds in conventional oven, spread almonds in single layer on baking sheet. Bake at 350° F. for 9 to 11 minutes, stirring occasionally, until golden brown. Cool.

To cook soup on the stove, increase water to 3 cups. Bring pumpkin, vegetable stock, and lentil mixture to a boil. Reduce heat and simmer 25 minutes, stirring frequently, until lentils are tender.

FAT PER SERVING: Saturated 1 gram; unsaturated 7–8 grams

Almond-Vegetable Soup

by Rowena Hubbard

SERVES 4

¾ cup whole natural almonds, toasted
1 onion, cut into narrow wedges
½ cup sliced celery
1 green bell pepper, cut into slivers
2 tablespoons extra-virgin olive oil, sesame (not toasted), or almond oil
1 cup miso broth (page 295) or vegetable stock (page 267)
½ cup dry white wine
1 medium clove garlic, minced
1 teaspoon basil, crumbled
½ teaspoon oregano, crumbled, or fresh oregano leaves
⅛ teaspoon pepper
1 medium tomato, cut into small chunks

Place almonds in food processor and process stop-and-go fashion, using double-bladed steel knife, until coarsely chopped. Sauté onion, celery, and green pepper in oil just until tender-crisp. Mix in stock or broth, wine, garlic, basil, oregano, and pepper. Heat through. Add tomato and heat through. Ladle into soup bowls. Spoon almonds into centers of bowls.

FAT PER SERVING: Saturated 2–3 grams; unsaturated 14–18 grams

Southwestern Corn Soup

by Rowena Hubbard

SERVES 4

¾ cup slivered almonds
4–5 ears fresh corn
  2 tablespoons extra-virgin olive oil
  ½ cup each chopped carrots, celery, and onions
  1 clove garlic, minced
  1 teaspoon ground cumin
  3 cups miso broth (page 295) or vegetable stock (page 267)
  ½ teaspoon ground white pepper
    Fresh Garden Salsa (page 235)

Spread almonds in single layer on baking sheet. Bake at 375° F., 6 to 8 minutes, until golden brown; cool. Slice corn kernels from ears; set aside. Pour oil into large saucepan. Add carrots, celery, and onions; cook over low heat, stirring occasionally until soft but not browned. Stir in garlic and cumin; cook 1 minute. Add broth or stock, corn kernels, and pepper. Simmer 20 to 25 minutes until corn is very tender. Transfer to a food processor or blender. Add toasted almonds. Process until smooth. Serve hot or cold, topped with Fresh Garden Salsa.

FAT PER SERVING: Saturated 2–3 grams; unsaturated 14–18 grams

Miso Broth

by Gene Spiller

A simple, instant broth can be made using miso, for a wonderful warm drink. Place from one teaspoon to one tablespoon of miso paste—whichever type of miso you like best—in a cup of warm or hot water. Stir and drink. You may vary this in many ways by adding some precooked vegetables or some vegetable soup stock.

A few pieces of a good whole-grain bread—fresh or toasted—in this broth give you a great grain-bean combination. Or you can merge the Mediterranean with the Oriental by using some Bruschettes—whole-grain bread slices toasted at a low temperature in the oven (page 356). For a true Oriental soup you can add some precooked brown rice. Remember that miso gives foods a wonderful flavor in place of salt or meat stock.

Serve cold for a summer day pick-me-up instead of a sweet drink. Some dry miso products are available in individual serving packets that are wonderful for travel.

FAT PER SERVING: Traces

Miso Soup

by Jody Main

*T*his is a great Asian soup that is easy to prepare. Rich and flavorful, Miso Soup is perfect as a breakfast broth, an afternoon revitalizer, or served with the evening meal. Kombu is a sea vegetable that is found in many specialty stores. You may replace it with another available sea vegetable. Kombu is mild in flavor but adds depth and character to miso soups and other soups and bean dishes.

SERVES 4

1 6-inch strand of kombu
4 cups water
4 tablespoons red miso
¼ cake tofu, cut into small ¼ inch cubes
1 scallion, sliced thin

Simmer kombu and water for 10 minutes. Turn off heat and remove kombu. Stir in miso, add tofu, sprinkle with scallions, and serve.

FAT PER SERVING: Traces

Grains and Pasta

RICE, QUINOA, AND OTHER WHOLE GRAINS

Basic Brown Rice

by Deborah Madison

*T*his method works for long-grain, short-grain, and brown basmati rice and should
yield perfect rice every time. Using a good heavy pan with a lid that fits well is
most important for making perfect rice. Try different varieties of rice for subtle differences in taste.

MAKES ABOUT 2 CUPS COOKED RICE

1 cup rice
2 cups water
¼–½ teaspoon salt, or salt to taste

Rinse the rice well and pour off the water. Discard any chaff or damaged
grains. Put the rice in a pot, add the water and salt, and bring to a boil.
Turn the heat to low, put on the lid, and cook 40 minutes. When rice is
done, all the water will be absorbed and the rice will be tender and a
little chewy. Using a fork, lightly break up the grains and transfer them
to a serving dish.

TROUBLESHOOTING

If not all the liquid has been absorbed but the rice is done (the heat was perhaps too low), remove the lid and cook a few more minutes or until the excess liquid has cooked off.

If the rice isn't done to your satisfaction but the water has cooked off (perhaps the heat was a little too high or the lid didn't fit well), add more water in small increments—say two tablespoons at a time—cover and continue cooking until the rice is done.

VARIATIONS

1. Cook the rice with a little olive oil and chopped herbs, such as marjoram and thyme, and freshly ground pepper.

2. Sauté the rice first for 4–5 minutes in a few teaspoons olive oil with herbs, salt and pepper, a sliver of garlic, then add the water and cook as above.

FAT PER SERVING: None

Rice with Fennel and Cheese

by Deborah Madison

*F*ontina cheese is wonderful with the fennel, but it is one of the fattier cheeses, so it is used here in combination with a low-fat mozzarella and Parmesan Reggiano.

Fennel is most available in the spring and fall. It is commonly sold by the name anise. When it's not available, try the same rice dish with other vegetables, such as cubes of winter squash or summer squash, celery root or corn.

SERVES 4 TO 6

1½ cups long-grain brown rice
2 fennel bulbs (about 6 ounces each)
3–4 tablespoons olive oil
1 medium onion or 2 leeks (white part only), finely chopped
½ teaspoon fennel seeds
2 tablespoons each chopped parsley and fennel greens
  salt and pepper
½ cup white wine
1 cup water
2 ounces low-fat mozzarella cheese, cut in cubes or coarsely grated
½ ounce fontina cheese, grated
2 tablespoons almonds, roasted and chopped
1 ounce Parmesan Reggiano

1. Cook the rice according to the instructions on page 297. While the rice is cooking, pull off the outer leaves of the fennel if they are bruised. Quarter the bulbs and remove the cores. Cut into pieces about ¼ inch square.
2. Warm the oil in a sauté pan. Add the fennel, onion or leeks, fennel seeds, and half the fresh herbs. Season with salt and pepper, then pour in the wine and simmer until the liquid is reduced to a syrupy glaze. Add the water and continue cooking until the vegetables are tender.
3. Toss the cooked rice with the fontina and mozzarella along with the vegetables and remaining herbs. Garnish with the toasted almonds and plenty of black pepper. Serve with Parmesan Reggiano shaved or finely grated over the rice.

FAT PER SERVING **(6 SERVINGS):** Saturated 1.5 grams; unsaturated 5–6 grams

Sunflower Rice

by Jody Main

*T*his is a crunchy, delightful dish that combines the rice with a seed rich in unsaturated fat. You can choose monounsaturated or polyunsaturated sunflower seeds.

SERVES 4

1 cup long-grain brown rice
2 cups water
1 scallion, sliced
1 tablespoon sesame oil
1 tablespoon natural soy sauce
1 cup baby sunflower sprouts (page 217) (from about ½ cup raw whole, hulled sunflower seeds)

Rinse rice. Bring water to a boil, add rice, lower heat, and simmer on low, covered, for 30–45 minutes until water is absorbed. Toss with scallion, sesame oil, soy sauce, and sunflower sprouts. Serve immediately.

FAT PER SERVING: (varies with degree of sprouting of sunflowers)
Saturated 0.5 gram; unsaturated 3 grams

Wehani Pilaf

by Jody Main

*W*ehani rice is a beautiful raspberry-colored rice developed from the aromatic basmati rice. Wehani fills the house with the aroma of popcorn as it cooks. Its festive color makes wehani a lovely holiday dish.

SERVES 8

1 cup wehani rice
1 onion, finely chopped
2 cups vegetable stock (page 267) or water
¼ cup currants
½ cup walnuts, finely chopped
1 tablespoon extra-virgin olive oil

Bring the rice and onion to a boil in the 2 cups of water or vegetable stock. Turn down heat and simmer gently, covered, for 1 hour or until water is absorbed. Remove from heat, add the currants and olive oil, and let steam for 15 minutes. Toss in walnuts and serve immediately.

Basmati, an aromatic rice, or long-grain brown rice may be used in place of wehani.

FAT PER SERVING: Saturated 0.5 gram; unsaturated 5–6 grams

Sprouted-Grain Pilaf

by Jody Main

*T*his is a flavorful, rich, and nutty grain dish. It is wonderful served as a main course with sizzling sautéed mushrooms.

SERVES 4

⅓ cup long-grain brown rice
⅛ cup lentils
1 tablespoon wheat berries
1 tablespoon sesame seeds
1 cup water

Soak the rice, lentils, wheat berries, and sesame seeds overnight. Rinse and drain several times the next day (see page 216, "How to Sprout Seeds," for more information). That evening, the sprouts are just budding and ready to cook. The ½ cup seed mixture will grow to 1⅓ cups of sprouts. Bring the water with the sprouts to a boil, turn the heat down to low, cover, and let simmer gently for 20 minutes. Remove from heat and leave covered for another 10 minutes or until the water has been absorbed by the sprouted seeds. Fluff with a fork and serve.

FAT PER SERVING: Saturated traces; unsaturated 0.5–1 gram

Millet Pilaf

by Deborah Madison

*M*illet makes a lovely golden pilaf, but it behaves differently from rice and wheat in that its grains do not come out light and distinctly separate. Millet also absorbs much more liquid than other grains do. A good juicy vegetable stew with a wonderful tomato broth or grilled tomatoes would be ideal to serve in tandem. Roasted peppers or finely diced tomato added at the end make a good-tasting and good-looking garnish.

For best results in cooking millet as well as other grains, make sure your pot has a tight-fitting lid so that the steam will be trapped.

SERVES 4

3–4 tablespoons olive or light sesame oil
  1 cup millet
  1 small onion, finely diced
  ⅛ teaspoon saffron threads or powdered saffron
  1 bay leaf
  ¼ teaspoon turmeric
  2 teaspoons marjoram leaves, finely chopped, or ½ teaspoon dried
  2 tablespoons parsley, finely chopped
  2 tablespoons basil leaves, or 1 teaspoon dried
    salt and pepper
  2 cups water
  ½ cup diced roasted peppers (optional)
  ½ cup diced tomatoes (optional)
    Fresh herbs for garnish

1. Warm half the oil in a skillet, add the millet, and stir over a medium heat until the grains have begun to color and pop, about 4 minutes. Remove from the heat and set aside in a bowl.

2. Heat the remaining oil in the same skillet and add the onion, saffron, bay leaf, turmeric, and herbs. Cook over medium heat until the onion is thoroughly warm, about 5 minutes. Season with salt and a few twists of pepper.

3. Add the toasted millet to the sautéed mixture and pour in the water. Give a stir, bring to a boil, then cover and adjust the heat to very low. Cook for 40 minutes, then remove the lid and taste the grain to make sure it is done. If it isn't quite done but the water has been absorbed, add 2 or 3 tablespoons of water, cover, and continue to cook another 5 minutes or until done.

4. When done, add the peppers and tomatoes, if using, and gently loosen the grains with a fork and heap them into a serving dish. Garnish with the fresh herbs and serve.

FAT PER SERVING: Saturated 1–1.5 grams; unsaturated 6–8 grams

Basic Quinoa or Quinoa Stuffing

by Jody Main

This is a basic quinoa recipe to enjoy as a main grain dish or as a good stuffing in other recipes.

SERVES 4 AS A MAIN DISH

1 cup minced onion
2 tablespoons extra-virgin olive oil
1 cup minced celery
2 cups minced mushrooms
1 cup quinoa, rinsed well
2 cups water
2 tablespoons fresh chopped parsley
1 teaspoon fresh chopped oregano or sage
2 teaspoons natural soy sauce

Sauté onion in olive oil for 1 minute. Add celery and sauté for another minute. Add mushrooms and sauté for another minute. Add the remaining ingredients and bring to a boil. Turn down heat, cover, and simmer gently for 15 minutes. Turn off heat and let steam for another 10 minutes. Fluff with a fork and serve or fill a prebaked squash and reheat at 350° F for 15–30 minutes or until hot.

FAT PER SERVING: Saturated 0.5–1 gram; unsaturated 4–5 grams

POLENTA

by Deborah Madison

Polenta is a wonderful food to have in your repertoire. It is versatile, delicious, inexpensive, and easy to make. Once cooked, it can be eaten while soft or left to harden and later heated and used to accompany other dishes, such as a sauté of wild mushrooms or greens with garlic. Firm polenta can also be sliced, layered with a tomato sauce and cheeses, and baked into a fragrant casserole. Its uses are virtually unlimited and a glance at Italian cookbooks, especially those on Northern Italy where polenta is a staple food, will yield many recipes and ideas. It has become so popular in America that cookbooks on contemporary American cooking, especially vegetarian books, also have recipes for dishes based on polenta.

Many recipes will undoubtedly call for large quantities of creamy cheeses, for fontina, gorgonzola, and Tallegio cheese are all wonderful with polenta. You should be prepared to scale the amounts way down, as such cheeses are borderline tier-five cheeses, at the limit of fat content allowed on the Superpyramid. Use these cheeses in recipes only occasionally. Polenta is the perfect medium for cheese—the mildness of the corn doesn't obscure the flavors of the cheeses, which helps their taste go further than if they were used with more strongly flavored foods. Although you won't be using them with abandon, combining the high-fat cheeses with some lower-fat cheeses such as low-fat mozzarella or ricotta will help extend the "cheesiness" of the dish.

And don't forget that polenta by itself, without cheese, simply grilled or broiled, makes a wonderful accompaniment to many vegetable dishes.

To make polenta to use later, pour the warm polenta as soon as it's finished cooking onto a sheet pan that has been rinsed with water but not dried. Spread the polenta out with a metal spatula as soon as it hits the pan for it will set rather quickly. If you spread it thinly (a half-inch or less), you can later cut out pieces with a biscuit cutter, overlap them in a gratin dish, and bake with tomato sauce and grated cheese. You can also pour the polenta into a bread pan (easier than spreading it out on a sheet pan) and when you unmold it later you'll have a loaf shape from which to cut thick or thin slices. It will take longer to cool and set but is very convenient to store, and will be easy to take on a picnic or to slice and grill over the coals. Similarly, you can pour warm polenta into a casserole or any other dish that suits your fancy.

Basic Polenta

by Deborah Madison

*P*olenta *can be served as soon as it has finished cooking or poured into a dish, left to harden, and later baked, fried, or grilled and served with vegetable accompaniments.*

Try to use a coarse cornmeal made from whole corn. It's often available in natural food stores.

SERVES 4 TO 6

4 cups water
1 teaspoon salt
1 ½ cups coarse cornmeal or polenta
   salt and pepper to taste
   ¼ to ½ cup grated Parmesan cheese (optional)

1. Bring the water to a boil in a heavy, roomy saucepan, then add the salt. Pour the polenta in a thin, steady stream, stirring while you do so. Use a wooden spoon rather than a whisk because the polenta will soon become quite thick.
2. Cook over a low heat, stirring frequently, for about 25 minutes.
3. When done, remove from the heat and season with salt and pepper. Stir in the cheese, if using. Pour onto heated plates and serve.

If you intend to serve it in the soft form but aren't quite ready for it, hold the polenta in a double-boiler.

FAT PER SERVING (4 SERVINGS): With ¼ cup Parmesan Reggiano (add some olive oil to increase unsaturated fat) saturated 1–2 grams; unsaturated 0.5–1 grams

Soft Polenta with Fontina and Gorgonzola

by Deborah Madison

*T*his is a recipe with two cheeses that are at the limit of tier-five cheeses for fat content. Use this for a very occasional change and not more than once a month. When you use this recipe, be sure the rest of the meal is free from other animal fats. Notice that the recipe contains more saturated than unsaturated fat. Combine it with a salad dressed with an olive oil dressing or other source of unsaturated oils. You may also choose low-fat cheeses from tier four and just a trace of gorgonzola and fontina cheese.

SERVES 6 TO 8

½ cup coarsely grated fontina or Gruyère cheese
½ cup gorgonzola
⅓ cup grated Parmesan Reggiano

Stir cheeses into Basic Polenta (page 306). Season with pepper and serve right away.

This polenta, hardened then sliced, makes a wonderful foundation for gratins and casseroles, or can be served broiled with sautéed tomatoes or a fresh tomato sauce.

FAT PER SERVING (6 SERVINGS): Saturated 10–11 grams; unsaturated 6–7 grams
(If you replace the fontina and gorgonzola cheeses—except for a trace for flavor—with low-fat mozzarella: saturated 6–7 grams; unsaturated 3–4)

Soft Polenta with Bread Crumbs and Parmesan

by Deborah Madison

Moisten a half-cup of fresh bread crumbs with a little olive oil, then toast them in the oven or brown them in a skillet. When cool, toss with a few tablespoons of freshly grated Parmesan cheese and finely chopped parsley, and season with salt and pepper. Sprinkle this on soft Basic Polenta (page 306).

FAT PER SERVING: Saturated 1–2 grams; unsaturated 2–4 grams (depends on amounts of cheese and oil used)

Soft Polenta with Parmesan Reggiano

by Deborah Madison

Use a vegetable peeler to remove large, thin shavings from a piece of good Parmesan Reggiano. Pile it over the warm soft polenta (page 306), drizzle with extra-virgin olive oil and freshly milled pepper, and serve right away. This is simple but very delicious.

FAT PER SERVING: Saturated 1–2 grams; unsaturated 2–4 grams (depends on amounts of cheese and oil used)

Polenta Gratin with Mushrooms

by Deborah Madison

*H*ere's an example of a simple gratin that can be made with polenta and tomato sauce. The original recipe, from **The Greens Cookbook,** *was also embellished with creamy fontina and gorgonzola cheeses. This version uses far less cheese and relies instead on a garnish of sautéed mushrooms for a strong, complementary flavor. The mushrooms could be sautéed, then layered with the polenta, or served on the side, as they are here. Spinach and other greens, quickly sautéed with garlic, are also very good alongside this gratin.*

This is the kind of dish that can be made easily from leftovers. With a little polenta and tomato sauce in the refrigerator, you can make a meal for one or two in a flash, or start from scratch and make it for six.

If you have chosen fontina cheese, do not use this recipe more than once a month.

SERVES 4 TO 6

    Fresh Tomato Sauce (page 227)
½ teaspoon finely chopped rosemary, or 2 teaspoons marjoram leaves, or
    a pinch of thyme
    Basic Polenta (page 306)
  2 ounces grated fontina or Parmesan cheese
  1 pound fresh mushrooms, thinly sliced
  2 tablespoons olive oil, plus some for brushing the dish
  2 cloves garlic, finely chopped
2–3 tablespoons chopped parsley
  ¼ cup red or white wine
    freshly ground pepper

1. Season the fresh tomato sauce with herbs.

2. Make the polenta according to the directions. When it is finished cooking, pour it onto a sheet pan or other convenient pan and set aside until it has cooled and hardened, about ½ hour. Cut into pieces about ½-inch thick and three inches long, or whatever suits your fancy.

3. Put about ½ cup of the sauce in the bottom of a gratin dish that has been lightly brushed with oil. Arrange the sliced polenta over the sauce in overlapping layers. (There may be more polenta than you can use.) Spoon the remaining sauce in between the pieces of polenta and scatter the cheese over all. Bake in a 400° F. oven until the gratin is hot and bubbling, about 25 minutes.

4. As soon as the gratin has finished baking, heat the olive oil in a skillet and, when hot, add the mushrooms. Immediately stir to coat them with the oil. After about 4 minutes, when the mushrooms are warm and have begun to release their liquid, add the garlic, half the parsley, and the wine. Continue to sauté until the mushrooms are done, another 5 minutes or less, depending on how you like them. Season with pepper.

5. Scatter the mushroom mixture over the top of the gratin or serve the gratin on individual plates with the mushrooms scattered around each portion. Sprinkle the remaining parsley over the whole and season with plenty of freshly ground pepper.

FAT PER SERVING (**4** SERVINGS): Saturated 2–3 grams; unsaturated 4–5 grams

COUSCOUS

by Deborah Madison

Couscous comes to us from North Africa. According to Gilda Angel, author of *Sephardic Holiday Cooking,* it is actually a kind of pasta made from the by-products of wheat milling. Usually the *middlings* that remain from milling are ground, moistened, and rolled into tiny pellets that look like a grain. Real couscous made from middlings* is high in protein and other nutrients. For those who can't eat wheat, some new couscous-like products made from brown rice are available in natural or specialty food stores.

Most couscous available in the market is the instant kind, which is cooked by adding boiling water and allowing it to stand. The noninstant kind is cooked by steaming over water or broth several times and rubbing the grains between steamings to break them up. It is a more complicated procedure but yields a light, tender pile of grain. Those wishing to know more about cooking couscous in the traditional way should see Paula Wolfert's *Couscous and Other Good Foods from Morocco.* Changes in any recipes from other books should be made to fit the Superpyramid plan (see page 400, on adapting recipes).

If you're using instant varieties of couscous, follow the instructions on the box. If you're buying in bulk, the method of cooking is to use ¾ cups water to 1 cup grain, bring it to a boil, pour over the grain, cover, and let stand 10–15 minutes or until all the water is absorbed. Then lightly break up the grains with a fork and serve.

Couscous is mild and delicate. It is traditionally served with stews made of meat, fish, and fowl and vegetables, which may be dry or soupy, with a rich flavorful broth that is absorbed by the grain. In the Superpyramid, use couscous with a small portion of fish or very little lean meat or poultry. For a vegetarian version of this couscous, see the Spicy Artichoke and Carrot Stew (page 344).

FAT PER SERVING: Traces

---

* Middlings are high in nutrients as they contain the germ and bran and other outer layers of the grain and less of the white core of the grain (endosperm). Use products made with middlings freely as you would use a whole-grain flour.

Falafel Patties

by Deborah Madison

*F*alafel is a tasty mixture of flours made from chickpeas, yellow peas, and wheat, seasoned with herbs and spices. It can be made from scratch, but the mixture can also be bought both in boxes and in bulk from natural food stores. It is a true convenience food—you simply add water, then shape the dough into small patties and fry them in oil. Falafel is a delicious traditional Middle Eastern food that is excellent in sandwiches or eaten with an accompaniment of garnishes, as below.

SERVES 4

1½ cups whole-grain falafel mix (with no fats added)
1⅛ cups water
    sesame or olive oil

Combine the falafel mix and water and stir together until well mixed. Let stand 15 minutes or until the liquid is absorbed, then shape the mixture into balls and press into patties. Make them any size you like, but since they will be only shallow-fried rather than deep-fried, a thinner patty will work better than a thick one.

Pour enough oil into a heavy frying pan to lightly cover the surface. When it's hot enough to sizzle a drop of water, add the patties and cook on both sides until golden.

VARIATION

Instead of frying the falafel patties, place in a baking pan with a small amount of olive or sesame oil, according to your taste, and bake for 20 or 25 minutes at 350° F.

FAT PER SERVING: Using a thin layer of oil in frying pan: saturated 0.5 gram; unsaturated 3–4 grams

Falafel Plate

by Deborah Madison

*H*ere are some possible combinations you might use in putting together a falafel plate. The Lebanese Tarator Sauce is particularly delicious with falafel, and the Yogurt Dressing with Tahini would also be good.

Falafel Patties (above)

Lebanese Tarator Sauce (page 226) or Yogurt Dressing with Tahini (page 225)

roasted peppers cut in strips (page 342)

Cracked-Wheat Salad (page 252)

cucumbers or Cucumber Salad with Yogurt Dressing (page 247)

ripe tomatoes

radishes

olives

whole-wheat pita bread

FAT PER SERVING: Depends on sauce used; add amount from sauce to the amount in the Falafel Patties.

Quesadillas

by Jody Main

Quesadillas are a wonderful quick meal that can be made in an iron skillet, in the microwave, or, for larger quantities, in the oven.

SKILLET

Heat a whole-grain tortilla on a hot iron skillet. Turn and spread with roasted peppers (page 342) and sprinkle with low-fat mozzarella cheese. Fold tortilla over and heat until the cheese has melted.

MICROWAVE

Lay tortilla on a microwave-safe plate. Spread with roasted peppers and sprinkle with low-fat mozzarella cheese. Fold tortilla in half and microwave for 2 minutes or until cheese has melted.

OVEN

Lay tortillas on a large cookie sheet. Spread with roasted peppers and low-fat mozzarella cheese. Fold over and bake in a preheated 350° F. oven for 3–10 minutes, until cheese has melted.

VARIATION

Hot sauce, fresh chopped cilantro, chopped onion, avocado, and chopped fresh tomatoes may be added. Delicious served with a scoop of your favorite beans.

FAT PER SERVING: With 1 ounce low-fat mozzarella: saturated 3 grams; unsaturated 1.5 grams

PASTAS

Whole Durum Wheat Pasta

by Gene Spiller

*M*aking *your own whole durum wheat pasta gives you a delightfully flavorful base to a meal with only a trace of mostly unsaturated fat. Start with durum wheat berries if possible, and grind them into flour just before making the pasta. Otherwise choose a good, freshly ground whole-grain durum wheat flour. The amounts suggested are easily worked by hand. If the amounts are doubled, work with half the dough at a time to shape the pasta.*

SERVES 2–3

1 cup freshly milled whole durum wheat flour
3 egg whites

1. Lightly beat the egg whites. Mound the flour into a pile, make a well in the middle, and add the egg whites. Working from the center gradually combine flour and egg whites, with spoon or hands, until a fairly stiff dough is formed. Form the dough in a ball and leave in a covered bowl for 20–40 minutes to allow the flour to absorb the moisture fully.
2. Roll dough out into a rectangle on a lightly floured wooden board. Turn dough over several times while rolling out as thinly as possible, without causing the dough to tear. Use a wheel-style cutter to cut strips of pasta. Alternatively, loosely roll up the dough, as though it was a jelly roll. Cut slices from the roll and uncurl them to form long strands of pasta.
3. Bring at least 2 quarts of water containing about ½ teaspoon salt and herbs (for example, oregano) according to taste, to a full rolling boil. Add the pasta and briefly, gently stir to separate the pasta strands. Boil, uncovered, for 10–12 minutes. Strain off the water through a colander. Remove herb stems. Gently toss the pasta with a few drops of olive oil or one of the sauces in the sauce section of the Superpyramid Kitchen.

VARIATIONS
Mix some other flour with the durum wheat flour. Amaranth, teff, millet, soy, and others make excellent pasta. Experiment with the amount of flour needed as you change your flour mixture.

FAT PER SERVING: Without dressing: traces for whole-grain flour, mostly unsaturated

Bean and Pasta Gratin

by Deborah Madison

*B*eans and pasta are commonly combined in soups, but there's no reason to limit this combination to soups alone. Baked together, beans and pasta make a succulent main dish, and this gratin sparkles with the addition of fragrant pesto and creamy ricotta cheese. The gratin can be set up ahead of time and baked later in the day or the next day.

Serve this with something fresh and simple—crisp romaine hearts, a raw fennel salad, or slices of tomatoes.

SERVES 4 TO 6

1 cup dried navy or cannellini beans, soaked overnight
6 cups water
⅓ cup plus 1 tablespoon olive oil
1 small onion, finely chopped
1 bay leaf and a pinch of dried thyme
1 teaspoon salt
3 medium garlic cloves, coarsely chopped
1 cup each loosely packed basil and parsley leaves
   approximately ½ cup or 1½ ounces grated Parmesan cheese
   freshly ground pepper
1½ cups small, dried pasta shapes such as shells or butterflies
½ cup low-fat ricotta cheese
⅔ cup bread crumbs tossed with 1 tablespoon olive oil

1. Parboil the beans according to the directions on page 327, then drain.
2. Heat the tablespoon of oil with the onion, bay leaf, and thyme and cook until softened, about 5 minutes. Add the drained beans, water, bring to a boil, then reduce the heat and simmer until the beans are nearly tender, about 1¼ hours. Stir in salt and continue cooking until the beans are done, but not mushy, another 15 minutes or so. Drain, but reserve the cooking water.
3. Using a food processor, pulse the garlic, basil, and parsley until coarsely chopped. Scrape down the sides, then, with the machine on, gradually add the ⅓ cup olive oil and the Parmesan. Process just long enough to have a rough puree. Season to taste with salt and pepper.
4. Preheat the oven to 350° F. Cook the pasta in a large pot of boiling

salted water. Remove while it is still a little firm and rinse immediately with cold water to stop the cooking. Drain and combine with the beans along with the basil sauce and enough broth to ensure that everything is very moist. Season the whole mixture again with salt and pepper, if needed.

5. Pour into a lightly oiled gratin dish. Drop spoonfuls of the ricotta into the beans, poking it beneath the surface. Sprinkle the bread crumbs evenly over the gratin and bake about 35 minutes, or until browned on top and bubbling around the edges. Let stand 10 minutes before serving.

FAT PER SERVING (6 SERVINGS): Saturated 3–4 grams; unsaturated 9–11 grams

Whole-Wheat Spaghetti with Arugula

by Deborah Madison

The spicy hotness of the arugula leaves and chili flakes go well with the nuttiness of the whole-wheat pasta. Make this dish when you have plenty of arugula in your garden or when it's inexpensive in the market as you'll want to use a lot of it. If getting handfuls of arugula is out of the question, try using another strong green such as mustard or turnip greens, kale, escarole, or a mixture. For pasta, choose a good-quality whole-wheat spaghetti that has good texture and a strong wheat flavor.

SERVES 4

Salt
1 pound whole-wheat spaghetti
3 tablespoons olive oil
2 large garlic cloves, thinly sliced
2 pinches red pepper flakes
4–6 cups arugula leaves or a mixture of greens (see above), washed and roughly chopped
⅓ cup whole-grain bread crumbs, toasted
freshly ground pepper
freshly grated Parmesan Reggiano (optional)
1 tablespoon extra-virgin olive oil (to drizzle on pasta when serving)

1. Bring a large pot of water to a boil, add salt to taste, then the pasta. Give it a stir, then cook until it is al dente. While the pasta is cooking, prepare the greens.

2. Warm the olive oil in a wide skillet with the garlic and pepper flakes. When you can begin to smell the garlic, add the greens and a little water from the pasta pot. Salt lightly. Stew the greens on a medium flame until they are tender—1 or 2 minutes for arugula, about 5–7 minutes for tougher greens. Taste to be sure they're as done as you like.

3. When the pasta is done, drain it and add it immediately to the pan with the arugula. Toss everything together, then garnish with the bread crumbs, black pepper, and the cheese. Serve with spoonful of extra-virgin olive oil drizzled over all.

VARIATION

Sautéed garlic has a fairly strong aroma that is not to everyone's liking. By boiling the garlic instead of sautéing it you have a much milder flavor but still a delightful dish.

1. Bring a large pot of water to a boil, add salt to taste, then the pasta. Add the garlic so it will flavor the pasta as it cooks. Give it a stir, then cook until it is al dente. When the pasta is cooking, prepare the greens.

2. Warm the olive oil with some water from the pasta pot in a wide skillet *without the garlic*. Add the pepper flakes and the greens. Salt lightly. Stew the greens on a medium flame until they are tender—1 or 2 minutes for arugula, about 5–7 minutes for tougher greens. Taste to be sure they're as done as you like.

FAT PER SERVING: Saturated 1.5–2 grams; unsaturated 6–8 grams

Buckwheat Noodles with Savoy Cabbage

by Deborah Madison

*B*uckwheat, both in the form of noodles and a kind of polenta, is found in the cooking of Northern Italy. It's nearly impossible to get Italian buckwheat noodles here, but Japanese soba noodles make an excellent substitute. You could also make your own pasta using a portion of buckwheat flour mixed with wheat. (Modify the basic noodle recipe on page 315 by mixing some buckwheat flour into the whole-wheat flour). Be sure the flours are whole grain if you plan to make the noodles yourself.

The crinkly-leafed savoy cabbage is preferable for its sweetness and delicacy. If that isn't available, use napa cabbage, a crinkly Asian variety that also has a delicate taste and texture, or your regular smooth-leafed green cabbage.

SERVES 4

    1 package buckwheat noodles (10 or 12 ounces)
    2 large garlic cloves, thinly sliced
    5 sage leaves or 1 teaspoon dried sage
    ½ teaspoon dried oregano or marjoram
1–1½ pounds savoy or napa cabbage, cored and thinly sliced
    ¼ cup Italian parsley, finely chopped
    1 bunch scallions, including some of the green, sliced in rounds
3–4 tablespoons olive oil
    salt and pepper
    1 ounce grated low-fat cheese

1. Bring a large pot of water to a boil for the pasta. While it is heating, cut the vegetables as suggested.

2. Warm the oil in a large skillet with the garlic, sage leaves, and oregano or marjoram. Once the garlic has taken some color, discard it. Don't let it brown.

3. Add the cabbage, parsley, and scallions and sauté over a medium heat. Ladle in a little of the pasta water to keep it from sticking and to make a little sauce. Season with salt and pepper and cook until the cabbage is tender.

4. When the water is boiling, add salt to taste, then the pasta, and cook until it is al dente. Drain the pasta and add it directly to the pan with the vegetables. Add the cheese and plenty of pepper, toss everything together, and serve.

FAT PER SERVING: Saturated 1.5–2 grams; unsaturated 7–8 grams

Spinach or Whole-Wheat Pasta with Ricotta and Walnuts

by Deborah Madison

Ricotta cheese makes a natural pairing with both whole-wheat and spinach pasta. Use the finest-grained low-fat ricotta you can find and have it at room temperature before you begin as the ricotta is merely warmed rather than cooked.

SERVES 4

Salt
12 ounces dried spinach pasta or whole-wheat pasta
¼ cup walnuts
1 cup low-fat ricotta cheese
¼ cup grated Parmesan cheese
2 tablespoons parsley, finely chopped
2 tablespoons chives, finely sliced
1 tablespoon fresh marjoram, finely chopped
pepper
additional Parmesan cheese

1. Bring a large pot of water to a boil, add salt to taste, then the pasta, and cook until it is al dente. While the water is heating and the pasta is cooking, prepare the sauce.
2. Toast the walnuts in a moderate oven (or toaster oven) until they smell toasty, about 7 minutes, then remove and chop finely.
3. Mix the ricotta with half of the walnuts, the grated cheese, and most of the herbs, reserving a few for garnish. Stir in a cup of the pasta water

or enough to make it about the thickness of cream, and season with salt and pepper. Transfer to a large skillet and keep warm over a low flame.
4. As soon as the pasta is done, add it to the ricotta mixture and toss gently. Garnish with remaining walnuts and herbs, a dusting of additional Parmesan, and plenty of freshly ground pepper.

FAT PER SERVING: Saturated 5–6 grams; unsaturated 7–9 grams (depends on amount of Parmesan used)

Pasta and Beans
(*Pasta asciutta con fagioli*)

by Gene Spiller

This is a simple recipe that can be prepared with little effort. While the Italian pasta e fagioli (pasta and beans) is really a soup (page 286), beans and pastas make wonderful combinations without any broth. The Italians call it pasta asciutta literally "dry pasta." Use spaghetti, noodles, rotini, or any other shape of pasta.

SERVES 2

   Salt
½ pound of your favorite whole-grain pasta
   sage and rosemary
2 or 3 garlic cloves, peeled (optional)
2 teaspoons Parmesan Reggiano (1 teaspoon per serving)
2 tablespoons extra-virgin olive oil
½ cup pinto or other beans separately cooked with herbs (page 327)

Bring water to a boil in a large pot and salt the water. Add the pasta, sage, rosemary, and garlic cloves. Cook to taste, stirring occasionally. When cooked, drain the water but remove the garlic as you drain the water.

When cooked and drained, add the warm beans and toss together with the pasta. Add the oil and sprinkle the Parmesan just before serving.

This is a delightful dish that can be varied in many ways. It's a basic Superpyramid dish.

FAT PER SERVING: With Parmesan: saturated 1.5–2 grams; unsaturated 7–8 grams

Gnocchi alla Romana (Roman Gnocchi)

adapted to the Superpyramid by Gene Spiller from a recipe by Pellegrino Artusi

*T*his is an old Italian recipe with many variations. It requires total dedication during the first stage of the cooking process. *The original idea—extensively modified for this book—came from a classic nineteenth-century Italian book by Pellegrino Artusi.**

SERVES 4 (MAKES 12 LARGE GNOCCHI)

1 cup (5 ounces) whole-grain durum wheat flour
2 cups (1 pint) low-fat or nonfat milk
1 whole egg (or two whites)
2 egg whites (in addition to the above)
4 tablespoons Parmesan Reggiano cheese
  Salt, if desired (the Parmesan cheese should supply enough salt)
2 tablespoons extra-virgin olive oil

TO MAKE THE BATTER

The gnocchi batter is best made ahead of time so that it will be cool enough to shape the gnocchi before the final baking step. Add flour to a cooking pot (1½–2-quart size) and add a few tablespoons of milk and then mix well, until all the milk has been added and a thin, smooth mixture has been produced. Lightly beat egg and egg whites together and stir them into the flour and milk mixture. Gradually heat the batter on a medium-hot setting of the stovetop and protect it from scorching by using a heat dispersing grid. Stir constantly during this cooking step. Cook the batter until it boils, thickens to a dough consistency, and becomes very smooth. During the last two minutes of cooking add cheese and salt according to taste. Stir well and allow to cool to room temperature.

TO SHAPE AND BAKE THE GNOCCHI

Preheat oven and a pizza stone at 375° F. (The pizza stone is not essential, but without one the baking time may be a little different.) Coat a baking dish (11x9x2 inches) with olive oil. Spoon the gnocchi batter into baking dish in form of twelve oval patties, allowing a heaped tablespoon of batter for each. Indent center of each with finger tip. Place baking dish on preheated pizza stone. Bake at 375° F. for 20–30 minutes, until lightly browned. Serve in place of pasta.

FAT PER SERVING: With one whole egg and 1 percent low-fat milk: saturated 4 grams; unsaturated 5–6 grams; cholesterol 70–80 mg

With no egg and nonfat milk: saturated 2 grams; unsaturated 4–5 grams; cholesterol traces

---

* Pellegrino Artusi, *L'Arte di Mangiar Bene*—a nineteenth-century Italian classic cookbook that has been reprinted 107 times. The recipe has been changed in a major way from the Northern Italian ingredients of Artusi, who used large amounts of butter and whole milk.

Gnocchi di Patate (Potato gnocchi)

adapted to the Superpyramid by Gene Spiller from a recipe by Pellegrino Artusi

*T*his is another old Italian recipe that is so simple—potatoes and flour—that no changes were needed except for the type of wheat flour. The original recipe can be found in the cookbook by Pellegrino Artusi already quoted, under gnocchi alla romana.

SERVES 4

1 pound yellow potatoes
1 cup whole durum wheat flour
½ teaspoon salt each 2 quarts of cooking water
1 tablespoon extra-virgin olive oil to coat baking dish

Peel and boil the potatoes in a pot of water until tender. Drain them well, mash, and allow to cool. Combine mashed potatoes and whole durum wheat flour and work them together very well with a fork until you have a smooth, stiff mixture. Place the dough on a wooden board and shape it by hand into rolls about ½ inch thick. Cut the roll so that each gnocchi is about 1 inch long. Make an indentation with a finger in the middle of each gnocchi. Cook in salted, vigorously boiling water for about 3 minutes: they are cooked when they float to the top. If you cook them for too long they will disintegrate! Remove from the boiling water with a perforated spoon. Place in an oven-safe dish coated with a thin layer of olive oil and *dry* in an oven preheated to 300° F. for about 5–10 minutes. Turn the gnocchi over to dry them evenly if you wish. Serve with any good pasta sauce or simply with some olive oil and fresh herbs. You may also add a few leaves of sage or rosemary to the boiling water.

Artusi tells a story in his book about a reader who tried this recipe and when she looked for the gnocchi in the cooking pot, she did not find anything because she had not used enough flour to hold the potatoes together and she had cooked them for too long. Elizabeth David in her beautiful book *Italian Food* uses eggs and butter in her gnocchi recipe. You may want to experiment with egg whites and a few drops of olive oil in the potato-flour mixture.

FAT PER SERVING: Without sauce: traces
With sauce: see under Sauces

Ravioli

Ravioli are a classic Mediterranean way to eat grains with vegetables, cheeses, and meats. In the Superpyramid the choices are vegetables and a low-fat or nonfat cheese or a small amount of Parmesan Reggiano.

Use the kind of dough described on page 315 or other whole-grain pasta dough and use fillings based on cooked pureed vegetables such as squash, spinach, carrots, or a mixture of them, with some cheese added and salt to taste. Cook as you cook pasta. Follow instructions given in a good cookbook such as Deborah Madison's *The Savory Way.*

Top Ten Cereal with Fruits and Nuts

by Monica Spiller

This is a combination of ten flaked whole grains, dried fruits, and ground nuts that is delicious served with milk or yogurt and perhaps a little honey. Prepared ahead of time, it is definitely something to look forward to as an instant breakfast or snack.

MAKES ABOUT 5 CUPS (5–10 SERVINGS)

½ cup each of the following:
  flaked whole wheat
  flaked whole rye
  rolled oats
  flaked barley
  whole dates
  dried apple rings
  Thompson seedless raisins
  manukka or other raisins
  filberts (without shells)
  almonds (without shells)

Add flaked whole grains to a large (4-quart) mixing bowl. Pit and remove hard ends from dates; snip or chop them into raisin-sized pieces; add to mixture. Snip or chop apples into raisin-sized pieces, discard any residual core, and add to mixture. Separate raisins and remove any remaining stems before adding to the mixture. Chop the filberts and almonds almost to a powder, using a food processor. Add the finely chopped nuts. Toss and stir the mixture until all ingredients are evenly distributed. Store, refrigerated, in a well-closed glass jar or plastic tub.

FAT PER ½ CUP BEFORE ADDING MILK OR YOGURT: Saturated 1–2 grams; unsaturated 15–17 grams

Beans, Lentils, and Peas

BASIC BEAN, LENTIL, AND PEA PREPARATION
by Deborah Madison

Along with grains and yogurt, beans and other legumes are among the basic foods of the Superpyramid. As with varieties of apples, lettuces, and so many foods, both new and old revived varieties of beans are beginning to appear on the market. Although beans are a dried food, there's quite a difference between this year's dried bean and a bean that's been sitting around for perhaps years. The older they are, the more difficult it is to cook beans properly, and the more time it takes. When shopping, try to buy beans in bulk bins so you can actually look at them and handle them. Dried beans should be whole and smooth, not cracked, split, broken up, or shriveled.

Before cooking legumes, go through them carefully and remove any little pebbles, grains of sand, or discolored or broken grains. Rinse them well for they are frequently dusty, and for best results cover them with water and let them stand for 6 hours or, better yet, overnight before cooking. This allows moisture to seep into the bean and the soaking softens the skin as well. You may go beyond this and let the bean begin to sprout for another twenty-four hours (see pages 216–17).

When you're ready to cook the beans, drain off the soaking water, cover with fresh water, and bring to a boil. Boil vigorously for about 5 minutes, then pour off the water and rinse. This helps rid the beans of the sugars that cause gas for people not used to eating beans. If you don't have this problem, the blanching step can be omitted.

After rinsing the beans, cover them again with plenty of fresh water, enough to cover by a few inches. (Since they've soaked, they've already absorbed quite a bit of moisture.) Bring to a boil, then lower the heat and simmer until the beans are tender but not quite done. If any scum rises to the surface, just skim it off. Usually this will have happened during the first boiling. For most beans, cooking will take about an hour —longer at high altitudes. Aromatics, such as whole garlic cloves, sage, rosemary, parsley, thyme, and olive oil, can be added while the beans are cooking. However, salt should not be added until the beans are nearly done as it works against absorption and slows down the cooking process.

The beans are done when they are tender but still hold their shape. Some people prefer them firmer than others do, but if carefully cooked, the finished beans will be whole and intact. (If the beans were very old to begin with, this may be impossible, especially if the soaking was skipped.) Be sure to save the broth for other recipes.

Using a pressure cooker is a great way to cook beans on the spur of the moment without going through the soaking routine. It is fast and efficient and with the new pressure cookers it is also safe and easy. It's a little harder to cook the beans so that they don't break, particularly if the soaking has been skipped, but this may not be important for everyone. The pressure cooker does allow one to cook beans without planning ahead, and you can still parboil them to get rid of the sugars. This may well be your most useful piece of cooking equipment if you eat a lot of legumes.

FAT PER SERVING: There is no fat in beans, except soybeans. Fat content of recipes depends on oil or other additions.

Pumpkin Stew with Hominy and Pinto Beans

by Deborah Madison

*T*his *is a warm and spicy dish for fall and winter. Hominy (or posole) is corn that has been treated with lime. It has a very characteristic taste because of the lime, that goes well with pumpkin and squash, chili, and beans. The dried hominy needs to be treated like beans—soaked overnight then cooked for several hours. A pressure cooker is of great help here.*

As with most stews and soups, this one tastes even better the next day. Serve it in bowls by itself or on a plate with rice or couscous. If you like the added zest of a fresh green salsa, serve the Tomatillo Salsa (page 228) alongside.

SERVES 4 TO 6

½ cup Spiced Yogurt (page 276)
1 cup dried hominy soaked overnight and cooked until tender
1 pound pumpkin or winter squash, cut into cubes and peeled
2 tablespoons olive or sesame oil
1 yellow onion, cut into ½-inch squares
1 teaspoon oregano
  salt
1 large clove garlic, minced
1–2 tablespoons red chili powder (preferably New Mexican)
1 tablespoon whole-wheat flour
1 quart water (or bean broth or vegetable stock)
1 large bell pepper, cut into ½-inch squares (red, yellow, or green)
1 cup cooked pinto beans
¼ cup chopped cilantro
  cilantro leaves for garnish

1. Make the Spiced Yogurt as for the Split-Pea Soup with Yogurt and let it stand at room temperature while you make the stew.
2. Prepare the hominy and the pumpkin, then warm the oil in a wide pan or soup pot and add the onion, squash, and oregano. Salt lightly and cook over medium heat for about 5 minutes.
3. Add the garlic, chili powder, and flour and mix well with the onion mixture. Next add the hominy and the water, stir well again, then lower the heat and simmer for about 45 minutes or until the pumpkin is about done.

4. Add the diced pepper and the beans, and continue cooking until the pumpkin is done and the pepper is tender. Taste for salt and season as needed. Stir in the cilantro. Pass the yogurt separately or stir it into the stew before serving.

FAT PER SERVING (4 SERVINGS): With nonfat yogurt: saturated 0.5 gram; unsaturated 4–5 grams

Lentils with Rice and Onions

by Deborah Madison

This is a combination that appears in different dishes on the North African side of the Mediterranean and, in more spicy versions, in India. It is usually made with white rice—here it's made with long-grain brown rice.

Fried onions make a succulent garnish to an otherwise simple dish. Grilled or broiled tomatoes, fried pumpkin, and roasted peppers would also make good garnishes, or they could be brought together on a singular colorful plate. If you like spicier foods, stir in a little Tunisian Hot Pepper Sauce at the end or serve it alongside, along with a cooling dollop of yogurt.

SERVES 4

    1 cup brown lentils
    salt
    bay leaf
    two parsley sprigs
    1 cup long-grain brown rice
1½ tablespoons olive oil
    2 large onions, thinly sliced
    2 tablespoons finely chopped parsley
    Tunisian Hot Pepper Sauce (Harissa) (page 234) (optional)
    nonfat yogurt

1. Rinse the lentils, then put them in a pot, cover with 2½ cups water, add 1 teaspoon salt, the bay leaf, and parsley, and bring to a boil. Lower the heat to a simmer and cook until the lentils are tender, about 25 minutes. Drain but reserve the liquid.

2. Cook the rice according to the instructions for Basic Brown Rice on page 297.

3. Combine the cooked rice and lentils in a single large pan, moisten with cooking water from the lentils, and heat together. Taste for salt and season, if needed. While they are heating, prepare the onions.

4. In another pan, warm the oil. When hot, add the onions. Fry until they are nicely browned, stirring frequently.

5. Serve the warm rice and lentils in a platter and scatter the onions and chopped parsley over the top. Serve a little yogurt or yogurt dressing on the side, and red chili paste or Tunisian Hot Pepper Sauce, if desired.

FAT PER SERVING: Saturated 0.5 gram; unsaturated 3–4 grams

Chickpeas with Tahini (Hummus bi Tahini)

by Deborah Madison

*C*ommonly called hummus, *this spread is now well known in much of the United States. Creamy and buff-colored, hummus combines chickpeas with sesame paste (tahini) to make a rich mixture that can be served as a spread for breads and crackers and as a condiment for all kinds of fresh vegetables and cooked grains. The tahini, or sesame paste, can be bought in health food stores or in Middle Eastern markets.*

FOR ABOUT 1 CUP

1 cup cooked chickpeas
1 clove garlic
3 tablespoons tahini
  juice of 1 lemon, or to taste
  salt to taste
1 tablespoon extra-virgin olive oil
  paprika
  chopped parsley

1. Put the cooked chickpeas in the work bowl of a food processor with the garlic and tahini and puree the mixture. It may be necessary to add some of the cooking liquid from the chick-peas (or water, if you've used canned ones) to make them easy to puree. When smooth, add the lemon juice and salt to taste.

2. To serve, mound the hummus in a bowl, make a shallow depression with the back of a spoon and fill it with olive oil. Garnish with a sprinkling of paprika and parsley.

FAT PER CUP: approximate; tahinis vary in fat content
Saturated 3–4 grams; unsaturated 24–28 grams

White Bean Puree with Rosemary

by Deborah Madison

This Tuscan dish is served on bread that has been lightly toasted, brushed with olive oil, and rubbed with fresh garlic. In restaurants, it is typically served with wine as a little nibble before the first course, making a simple but flavorful hors d'oeuvre. It could also be included on a plate with fresh or cooked vegetables dressed in a vinaigrette, with olives, roasted peppers, and the like.

A puree is not too far from a soup. The combination of white beans, garlic, and rosemary, thinned to a soup consistency with bean broth and served with small, toasted croutons, would be a delicious variation on this recipe. Include some pasta in the soup, and you have pasta e fagioli.

MAKES ABOUT 1 CUP

1½ cups cooked white beans (cannellini, great northerns, or navy)
2–3 tablespoons olive oil
2 cloves garlic, finely chopped
2–3 teaspoons rosemary, finely chopped
    salt and pepper

¼ cup cooking liquid from the beans, or more, as needed

    lightly toasted croutons, brushed with extra-virgin olive oil and rubbed with garlic (page 356)

    branches of rosemary for garnish

    lemon wedges, black olives for garnish (optional)

1. Drain the cooked beans but reserve the liquid.

2. Warm the oil in a skillet with garlic and rosemary. Cook gently for several minutes, then add the beans. Season with salt and pepper, to taste, and add the ¼ cup of liquid.

3. Simmer gently for about 10 minutes, adding more liquid as necessary to keep the beans moist, then start mashing them with a fork. Keep mashing over the heat until the beans have broken down into a rough puree. There should be some texture remaining.

4. Taste and season again with salt and pepper. Spread on the croutons, drizzle with oil and freshly milled pepper. Serve on a plate garnished with branches of rosemary and, if you like, wedges of lemon and black olives.

VARIATIONS

Other seasonings and methods can be used with white beans. Treat them similarly to Hummus (page 331) and season the puree with lemon juice, paprika, or cayenne and freshly chopped parsley or dill. Serve with crackers, pita bread, and vegetables like fresh cucumbers, peppers, and tomatoes.

FAT PER CUP: With 2 tablespoons olive oil: saturated 1.5–2 grams; unsaturated 10–12 grams

Savory Soybeans

by Jody Main

*D*elicious as a sandwich spread, savory soybeans are also wonderful served on a bed of lettuce with whole-grain crackers. Top with a sprinkle of salsa or fresh chopped cilantro.

SERVES 4

3 cups baby soybean sprouts (page 217) (from about 1 cup dry whole soybeans)
1 cup grated celery
1 clove grated garlic
2 tablespoons grated onion
2 tablespoons grated carrot
¼ cup minced fresh parsley
2 tablespoons minced fresh oregano, marjoram, dill, or basil
2 tablespoons whole-grain toasted bread crumbs (you can use bruschettes, page 356)
2 tablespoons natural soy sauce
2 tablespoons nonfat plain yogurt
dash each white pepper and cayenne

Simmer baby soybean sprouts over medium-low heat with 8 cups of water until tender, about 2½ hours. Add water as necessary. Drain and mash coarsely with a fork while still warm. Leave some beans whole for good texture. Combine with remaining ingredients and refrigerate a few hours before serving, allowing the flavors to marry.

FAT PER SERVING: Saturated trace; unsaturated 2–3 grams (depends on degree of sprouting of soybeans)

Sprouted Black Beans in a Pot

by Jody Main

Cooked sprouted beans are rich, sweet, and creamy. They are good served over rice, on a tostada, or in burritos. Cooking time for sprouted beans is much shorter than for dry beans. Pinto and other beans are just as good in this recipe.

SERVES 4

1 cup black beans (to sprout to about 3 cups)
3 cups water (for cooking)
2 cloves garlic, crushed

Sprout the beans until a bud forms (1–2 days; see pages 216–17 for more details on sprouting seeds). Cook with water and garlic on medium-low heat for 1 hour. Stir frequently and check often the last half hour, adding water as necessary.

VARIATION

For a delicious black bean soup, add 1 tablespoon balsamic vinegar or fresh lemon juice, a chopped red pepper, and a dash of cayenne. Simmer for 2 hours instead of 1, adding water if needed. Serve with roasted sunflower seeds and a dusting of Parmesan cheese.

FAT PER SERVING: Saturated trace; unsaturated 2 grams (depends on degree of sprouting of beans)

Lentil Sprout Pilaf

by Jody Main

*T*his savory dish is quite nice served with roasted vegetables and a fresh green salad.

SERVES 4

1 cup long-grain brown rice
1 tablespoon extra-virgin olive oil
2 cloves garlic, crushed
1 cup lentil sprouts (see page 217) equal to about ½ cup dry lentils
1 onion, chopped
3 tomatoes, chopped

Combine ingredients and simmer, covered, on low heat for 1 hour or until liquid is absorbed.

FAT PER SERVING: Saturated trace; unsaturated 2–3 grams

Tofu Cutlets

by Jody Main

These are tender and flavorful cutlets with a thin, chewy crust and an almost custard-like center. Broiled tofu is wonderful served with a grain pilaf and fresh vegetables. Chilled, the cutlets are great in sandwiches and sliced in salads. These are very versatile and easy to make, and you will want to have them on hand.

SERVES 4

1 cake (10 ounces) medium or firm tofu
1 or 2 tablespoons extra-virgin olive oil
1 tablespoon natural light soy sauce
1 tablespoon mirin (Japanese cooking wine)
1 clove garlic, crushed
   dash each white pepper and paprika

1. Slice tofu cake lengthwise into 4 thin, large, flat pieces. Cut these in half to make 8 pieces approximately. Adapt these sizes to the kind of tofu you like best, as some tofus come in cakes of different size.
2. Blend remaining ingredients and pour over tofu. Turn tofu over several times to cover. Marinate at least 1 hour.
3. Broil (or sauté) until golden on both sides. This takes about 3 minutes per side. The cutlets will turn tough if overcooked. Serve immediately or refrigerate until ready to use.

FAT PER SERVING: Saturated 2–3 grams; unsaturated 10–12 grams

Tofu Kabobs

by Jody Main

*T*his is a festive dish to be served over a nice pilaf. Broiling marinated tofu gives it a delightful roasted flavor. Make sure the tofu is about 4 inches from the flame to ensure even browning instead of burning.

SERVES 4

4 small red potatoes, cooked
1 sweet red pepper
1 cake (10 ounces) firm tofu
1 onion
12 small mushrooms
   miso sauce (page 238)
4 12-inch skewers

Cut the potatoes, red pepper, tofu, and onion into 1-inch squares or pieces. Alternate the vegetables and tofu onto 4 skewers or in a pan and lightly brush with the miso sauce. Set aside for about an hour. Broil for 10–15 minutes, turning them as they become light brown. Serve with the leftover miso sauce for dipping.

FAT PER SERVING: Saturated 1.5–2 grams; unsaturated 8–9 grams

Deviled Tofu

by Jody Main

*T*his is a savory sandwich spread much like egg salad in taste and texture. It is also wonderful on crackers and topped with alfalfa sprouts or served nestled in fresh spinach with whole-grain crackers on the side.

SERVES 4

1 cake (10 ounces) regular or firm tofu
2 stalks celery, minced
1 tablespoon minced onion
1 tablespoon minced parsley
1 teaspoon minced oregano
1 tablespoon natural soy sauce
   dash of cayenne

Rinse tofu and dry with a towel. Coarsely mash tofu with a fork. Combine all ingredients in a food processor and whiz around a few times until mixture is blended and holds together but is still coarse. Watch closely. Refrigerate a few hours for flavor to marry.

VARIATION
Tofu patties can be made by adding two egg whites and some whole-grain bread crumbs or cracker crumbs to the deviled tofu. Form into patties and sauté on a lightly oiled skillet until golden on both sides.

FAT PER SERVING: Saturated 1.5–2 grams; unsaturated 8–9 grams

Cooked Vegetables

INTRODUCTION

As vegetables are on the second tier of the Superpyramid, it's important to enjoy them in many different ways. Some of these vegetables—like potatoes—are on the first tier and can be used occasionally as an alternative to grains. Although raw vegetables should be our first choice, many vegetables need to be cooked, which can be done in an appealing and yet simple way.

Roasted Vegetables

by Jody Main

*T*his is an example of a delicious mixture of roasted vegetables. Roasting vegetables brings out their rich flavor. Served with a fresh salad and some whole-grain bread, roasted vegetables make a hearty winter meal.

SERVES 4

3 medium fennels
6 baby turnips
3 parsnips
12 cloves garlic
    extra-virgin olive oil
    balsamic vinegar

Wash fennel, turnips, and parsnips and slice into small pieces. Crush 3 garlic cloves and add to vegetables along with the remaining unpeeled cloves. Drizzle with extra-virgin olive oil. Turn vegetables until lightly coated and fragrant. Place roasting pan in a preheated 350° F. oven and roast 30 minutes to 1 hour, until tender. Splash with balsamic vinegar to taste. Serve immediately or let set until at room temperature. You can use this recipe for many other root vegetables like beets and carrots.

FAT CONTENT: Depends on amount of olive oil used (see page 219)

Roasted Peppers

by Deborah Madison

*T*his is a most useful condiment, one you will be sure to use often. Roasting or grilling peppers brings out their inherent sweetness; when grilled over the fire, they take on a faintly smoky flavor as well.

These peppers can be used as an appetizer salad, seasoned with garlic and herbs, served with anchovies, olives, capers, and possibly large shavings of Parmesan Reggiano, or presented with just a little extra-virgin olive oil and a splash of vinegar or squeeze of lemon. Roasted peppers can also be used as a garnish, with green salads, for example, or as part of an antipasto or summer salad plate. Diced, they make a rich colorful addition to lentil-and-bean salads of all kinds, to rice salads and pilafs, and are wonderful tossed in pasta with a spoonful of Aioli or Salsa Verde. Combined with olive paste on a crouton, they make a delicious appetizer. The possibilities are virtually endless. Covered with oil and refrigerated, they'll keep for weeks.

Summer and fall are when big, sweet bell peppers are at their best. Use heavy red or yellow bell peppers for they have the thickest flesh. Green peppers can also be grilled, but their flesh is thinner and more likely to burn, and they aren't as sweet. It's easiest if you can use peppers with large flat surfaces rather than those that are small and convoluted—they'll grill much more evenly.

ON THE GRILL

1. Slice the ends off the peppers, make a cut down one side, and open them up. You'll have one large, long strip of pepper. Cut away the membranes and remove the seeds. Where the peppers curve inward at the bottom make a cut with the knife and gently press them open so that they'll lie flat on the grill.

2. Brush the peppers on both sides with a light oil.

3. Roast over a charcoal fire on both sides. When the skin appears wrinkled and loose (and possibly charred) and the peppers have become soft, transfer them to a bowl, cover with a plate, and let stand for 10 minutes, or until cool, to steam. This makes the skins easier to remove.

4. When cool, remove the skins. They should just come right off, or you may need to work at parts of them with a knife. Try to resist rinsing them under water as much of the flavor will be washed away. Cut the peppers into strips and put them in a bowl with a few slivers of garlic and extra-virgin olive oil to moisten until ready to use. Be sure to use the syrupy liquid that comes off the peppers after they have steamed; it is very sweet and delicious.

IN THE OVEN

Prepare the peppers as above—open them up and brush them with oil —then place on a sheet pan and roast in a hot oven until the skins are blistered. Remove to a bowl, allow to steam, and proceed as above. The peppers can also be cooked under the broiler but it takes more watching. The skin side can char as it will be removed, but the inside shouldn't.

ON A GAS RANGE

This method is most tedious, but it yields a fine-tasting pepper with a smoky flavor.

1. Leave the peppers whole and set them directly on the gas burner. Turn them frequently with a pair of tongs so that the skins char black all over the surface.

2. When the peppers are completely charred, transfer them to a bowl, set a plate over the top, and allow to sit for at least 10 minutes or until cool.

3. Remove the burned skins by hand or with a small knife, then cut the peppers open, remove the seeds and veins, and use as desired.

FAT PER SERVING: Depends on amount of oil or sauce used (see Sauces)

Spicy Artichoke and Carrot Stew

by Deborah Madison

*A*rtichokes make an unusual and hearty stew. This one is seasoned with saffron, turmeric, and paprika and laced with olives, making a rich, spicy sauce. Fresh artichokes are preferable, but frozen ones will do if they're rinsed first.

Serve the stew with mound of couscous, rice, or the Millet Pilaf (page 302). The Orange Salad with Pomegranates and Olives (page 245) or Oranges with Cointreau (page 389) would both make good accompaniments, particularly in winter.

SERVES 4 TO 6

    4 large artichokes or 1 package frozen artichoke hearts
       juice of two lemons (if using fresh artichokes)
    2 tablespoons olive oil
    1 large onion, finely diced
    ¼ teaspoon turmeric
    ¼ teaspoon cinnamon
    1 teaspoon hot paprika
    ½ teaspoon ground cumin
    ½ teaspoon freshly ground pepper
    4 branches cilantro
    4 branches parsley
    ⅛ teaspoon saffron threads covered with a few tablespoons boiling water
    4 medium-sized carrots cut into 2-inch lengths, then halved, lengthwise
       salt
1½ cups water
    ⅓ cup Moroccan black olives or Kalamata olives
       cilantro leaves for garnish

1. Trim the artichokes down to the hearts by breaking off the tough outer leaves. Slice off the inner cone of remaining leaves and trim the outside with a paring knife. Slice the hearts into quarters or eighths and remove the chokes. As you work, put the finished pieces in a bowl of water with the juice of the two lemons. If using frozen artichokes, rinse them briefly with warm water, then set them aside to thaw.

2. Warm the olive oil in a large sauté pan and add the onion, the spices, the cilantro, and parsley. Stir together and cook over medium heat for about 5 minutes, then add the saffron along with the soaking liquid. Add the artichokes and the carrots and season with salt. Pour in the water, cover the pan, and cook over a low heat until the artichokes and carrots are tender, about 30 minutes.

3. Add the olives during the last 10 minutes of cooking.

4. Serve garnished with branches of cilantro.

VARIATIONS

1. Include some chickpeas in the stew and use their cooking liquid in place of the water.

2. Add a grilled or roasted tomato, chopped up or blended, to the onion and spice mixture.

3. If fresh peas are available, add a handful at the end of the cooking.

FAT PER SERVING (4 SERVINGS): Saturated 0.5–1 gram; unsaturated 5–7 grams (varies with size of olives)

COOKING WINTER SQUASHES
by Jody Main and Gene Spiller

Winter squashes come in many colorful and fanciful shapes and range in flavor and texture from subtle and very mild to sweet and chestnut-flavored. Some of them are so sweet and flavorful that they do not need any sauce or dressing.

Winter squash will store for several months if kept in a cool, dry area. Winter squash can be steamed or baked whole or halved. The timing depends on the size of the squash, but generally plan on 30 minutes to 1 hour in a regular oven. To bake whole, probably the best and easiest way to preserve the aroma and texture is to pierce several holes in the squash for the steam to escape. Place in a 350° F. oven and bake until tender. In a microwave, squash will cook in 10–20 minutes depending on size; this is an easy way to prepare a squash in a short time.

After the squash is baked, slice in half and scoop out the seeds and the fibers that surround the seeds. A good flavorful squash such as a buttercup can then be cut and eaten as is after it has cooled. If not sweet enough for you, add a trace of honey or brown sugar or *vino cotto* (page 153). Or you may stuff it with hot homemade applesauce, cranberry sauce, or nut or sesame butter. Leftover winter squash is wonderful and can be kept in the refrigerator for a couple of days.

Another nice way to bake winter squash (although it loses some of the wonderful aroma) is to cut it and clean it before baking. When you're cutting the squash, slice the end off first. This makes slicing the squash in half easier. Scoop out the seeds and fibers and rub the pulp with a little virgin olive oil.

Place facedown in a baking dish in the oven and cook until tender (about 30 minutes).

Twice-Baked Delicata Squash

by Jody Main

*T*his dish combines the seasonal fruits of winter squash and pears. Choose smaller squash so that each serving is half a squash with a surprisingly savory and fluffy filling.

SERVES 6

3 small delicata squash
2 pears, peeled, cored, and grated
1 clove garlic, crushed
  dash of pepper
  dash of cayenne

Poke a few holes in squash and bake in a baking dish at 350° F. for about 30 minutes or until tender when pierced with a knife. Cut squash in half lengthwise and remove seeds and fibers. Spoon out pulp, being careful not to rip outer shell. Blend squash pulp with remaining ingredients with a hand mixer or food processor and refill shells. Place filled squash under a broiler until hot and the peaks turn golden, about 15 minutes.

FAT PER SERVING: None

Kabocha Squash with Applesauce

by Jody Main

Kabocha squash is a rich, nutty, and sweet-tasting variety with a velvety dense texture. The fragrant applesauce combines well to make this dish perfect for a fancy meal.

SERVES 4

1 large or 2 small kabocha squash
6 assorted apples for a nice bouquet
   fresh or bottled apple juice
   cinnamon to taste

1. Poke a few holes in the kabocha and bake in a baking dish at 350° F. until tender when pierced with a knife, about 45 minutes. Remove from oven, cut in half, and remove seeds and the fibers that surround the seeds.
2. While squash is baking, core and coarsely chop unpeeled apples. Place in a heavy saucepan and pour in apple juice to almost cover. Stir in 1 teaspoon cinnamon or more to taste. Bring to a boil, turn down heat, and simmer gently for about 15 minutes until the apples are tender and the sauce is thickened. Lightly crush apples halfway through cooking.
3. Fill cavities of kabocha with the hot applesauce and serve.

FAT PER SERVING: None

Delicata Squash with Walnut Sauce

by Jody Main

*M*any *traditional Native American dishes combine the sweetness of winter squash with the rich taste of nuts. Ground almonds and any winter squash may be substituted in this recipe.*

SERVES 4

2 medium size delicata, sweet dumpling, or acorn squash
½ cup coarsely chopped walnuts
2 tablespoons maple syrup

Pierce a few holes in each squash and place on a baking dish. Bake whole in a 350° F. oven for 45 minutes or until tender when pierced with a knife. While squash is cooling, simmer gently the walnuts and syrup for a few minutes. Cut squash in half and scoop out seeds and fibers. Spoon walnut sauce into cavities and serve immediately.

FAT PER SERVING: Saturated 0.5–1 gram; unsaturated 7–8 grams

Blue Hubbard Squash with Pear Sauce

by Jody Main

*P*ear *sauce is a wonderful flavor for winter squashes. Any winter squash may be substituted for the blue hubbard. Good choices are kabocha and buttercup.*

SERVES 8 OR MORE, DEPENDING ON SIZE OF SQUASH

1 baby blue hubbard squash (or other winter squash)
4 pears
1 cup unsweetened pear or apple juice
2 tablespoons maple syrup
  almond oil or extra-virgin olive oil

1. Cut squash in half, remove seeds and fibers, rub cut end with oil and place face down on baking dish. Bake for about 30 minutes in an oven preheated 325° F. oven, or until squash is tender when pierced with a knife.

2. While squash is baking, wash, core and cut unpeeled pears into small pieces. Combine with juice and maple syrup in a heavy saucepan. Cover and simmer on low for 15 minutes or until tender. Lightly crush pears halfway through cooking.

3. Spoon hot pear sauce into squash cavities.

FAT PER TABLESPOON OF OIL: Saturated 1–1.5 grams; unsaturated 8–9 grams

Cranberry-Blackberry Compote

by Jody Main

Natural sweeteners are used to make this delicious and beautiful fruit dish. Serve on baked squash.

SERVES 12

3 cups (12-ounce package) cranberries
2 cups blackberries
6 ounce cranberry nectar concentrate or *vino cotto* (page 153)
½ cup honey

While stirring and mixing, bring ingredients to a boil. Turn down heat and gently simmer, covered, for a few minutes until the cranberries have popped. Remove cover and simmer until thick, 5–10 minutes. Serve warm or cold.

FAT PER SERVING: None

Almond Eggplant Appetizer

by Rowena Hubbard

MAKES 1 QUART

1 large eggplant (approximately 1 pound)
¼ cup almond or extra-virgin olive oil
   salt to taste
2 medium onions, chopped
1 cup sliced celery
1 clove garlic, minced
1–2 cups stewed tomatoes
1 jar (3 ounces) capers, undrained
1 cup Greek olives with pits removed
¼ cup red wine vinegar
1 teaspoon basil (or a few leaves fresh basil)
1 teaspoon oregano (or a few leaves fresh oregano)

Dice eggplant into 1½-by-½-inch pieces, leaving skin on. Sauté eggplant in oil until golden. Sprinkle salt to taste during cooking—remember that the Greek olives may supply sufficient salt. Remove from pan and set aside. Add onions, celery, and garlic to pan; cook until just tender. Add eggplant, tomatoes, capers, olives, vinegar, basil, and oregano. Simmer 20 minutes. Chill 4 hours or overnight for flavors to blend. Serve as an appetizer or use as a spread with toasted whole-grain bread, sprinkled lightly with Parmesan cheese.

This mixture keeps well in tightly covered containers in refrigerator for 3 to 4 weeks.

FAT PER SERVING: Saturated 2–3 grams; unsaturated 15–17 grams (very approximate, depending on size of olives and their preparation)

Sandwiches and Croutons

INTRODUCTION

Sandwiches always make an easy informal meal, and many of the spreads and sauces go very well with fresh vegetables. For bread, try the commercially made whole-wheat pita pocket breads, as they are available most everywhere and taste great with the Mediterranean sauces and fillings given here. Better yet, make your own (pages 440 and 467). You could of course use other whole-grain breads if you prefer.

Whole-wheat breads toasted, brushed with olive oil, and rubbed with a clove of garlic serve well as appetizers and light meals. Cover them thinly with a spread such as the White Bean Spread or Olive Paste, then garnish them with fresh herbs or low-fat mozzarella cheese and tomatoes. Serve these with wine before a meal, with soup for lunch or dinner, or by themselves as the main part of a meal or a snack.

As you become familiar with some of the basic Mediterranean sauces and spreads you will see how well and how easily they work together, and sandwich combinations will naturally suggest themselves to you.

Find a good, true whole-grain bread in a good bakery or store or bake your own. Nothing is better than a loaf of homemade bread.

In the section on Sauces, Salad Dressings, and Spreads, the following spreads are wonderful on any kind of whole-grain breads in whichever form you like—whether slices from a regular loaf, pita breads, tortillas, or bruschettes.

Pesto (page 220)
Greek Garlic Sauce (Skordalia) (page 221)
Olive Paste (Tapenade) (page 222)
Lebanese Tarator Sauce (page 226)
Tomatillo Salsa (page 228)
Roasted Eggplant Spread (page 229)
Green Herb Sauce (Salsa Verde) (page 230)
Garlic Mayonnaise (with or without egg yolks) (page 232)
Tunisian Hot Pepper Sauce (Harissa) (page 234)

Falafel Sandwiches

by Deborah Madison

*F*alafel, patties made of a mixture of chickpea flour and spices, is a very satisfying dish. The little patties fit perfectly into a pita bread, or they can be served on a plate with the same sauces and accompaniments, with the pita on the side for a slightly more formal presentation. This type of sandwich is already a part of our culture—it can be bought from pushcarts all over New York and it makes an inexpensive and good on-the-spot meal.

FOR 2 SANDWICHES

2 whole-wheat pita breads
   Falafel Patties (page 312)
1 firm, ripe tomato, sliced
1 small cucumber, sliced
2 handfuls shredded romaine lettuce
   Lebanese Tarator Sauce (page 226) or nonfat Yogurt Dressing with
      Lemon and Tahini (page 225)

Shape the falafel into disklike patties and fry it according to the instructions. Let drain on a paper towel. Fill the pita halves with the patties, sliced tomatoes and cucumbers, a handful of lettuce, and a generous amount of the dressing. Serve and eat right away.

FAT PER SANDWICH: See dressing used

PITA SANDWICHES

by Deborah Madison

Pita, or pocket bread, makes an obvious container for sandwich fillings. Pita bread can be made from most bread doughs—it's a matter of rolling, shaping, and baking it properly, which takes a bit of practice to perfect. Fortunately, good whole-wheat pita bread is available to buy most everywhere, but if you want to know more about making pita or pocket bread yourself, see pages 440 and 467 of the *Superpyramid Bakery*, or take a look at *The Fannie Farmer Baking Book* or other books on breads.

Fillings for pita breads might include mixtures of fresh vegetables, grilled or roasted eggplant with tarator sauce or skordalia, hummus with lettuce and tomato, patties made of falafel and roasted peppers with tapenade, avocados and tomatoes with the tomatillo salsa, etc. Virtually all of the recipes for the sauces are delicious in the sandwiches. Your imagination, perhaps aided with what's in the refrigerator, should guide you to innumerable tasty sandwiches. Here are a few ideas to start with:

Pita Sandwich with Vegetables and Feta Cheese

by Deborah Madison

FOR 2 SANDWICHES

½ bunch scallions, the white part and some of the green, sliced
½ small bell pepper (any color), thinly sliced
1 small cucumber, peeled, seeded, and diced
2 ounces feta cheese, crumbled
6 Kalamata olives, pitted and chopped
2 radishes, diced
1 tablespoon parsley, chopped
1 tablespoon additional herbs, such as mint, marjoram, basil, or a mixture, chopped
   lemon vinaigrette (page 241) or Lebanese Tarator Sauce (page 226)
   freshly ground black pepper
4 large lettuce leaves
2 whole-wheat pita breads, cut in half
1–2 tomatoes, sliced

1. Combine the scallions, pepper, cucumber, feta cheese, olives, and radishes in a bowl with the herbs and toss with enough vinaigrette or tarator sauce to moisten. Season with pepper.

2. Line each pita half with a lettuce leaf and stuff the salad mixture on top of it to keep the bread from getting too soft. Slide the tomato slices on top of the vegetable mixture. Serve and eat right away.

FAT PER SANDWICH: Saturated 4–5 grams; unsaturated 2.5–3 grams
With low-fat mozzarella cheese: saturated 1 gram; unsaturated 2.5–3 grams

Pita Sandwiches with Hummus and Yogurt Dressing

by Deborah Madison

*H*ummus *is often served with pita bread as an appetizer. It can also be used as stuffing. Hummus needs the tartness of the yogurt and something cool and moist, like sliced cucumbers or chopped romaine lettuce, to contrast with its more solid texture.*

FOR 2 SANDWICHES

2 whole-wheat pita breads, halved
1 cup Chickpeas with Tahini (Hummus bi Tahini) (page 331)
1 large cucumber, thinly sliced, and/or two handfuls chopped lettuce leaves
2 tablespoons chopped parsley and mint, mixed
  Yogurt Dressing (page 223)
  olives and radishes, for garnish

Line each of the pita halves with a quarter of the hummus. Stuff in the cucumber and/or lettuce leaves, tossed with the herbs. Drizzle the yogurt dressing into the sandwiches. Serve garnished with olives and garden radishes.

FAT PER SANDWICH: Saturated 1–1.5 grams; unsaturated 7–11 grams

Tempeh Sandwich with Sprouts

by Gene Spiller

This delicious sandwich combines Western and Oriental tastes. Try it open-face or as a regular sandwich.

  1 (for open-faced) or 2 slices whole-grain bread
  ¼ avocado or 1–2 teaspoons Olive Paste (page 222)
  1 3-ounce tempeh patty broiled for 3 or 4 minutes, according to instructions on tempeh package
  a handful of sprouts of your choice
1–2 slices ripe tomato
1–2 leaves of dark green lettuce or radicchio
  1 ounce low-fat mozzarella cheese or other cheese (optional)

Wonderful without any further preparation, or place in the oven at 350° F. for 3–4 minutes.

FAT PER SANDWICH (TEMPEH FAT CONTENT VARIES DEPENDING ON TYPE): Without cheese: saturated 2.5–5 grams; unsaturated 10–12 grams
With low-fat mozzarella cheese: saturated 4–6 grams; unsaturated 11–17 grams

CROUTONS AND OPEN-FACED SANDWICHES

Here are a few suggestions for croutons, bruschettes, and open-faced sandwiches. Most begin with toasted bread. One way is to grill thick slices of bread over the coals until they are marked on the outside but still soft inside. If you prefer bruschettes, these in the true Italian definition are dry and slightly toasted through. Choose whichever you like best, but be sure the bread is whole-grain.

Toasted Croutons

by Deborah Madison

Slice as many pieces of bread as you wish to use. Toast on both sides in a toaster, oven, or over a charcoal fire. As soon as they are done, brush them lightly with a flavorful extra-virgin olive oil and rub the warm surface with a fat clove of garlic that has been cut in half. (At this point they will smell wonderful.) They can be eaten without further adornment, or used as the foundation for any of the ideas suggested below. They can also be covered, while warm, with shavings of Parmesan Reggiano and eaten alongside or floated in a bowl of soup.

FAT PER SERVING: Depends on amount of olive oil (page 219) and type of bread used. Homemade breads from the Superpyramid Bakery have only traces of fat from the germ.

Bruschettes

by Gene Spiller

Bruschettes are a Southern Italian bread that is prepared by slowly drying slices of bread—of whichever type you choose—at a lower temperature than typical toast or croutons. The bread does not turn dark and it becomes quite dry so that it keeps for a long time and can be taken camping or on backpack trips or kept around for a wonderful snack. One easy way to prepare bruschettes is to place slices of whole-grain bread in the oven at a low temperature (about 200–250° F.) until they are quite dry. You can use them as crunchy bread like Swedish dry rye breads. They are wonderful with the same spreads and fillings used for croutons and other open-faced sandwiches. Any of the recipes that follow can be used for bruschettes as well as for croutons.

FAT PER SERVING: Depends on bread used. Homemade breads from the Superpyramid Bakery have only traces of fat from the germ.

Avocado Open-faced Sandwich with Tomatillo Salsa

by Deborah Madison

This is good on both bread and toasted croutons. Whichever you choose, cover with thin slices of avocado. Drizzle Tomatillo Salsa (page 228) or Green Herb Sauce (page 230) over the top. Add freshly ground pepper and serve. If you don't have the salsa on hand, squeeze a lime over the avocado and garnish with minced green chili, onions, and cilantro.

FAT PER SANDWICH: For 1 ounce avocado and small amount of tomatillo sauce: saturated 0.5–1 grams; unsaturated 3–4 grams

Open-faced Sandwich with Olive Paste and Low-fat Mozzarella Cheese

by Deborah Madison

Cover a long crouton (page 356) or a slice of bread with a layer of Olive Paste (page 222), then with thin slices or coarsely grated low-fat mozzarella cheese. If you like, slip a few onion rings, roasted peppers, or sliced tomatoes between the pieces of cheese. Put under the broiler or in toaster oven until the cheese is melted and bubbling. Serve hot, either whole or cut in finger-shaped pieces.

FAT PER SANDWICH: Approximately, per ounce of low-fat mozzarella: saturated 3–3.5 grams; unsaturated 2–2.5 grams (depends on amount of Olive Paste)

Croutons with Roasted Peppers and Yogurt Cheese

by Deborah Madison

Add some capers to the Roasted Peppers (page 342) along with freshly chopped garlic and fresh basil leaves, and a thin slice of lemon, finely chopped. Moisten with extra-virgin olive oil.

Spread croutons with a layer of Yogurt Cheese (page 363) and pile the seasoned peppers on top.

Or, spread the croutons with Olive Paste (222) and garnish with the peppers. In this case, omit the capers from the pepper mixture as they are already present in the olive paste.

FAT PER SERVING: With cheese made from nonfat milk: traces only. If you use Olive Paste see page 222 for fat content.

Croutons with White Bean Puree

by Deborah Madison

Cover croutons with a thick layer of the White Bean Puree with Rosemary on page 332. Drizzle with extra-virgin olive oil, freshly ground pepper, and a little finely chopped rosemary. Garnish the plate with branches of rosemary. If you have rosemary in your garden, use some of the lavender-blue flowers for a garnish as well.

FAT PER SERVING PER TABLESPOON OF OLIVE OIL: Saturated 0.8 gram; unsaturated 6 grams (depends on amount of olive oil)

Croutons with Ricotta and Marjoram

by Deborah Madison

Place ricotta in the oven or on the stove until it is warm, then spread on croutons and garnish with freshly chopped marjoram and a drizzle of extra-virgin olive oil. Serve while warm with a bowl of olives and a plate of fresh vegetables, for an appetizer. Or serve for dessert with crushed walnuts, instead of pepper, and slices of ripe pears.

FAT PER SERVING: With about 1 tablespoon of low-fat ricotta and 1 teaspoon of olive oil: Saturated 1–1.5 grams; unsaturated 3–4 grams (walnuts and olives will add more good unsaturated fat)

Croutons with Pesto

by Deborah Madison

Cover the croutons with a thin layer of pesto—the pesto seasoned with tomato (Pistou, page 289) or the green pesto (Pesto, page 220). Garnish with fresh leaves of any variety of basil and serve.

FAT PER SERVING: See spread used

Open-faced Sandwich with Pesto and Tomatoes

by Deborah Madison

Spread toasted croutons thinly with Pesto (page 220) and cover with overlapping slices of absolutely ripe tomatoes. Season with a pinch of salt and freshly ground pepper.

FAT PER SANDWICH: See Pesto

Croutons with Olive Paste

by Deborah Madison

Cover toasted croutons with a layer of Olive Paste (page 222). Garnish with chopped herbs—mainly parsley with a little thyme, basil, or marjoram—tossed with a pinch or two of grated lemon zest.

FAT PER SERVING: See Olive Paste

Croutons or Sandwich with Yogurt Cheese, Cucumbers, and Tomatoes

by Deborah Madison

Cover toasted croutons or piece of bread with a layer of nonfat Yogurt Cheese (page 363), sliced cucumbers, and tomatoes. Drizzle a little extra-virgin olive oil over the top and add a twist of freshly ground pepper. Serve with a wedge of lemon and a few olives on the side. If you like, add a sprinkling of freshly chopped herbs (parsley, basil, dill, lovage, marjoram, cilantro) or garnish with whole leaves slipped between the tomatoes and cucumbers.

FAT PER SERVING: Trace from olive oil

Yogurts

Yogurt is a basic tier-one food when nonfat or very low-fat. It's so important in the Superpyramid plan that we have gathered here a series of recipes for various foods in which yogurt is the major component. You'll also find yogurts used in a variety of other recipes throughout this recipe part of the book. Read again chapter 4, pages 81–91.

Basic Yogurt

For the best-flavored yogurt, choose the freshest possible nonhomogenized milk, although other milks such as homogenized, skimmed, and nonfat can certainly be used. If you use whole, nonhomogenized milk, remove the fat that floats on top. Even though milk has usually been pasteurized, to ensure success bring the milk to a full rolling boil before cooling it and combining it with the yogurt culture. Boiling kills bacteria still present in the milk, which although not harmful, may affect the final yogurt flavor and consistency. For a culture, use a favorite brand of plain yogurt—one whose label specifies that it contains active cultures—with the fewest possible ingredients. Always use fresh yogurt as the starter culture for a good-tasting and well-set yogurt. Use utensils that have been well washed, rinsed, and dried.

2–4 pints milk
   2 tablespoons fresh plain yogurt with active cultures
      insulated or heated yogurt container

1. Bring milk to a full rolling boil using half heat on burner or hotplate and a heat-dispersing grid, to avoid burning the milk. Boil milk in microwave oven if you have one. Allow the milk to cool down to about 115° F.
2. Stir the plain yogurt in a separate bowl until the yogurt is smooth and liquid. Spoon the skin off the top of the milk and mix in the yogurt culture. Stir well.
3. Pour the mixed milk and culture into a glass or plastic container. Place inside insulated or heated container. Leave it there to incubate for 6–24 hours. Once yogurt has set, it can be refrigerated.

Note: If the yogurt sets and is good tasting, then you can be sure that it has been properly made. If by chance it does not set after about 24 hours or if it has an off taste, the milk should be discarded and the process repeated with fresh ingredients.

VARIATIONS
For flavored yogurt, mix plain yogurt with jam, honey, vanilla flavoring, cinnamon, or your favorite flavoring.

FAT CONTENT OF YOGURTS
In some of the following recipes you won't find a fat analysis. The reason is simple: the fat content of yogurts, yogurt cheeses, and yogurt drinks depends on the milk used. Your first choice is a nonfat (or very low-fat) yogurt and *the fat content is practically zero;* for low-fat the total fat is about 1 to 1.5 percent and the saturated fat about 0.7 to 1 percent; for whole-milk yogurt total fat is about 3–3.5 percent with about 2–2.5 grams saturated. Because of this possible wide variation in fat content, some recipes in this section do not have a fat analysis. To translate the percentage given here to the recipes that follow, it's useful to think of percentages as the amount in approximately three ounces of yogurt. For recipes containing other sources of fat, a fat analysis is given.

Yogurt Cheese

by Deborah Madison

*T*his cheese—firm, creamy, and a little tart—is made by draining yogurt in a colander lined with cheesecloth. The longer it drains, the more firm it becomes. Yogurt cheese can be used both for savory dishes and for desserts. As a savory cheese it can be served with olive oil poured over the top, garnished with fresh herbs and coarse pepper. Or it can be used plain as a spread for toast, in sandwiches, or on a plate with fresh vegetables. It can also be mixed with other cheeses, such as goat cheeses, then used in various ways—as a filling for crepes, between layers of baked eggplant, or as a spread.

As a dessert, yogurt cheese is delicious with honey, fruit, and nuts. Form an attractive scoop of cheese on a dessert plate (a spring-loaded ice cream scoop works well) and drizzle it with your favorite honey. Add some fresh fruits in summer or dried fruits in winter, and a few roasted almonds.

The whey that drains off the cheese can be used in soups or in bread. It also makes a wonderful tart and refreshing beverage by itself. It's high in easily digestible proteins and calcium.

MAKES ABOUT 2 CUPS

1 quart yogurt
½ teaspoon salt (optional)
cheesecloth

1. Line a colander with two or three layers of cheesecloth, first rinsed in cold water. Pour the yogurt in, fold the ends of the cheesecloth over the top, then refrigerate with something underneath to catch the liquid. If the colander does not have a raised bottom or feet, place it on a small, inverted bowl to let the whey drain off. Leave overnight.
2. The next day, pull back the cheesecloth and check the thickness of the cheese. If you want a firmer cheese, let it continue to drain until it is the thickness you like.
3. Turn the cheese out of the cheesecloth onto a plate. (This makes a pretty presentation in itself with the fine pattern of the cloth imprinted in the cheese.) Store, covered, in the refrigerator, until ready to serve. The yogurt cheese will last a week or more.

Yogurt Sauce with Mint

by Deborah Madison

½ cup low-fat or nonfat yogurt
2–3 tablespoons honey, to taste
  1 tablespoon finely chopped mint leaves
½ tablespoon grated orange zest

Combine ingredients and let stand for at least half an hour for mint to release its flavor. Add to Fruit Plate (see page 384), to taste.

Yogurt Drink with Fresh Mint

by Deborah Madison

Yogurt is used as a drink throughout the Middle East. It is very refreshing, like buttermilk, and usually flavored with fresh mint. Be sure to use yogurt that isn't stabilized with gelatin or flavored with fruit. You can add your own seasonal fruits when they are at their best.

MAKES 2 TALL GLASSES

2 cups low-fat yogurt
1 cup cold water or ice
  pinch of salt
1 tablespoon or more dried or fresh mint, to taste

Combine the yogurt and water or ice in a blender, add the salt and mint, and puree. Taste and add more mint if you like.
   Its flavor will come out as it sits. Refrigerate until ready to serve.

Yogurt Drink with Fruit

by Deborah Madison

In a food processor or blender, whiz 2 cups low-fat yogurt and 1 cup water or ice with ripe stone fruits, such as nectarines, peaches, and apricots. A drop or two of almond extract will enhance the flavor of these fruits. Or use tropical fruits, such as mango, banana, papaya, and passion fruit. If the stone fruits are organic, there's no need to peel them. Just be sure they are ripe and the pits have been removed.

Yogurt Drink with Berries and Bananas

by Deborah Madison

This could also be served as a dessert poured over whole berries in a brandy snifter or wineglass.

MAKES ABOUT 4 CUPS

1 banana
1 cup raspberries, blackberries, or strawberries
¼ cup passion fruit or grenadine syrup or ½ cup freshly squeezed orange juice
2 cups nonfat or low-fat yogurt
¼ teaspoon vanilla

Combine everything in a blender or food processor and puree. Chill and serve very cold in tall glasses with a garnish of berries or mint leaves.

Egg Dishes
for Breakfast,
Lunch, and
Dinner

FAT AND CHOLESTEROL ANALYSES
FOR EGG DISHES

All the egg dishes in this section use either only egg whites or a limited amount of egg yolk. If there are egg yolks, the amount of cholesterol per serving is listed at the end of the recipe. When you decrease your intake of meats, poultry, and fish it's important to eat some of these egg dishes to make your Superpyramid Program successful. One egg yolk, depending on size of egg and sometimes the way the chickens are fed, contains 200 to 250 mg of cholesterol. In the recipes that follow, each serving never contains more than one egg yolk.

Superpyramid Scrambled Eggs

by Gene Spiller

*T*his is a basic egg dish that can be varied in many ways by adding different ingredients.

SERVES 2

1–2 tablespoons water
  1 tablespoon extra-virgin olive oil
  4 egg whites from large eggs (or 3 from extra-large eggs)
  1 egg yolk (optional)
    herb(s) of your choice (e.g., sage, thyme, rosemary)
    salt to taste

1. Heat water and olive oil (if you prefer use only olive oil) in a frying pan. (Do not overheat).

2. Beat the eggs (with the water if not used in pan) in a bowl, add any herbs, trace of salt to taste, and pour the mixture into the frying pan. Stir gently while the eggs are cooking to prevent sticking. Cook to desired consistency. Serve warm. This is a very plain dish unless you use herbs to enhance the flavor or have some additional ingredients (see variations below). Great on whole-grain toast as an open sandwich. If you eliminate the egg yolk the color is very pale and you should add some colorful ingredients such as fresh tomatoes, tomato sauce, or olive paste (see Variations).

VARIATIONS

The number of variations is almost endless—use your imagination. If you use very flavorful variations, you may want to leave out the egg yolk.

With Tomatoes Add some fresh, peeled ripe tomatoes in small pieces as you begin to cook the eggs.

With Avocado When the eggs are cooked, add a few slices of a ripe avocado.

368 A THE SUPERPYRAMID EATING PROGRAM

With Olive Paste Do not use any salt and add some Olive Paste (page 222) or chopped, pitted olives when the eggs are almost cooked.

With Apples This is a sweet variation. Add one sliced apple and serve with some brown sugar or honey. Leave out herbs for this variation.

With Low-fat Cheese Add some small pieces of a low-fat cheese—such as low-fat mozzarella—or grate some Parmesan Reggiano and mix with the eggs when they are almost cooked. If you use a regular, salted cheese do not add any salt to the eggs.

FAT PER SERVING FOR THE BASIC RECIPE: Without egg yolk: saturated traces; unsaturated 2–3 grams
With one egg yolk: saturated 2–3 grams; unsaturated 5–6 grams; 100–130 grams cholesterol

Superpyramid Parmesan Cheese Omelet

by Gene Spiller

A wonderful breakfast omelet that can be varied in many ways. Combined with good whole-grain breads, this gives you a good supply of energy and protein for the day.

SERVES 2

> 4 egg whites
> herb(s) of your choice (e.g., sage, thyme, rosemary), preferably fresh
> 1–2 tablespoons water
> 1 egg yolk (optional)
> 2 tablespoons extra-virgin olive oil
> 2 tablespoons Parmesan Reggiano cheese (see variations for other cheeses)
> 1 ripe slice avocado, tomato, or freshly made tomato sauce
> (no salt, as the Parmesan cheese supplies enough flavor)

Beat the eggs with the herbs in a bowl with 1 or 2 tablespoons of water. If you wish you can add one egg yolk. Heat the olive oil in an omelet pan and when it's hot pour in the eggs. Cook as a normal omelet, by shaking the pan back and forth a few times (see a good cookbook such as Deborah Madison, *The Savory Way*, for techniques on omelet cooking). When the omelet is partially cooked add the Parmesan or other cheese and cook until the eggs are set. You may slice an avocado or tomato on top just before serving, or top with a dollop of fresh tomato sauce.

VARIATIONS

1. Replace Parmesan cheese with either 1 ounce Yogurt Cheese (page 363), in which case you may want to add some salt, or 1 ounce low-fat mozzarella cheese in small pieces.
2. For a more complete meal, add some tender spinach leaves (or other green leaf such as arugula) without hard stems before cooking. If you choose a tough leaf, precook the leaf for a few minutes with a trace of water in a separate pan.
4. Add one egg yolk for color.

FAT PER SERVING: With a teaspoon of Parmesan per serving: saturated 2–2.5 grams; unsaturated 7–8 grams
With nonfat yogurt cheese: saturated 0.5 gram; unsaturated 7–8 grams
With low-fat mozzarella cheese: saturated 4 grams; unsaturated 7–8 grams
With ½ avocado: saturated 3 grams; unsaturated 15–20 grams
If one large egg yolk added for 2 servings: cholesterol about 100–130 mg per serving

Orange Marmalade Omelet

by Gene Spiller

A wonderful breakfast omelet if you want something sweet. It can be varied in many ways by replacing the orange marmalade with other fruit preserves or jams.

SERVES 2

   4 egg whites
1–2 tablespoons water
3–4 tablespoons orange marmalade or other fruit jam or preserve
   1 tablespoon sesame or almond oil

Beat the eggs with 1 or 2 tablespoons of water. If you wish, you can add one egg yolk. Warm a sweet-tasting oil (almond or sesame oil) in an omelet pan and when it's hot, pour in the eggs. Cook as a normal omelet, by shaking the pan back and forth a few times (see a good cookbook such as Deborah Madison's *The Savory Way* for techniques on omelet cooking). When the omelet is almost cooked, place the orange marmalade (or other jam or preserve) in the middle and fold the omelet on top of the marmalade. Serve warm.

FAT PER SERVING: Saturated 0.5 gram; unsaturated 4–6 grams

Savory Baked Egg-Tofu Patties

by Gene and Monica Spiller

*T*asty main dish to serve for dinner accompanied by seasonal vegetables and a mixture of wild and brown rice.

FOR 4 TOFU PATTIES (SERVES 2)

1 cup mashed soft tofu
4 tablespoons nonfat yogurt
4 large egg whites
1 cup raw wheat germ
4 teaspoons fresh thyme
  salt to taste
1 tablespoon olive oil
4 teaspoons grated low-fat cheese
4 mushrooms
2 lemons

Finely mash tofu and mix with yogurt in mixing bowl. Lightly beat egg whites and add to tofu mixture. Add wheat germ, thyme, and salt. Mix well. Lightly coat a baking dish with olive oil. Spoon the mixture into dish in form of 4 round patties. Decorate with grated cheese and sliced mushrooms. Bake in preheated oven at 350–375° F. for 20–30 minutes. Cut lemons into halves and remove pips. Serve with lemon halves to be squeezed onto tofu cakes. You may want to experiment with soft and hard tofus (page 215).

FAT PER SERVING: Saturated 1.5–2 grams; unsaturated 8–9 grams

Herb Patties

by Gene and Monica Spiller

Richly herbed patties for dinner. Serve with salad and cooked vegetables and a grain of your choice.

SERVES 4

4 egg whites
2 cups wheat germ, preferably raw
1 cup plain nonfat yogurt
   finely ground salt to taste
   a sprig each of fresh chives, curly parsley, sage, rosemary, and thyme
1 tablespoon olive oil
1 lemon (slices or juice)

Lightly beat egg whites and mix them together with wheat germ and yogurt. Add salt and mix well. Finely chop chives and parsley and mix in well. Coat a baking dish with olive oil. Spoon the mixture into baking dish in the form of 4 round patties. Lay sage, rosemary, and thyme leaves between the patties. Bake in preheated oven at 325° F. for 20–30 minutes. To serve, transfer patties to a clean, warm dish and decorate with fresh parsley and lemon slices.

FAT PER SERVING: Saturated 1.5 grams; unsaturated 6 grams

VARIATION
Add some grated low-fat mozzarella or Parmesan Reggiano to the egg whites at mixing time.

Fish and Poultry Recipes, with Some Suggestions on Red Meats

INTRODUCTION

No recipe in the previous sections of the Superpyramid Kitchen contained any meat, fish, or poultry: All these are optional foods in this program.

Remember: You do not have to eat any of the foods in this section of the Superpyramid Kitchen. If you choose to eat fish, poultry, or red meats, remember that fish is an option on the third tier and poultry and meats are an option on the fourth tier. This means that fish should be your first choice; you can eat it more liberally, as long as it does not become your main source of energy. Remember that fish contains those good omega-3 oils.

The number of recipes for fish and poultry in this section are very few. No recipes are given for red meat—only a few preparation and shopping tips—for two reasons: Most people know how to prepare a lean piece of red meat and omitting recipes de-emphasizes red meat as a regular part of meals.

SERVING SIZES

In the Superpyramid the serving sizes of meat and poultry are smaller than serving sizes in standard cookbooks or listings of food nutrients in food tables. A serving of steak, for example, in the Superpyramid should be 2–3 ounces, compared to 6–10 ounces in a typical serving. A serving of fish should be about 2–4 ounces. Analyses at the end of each recipe are based on small serving sizes.

Poached Salmon

by Jody Main

SERVES 4

½ cup water
½ cup dry white wine or white zinfandel
2 cloves garlic, thinly sliced
2 tablespoons fresh dill, chopped, or 1 teaspoon dry dill
2 fresh salmon steaks, rinsed and patted dry
1 teaspoon Dijon mustard
1 tablespoon plain nonfat yogurt

1. Bring water, wine, garlic, and dill to a boil. Add salmon, cover, lower heat, and simmer (poach) gently for 10 minutes or until salmon flakes when tested with a fork. Turn off heat and remove salmon from pan.
2. Reduce liquid to about ½ cup, remove from heat, and add mustard and yogurt. Whirl in a blender or food processor for a few seconds to puree garlic into sauce. Remove the center bone from each salmon steak, dividing each in half.
3. Place salmon onto a small platter and ladle with sauce. Serve with a light grain dish and steamed asparagus with fresh lemon juice for a very elegant meal. The poached salmon is also wonderful placed over a bed of hot whole-grain pasta. Ladle with sauce and serve with a green salad with slivers of fresh fennel.

FAT PER SERVING (FOUR 5-OUNCE SERVINGS): Saturated 1 gram; unsaturated 5–6 grams

Broiled Fillet of Sole Amandine

by Jody Main

*T**his elegant dish is a good choice for dinner parties.*

SERVES 8

1 pound fresh fillet of sole
  juice of ½ fresh lemon
1 tablespoon extra-virgin olive oil
2 cloves garlic, crushed
1 teaspoon mirin (Japanese cooking wine)
1 teaspoon soy sauce
1 teaspoon paprika
2 tablespoons slivered almonds
½ lemon, sliced

1. Wash fillets, remove bones, pat dry, place in baking pan, and drizzle with lemon juice. Blend oil, garlic, mirin, and soy sauce and lightly brush fillets on both sides. Sprinkle with paprika and then with the almond slivers.

2. Preheat broiler for a few minutes until hot. Broil fillets, 3–4 inches from the flame, for about 5 minutes or until they begin to crisp around the edges. Be sure the fish does not cook too dry and that the almonds do not burn. Serve with slices of lemon. Combines well with Wehani Pilaf (page 301).

FAT PER SERVING: Saturated traces; unsaturated 0.5–1 gram

Baked Red Snapper on Garlic Toasts

by Rowena Hubbard

SERVES 8

RED SNAPPER

1 pound red snapper fillet, cut into 8 portions
3 tablespoons dry white wine
1 teaspoon grated lemon peel
2 teaspoons chopped fresh dill, or 1 teaspoon dried dill weed
¼ cup each, carrot and zucchini julienne
¼ cup sliced natural almonds, toasted
2 tablespoons olive oil
    Roasted Garlic Toast (below)

Cut eight 12-x-12-inch squares of baking parchment paper. Place one portion of fish in center of each square. Sprinkle with wine, lemon peel, and dill. Toss carrots and zucchini with almonds. Divide mixture evenly over fish. Drizzle with olive oil. Fold edges of paper over top of fish; crimp edges together around fish to seal. Place packages on baking sheet; bake at 375° F. for 8 minutes, or until fish is cooked through. Arrange 1 slice of Roasted Garlic Toast on each of 8 plates. Spoon fish and all juice in each package onto toast to serve.

Roasted Garlic Toast

1 head garlic, outer skins removed
2 tablespoons dry white wine
2 tablespoons olive oil
8 slices whole-grain bread, toasted

Place garlic head in glass measuring cup; drizzle with wine and olive oil. Cover; microwave on high power for 4 minutes. Remove from oven and cool, covered, 5 minutes. Squeeze garlic cloves from skins. Mash cloves onto one side of toast slices before serving.

FAT PER SERVING (FISH): Saturated 1 gram; unsaturated 5–7 grams

FAT PER 1 SLICE OF TOAST: Saturated 0.3 gram; unsaturated 1.5–2 grams

Roast Turkey with Aromatic Gravy

by Jody Main

This is a basic turkey recipe. The roasted garlic cloves, when individually squeezed from their skins onto bread, are creamy, mild, and delicious.

SERVINGS DEPEND ON SIZE OF TURKEY

    1 turkey
     paprika
    4 onions, quartered
    4 parsnips or carrots, cut in 2-inch pieces
    2 fennel bulbs, quartered
½–1 pound whole fresh mushrooms
    6 stalks celery, cut in 2-inch pieces
3–4 whole heads of garlic, unpeeled

1. Rinse turkey, pat dry, and lay in a large roasting pan. Sprinkle liberally with paprika. Fill cavities with washed, trimmed, and cut vegetables. Lay remaining vegetables around turkey to flavor the gravy. Add 1 quart water and place in a preheated 400° F. oven for 30 minutes. Lower oven temperature to 325° F., loosely cover with foil, and roast 20 minutes per pound or until done. The drumstick should readily move.

2. Remove turkey from roasting pan onto a large platter and surround it with vegetables that are still intact, including the garlic. Pour juices through a colander into a tall mason-type jar. Remove the fat that has risen to the surface with a small ladle and return juices to the roasting pan. Bring to a simmer on the stove.

3. Reduce liquid and season to taste. Serve turkey and vegetables with the aromatic gravy on the side.

FAT PER SERVING (ABOUT 4 OUNCES): Saturated 1–2 grams; unsaturated 2–3 grams

Chicken and Roman Ground Almond Soup or Stew

by Rowena Hubbard

SERVES 10

2½ pounds lean boneless chicken parts without skin
  4 cups water
  1 stalk celery, halved
  1 carrot, sliced
  3 parsley sprigs
  1 bay leaf
  2 teaspoons seasoned salt
  1 cup stewed tomatoes
½ cup chopped onion
½ cup slivered almonds, lightly toasted and ground*
  1 eggplant (about 1 pound), sliced ½ inch thick
  1 medium green bell pepper, cut into strips
⅛ teaspoon ground pepper
    hot steamed brown rice
    toasted sliced almonds, for garnish

1. In large pot, combine chicken, water, celery, carrot, parsley, bay leaf, and salt. Bring to boil, reduce heat, and simmer until chicken is tender, about 30 minutes.
2. Strain stock; cool and chill. Discard celery, carrot, parsley, and bay leaf.
3. Cool chicken; slice chicken into bite-size pieces.
4. Skim fat from stock. Return stock to pot with chicken, tomatoes, and onions; heat to simmering. Add almonds, eggplant, green pepper, and ground pepper. Simmer 40 minutes or until eggplant is tender.
5. Serve in soup bowls over hot steamed rice. Garnish with toasted sliced almonds.

FAT PER SERVING: Saturated 2–3 grams; unsaturated 7–10 grams

---

* Toast almonds by spreading in a single layer on a baking sheet. Bake at 350° F., 9–11 minutes, until lightly browned. Remove and cool. Almonds will continue to toast slightly during cooling.

Savory Chicken

by Jody Main

*T*his is a basic recipe for chicken breasts.

SERVES 8

8 chicken breasts, boned and skinned
2 cloves crushed garlic
   paprika
2 cups chicken stock
½ cup white wine
½ teaspoon or a few leaves fresh rosemary
2 tablespoons whole-wheat pastry (or fine) flour
12 shiitaki or other mushrooms

Place chicken in a broiling pan. Rub with garlic and sprinkle with paprika. Broil about 10 minutes, until the top turns golden. In a heavy saucepan bring stock, wine, rosemary, and flour to a boil while stirring with a whisk. Add mushrooms and bring to a boil again, stirring. Add chicken breasts and bring to a boil, lower heat, cover, and simmer gently for 30 minutes. Serve with whole-grain pasta or rice or other whole grain.

FAT PER SUPERPYRAMID SERVING (1 CHICKEN BREAST): Saturated 0.5–1 gram; unsaturated 1.5–3 grams

BEEF AND OTHER MEATS

Beef, lamb, pork, and similar meats are optional on the fourth tier of the Superpyramid. If you choose to eat them, eat only very small amounts. They should never, never be your main source of energy. Reread chapter 7. Remember that lean poultry has a better balance of fats.

Buying Meats

Buy only extremely lean cuts. The appearance of meats that have not been ground reveals extra fat much more than ground meats do. Ask a reliable market to recommend their leanest cuts. First of all, be sure that there is no visible fat or that whatever fat is visible is easy to trim off. For beef, pork, or lamb, usually the *loin* cuts are a good lean choice, as is top round for beef and rib cuts for lamb. For ground beef or other ground meat some markets now offer extra-lean or super-lean classifications; these should be the only ones to buy. Labels are getting better as the meat industry has become conscious of the need for leaner meats. If you find beef raised on an open pasture—which means grass-fed— buy it, as it may have a better fat composition.

Cooking and Serving Tips

Broiling is a good way to cook meat. Let the fat drip down so it can be eliminated as much as possible *but not on hot charcoal or other hot burner as the fumes produced by the burning fat are very undesirable.* One serving should not exceed 2–3 ounces of lean meat. Eat red meats as a *side* dish to a large plate of rice or other grain. In Mediterranean countries beef is often boiled in a pot full of water. This removes some of the fat (be sure to discard the water and not to use it as a soup stock!) and is a good option. Flavor the water with salt and herbs such as rosemary or sage.

Desserts

MEDITERRANEAN DESSERTS
by Deborah Madison

lthough the Mediterranean countries all produce sweet crea-
tions made with white flour, sugar, cream, and eggs, simple
desserts of fruit and cheeses are also traditional. Those who
have traveled in Europe have probably had the pleasure of being served
a basket of perfect white peaches, a dessert bowl of sweet berries, a
flawless pear, or a cluster of grapes and found it completely satisfying.
It is a way of eating that is easy to adapt to.

One approach to desserts in the Superpyramid plan is to leave pastries
behind and go on in the direction of fruits, some low-fat cheese desserts,
and occasionally a small piece of a low- or medium-fat cheese such as
low-fat mozzarella or Parmesan, to accompany a choice pear. Certainly
the preparation of fruit is very easy. Fruit is naturally beautiful and it
can be served simply whole at the table, with a fruit knife for each
person, or it can be peeled and sliced by the cook. Different fruits combined with one another make beautiful arrangements.

If fruit is delicious to begin with, nothing need be done to improve it.
The difficult part is finding good fruit, and to succeed with the search is
to find yourself involved with the change that's gradually taking place in
agriculture—the emergence of local organic farmers, farming with traditional methods. The products of these farmers are always most re-
warding for freshness and flavor. For the most part the supermarket is
a poor source of good fruit. Most of it is picked too green ever to ripen
and it is heavily treated with chemicals, both of which impede flavor.

Fresh Yogurt Cheese with Summer Fruits

by Deborah Madison

This is the simplest of summer desserts—a scoop of fresh cheese and ripe berries. A little brown sugar sprinkled over the berries helps bring out their juices and sweeten those that are tart.

SERVES 4

1 cup nonfat Yogurt Cheese (page 363)
1 pint or more ripe berries (blackberries, olallieberries, raspberries, blueberries, etc.)
  honey or dark brown sugar, to taste
  edible blossoms, if available, such as rose geranium, pineapple sage, violets, or rose petals

Make an attractive mound of cheese on each of four plates. Surround with berries sprinkled with a little brown sugar. Garnish with blossoms, if available, either finely cut into a colorful confetti or tucked on the side among the fruits.

VARIATIONS

Use low-fat ricotta instead of the yogurt cheese. The ricotta doesn't have the tartness of yogurt and may be preferable to some for that reason. There will be slightly more saturated fat this way.

Or you may thin ricotta with yogurt or yogurt cheese and press it into little heart-shaped cheese molds, first lined with cheesecloth. For a delicate flavor, set a few rose geranium leaves on the cheesecloth before adding the cheese. Turn them out the next day on a pretty plate and serve with the berries and blossoms.

Instead of brown sugar, drizzle a little honey over the cheese and berries, unless they're already very sweet.

FAT ANALYSIS PER SERVING: With nonfat yogurt cheese: traces only
With low-fat ricotta cheese, 2 tablespoons per serving: saturated 1–2 grams; unsaturated 0.5–1 gram

Yogurt Cheese with Honey, Almonds, and Fruit

by Deborah Madison

*U*se a spring-loaded oval ice-cream scooper to make a beautiful mound of nonfat yogurt cheese. Or simply use two spoons to form an attractive shape. Use a honey with a special flavor, such as lavender honey from Provence, the wonderful Greek thyme-scented honey, or any good local honey. Choose your own favorite.

Scoop some nonfat Yogurt Cheese (page 363) on a plate and drizzle honey over the top. Garnish with a few toasted almonds and slices of seasonal fruit, such as juicy Comice or Bartlett pears, fresh figs and raspberries, or dried figs in the winter.

FAT PER SERVING: With 6 or 7 almonds: saturated trace, unsaturated 4 grams

Firm Ricotta Cheese and Pine Nuts

by Deborah Madison

*L*ow-fat ricotta cheese, like yogurt, can be pressed so that it becomes firm enough to slice, more like some Italian ricotta cheeses. Line a colander with a double layer of cheesecloth and place the ricotta in it. Fold the ends of the cloth over the cheese, place a heavy object (such as a can of olive oil) on top, and set in a bowl to drain overnight in the refrigerator. Unmold the next day. It should be thick enough to slice in wedges and serve.

Toast a spoonful of pine nuts per person in a dry pan until they are nicely colored, then remove them so that they don't continue to darken. Scatter them over a slice of cheese and drizzle with honey.

VARIATIONS

Use chopped toasted or raw almonds instead of pine nuts, or new crop walnuts, simply cracked and shelled. Instead of a drizzle of honey, you could serve a piece of honeycomb alongside the cheese.

In addition to nuts, serve the cheese with dried fruits, such as dates, figs, big monuka raisins, and apricots.

For a lower-fat variation use nonfat yogurt cheese with pine nuts or other nuts and use soft ricotta cheese rather than pressed.

FAT PER SERVING (ABOUT 2 OUNCES CHEESE OR YOGURT CHEESE): With low-fat ricotta: saturated 2–4 grams, unsaturated 3–5 grams
With nonfat yogurt cheese: saturated traces; unsaturated 3–4 grams

Fruit Plate with Yogurt and Mint

by Deborah Madison

A plate of perfectly ripened fruits makes an exquisite dessert or salad. Most fruits are lovely with a flavored nonfat yogurt sauce. Apples, grapes, and apricots are the few exceptions, but it's always a matter of personal choice. The really crucial point is to choose fruit that is fully ripe and flavorful. And the second crucial point is to limit yourself to five or six choices so that the plate doesn't become overcrowded.

Here are a few suggestions of fruits to use:

kiwi fruit, peeled and sliced thinly in rounds
tangerines, oranges, and grapefruit, peeled and sliced in
   rounds or in sections
pineapple, peeled, cored, and thinly sliced
figs, peeled or not, halved or sliced in rounds
peaches and nectarines, sliced
Italian prune-plums, halved or quartered
blackberries, raspberries, blueberries, left whole
strawberries, rinsed if necessary
mulberries, left whole

Yogurt Sauce with Mint (page 364)

Arrange beautifully sliced and whole fruits on dessert plates and drizzle the yogurt in a thin stream over them, garnishing, not covering, the fruit. Garnish the plate with additional mint leaves.

FAT PER SERVING: None with nonfat yogurt

Almond-Hazelnut Delight

by Gene Spiller

A *great dessert to crown a sophisticated dinner.*

SERVES 4

 4 large egg whites
 2 cups wheat germ, preferably raw
 1 cup plain yogurt
 1 teaspoon vanilla
2–3 tablespoons honey or brown sugar (or sweeten to taste)
 ½ cup ground almonds or hazelnuts (can be made in a food processor
  from whole raw almonds or hazelnuts)
 1 tablespoon almond or hazelnut oil

Lightly beat egg whites and mix them together with the wheat germ, yogurt, vanilla, and honey or brown sugar. After you have beaten the eggs well, add the ground almonds or hazelnuts (or a mixture of the two) and mix well. Coat a baking dish with a mild oil such as almond oil. Spoon the mixture into baking dish in the form of patties. You may also pour it into the pan to make a single flat cake and serve it in the baking dish, slicing it as desired. Bake in preheated oven at 325° F. for 20–30 minutes.

 Serve with some jam or sliced sweet fresh fruit or cooked dry fruit.

VARIATIONS

Add some dry fruits such as raisins to the mix when you add the almonds or hazelnuts. Or after 15 minutes of cooking, when the eggs are set, place a few slices of fresh sweet fruits such as peaches on top, then let it cook for another 10 minutes.

FAT PER SERVING: Saturated 2–3 grams; unsaturated 10–15 grams

Fruit Salad with Baby Sprouted Seeds and Almonds

by Jody Main

Sprouted seeds and nuts blended with fresh seasonal fruit is a wonderful luncheon meal or evening dessert. You can substitute your choice of fresh fruit in season for the figs and grapes in this recipe.

SERVES 12

1½ cups baby sunflower and pumpkin sprouts (pages 216, 217)
   2 cups almond sprouts (page 216)
   4 cups fresh ripe figs
   4 cups seedless grapes

Gently blend the fruit and sprouts. Be sure not to crush the fruit.

FAT ANALYSIS PER SERVING: Saturated 1–2 grams; unsaturated 2–8 grams (depends on degree of sprouting of seeds)

Cinnamon-Cardamom Ice Milk

by Deborah Madison

This ice milk is fragrant with spices. Fresh or candied blossoms and pistachio nuts, finely chopped, make a fitting garnish or addition, once the milk is frozen. It can be made either in an ice-cream freezer or in the freezer compartment of the refrigerator.

MAKES ABOUT 3½ CUPS

    3 cups low-fat milk
    3 cinnamon sticks
     zest of 1 lemon
    1 teaspoon cardamom seeds (can be in pods)
     two cloves
½–¾ cup honey
        garnishes: chopped pistachio nuts, chopped toasted almonds, candied
        rose petals, or violets chopped and sprinkled over the top

1. Combine all the ingredients except the garnishes in a soup pot. Bring to a boil, lower the heat to the lowest flame possible, and continue heating for another 20 minutes, then remove from the heat and allow to cool to room temperature.

2. Pour the flavored milk through a sieve and discard the spices and lemon peel. Freeze in an ice-cream freezer according to the instructions, or put in the freezer in a shallow pan until set. Once the ice milk is frozen in the pan, break it into chunks, then work in the food processor until it is completely smooth. Return to the freezer until ready to use.

3. To serve, scoop into tall glasses and serve with any of the suggested garnishes. Or scatter chopped rose petals and pistachio nuts over the surface of the ice milk before scooping, and bits of color, flavor, and texture will be rolled into each mouthful.

FAT PER CUP: With 2% low-fat milk: saturated 3 grams, unsaturated 2–3 grams

Pears with Gorgonzola

by Deborah Madison

*R*emember *that gorgonzola is similar to blue cheese in fat content and is a border-line tier-five food,* to be used only occasionally. *Pears with gorgonzola is a delectable combination, whether in a salad (with endive and walnut), on a sandwich (the cheese spread on grilled bread and the pear sliced on the top), or as a dessert, the cheese beaten until smooth and piled into the hollowed center of a perfectly ripe, peeled pear.*

To make the gorgonzola cheese more compatible with the Superpyramid, mix it with twice as much low-fat ricotta cheese. Do not exceed one tablespoon of gorgonzola.

Choose a firm but juicy pear, such as a Comice or a Bartlett. Peel the pear and remove the stem and core with a pointed teaspoon or a pear corer. Fill the cavity with the cheese and serve right away with a few fresh walnuts on the side.

Eat only occasionally, for a change. This recipe has more saturated than unsaturated fat.

VARIATION
Replace the gorgonzola cheese entirely with low-fat ricotta.

FAT ANALYSIS PER SERVING: Saturated 3 grams; unsaturated 1–1.5 grams (based on the equivalent of 2 tablespoons low-fat ricotta and 1 tablespoon gorgonzola)

Fruits with Liqueurs

by Deborah Madison

A simple fruit dessert can be made by flavoring fruits with a few drops of liqueur, either one with the same flavoring or one that contrasts and complements in a pleasing way. If liqueurs aren't in your diet plan, the same fruit plates make excellent desserts providing the fruit is of the most flavorful quality.

Important: Note that only a few drops of liqueur are used as a flavoring, in an amount that supplies hardly any alcohol at all.

Oranges with Cointreau

by Deborah Madison

Peel one or two navel oranges per person, removing all the white pith as you do so, then slice them in rounds and arrange them attractively on a pretty plate. Sprinkle a little Cointreau or Grand Marnier over the top and serve.

Or make a mixture of citrus, using tangerines, ruby grapefruits, blood oranges, and navels. Slice them in rounds and remove the seeds, or if you prefer, section each fruit. Be sure to catch the juice in a bowl as you work, and pour it, along with the liqueur, over the fruit. Pomegranate seeds and fresh mint leaves would make a seasonal and beautiful garnish.

NO FAT

Melon with Anise Liqueur

by Deborah Madison

Melons are ideal to pair with anise liqueurs. Cut chilled melons into wedges, then remove the skins. Dilute one or two teaspoons of anisette or Pernod with half as much water, pour over the melon, and serve.

NO FAT

Berries with Kirsch or Grand Marnier

by Deborah Madison

A ll berries are happily complemented with these two liqueurs. Lightly sugar the berries first, then toss with a little kirsch, Grand Marnier, or Cointreau. Let stand for a half hour or more for the flavors to absorb and serve alone, with yogurt cheese, or inside the cavity of a small cantaloupe or other melon.

NO FAT

Pineapple with Kirsch and Honey

by Deborah Madison

C hoose a ripe, fragrant pineapple, cut off the skin, and remove the eyes with the tip of a vegetable peeler. Cut the pineapple in rounds about ½ inch thick, then remove the core from each piece. Drizzle honey over the pineapple and add a few drops of kirsch and a garnish of fresh mint or lemon verbena leaves. Serve chilled, or heat the pineapple with the honey until it is hot and bubbling, then serve with a few drops of kirsch. (Heating is a good method if your pineapple isn't quite ripe enough.)

NO FAT

Pears with Ginger-Cardamom Cream

by Deborah Madison

*T*his cream goes well with pears, peaches, fresh figs, bananas, and other soft fruits. The flavor of the fresh ginger permeates the entire cream and the little nuggets of crystallized ginger make a spicy accent. If you're not using crystallized ginger, sweeten the cream with honey or maple syrup to taste.

Use ripe Bartlett or Comice pears. If the fruit is organic, you can leave the skins on. They are sometimes quite beautiful, especially when they're red.

SERVES 4

1 cup low-fat cottage cheese
1–2 tablespoons nonfat (or low-fat) yogurt
¼ teaspoon ground cardamom
½ teaspoon freshly grated ginger
2 pieces candied ginger, finely diced

1. Put the cottage cheese in a food processor with the yogurt and work until it is creamy and smooth.
2. Remove and add the cardamom, grated ginger, and candied ginger. Let stand in the refrigerator for a half-hour or longer for the flavors to merge. Serve chilled.
3. Halve the four pears and remove the cores with a melon baller or other special tool designed for the purpose. Set two halves on a plate and fill them with the Ginger-Cardamom Cream.

FAT PER CUP: With 1 percent low-fat cottage cheese: saturated 1.5–2 grams; unsaturated 0.5–1 gram

OTHER DESSERTS

For other desserts see The Superpyramid Bakery for pies, biscotti, raisin cake, and desserts based on grains. See Egg Dishes for baked-egg desserts.

Superpyramid Menus

These menus are just a few out of thousands of possible choices. Using the recipes from the Superpyramid Kitchen you can create an endless number of great meals for all tastes. As you plan a menu, always project in your mind the picture of the Superpyramid and base your menus on the foods on *tiers one and two*. Then add—at least at one or two of your meals—some foods from *tier three* such as nuts or olive oil. Use foods from *tiers four and five* to round out your daily Superpyramid. In your choice of *beverages*, remember that a beverage can be just a pleasant hot drink—such as tea—or can be an actual part of your Superpyramid choices—such as a glass of fresh orange juice or buttermilk.

Superpyramid Breakfast Menus

▲ *1* ▲

hot porridge from rolled or steel-cut oats
milk
raisins and honey
fresh fruit in season

▲ *2* ▲

fresh fruit in season
Top Ten Cereal (page 325) with yogurt and honey

▲ *3* ▲

Bread and Milk Breakfast*
(whole-grain toast, fresh whole-grain bread, or muffins broken up into a bowl of
milk, sweetened with honey or vino cotto)
fresh fruit juice or fresh fruit

▲ *4* ▲

Omelet (page 368)
sliced tomatoes in season
whole-wheat bread
yogurt or buttermilk

---

* This is an old-fashioned breakfast that is extremely nourishing. Break the bread into small pieces and place them in the bowl with the milk. Eat with a spoon as though you were eating a breakfast cereal. For some reason, this simple breakfast has been forgotten! It's fast to prepare—a truly *instant breakfast*—and well balanced. You may add a little coffee or black tea to your milk. For extra fun buy a special large cup or bowl for this taste treat. Placing bread in a bowl with milk should be just as acceptable as placing a prepared cereal in a bowl with milk! *Option:* replace the milk with almond or soy milk.

▲ *5* ▲

Scrambled Eggs (page 367)
fresh mixed green leaves
whole-grain toast or whole-wheat muffin
yogurt or buttermilk

▲ *6* ▲

boiled eggs
(eat whites only; small portion of yolk optional)
whole-grain toast
fresh fruit in season with yogurt

▲ *7* ▲

fresh mixed green leaves
large cup nonfat yogurt with honey
whole-grain toast with orange marmalade

▲

Beverages

Light tea with milk (black, green or herbal, honey optional) or moderate amount
of arabica coffee or roasted chicory or barley or glass of low-fat milk or buttermilk
or fresh fruit or vegetable juice.

Superpyramid Lunch Menus

▲ *1* ▲

Avocado Open-faced Sandwich with Tomatillo Salsa (page 358)
cup of yogurt flavored to your taste
fruit salad

▲ *2* ▲

Green Salad (page 243)
1–2 slices of low-fat cheese
whole-grain bun or toast with a few drops of olive oil
fruit

▲ *3* ▲

Roasted Vegetables (page 341)
whole-grain bun or toast with a few drops of olive oil
nonfat yogurt with honey
fruit

▲ *4* ▲

Leek, Mushroom, and Potato Soup (page 272)
toasted whole-grain bread or croutons in soup
Yogurt Cheese (page 363)
fruit

▲ 5 ▲

Salad of Mixed Tomatoes with Olive Oil, Herbs, and Capers (page 244)
Miso Broth (page 295) or Miso Soup (page 296)
whole-grain bread or croutons in broth
fruit and nuts

▲ 6 ▲

Tempeh Salad (page 260)
whole-grain croutons
fruit

▲ 7 ▲

Pita Sandwich (page 353)
yogurt with fresh fruit

▲ 8 ▲

Split-Pea Soup with Yogurt (page 276)
whole-grain bun with olive oil
fruit

▲

Beverages

Light tea with milk (black, green or herbal, honey optional) or moderate amount of arabica coffee or roasted chicory or barley or glass of low-fat milk or buttermilk or fresh fruit or vegetable juice.

Superpyramid Dinner Menus

▲ *1* ▲

Green Salad (page 243)

Basic Brown Rice (page 297)
Pumpkin Stew with Hominy and Pinto Beans (page 329)
Roasted Peppers (page 342)

yogurt with fresh fruit

▲ *2* ▲

Green Salad (page 243)

Bean and Pasta Gratin (page 316)
Roasted Vegetables (page 341)

Fruit Plate with Yogurt and Mint (page 384)

▲ *3* ▲

Quinoa with Pistachios, Dried Apricots, and Cumin Vinaigrette (page 254)

Tofu Cutlets (page 337)
whole-grain buns with a small dish of olive oil on the side

fresh fruit

▲ *4* ▲

Lentil Salad with Roasted Peppers and Mint (page 256)

Pita Sandwich (page 353)
Baked Winter Squash (page 345)

Yogurt Cheese (page 363)
fruit salad

▲ *5* ▲

Green Salad (page 243)

White Bean and Pasta Soup with Sage (page 286)
Herb Patties (page 372)

Yogurt Cheese with Honey, Almonds, and Fruit (page 383)
fruit

▲ *6* ▲

Cucumber Salad (page 247)

low-fat cheese or Yogurt Cheese (page 363)
Lentils with Rice and Onions (page 330)
whole-grain buns

fruit

▲ *7* ▲

Zucchini Vinaigrette (page 265)

Polenta (page 306)
Black Bean Chili (page 280)

Fruit Plate with Yogurt and Mint (page 384)

▲ *8* ▲

Green Salad (page 243)

fish or poultry (pages 374–79) (small serving)
baked potato
whole-grain bread
baked carrots and broccoli

Apple Pie (page 452)

▲ *9* ▲

Green Salad (page 243)

Sunflower Rice (page 300)
Pumpkin Stew with Hominy and Pinto Beans (page 329)

Yogurt Cheese with Honey, Almonds, and Fruit (page 383)

▲ *10* ▲

Summer Vegetable Antipasto (page 248)

Gnocchi di Patate (page 324)
cooked eggplant

Almond-Hazelnut Delight (page 385)
fresh fruit

▲ *11* ▲

Green Salad (page 243)

Split-Pea Soup with Wild Rice (page 290)
Twice-Baked Delicata Squash (page 346)

Ricotta Cheese with Pine Nuts (page 383)

▲
Beverages

Avoid tea or coffee in the evening. Choose a natural, light wine in moderation (1–2 wineglasses), low-fat buttermilk, fresh vegetable or fruit juice, herb tea, sparkling water, or just plain spring water. Choose buttermilk or related drink whenever there are no milk products such as yogurt on the menu.

Some Final Thoughts

Notice now many of the lunch and dinner menus start with a green salad. Remember how much you can vary this kind of salad. Similarly, you can vary cooked vegetable dishes by choosing different vegetables in season. Green salads and cooked vegetables are basic to Superpyramid dinners. Combine them with a main grain dish or sufficient bread and a dish based on legumes (especially beans and lentils) and some yogurt or low-fat cheese or egg dish. If not on the menu, you can always add some fruit or fruit-based dessert.

Sometimes a dessert is high in energy and protein foods from tiers one, two, and three. In such case earlier courses can and should be lighter. Use dinner menu number 10 as an example.

Consider the entire day as a Superpyramid day. Your choices of breakfast, lunch, and dinner menus should not be made in isolation but should be integrated to make a beautiful-looking Superpyramid when taken together.

ADAPTING RECIPES FROM OTHER COOKBOOKS

If you want to adapt recipes from other cookbooks to the Superpyramid Program, here are a few simple rules to follow. An example of how well it can be done is demonstrated in our gnocchi recipes (pages 322–24), which we have adapted from a Northern Italian nineteenth-century cookbook by Artusi, a cook who loved to use large amounts of butter, lard, and refined flours. Many cookbooks on Mediterranean, Mexican, Middle Eastern, Chinese, and Indian cookery have recipes that you can easily adapt to the Superpyramid Program.

Many recipes in the books listed in the following pages are already very good. Preferably avoid all recipes containing red meats or poultry. Choose instead recipes high in whole grains, beans, vegetables, and fruit, which use olive or similar oils and nonfat or low-fat milk, yogurt, or cheeses. Before you try to adapt recipes from other books, use the recipes in the Superpyramid Kitchen section of this book. You'll soon become an expert at recognizing how to adapt other recipes.

A few things you may need to do:

1. Replace refined grains and white flours with whole grains or whole-grain flours.
2. Make the grains and beans the main part of a dish, with poultry, meat, or fish playing a minor role.
3. Use low-fat or nonfat cheeses. Substitute yogurt or low-fat milks for cream.
4. Replace animal fats with vegetable oils.
5. Add garlic or onion and herbs for flavor whenever possible and limit the amount of salt.
6. Avoid all recipes that require prolonged or deep frying.
7. Prepare your food fresh, avoid leftovers.
8. Use honey, brown sugar, maple syrup, or molasses in place of refined sugars.

The
Superpyramid
Bakery

▲

Breads, Muffins, Scones, Pies, and Other Baked Products

THE STAFF OF LIFE

L et's remember that bread is the most basic food of mankind. The term staff of life is historically related more to bread than to any other grain food.

Because of this, this section on breads and breadmaking is a key section of the Superpyramid Kitchen. It may seem as though it takes time to make a loaf of naturally leavened bread, but breadmaking is an experience that can change your life and your approach to foods and meal design. An excellent book on whole-grain breadmaking is *The Laurel's Kitchen Bread Book*, which we highly recommend to anyone serious about a Superpyramid way of eating. In it you'll find recipes for whole-grain breads leavened with bakers' yeast alone, as well as with a variety of sourdough starters that provide valuable *lactic* fermentation for whole-wheat breads. Because there are such excellent books on general bread-making, we'll focus on one natural leavening—barm—and its use to make a variety of breads and baked products including pies without solid, saturated fats.

Barm leavening involves both yeast and lactic fermentations. The lactic fermentation gives mild fruity and buttery flavor to the breads, especially when they are made from whole-wheat flours, and some research suggests that the acidity of the lactic fermentation of the barm may allow the release of precious bound minerals from the bran of the grains, over and above those released by yeast fermentation.

The Superpyramid Bakery section was prepared by Monica Spiller and adapted from *The Barm Bakers' Book*.

> **M**ake bread with barm, bakers' yeast, sourdough starters, or whatever method you choose, but find the time to make bread even if only once in a while. No matter how busy you are you'll find this a most rewarding experience that will give you a deeper sense of the wonders of the staff of life.

Fat Content of Breads

If no oils are added, the fat content of breads made the Superpyramid Bakery way is about 1 gram saturated and 7–8 grams unsaturated fat per pound. This is equal to about 1.5–2 grams fat percent or about 0.5 gram per ounce. The fat content given after the bread recipes is—as in the Superpyramid Kitchen—intended for guidance only, as all natural foods vary in fat content. In general, the fat content of Superpyramid Bakery breads is insignificant, unless oils are added.

When shopping, remember that fat—often saturated or hydrogenated fat—is frequently added to commercial breads and you should read the label carefully. In the Superpyramid Bakery only good oils and nuts are used.

BARM AS A NATURAL LEAVENING

The making of bread with some kind of fermented grains must be as old as the preparation of grains for human food. The fermentation must have been spontaneous since all grains, like other fruits and seeds, have a natural bloom of microorganisms on their surface, waiting to spring into action when the grains are ground up and the nutrients inside are made available. The natural bloom on grains consists mainly of a mixture of yeasts and lactic bacteria. A concentrated growth of these microorganisms in a dough or batter of whole-grain flour and water served for thousands of years as a leavening or raising agent for breads. An old English name for this mixture was *barm*; in France the word used was *levain*; in Italy *biga*; in Belgium *desem*; and so on.

Barm leavening was always available in the form of part of the previous batch of bread or ale. The yeasts in barms produce plenty of carbon dioxide gas as they grow and so give breads their spongy texture. The lactic bacteria produce lactic acid and flavorful esters in the presence of the yeasts. Doughs and batters leavened with barm are therefore much more acidic and aromatic than doughs leavened with modern bakers' yeast alone. The advantages of barm-leavened, acidic doughs are in the self-preserving properties of the finished bread against molding and the increased digestibility of the minerals in the bran of the grain, as well as in the lovely flavors imparted by the lactic fermentation. A recipe for making your own barm, as well as refreshing it and so continuing the barm leavening, is included in this section.*

Barm Alternatives

Sourdough starters made with whole-grain flours can be used as a substitute for barm. Most available sourdough starters, which can supply the flavorful lactic fermentation, are used with bakers' yeast. However, the flavor development in final breads made with a sourdough may be quite different from the flavor of barm breads.

HOW TO MAKE BARM BREADS

Before learning the detail of barm breadmaking, choose the recipe for a bread that you would like to make. The easiest recipes are those made with soft wheats (pages 449–61).

- ▲ A *description of barm* is given on page 406.
- ▲ Some suggestions on the *selection of ingredients* for barm breadmaking are given on pages 408–17.
- ▲ Variations on *breadmaking techniques* as applied to whole-grain barm breads are given on pages 417–24.
- ▲ Before making barm breads it is necessary to obtain some barm starter. Dried barm can be purchased or you can make your own barm starter (pages 424–28). Beyond acquiring the barm starter there are *three main steps in barm breadmaking:*

Step 1: Taking care of the barm starter: continuing the barm by refreshment and storing it between baking days (see pages 429–31).

Step 2: Bringing the barm to a peak of gassing ability and flavor in the form of a barm sponge (see pages 432–36) ready to be used in the final bread recipe.

---

* The recipes in this section of the book and the production of barm are intended for home use. Commercial use is protected by various patents (page 476), and permission must be obtained for such use.

Step 3: The final breadmaking (see pages 440–67 for recipes).

▲ Sample schedules for use in planning for barm breadmaking are given on pages 436–39.

KEEPING BARM BREADMAKING SIMPLE

For the busy parent or career person, the idea of using barm may at first glance appear to be complex and time-consuming. Dried barm (if you have chosen not to make your own) and freshly ground whole-grain flour must be searched for, but they are available (Sources, page 477). Once past that stage, the barm can be continued indefinitely. In practice, the actual breadmaking stage requires just the same hands-on time as for baking powder or yeast-leavened breads. The waiting time for the barm and sponge is to allow the buildup of a high concentration of the acids and flavor compounds provided by the lactic fermentation. There is a little additional work in refreshing the barm and preparing the barm sponge, but these can be one and the same task, which is as simple as any cooking task can be: Flour and water are mixed into the continuous barm so that it is doubled in amount and maintains the soft batter texture, and then a small amount of honey is added. Barm breadmaking is a very forgiving art, and the purpose of exact recipes is to allow the baker to produce a pleasing result at the first attempt. For those who would like to bypass the measuring and exactness there are only three requirements: that the continuous barm has a pleasing aroma, that it is very bubbly, and that it is sufficiently acidic before refreshing it or using it to make barm sponge.

The most undemanding barm breads to make are those from soft wheats. For example, muffins and scones (American biscuits) are both made in the same way as baking powder quick breads, except that the leavening is a barm sponge and there is a wait of 45 minutes between shaping and baking.

WHOLE GRAINS AND WHOLE-GRAIN FLOURS FOR USE WITH BARM LEAVENING

In order to make barm leavening successfully, the whole grains need to have their natural bloom of yeasts and lactic bacteria intact and for this to be so, the grain must not be too old and it must never have been treated physically or chemically in any way that would destroy the bloom of microorganisms on the grains. Similarly, when barm is refreshed it is better to use whole grains and whole-grain flour, which have no residues that could stop the growth of the barm microorganisms. Otherwise the choice of whole grains and whole-grain flours depends on availability and what it is that you would like to make from them. (You may want to go back and read again some of the points made on grains in chapter 4 as well.)

Wheat

More wheat is grown and eaten throughout the world than any other grain. Wheat is grown in widely different climates. The wheat types grown in Mediterranean regions are quite different from those grown in temperate British or continental Russian climates. Because of the variety of climate in North America, practically all the different types of wheat are available on this continent and it is possible to make the breads of almost any land by using a wheat type typical of that land.

Available wheat species can be divided into two groups: the *bread wheats* and the *pasta wheats*. These names suggest that only the bread wheats are suitable for bread and yet in the Mediterranean countries such as Algeria, Morocco, and southern Italy where *pasta wheats* predominate, delicious breads such as the Italian focaccia are made from their local *pasta wheats*. The *bread wheats* are further classified as possessing hard or soft kernels, and strong or weak gluten. To the baker this may suggest that they are only suitable for breads if they are hard-kerneled and with a strong gluten, and only suitable for cakes and pastries if they are soft-kerneled and with a weak gluten. In fact, however, all varieties of wheat can be used to make breads of some kind. There are recipes following in this section that will allow any whole-wheat flour to be made into a bread. What is important, is to be able to decide which recipe is suitable for the wheat flour that you have, so that you will be pleased with the result.

Hard Wheat

The hard, red or white, wheat with high protein and strong gluten is the wheat used to make the whole-wheat flours most desired by professional bakers. They use it to make breads with the open spongy texture that we take for granted in professionally made breads. In some ways this is the most difficult flour to use, since the strong gluten must be worked or kneaded very well to produce a light spongy texture in the finished bread. The kneading can be managed quite easily by hand provided the dough piece is of a reasonable size, or it can be done with a dough-hook attachment in a food mixer, a food processor, or automatic breadmaking machine. This hard, high-protein wheat as grain or flour is not always easily available to the home baker; it is often necessary to special-order it in twenty-five or fifty-pound bags. Storing small quantities of whole grain in a closed plastic container, in a cool room at home is easy, but storing such large amounts of whole wheat in the form of flour at home is not recommended. Whole-grain flour is best used to make bread while it is still fresh and preferably on the same day that it is ground into flour. In most supermarkets, small bags (5 pounds) of whole-wheat flour with the description "Best for Bread" on the label, prepared from hard red, high-protein wheat, are usually available, the disadvantage being only that the flour is not freshly ground on the day that you choose to bake.

Lower-protein hard red or white wheats are usually much more readily available to the home baker. They are produced in years when the growing conditions are less than ideal or from less successful hard-wheat varieties. Breads from these wheats, rather than from the super high-protein wheats, are actually easier to make since the weaker gluten requires a much shorter kneading time; it probably will not be possible to obtain quite such a light texture, but breads made with these wheats will still be delicious and interesting.

Soft Wheat

Soft, red or white, wheats are usually easily available as whole grains and as whole-wheat flours; the flours are often sold as cake or pastry flour. These wheats need very little mixing and certainly no vigorous kneading. Soft wheats are renowned for their flavor and for the texture they give to pastry, cookies, scones (American biscuits), cakes, and cake-textured breads and you will probably recognize that each of these is conventionally made with baking powder leavening or no leavening at all. The soft-wheat recipes that follow make use of a barm leavening, with the idea of increasing the nutrient availability from the whole-grain flours used, reducing the sodium introduced by baking powders, as well as creating a delicious new range of flavor for traditionally homemade pies, scones, and cake-textured breads. Hands-on time for these recipes is essentially the same as for the corresponding baking-powder recipes; additional time is needed to prepare the barm sponge and to wait for some rising between mixing and baking, both of which are easily accomplished.

▲

Types of Wheat Available

▲

BREAD WHEATS

High-protein, hard, red or white wheat	high protein (above 15%*), strong gluten	hearth breads and pan breads
Hard, red or white wheat	lower protein (12%–14%*), weaker gluten	hearth breads and pan breads
Soft, red or white wheat	lower protein (9%–11%*), weak gluten	flat breads, pastries, cakes, and cookies
Spelt	high protein, weak gluten	flatbreads, pastries, cakes

▲

PASTA WHEATS

Durum wheat	high protein (15%–17%*), variable-strength gluten	pasta, flat breads, pastries
Kamut wheat	high protein, variable-strength gluten	pasta, flat breads, pastries

* based on a 10% moisture content

In Europe the term "hard" is used to describe pasta wheat and "soft" to describe bread wheat; according to the Europeans any relatively hard-kerneled bread wheat is still considered to be softer-kerneled than the pasta wheat. In this book, only the American terminology given above is being used.

Spelt

Spelt wheat has been grown in central Europe for centuries and is well known there for making delicious cakes; the grain is fairly soft and large so that whole-grain spelt flour was traditionally prepared using stone mills. Spelt wheat is exceptional in that it is not easily removed from its husk and the ear of spelt wheat must be sent through a special dehusking machine to release the spelt wheat grains. There is the possibility of damage to the germ of the grain during this process. This may reduce the keeping properties of the whole-grain spelt slightly, in comparison with other wheats, and its ability to sprout may also be impaired, but these are very minor disadvantages. The advantages for spelt are its higher protein content than soft wheats and its good flavor. Whole-grain spelt flour has very similar characteristics to soft-wheat flour and can be used in most recipes that call for whole-grain soft wheat flour.

Durum Wheat

Durum wheat is so called because its grain is very hard; the flours produced from it are quite granular in texture. The flour is usually golden yellow, which gives a lovely color to breads made with durum wheat. Their flavor is sweet, and the protein content is high. The durum wheat flour characteristics of being slow to absorb the liquids and having a variable gluten strength do not present a problem; it is necessary only to mix a durum wheat dough just to combine the ingredients and then to wait for liquids to be absorbed, before kneading just a little and then shaping the final bread. Several traditional durum wheat breads are sourdough leavened and the recipes given here with a barm leavening are in keeping with that tradition.

Kamut

The grain *kamut* is a wheat species closely related to durum wheat and it has all the same attributes of golden color, sweet flavor, high protein, and variable-strength gluten. Any recipe developed for durum wheat can, in general, be used for kamut. Kamut is a distinct wheat species, characterized by the enormous size of its grain. The name *kamut* is Egyptian and is being used in recent promotions of this extraordinary wheat.

Rye, Oats, and Barley

All of these grains have a weak gluten structure and so are usually either mixed in a small amount with a high-protein hard wheat flour to make a light bread or treated similarly to a weak gluten wheat and made up into cakelike loaves or flat breads. Rye, oats, and barley each add distinctive texture and flavor to breads and so are often included to bring variety to recipes.

Flour

Although a busy life-style may give you less time than you want in the kitchen, it's ideal if you can use freshly ground whole-grain flour whenever you choose to bake. If it is at all possible, buy your wheat as the whole grain, store it as such in a well-closed container in a cool room, and then grind it to flour in a home mill, preferably on the day of baking. If you are fortunate enough to live near a store that sells and freshly grinds grain for you, you'll save some effort. Modern mills for home use are almost all electrically driven but if you have an heirloom quern—an ancient-style hand-driven mill—then you will surely enjoy the waist-trimming exercise of hand grinding your grain. This way, the flour is coolly produced and retains the highest possible number of nutrients in the process.

Sprouted Grains and Malt

Freshly sprouted wheat is used in the production of a whole-wheat barm from whole wheat. The barm microorganisms apparently thrive in the presence of the extra nutrients supplied by the sprouted wheat. Rather than continue the barm by refreshment with fresh wheat sprouts mixed with whole-grain flour, the sprouts can be dried and ground into a *sprouted-wheat flour*. The sprouted-wheat flour can be kept in a closed container, in a cool place, until it is needed as a replacement for freshly sprouted wheat when the barm is to be refreshed or a bread is being made. The amount of sprouted-wheat flour recommended in most recipes is 1 percent of the flour amount, or 1–2 teaspoons per pound of whole-grain flour.

When grains are sprouted, there is a release of enzymes, some of which are capable of transforming the grain starch into the sugar called *maltose*. If these sprouted grains are gently heated, the enzymes are able to transform a high proportion of the starch into maltose, and the resulting treated grain is known as a *malt*. Maltose is especially well used by the barm lactic bacteria. Malted wheat flour can be made at home by sprouting wheat, lightly roasting it, and then grinding the treated grain into a flour. *Barley malt* is the most usual malt made commercially, because it is used in making beers and in the making of bread from modern bakers' yeast. Barley malts are frequently extracted with water; the extract is concentrated to give a *barley malt (extract) syrup*. Drying of barley malt extract yields *barley malt (extract) powder*.

The enzymes that transform starch into maltose are known as *diastatic enzymes*. If they are allowed to remain active by using low-temperature drying of the malted grain, the malt is said to be *diastatic*. However, if the malted grain is dried at a higher temperature or is roasted, then the diastatic enzymes will be destroyed and the malt will be *nondiastatic*. The particular malt used in the following recipes is *nondiastatic barley malt (extract) powder*. It has been chosen because it is fairly readily available. Barley malt powder absorbs moisture extraordinarily well and needs to be stored in an airtight container, such as a screw-capped glass jar, rather than the small plastic bag in which it is often sold to the home baker. *Nondiastatic barley malt syrup* can be substituted for nondiastatic barley malt powder in the following recipes. Diastatic malt is not recommended in these barm-bread recipes because sprouted grains are already included and these are expected to supply enough diastatic activity. Excessive amounts of diastatic enzymes supplied by diastatic malt or fresh sprouts can sometimes result in breads with an unintentionally sticky texture. This can of course be turned to good effect if a sweet gooey bread is the goal.

OTHER INGREDIENTS FOR BARM BREADS
Water
Water is usually a major ingredient in bread and it is well worth the effort to use good-tasting potable water free from disinfectant chemicals such as chlorine or halazone. Not only can these chemicals spoil the taste of the finished bread but there is the risk that the barm microorganisms will be adversely affected, and the bread will not be as light or as well acidified as expected. If necessary, disinfecting chemicals can be removed from the water using an activated carbon filter. Completely purified or distilled water is not recommended since normal drinking water is a valuable source of minerals for the barm microorganisms.

Milk
Any milk for baking, even if it has been pasteurized, should be brought to a full rolling boil and then cooled down to the dough temperature, before addition to a barm-leavened dough. This is so no unwanted microorganisms that might compete with the barm microorganisms will be introduced.

Yogurt and Buttermilk
Although both yogurt and buttermilk contain their own set of lactic bacteria and are already distinctly acidic, their addition to barm-leavened breads results in an enhanced barm bread quality; the barm leav-

ening seems to be favorably affected. Since yogurt and buttermilk are generally stored in the refrigerator, it is a good idea to measure amounts for recipes well ahead of time and to allow them to warm to dough temperature before adding them to a barm dough. In a Superpyramid recipe these products should be nonfat or low-fat.

Honey

Honey must surely have been used in ancient times for barm-leavened breads and cakes. Honey is predominantly a mixture of the two simple sugars glucose and fructose, which in turn are very easily used by the barm microorganisms. The generous use of honey whenever barm is refreshed seems to enhance the effect of the barm as a leavening. Barm breads, made with honey according to the recipes in this section, can rise to double after mixing the dough in as little as 45 minutes and usually within 75 minutes at 86° F. (30° C.).

Fruit Sweeteners

Grape (vino cotto), raisin, and fig juice concentrates (page 153) contain as much as 70 percent sugars, almost all in the form of a mixture of glucose and fructose, both of which are well used by the barm micro-organisms. These fruit juice concentrates are therefore recommended as sweeteners in recipes using barm leavening. Fruit juice concentrates can add delicious alternative flavors and texture to breads. If fruit juice concentrate is used as an alternative to honey, then more must be used because fruit juice sweeteners contain a lower concentration of sugars than honey (83 percent sugars in honey) and correspondingly more water. As an approximate guide, 1 tablespoon (40 grams) honey could be replaced by 3–4 tablespoons (47 grams) of fruit juice concentrate. When this much fruit juice concentrate is used, it adds an extra 1–2 teaspoons (7 grams) water. The liquid in the recipe can be correspondingly reduced; this extra water can usually be ignored, unless a larger amount of fruit juice concentrate is used or the recipe is being scaled up for a large batch.

Salt

The amount of sea salt (page 166) suggested in the following recipes is a level ½ teaspoon (2 grams or 0.3 percent of flour weight) in a 1 kg (2¼-pound) loaf. This can be compared with zero salt as used by the Tuscan Italians in their local breads (see The Italian Baker by Carol Field, New York: Harper and Row, 1985), 2 level teaspoons (7.5 grams or 1 percent of flour weight) of salt in a 1 kilogram loaf of French country bread (*The Breads of France* by Bernard Clayton, New York: Bobbs-Merrill, 1978), and 4 level teaspoons (15 grams or 2 percent of flour weight) of salt in a 1 kilogram loaf, which is the maximum recommended for use by American bakers (*Baking Science and Technology*, Vol. I, by E. J. Pyler, Merriam, Kansas: Sosland Publishing Company, 1988). When adding salt to barm-leavened doughs, dissolve it in at least some of the ingredient liquid before adding it to the dough. Salt should always be used sparingly in any Superpyramid recipe.

Oils

Olive oil is almost always suggested when oil is an ingredient in the following recipes. Other oils could easily be substituted, with the caution that the flavor of a bread could be dramatically changed if a strongly flavored oil such as sesame oil is used. The way in which an oil is incorporated into the bread can have a dramatic effect on the texture of the finished bread. Possibly the best method to incorporate the oil is to rub it into the flour right at the beginning of a recipe, either by hand (lifting the flour and oil from the bowl with both hands and rubbing them together between thumbs and fingers, allowing the mixture to fall back into the bowl and repeating the process until the flour and oil are one, in fine crumblike granules) or by using a food processor. Rubbing in the oil is the method of choice when mixing and kneading are to be kept to a minimum, in soft-wheat recipes, for example. If the recipe calls for kneading the dough very thoroughly, then the oil can simply be added along with the rest of the ingredients because it will, in any case, be very well incorporated during the kneading process. However, most hard-wheat recipes still do suggest rubbing the oil into the flour. A third method is to work the oil into the finished dough just before finally shaping the bread and this may be appropriate to give a particular texture.

Dried Fruit

Raisins and other dried fruits such as currants, prunes, apricots, peaches, cherries, figs, apples, and tomatoes make delicious additions to breads.

All these dried fruits are juicier in the breads if they have been soaked, half an hour to four hours or sometimes more, ahead of time in hot water and then drained just before addition to the bread. The only difficulty is that the dried fruit becomes very soft and delicate after soaking and should be mixed quite gently into the dough, to avoid breaking up the fruit. In any case these rehydrated fruits should not be added to the dough until all the vigorous kneading is completed. One technique for incorporating the soft rehydrated fruit is to flatten the dough into a rectangle, spread the soft fruit evenly over all the dough, and roll it up like a jelly roll. Then proceed to knead gently with a normal kneading motion until the fruit is evenly distributed throughout the dough.

VARIATIONS ON SOME ANCIENT TECHNIQUES FOR BREADMAKING

Measuring the Acidity of the Barm

Bakers of barm breads in ancient times must have used the aroma, appearance, and texture of the barm batter or dough in order to judge when it was ready to be used in the next stage of preparing a bread, and they would surely pass such knowledge on to their apprentices. Without this experience we need to use other ways to be sure that the fermentation system is a healthy one. When refreshed barm is healthy and ready to be refreshed further, it is distinctly acidic. Bacteria that are unhealthy to humans do not grow under such acid conditions. *The acidity or pH value for refreshed barm that is ready for further refreshment is pH 3.5–4.* The use of pH paper is suggested as an easy method for measuring the acidity of barm. These pH papers have been impregnated with dyes that change color according to the acidity, or pH, of the liquid with which they are in contact. The dyes may not be edible, so, whenever pH paper is to be used, spoon some barm out of the main batch and dab it onto the pH paper. Look for the color change, compare the color with the chart on the box, and determine the approximate pH value for the barm. The pH papers with the ability to change color in the pH range 3.0–5.5 are recommended for use with the barm.

Materials in Contact with Barm Doughs

For thousands of years barm bakers must have used wooden tubs to mix their dough, wooden or marble-topped benches to shape the dough, and unglazed ceramic tiles to bake the bread on. All of these materials are completely compatible with acidic barm doughs. Among the more modern materials, stainless steel, ovenproof glass and food-compatible plastics are also suitable for use with acidic barm doughs. However, aluminum, cast iron, tinned ware, galvanized iron, and lead-glazed ceramics are definitely *not* suitable for contact with the acidic barm dough and should be avoided: they are all capable of reacting with acids and could gradually dissolve in barm doughs.

Weighing and Measuring

The required consistency of the dough is usually described in the recipe. However, the recipes were developed with relatively dry grains and flour, in a dry climate. If these recipes are being made up in a humid climate, then it may be necessary to use both a little less water and correspondingly more flour to obtain the required consistency; in this way the overall weight of the dough produced will not be changed.

The recommended method for measuring out ingredients is by weighing in grams. Weighing, rather than measuring in cups and spoons, gives a better chance that the recipe will be reproduced from one time to another without surprises. For example, a cup of whole hard red wheat flour ranges from 135–166 grams (5.5 to 6.5 ounces), depending on the freshness of the flour and the way in which a cup is measured; a tablespoon of honey can be anything from 22–55 grams (less than one ounce to about two ounces), depending on the thickness of the honey and the generosity of the cook. Grams and kilograms, which are metric units, are included because these were the units used in developing the recipes and because metric units are fast becoming the units in everyday use in the U.S. All of the following recipes for barm-leavened breads were developed using a modern digital scale with a range from 0.1 to 5,000 grams. This is by no means essential to breadmaking, but if you are ready for one of these digital balances, then you will experience a revolutionary reduction in the time and effort usually given to weighing and measuring. Besides being able to choose whether to measure in grams or ounces, on this kind of scale, it is possible to place a mixing bowl or whatever directly onto the scale pan, and with the push of a button register its weight as zero and then add just the right number of grams of ingredient, whether liquid or solid. If you are not quite ready for a digital scale and already have a well-used scale that reads in grams, as well as pounds and ounces, that will still make it much easier to make breads predictably than measuring the ingredients with cups and spoons.

Temperature Measurement

When summer temperatures rise into the upper eighties (86° F. is approximately 30° C.), then at last breadmaking itself becomes liberated from the chore of finding the ideal warm place. In fact, it may be necessary to find a cooler place, at about 68° F. (approximately 20° C.), to keep the refreshed continuous barm. All equipment for barm bread-making should ideally be no cooler than 68° F. (20° C.) and preferably at 86° F. (30° C.). Water used in the recipes is usually recommended to be a little above 86° F. (30° C.). The hottest water ever recommended for use with the barm microorganisms is 104° F. (40° C.), and this is used to rehydrate dried barm; the hotter water is believed to be less damaging to the yeasts, while they rehydrate, than cooler water would be. A kitchen wall thermometer or thermostat is helpful for judging ambient temperatures. A thermometer, with a stainless-steel probe set beneath a dial, is valuable for judging the temperature of liquids and dough.

Mixing

The amounts given in the following recipes can be mixed by hand very easily. As always in breadmaking, a relatively large bowl compared with the volume of the starting ingredients is recommended, especially if the dough is to be left to rise to double its volume in the same bowl. A 4-quart (16-cup or 4-liter) capacity mixing bowl is recommended for recipes making up to 5 cups of dough (1¼ kilograms of finished bread). If a food mixer is used, then the manufacturer's instructions need to be referred to, and the recipe size proportioned to fit the mixing bowl size and the strength of the motor. Actual mixing (as opposed to kneading) is best achieved with the paddle supplied with food mixers. A food processor can also sometimes be used for mixing bread dough, by following the manufacturer's instructions.

First Rising

During the first rising the flour has time to fully absorb the added liquids. At the same time the barm yeast and bacteria grow vigorously in the presence of the freshly added honey and flour. The gas produced by the barm yeast fills out the dough and it rises. This first rise barely doubles the volume of the dough because the gluten network has not yet been developed by kneading, which is the next step.

There are three main considerations during the rising of bread dough: *maintaining the dough at a warm enough temperature* for the barm microorganisms to grow vigorously, *keeping the dough surface moist* so that it does not dry out during the rising, and *knowing when the dough has doubled in volume.*

The ideal rising temperature for barm breads is around 86° F. (30° C.), and it is well worthwhile finding or making such a place in your home before attempting to make barm breads.

If you plan to bake barm breads frequently then it is worth considering the purchase of a simple incubator, of the kind normally used in microbiological laboratories, and always keeping it at a temperature of 86° F. (30° C.).

Keeping the dough surface moist during rising is achieved by closing the bowl or container with a close-fitting plastic cover or lid, or with a clean damp cloth.

Knowing when the dough has doubled is easy to see if the dough is left to rise in a large measuring jug or tall tub-shaped container. A piece of dough weighing 2.2 pounds (1 kilogram) has a volume of 4 cups (1 quart or 1 liter) on rising to double will have a volume of 8 cups (2 quarts or 2 liters). So that *the minimum-sized, covered container for 4 cups (1 kilogram) dough during the first rising to double is 8 cups (2 quarts or 2 liters).*

Kneading

The word *kneading* is used here to mean the working of the bread dough, after it has been mixed and has had time to fully absorb the added liquids and to rise once. Kneading develops wheat gluten so that the finished bread will be soft and spongy in crumb texture. Only those breads made from high-protein hard wheat require really strong and prolonged kneading. Gluten development is achieved sooner with lower-protein hard wheats. Durum wheat and kamut require very little kneading, and soft wheats give better cakes and flat breads if they are not kneaded at all. When strong and prolonged kneading is necessary it can be done by hand, using a food mixer with a dough hook, in a food processor, or in an automatic breadmaking machine set to finish at the dough stage. Reference should be made to the manufacturer's instructions for kneading dough in any of these machines. The hand-kneading technique suggested here differs in two ways from the usual description of kneading for home bakers. The first difference is that the hands are kept slightly wet, with a little water, throughout the process to prevent them from sticking to the dough. The second difference is that the dough is worked without the addition of any flour, on a smooth surface made of stainless steel, plastic, or marble and of these three, marble seems to be the best. There are many ways to successfully manage the physical kneading process by hand and the following methods are offered for those who are beginners or those who would like to try a variation. In every method *kneading is completed when the dough can be spread out into a paper thin sheet when gently pulled between the hands.*

One-handed method for kneading a small piece of dough (2 cups, 500 grams or less) Place the dough piece on the working surface. Grasp the farthest end of the dough piece, with one hand only, and begin to roll it up using the fingertips and thumb. Tighten the roll by pushing with the heel of the hand. Tug on the opposite end of the dough with the other hand, if necessary. Continue until the dough is rolled up tightly, like a jelly roll.

Pick up the rolled dough at one end, turn it through 90°, and begin again to roll up the dough piece as before.

Repeat this process for 5–20 minutes. Gradually the texture of the dough will change from being stiff and unyielding to being so soft and stretchy that the roll will be very easily elongated.

Two-handed method for kneading a larger piece of dough (4 cups or 1 kilogram) Place the dough piece on the working surface. Grasp the farthest end of the dough piece with both hands, and continually try to roll it up using the fingertips and thumbs. Keep tightening the roll by pushing with the heels of the hands. Continue until the dough is an elongated roll.

Pick up the roll of dough at each end, and flap one end over the other to make a shorter dough piece, squeeze the dough piece together, and begin again to try to roll up the dough as before.

Repeat this process for 5–20 minutes. Gradually the texture of the dough will change from being stiff and unyielding to being so soft and stretchy that the roll will elongate very easily.

Resting the Dough

Doughs made with high-protein hard wheat have a strong gluten structure that is well developed as a result of prolonged kneading. Once kneading is stopped the gluten tends to shrink and stiffen in reaction to the process, but on standing undisturbed, or *resting*, for 10–20 minutes the soft stretchy texture returns and the dough can then be easily shaped into its final form without tearing the dough. A special resting step is not usually necessary unless the dough has been strongly kneaded.

Shaping the Dough

Shaping the dough for hearth breads can be done on a lightly floured work surface with flour-covered hands. When the shaping is finished the bread can be left, covered, for the final rise on a bed of flour, which will prevent the dough from sticking to the work surface. It should also be possible to slip an oven pele under the floured bread when the time comes to slide the loaf onto preheated tiles in the oven. A useful alternative to the floured work surface and floury hands is to use slightly wet hands and an unfloured work surface such as a marble slab, splashed occasionally with water to prevent the dough from sticking. Breads that are to be baked in pans are very conveniently handled in this way. Hearth breads can also be handled in this way with wet hands and can then be left for the final rise on nonstick kitchen parchment paper. The hearth bread and paper together can be transferred to the oven and removed from the oven with ease on a pele. The paper can easily be removed after baking.

The most frequent shaping for a dough piece from hard wheat is into a ball: Gather up the dough with both hands and form the ball by pulling dough from the top surface in a continuous film and tucking it under the dough piece, all the while turning the dough piece between both hands. Other shaping instructions are included in recipes.

Final Rising

After shaping the dough it should be covered and left to undergo the final rising, at about 86° F. (30° C.); most doughs should only be allowed to *nearly* double. In this way the dough will be able to expand still further in the oven and will be baked before it has had the chance to expand to the point of collapse. It is useful to realize that the strongest gluten doughs, after development by thorough kneading, can expand to triple before collapsing; they can therefore be allowed to expand to double or beyond in the final rise, and still have some expansion in reserve for the baking process.

Some ingenuity is needed to find covers suitable for the finally shaped dough while it rises. For example: Breads in loaf pans can be placed inside large clear polyethylene bags, which can be puffed up and then closed. Hearth loaves can be covered with an inverted 4-quart (4-liter) mixing bowl, which has been previously warmed to 86° F. (30° C.) Flat breads spread out on a floured board can be covered with a clean dry cloth.

Slashing

Just before putting loaves into the oven their surface can be cut or *slashed* with a sharp knife, to give the loaf extra outer surface to allow for the huge (we hope) expansion that occurs during baking. In this way the loaf splits along the guidelines of the slash rather than randomly and perhaps not so prettily.

Baking

Breads baked in an oven are most successful when there is an initially steamy atmosphere followed by a steady high temperature. With some easy additions, both of these requirements are achievable in a modern domestic oven, which would otherwise be too drying and unsteady in temperature to produce a well-baked loaf of bread. An initially steamy atmosphere can be created by baking breads underneath a preheated ceramic cover, or *cloche,* which is only a little bigger than the expected final volume of the loaf. In this way the water lost from the loaf as it initially heats up stays under the cloche and creates the required steamy atmosphere instead of escaping from the oven. As the baking continues the steam is reabsorbed into the bread. The cloche can be removed for the last 5 to 10 minutes of baking to allow a firm and crispy crust to form.

A steadier oven temperature can be achieved by lining the oven shelf, on which the breads are to be baked, with *ovenproof ceramic tiles* or *a pizza baking stone* and preheating them at the same time that the oven is being heated. Breads can be baked on these tiles or stone, with only a layer of flour or parchment paper between the bread and the tile or stone surface. If a cloche is used it can be preheated on top of the tiles and then placed on top of the bread being baked on the tiles. For panned loaves that are not easily covered by a cloche it is suggested that *unglazed terra cotta loaf pans* be used. A terra cotta loaf pan would also contain the dough during the final proof, and so would be at 68–86° F. (20–30° C.) when placed in the oven. For a nicely browned loaf in a terra cotta pan, bake it in a preheated oven, without the additional use of baking tiles, stone, or cloche.

The easiest and most thorough way to clean these ceramic tiles, baking stones, and terra cotta bread pans is to leave them in the oven during the self-cleaning cycle of the oven. The cleaning is so thorough that they look and feel like new again, and in some cases must be seasoned anew to prevent the dough from sticking.

When barm loaves are taken from the oven it is recommended that they be cooled on a wooden cooling rack.

Automatic Breadmaking

Provided the recipe is proportioned for the capacity of the breadmaker, the final mixture for barm breads can easily be made into a bread in an automatic breadmaker. For example, the largest loaf made in an automatic breadmaker (1½ pounds) is close to two-thirds (0.68) of the size of the 2¼-pound (1-kilogram) loaf ingredient amounts in this book. A smaller loaf in an automatic breadmaker (1 pound) could be made with a little less than half (0.45) of the 2¼-pounds (1-kilogram) loaf ingredient amounts in this book. If all your barm breadmaking is by machine, then all the recipes including continuous barms and barm sponges can be proportioned to match the final machine bread. An automatic breadmaker can also be used to make bread to the stage of shaping the dough for the final rise; this is ideal for baking such breads as hearth breads, pizza, and small buns. However, it is important to realize that automatic bread bakers are designed to make breads from strong gluten flours. Only the barm-bread recipes using the highest-protein hard wheat are recommended for bread machines.

Using and Storing Barm Breads

Barm breads are very good to eat for several days after they are made, especially if they are revived slice by slice by lightly or fully toasting. Barm breads still need to be protected from drying out by keeping them in a closed plastic bag at cool room temperatures. When fresh barm breads are not going to be eaten within a few days, they can be allowed to cool to room temperature, cut into half-kilogram pieces if necessary, and stored frozen in a well-closed, thick polyethylene freezer bag. These strong plastic bags are easily washed and reused. Barm breads keep very well this way and can be allowed to thaw inside the closed polyethylene bag at room temperature for a few hours before they are needed.

SOURCES OF BARM

The technology exists to produce barm in a dry form, and it is not necessary to start your own barm—you can simply rehydrate dried barm. However, making barm from the beginning is an amazingly absorbing task that spreads over about two weeks and yet does not demand a lot of hands-on time. There is no exact timing of the stages; these recipes give just one set of conditions known to work well. *Initial barms* can be made quite easily by creating the conditions of food, warmth, and moisture that allow a healthy growth of barm microorganisms. The microorganisms are already in existence as a bloom on the grain surface, provided the grains have not been treated physically or chemically to destroy this bloom.

The food for the microorganisms consists of nutrients that can be released from grains when they germinate or sprout; the sprouting process is accompanied by the release of enzymes that break down the grain to release sugars, minerals, and vitamins, among other things that are vital to the growing microorganisms. The method for a wheat barm begins, therefore, with the production of a good supply of freshly *sprouted wheat berries.* The continued growth of the barm is helped by *refreshment* with a continuing supply of nutrients from sprouted wheat in the form of *sprouted wheat flour* or *soaked wheat berries,* which by the end of their soaking time have produced a small but adequate proportion of sprouted wheat.

Freshly Sprouted Wheat

F or initial barm or for sprouted-wheat flour: Wheat berries can be sprouted on the stacked perforated trays that come with some food driers. In order to produce a cool, moist atmosphere surrounding the sprouting grain, the topmost and lowest trays can be left empty and the whole stack stood on a regular tray containing a small amount of water. A clean, wet cloth can then be draped over the stack in such a way that the ends dip into the water in the tray and keep the cloth constantly wet.

TO MAKE 2½ CUPS (300 GRAMS) FRESH WHEAT SPROUTS OR
1½ CUPS (185 GRAMS) DRIED SPROUTS

1 cup (200 grams) wheat berries
1 cup (250 grams) water at 68° F. (20° C.)

1. Mix whole-wheat berries with the water and then allow them to soak for 24 hours.
2. After the soaking time, drain the soaked wheat, remove any moldy or damaged wheat berries, and set to sprout on perforated trays kept in a very moist atmosphere at 68° F. (20° C.) Inspect the sprouting wheat daily. Allow the berries to sprout until the roots are ½ to 1 inch (1–2 centimeters) long and the plumule (leaf shoot) between a quarter of and the whole length of the berry (2–3 days). Again remove any moldy or damaged wheat berries. Ideally no moldy wheat berries will be seen, but if more than two or three are found, then the sprouting process should be begun again, with clean equipment and a new batch of wheat berries.

Sprouted-Wheat Flour

Sprouted-wheat flour can be made from any type of whole-wheat berries that have been sprouted and dried at a low temperature—below 104° F. (40° C.)—until they are brittle. In a recipe, it is preferable to use the sprouted wheat and flour from the same wheat type. However, there is another consideration as well: The hard wheats, even after sprouting and drying, are still a very hard grain to grind into flour. It is therefore recommended that soft white wheat be chosen to make sprouted-wheat flour, at home. Dried sprouts from soft white wheat can be ground to a flour very easily as needed, using a small marble mortar and pestle. The easiest way is to use a domestic grain mill although there is some risk that valuable factors in the sprouted wheat will be damaged by the heat generated during the grinding process.

MAKES 1 CUP (185 GRAMS)

2½ cups (300 grams) freshly sprouted wheat (page 425)

Dry sprouted wheat at 86–104° F. (30–40° C.) in a domestic food drier, until brittle (6–12 hours), and grind into flour. Store in a closed glass jar at cool room temperature.

Initial Barm from Wheat Berries

If you have been unable to purchase dried barm or would like to see for yourself how a barm can be started from wheat, this is the recipe for you.

MAKES 1 CUP (250 GRAMS)

1 cup (125 grams) freshly sprouted wheat (page 425)
½ cup (63 grams) whole-wheat flour
¼ cup (63 grams) water at room temperature

1. Grind freshly sprouted wheat berries to a paste, in a food processor, and mix with flour and water. Add more water if needed, to produce a medium thick batter. Observe pH (acidity, page 417) of a small amount of batter taken from the fresh mixture; pH will probably be between 5 and 6.

2. Loosely cover mixture and leave at 95–104° F. (35–40° C.) for 12 hours and then at 68–86° F. (20–30° C.) for 12 hours. Stir when mixture becomes bubbly and is well gassed.

3. Twenty-four hours after mixing, notice the aroma, which should be altogether pleasing, perhaps reminiscent of hay, perhaps buttery or fruity. Measure pH on small amount of initial barm mixture removed from container; it should already be less than 5. *An unpleasant smell or rising pH is reason to abandon the initial barm and to try again with clean utensils and another batch of grain.*

FIRST REFRESHMENT OF INITIAL BARM

MAKES 2 CUPS (500 GRAMS)

1 cup (250 grams) initial barm
⅔ cup (109 grams) whole-wheat flour including ½ teaspoon (1 gram)
   sprouted-wheat flour
⅔ cup (141 grams) water at 86–104° F. (30–40° C.)

1. Mix initial barm, flour, and water. Add extra water, if needed, to produce a medium-thick batter. Loosely cover and leave at room temperature, 68–86° F. (20–30° C.). Stir whenever barm becomes well gassed.

2. Keep the barm under these conditions for 2–3 days. Monitor pH and aroma every 24 hours. The barm will be ready for further refreshment when pH has been 3.5–4.0 for the previous 24 hours and the aroma is pleasantly fruity or buttery.

SECOND REFRESHMENT OF INITIAL BARM

MAKES 4 CUPS (1,000 GRAMS) TWICE-REFRESHED INITIAL BARM

2 cups (500 grams) once-refreshed initial barm (pH 3.5–4.0 for previous
   24 hours)
1⅓ cups (218 grams) whole-wheat flour including 1 teaspoon (2 grams)
   sprouted-wheat flour
1⅓ cups (282 grams) water at 86–104° F. (30–40° C.)

1. Mix together once-refreshed initial barm, flour, and water. Add extra water, if needed, to produce a medium-thick batter. Loosely cover and leave at room temperature, 68–86° F. (20–30° C.). Stir whenever barm becomes well gassed.

2. Keep the barm under these conditions for 1–3 days, and monitor pH and aroma every 24 hours. Ideally the pH will be 3.5–4.0 just 24 hours following the second refreshment and the barm can then be used as continuous barm suitable for making barm sponge or for further refreshment to make more continuous barm.

If, 24 hours after the second refreshment, the pH does not fall to 3.5–4.0, wait to refresh the barm further until pH has been 3.5–4.0 for 24 hours. Repeat the process of refreshment and monitoring, until the pH falls to 3.5–4.0 within 24 hours of refreshment, at which point it can be used as continuous barm. Unpleasantly smelling barm or barm remaining at pH values above 4.0 for more than 3 days should be discarded.

Rehydration of Dried Barm

*D*ried barm is the most convenient form of barm leavening to start barm baking with. It can be stored for a year or more at 68° F. (20° C.), provided it is kept unopened in its original container, which is under vacuum.

Once dried barm has been rehydrated, it can be used as continuous barm, but for better leavening and a larger supply of continuous barm, it is better to refresh it at least once. Allow 24 hours to complete the rehydration and another 24 hours for the refreshment.

MAKES 1 CUP (250 GRAMS) REHYDRATED BARM

1 cup (110 grams) dried barm
⅔ cup (145 grams) water at 104° F. (40° C.)

1. Stir together until a fairly smooth batter forms. Cover loosely and leave at 86° F. (30° C.) for 24 hours. Stir well at least twice during this time.

2. Rehydration can be regarded as successful if, at the end of this 24-hour period, the pH has fallen to 3.5–4.0, the mixture has produced plenty of gas bubbles and it has a pleasant aroma. Successfully rehydrated barm can be used as continuous barm, although its activity will be enhanced by further refreshment.

MAKING A BARM SPONGE

A barm sponge is prepared in readiness for the final breadmaking step using continuous barm that has been refreshed 24 hours ago. The ingredient proportions for barm sponge and continuous barm are identical. The only distinctions between barm refreshed to become sponge, rather than continuous barm, are in the length of fermentation time and the temperature. Barm sponge is kept either at 68° F. (20° C.) for 8–16 hours or at 86° F. (30° C.) for 4–8 hours before being mixed into the final bread dough, whereas continuous barm is kept at 68° F. (20° C.) for 24 hours before being refreshed again.

Wheat Barm Sponge

The whole-wheat flour in barm sponge can be from any kind of wheat, including spelt, kamut, durum, hard, and soft wheats. With these proportions, the hard wheats produce the thickest consistency, while the soft wheats give a thin batter.

MAKES 2 CUPS (500 GRAMS) WHEAT BARM SPONGE AFTER FERMENTATION

1 cup (250 grams) continuous wheat barm (page 430), last refreshed 24 hours ago and kept at 68° F. (20° C.)
⅔ cup (109 grams) whole-wheat flour, including ½ teaspoon (1 gram) sprouted-wheat flour
⅔ cup (141 grams) water at 68° F. (20° C.)
1 teaspoon (20 grams) honey

Mix all together to produce a medium-thick batter consistency. Stir well. Cover and allow to ferment for 4–8 hours at 86° F. (30° C.) or 8–16 hours at 68° F. (20° C.). Stir well once or twice during fermentation time.

MILK BARM SPONGE

In the wheat barm sponge recipe: For water, substitute low-fat or nonfat milk, freshly boiled and cooled to 68° F. (20° C.). The consistency is thicker than with water and it may be necessary to compensate for this by using slightly more milk.

BUTTERMILK BARM SPONGE

In the wheat barm sponge recipe: For water, substitute low-fat or nonfat buttermilk, at 68° F. (20° C.). The consistency is thicker than with water

REFRESHMENT OF REHYDRATED BARM

MAKES 2 CUPS (500 GRAMS) CONTINUOUS BARM, AFTER FERMENTATION

1 cup (250 grams) rehydrated barm (water added to dried barm 24 hours ago)
⅔ cup (110 grams) whole-wheat flour including ½ teaspoon (1 gram) sprouted-wheat flour
⅔ cup (140 grams) water at 68° F. (20° C.)
1 teaspoon (20 grams) honey

1. Mix all ingredients together very well. The consistency should be that of a medium thick batter. Leave in covered bowl at 68° F. (20° C.) for 24 hours. Stir well once or twice during this time.
2. Refreshment can be regarded as complete if, at the end of this time, the pH has fallen to 3.5–4.0, the mixture has produced plenty of gas bubbles and it has a pleasant aroma.

CONTINUING A BARM BY REFRESHMENT

Once a barm has been produced it can be refreshed innumerable times and still perform well as a leavening for barm breads. Although the recipes may look complex some practice will show otherwise. Refreshment of barm, whether to continue the barm or to make a sponge for breadmaking, is always such that the ratio of barm: flour: water is approximately 2:1:1 by weight. In other words, the starting amount of barm is refreshed to give double the amount, without changing consistency. The amounts of any honey or malt are proportioned to the amount of flour used in the refreshment. The quantities of refreshed continuous barm produced from each recipe are enough to use in the barm sponge recipes plus an amount of continuous barm that can be kept for the next cycle of barm breadmaking, using the same recipes over again.

Continuous Wheat Barm

Continuous wheat barm ready for refreshment can be any one of the following:

- ▲ Initial wheat barm refreshed successfully enough times that it can be considered the same as continuous barm (page 427).
- ▲ Dried wheat barm 24 hours following rehydration (page 428).
- ▲ Refrigerated continuous wheat barm, stored at 40° F. (4° C.) for up to 1 month (page 431).
- ▲ Continuous wheat barm kept at 68° F. (20° C.), refreshed 1–3 days previously (page 430).

Refreshment of Continuous Wheat Barm

MAKES 2 CUPS (500 GRAMS) CONTINUOUS WHEAT BARM AFTER FERMENTATION

1 cup (250 grams) continuous wheat barm (page 430)
⅔ cup (109 grams) whole-wheat flour including ½ teaspoon (1 gram) sprouted-wheat flour
⅔ cup (141 grams) water at 68° F. (20° C.)
1 teaspoon (20 grams) honey

1. Mix together continuous barm, flour, water, and honey. Loosely cover and leave to ferment at 68° F. (20° C.) for 24 hours. Stir 2–3 times.
2. After 24-hour fermentation time, measure pH on small amount of continuous barm taken from container; it should be 3.5–4.0. Notice the aroma; it should be very mild, pleasant, and fruity. The mixture should also be very well gassed. It is important that the refreshed barm should have all these three characteristics. *A higher pH value, unpleasant smell, or lack of gassing are reasons to discard that particular continuous barm batch.* Successfully refreshed continuous wheat barm can be used to make barm sponge or for making more refreshed continuous barm.

Wheat-Berry Continuous Barm Refreshment

MAKES 2 CUPS (500 GRAMS) WHEAT-BERRY CONTINUOUS BARM AFTER FERMENTATION

½ cup (109 grams) whole-wheat berries
⅔ cup (141 grams) water at 68° F. (20° C.)
1 cup (250 grams) continuous wheat barm (page 430)
1 teaspoon (20 grams) honey

1. Mix the whole-wheat berries in specified amount of water and leave to soak for 24 hours.
2. Grind together soaked wheat berries and remaining soaking water, in a food processor, to form a coarse batter. Mix together ground wheat berries, barm, and honey. Stir well. Cover and allow to ferment for 24 hours at 68° F. (20° C.). Stir 2–3 times during the fermentation period.
3. Make observations, on gassing ability, pH, and aroma, as for refreshment of continuous wheat barm.

Refrigerated Continuous Barm

When continuous barm has been successfully refreshed at 68° F. (20° C.) *(judging by its pH 3.5, pleasant aroma, and gassing ability 24 hours after refreshment)*, it can be covered and stored in a refrigerator at 40° F. (4° C.). Alternatively, it can be kept at cool room temperature, 68° F. (20° C.), for a total of 3 days following refreshment, before being refrigerated at 40° F. (4° C.). Refrigerated continuous barm is best used within 2 weeks but it can usually still be successfully refreshed again, even if it has been refrigerated for up to 1 month.

Note: Continuous barm should not be frozen. Barm microorganisms die when the continuous barm freezes solid at freezer temperatures, below 32° F. (0° C.).

and it may be necessary to compensate for this by using slightly more buttermilk.

Combined Refreshment and Wheat Barm Sponge Preparation— for Daily Breadmaking

MAKES 4 CUPS (1,000 GRAMS) REFRESHED CONTINUOUS WHEAT BARM OR WHEAT BARM SPONGE, AFTER FERMENTATION

2 cups (500 grams) continuous wheat barm (page 430), last refreshed 24 hours ago and kept at 68° F. (20° C.)

1⅓ cups (218 grams) whole-wheat flour including 1 teaspoon (2 grams) sprouted-wheat flour

1⅓ cups (282 grams) water at 68° F. (20° C.)

1 tablespoon (40 grams) honey

1. Mix all together to produce a medium-thick batter consistency. Stir well. Keep 2 cups (500 grams) in covered container, at 68° F. (20° C.) and allow to ferment for 24 hours as continuous barm ready for next day.
2. Use the remainder (2 cups or 500 grams) to prepare barm sponge: Cover and allow to ferment for 4–8 hours at 86° F. (30° C.) or 8–16 hours at 68° F. (20° C.). Stir well once or twice during fermentation time.

Wheat Barm Sponge— Machine Bread Amounts

A mounts are for bread machines that produce 1½-pound loaves.

MAKES 1⅓ CUPS (340 GRAMS) WHEAT BARM SPONGE, AFTER FERMENTATION

⅔ cup (170 grams) continuous wheat barm (page 430), last refreshed 24 hours ago and kept at 68° F. (20° C.)

½ cup (74 grams) whole-wheat flour including ½ teaspoon (1 gram) sprouted-wheat flour

⅜ cup (96 grams) water at 68° F. (20° C.)

1 teaspoon (14 grams) honey

Mix all together to produce a medium thick batter consistency. Stir well. Cover and allow to ferment for 4–8 hours at 86° F. (30° C.) or 8–16 hours at 68° F. (20° C.). Stir well once or twice during fermentation time.

Combined Refreshment and Wheat Barm Sponge Preparation—Amounts for Daily Machine Breadmaking

MAKES 2⅔ CUPS (680 GRAMS) REFRESHED CONTINUOUS WHEAT BARM OR WHEAT BARM SPONGE, AFTER FERMENTATION

1⅓ cups (340 grams) continuous wheat barm (page 430), last refreshed 24 hours ago and kept at 68° F. (20° C.)

1 cup (148 grams) whole-wheat flour including 1 teaspoon (1–2 grams) sprouted-wheat flour

¾ cup (192 grams) water at 68° F. (20° C.)

1–2 teaspoons (28 grams) honey

1. Mix all together to produce a medium thick batter consistency. Stir well.

2. Keep 1⅓ cups (340 grams) in covered container, at 68° F. (20° C.) and allow to ferment for 24 hours as continuous barm ready for next day.

3. Use the remainder (1⅓ cups or 340 grams) to prepare barm sponge: Cover and allow to ferment for 4–8 hours at 86° F. (30° C.) or 8–16 hours at 68° F. (20° C.). Stir well once or twice during fermentation time.

Wheat-Berry Barm Sponge

MAKES 2 CUPS (500 GRAMS) WHEAT-BERRY BARM SPONGE AFTER
FERMENTATION

½ cup (109 grams) whole-wheat berries
⅔ cup (141 grams) water at 68° F. (20° C.)
 1 cup (250 grams) wheat-berry continuous barm (page 431), last refreshed
    24 hours ago and kept at 68° F. (20° C.)
 1 teaspoon (20 grams) honey

1. Mix the whole-wheat berries in amount of water specified in recipe,
and soak for 24 hours.
2. Grind together soaked wheat berries and remaining soaking water,
in a food processor, to form a coarse batter.
3. Mix together ground wheat berries, barm, and honey. Stir well.
Cover and allow to ferment for 4–8 hours at 86° F. (30° C.) or for 8–16
hours at 68° F. (20° C.). Stir well once or twice during the fermentation
time.

Combined Refreshment and Wheat-Berry Barm-Sponge Preparation— Amounts for Daily Breadmaking

MAKES 4 CUPS (1,000 GRAMS) REFRESHED CONTINUOUS WHEAT-
BERRY BARM OR WHEAT-BERRY BARM SPONGE, AFTER
FERMENTATION

 1 cup (218 grams) whole-wheat berries
1⅓ cups (282 grams) water at 68° F. (20° C.)
 2 cups (500 grams) wheat-berry continuous barm (page 431), last
    refreshed 24 hours ago and kept at 68° F. (20° C.)
 1 tablespoon (40 grams) honey

1. Mix whole-wheat berries in amount of water specified in recipe, and soak for 24 hours.

2. Grind together soaked wheat berries and remaining soaking water, in a food processor, to form a coarse batter.

3. Mix together ground wheat berries, barm, and honey. Stir well.

4. Keep 2 cups (500 grams) in covered container, at 68° F. (20° C.) and allow to ferment for 24 hours as continuous barm ready for next day.

5. Use the remainder (2 cups or 500 grams) to prepare barm sponge: Cover and allow to ferment for 4–8 hours at 86° F. (30° C.) or for 8–16 hours at 68° F. (20° C.). Stir well once or twice during the fermentation time.

BARM BREADMAKING AS PART OF YOUR DAILY ROUTINE

The three stages of barm breadmaking are *refreshment, sponge preparation,* and finally *breadmaking.* There is a 24-hour interval between barm refreshment and the making of a sponge and a shorter interval (4–16 hours) between sponge preparation and making the bread. Final breadmaking takes 1½ to 4 hours according to the recipe. If wheat-berry barm is used, then a fourth step, *soaking* the wheat berries, would be introduced at the beginning of the cycle. An extra 24 hours would be needed, for the wheat berries to soak, before they could be used to refresh continuous barm. This may seem daunting until it is realized that wheat-berry soaking, barm refreshment, and barm sponge preparation each require only 5–10 minutes of hands-on time. For daily breadmaking, barm refreshment and barm sponge preparation are performed as a single task. Even the breadmaking stage can be handled with little hands-on time. The only real requirement is to be able to plan and then to stay with the chosen schedule.

A barm breadmaking schedule could begin with the refreshment of continuous barm in the early morning of the first day. The sponge would be made early in the morning of the second day; it would be kept at 86° F. (30° C.) for 4 hours and the bread would be made during the afternoon of the second day.

If evening refreshment of continuous barm in readiness for baking is preferred, then a differently patterned schedule is possible. The process would span three days, but the bread would be made in the morning on baking day: Continuous barm would be refreshed on the evening of the first day. The sponge would be made on the evening of the second day and then kept at only 68° F. (20° C.) overnight for 8–16 hours, in readiness for breadmaking on the morning of the third day.

REFRESHMENT OF REHYDRATED BARM

MAKES 2 CUPS (500 GRAMS) CONTINUOUS BARM,
AFTER FERMENTATION

1 cup (250 grams) rehydrated barm (water added to dried barm 24 hours
ago)
⅔ cup (110 grams) whole-wheat flour including ½ teaspoon (1 gram)
sprouted-wheat flour
⅔ cup (140 grams) water at 68° F. (20° C.)
1 teaspoon (20 grams) honey

1. Mix all ingredients together very well. The consistency should be that
of a medium thick batter. Leave in covered bowl at 68° F. (20° C.) for 24
hours. Stir well once or twice during this time.
2. Refreshment can be regarded as complete if, at the end of this time,
the pH has fallen to 3.5–4.0, the mixture has produced plenty of gas
bubbles and it has a pleasant aroma.

CONTINUING A BARM BY REFRESHMENT

Once a barm has been produced it can be refreshed innumerable times
and still perform well as a leavening for barm breads. Although the
recipes may look complex some practice will show otherwise. Refreshment of barm, whether to continue the barm or to make a sponge for
breadmaking, is always such that the ratio of barm: flour: water is approximately 2:1:1 by weight. In other words, the starting amount of
barm is refreshed to give double the amount, without changing consistency. The amounts of any honey or malt are proportioned to the
amount of flour used in the refreshment. The quantities of refreshed
continuous barm produced from each recipe are enough to use in the
barm sponge recipes plus an amount of continuous barm that can be
kept for the next cycle of barm breadmaking, using the same recipes
over again.

Continuous Wheat Barm

Continuous wheat barm ready for refreshment can be any one of the following:

- ▲ Initial wheat barm refreshed successfully enough times that it can be considered the same as continuous barm (page 427).
- ▲ Dried wheat barm 24 hours following rehydration (page 428).
- ▲ Refrigerated continuous wheat barm, stored at 40° F. (4° C.) for up to 1 month (page 431).
- ▲ Continuous wheat barm kept at 68° F. (20° C.), refreshed 1–3 days previously (page 430).

Refreshment of Continuous Wheat Barm

MAKES 2 CUPS (500 GRAMS) CONTINUOUS WHEAT BARM AFTER FERMENTATION

1 cup (250 grams) continuous wheat barm (page 430)
⅔ cup (109 grams) whole-wheat flour including ½ teaspoon (1 gram) sprouted-wheat flour
⅔ cup (141 grams) water at 68° F. (20° C.)
1 teaspoon (20 grams) honey

1. Mix together continuous barm, flour, water, and honey. Loosely cover and leave to ferment at 68° F. (20° C.) for 24 hours. Stir 2–3 times.
2. After 24-hour fermentation time, measure pH on small amount of continuous barm taken from container; it should be 3.5–4.0. Notice the aroma; it should be very mild, pleasant, and fruity. The mixture should also be very well gassed. It is important that the refreshed barm should have all these three characteristics. *A higher pH value, unpleasant smell, or lack of gassing are reasons to discard that particular continuous barm batch.* Successfully refreshed continuous wheat barm can be used to make barm sponge or for making more refreshed continuous barm.

Wheat-Berry Continuous Barm Refreshment

MAKES 2 CUPS (500 GRAMS) WHEAT-BERRY CONTINUOUS BARM
AFTER FERMENTATION

½ cup (109 grams) whole-wheat berries
⅔ cup (141 grams) water at 68° F. (20° C.)
 1 cup (250 grams) continuous wheat barm (page 430)
 1 teaspoon (20 grams) honey

1. Mix the whole-wheat berries in specified amount of water and leave to soak for 24 hours.
2. Grind together soaked wheat berries and remaining soaking water, in a food processor, to form a coarse batter. Mix together ground wheat berries, barm, and honey. Stir well. Cover and allow to ferment for 24 hours at 68° F. (20° C.). Stir 2–3 times during the fermentation period.
3. Make observations, on gassing ability, pH, and aroma, as for refreshment of continuous wheat barm.

Refrigerated Continuous Barm

When continuous barm has been successfully refreshed at 68° F. (20° C.) *(judging by its pH 3.5, pleasant aroma, and gassing ability 24 hours after refreshment)*, it can be covered and stored in a refrigerator at 40° F. (4° C.). Alternatively, it can be kept at cool room temperature, 68° F. (20° C.), for a total of 3 days following refreshment, before being refrigerated at 40° F. (4° C.). Refrigerated continuous barm is best used within 2 weeks but it can usually still be successfully refreshed again, even if it has been refrigerated for up to 1 month.

Note: Continuous barm should not be frozen. Barm microorganisms die when the continuous barm freezes solid at freezer temperatures, below 32° F. (0° C.).

MAKING A BARM SPONGE

A barm sponge is prepared in readiness for the final breadmaking step using continuous barm that has been refreshed 24 hours ago. The ingredient proportions for barm sponge and continuous barm are identical. The only distinctions between barm refreshed to become sponge, rather than continuous barm, are in the length of fermentation time and the temperature. Barm sponge is kept either at 68° F. (20° C.) for 8–16 hours or at 86° F. (30° C.) for 4–8 hours before being mixed into the final bread dough, whereas continuous barm is kept at 68° F. (20° C.) for 24 hours before being refreshed again.

Wheat Barm Sponge

*T*he whole-wheat flour in barm sponge can be from any kind of wheat, including spelt, kamut, durum, hard, and soft wheats. With these proportions, the hard wheats produce the thickest consistency, while the soft wheats give a thin batter.

MAKES 2 CUPS (500 GRAMS) WHEAT BARM SPONGE AFTER FERMEN-
TATION

1 cup (250 grams) continuous wheat barm (page 430), last refreshed 24 hours ago and kept at 68° F. (20° C.)

⅔ cup (109 grams) whole-wheat flour, including ½ teaspoon (1 gram) sprouted-wheat flour

⅔ cup (141 grams) water at 68° F. (20° C.)

1 teaspoon (20 grams) honey

Mix all together to produce a medium-thick batter consistency. Stir well. Cover and allow to ferment for 4–8 hours at 86° F. (30° C.) or 8–16 hours at 68° F. (20° C.). Stir well once or twice during fermentation time.

MILK BARM SPONGE

In the wheat barm sponge recipe: For water, substitute low-fat or nonfat milk, freshly boiled and cooled to 68° F. (20° C.). The consistency is thicker than with water and it may be necessary to compensate for this by using slightly more milk.

BUTTERMILK BARM SPONGE

In the wheat barm sponge recipe: For water, substitute low-fat or nonfat buttermilk, at 68° F. (20° C.). The consistency is thicker than with water

and it may be necessary to compensate for this by using slightly more buttermilk.

Combined Refreshment and Wheat Barm Sponge Preparation— for Daily Breadmaking

MAKES 4 CUPS (1,000 GRAMS) REFRESHED CONTINUOUS WHEAT BARM OR WHEAT BARM SPONGE, AFTER FERMENTATION

2 cups (500 grams) continuous wheat barm (page 430), last refreshed 24 hours ago and kept at 68° F. (20° C.)
1⅓ cups (218 grams) whole-wheat flour including 1 teaspoon (2 grams) sprouted-wheat flour
1⅓ cups (282 grams) water at 68° F. (20° C.)
1 tablespoon (40 grams) honey

1. Mix all together to produce a medium-thick batter consistency. Stir well. Keep 2 cups (500 grams) in covered container, at 68° F. (20° C.) and allow to ferment for 24 hours as continuous barm ready for next day.
2. Use the remainder (2 cups or 500 grams) to prepare barm sponge: Cover and allow to ferment for 4–8 hours at 86° F. (30° C.) or 8–16 hours at 68° F. (20° C.). Stir well once or twice during fermentation time.

Wheat Barm Sponge— Machine Bread Amounts

*A*mounts are for bread machines that produce 1½-pound loaves.

MAKES 1⅓ CUPS (340 GRAMS) WHEAT BARM SPONGE, AFTER FERMENTATION

⅔ cup (170 grams) continuous wheat barm (page 430), last refreshed 24 hours ago and kept at 68° F. (20° C.)

½ cup (74 grams) whole-wheat flour including ½ teaspoon (1 gram) sprouted-wheat flour

⅜ cup (96 grams) water at 68° F. (20° C.)

1 teaspoon (14 grams) honey

Mix all together to produce a medium thick batter consistency. Stir well. Cover and allow to ferment for 4–8 hours at 86° F. (30° C.) or 8–16 hours at 68° F. (20° C.). Stir well once or twice during fermentation time.

Combined Refreshment and Wheat Barm Sponge Preparation—Amounts for Daily Machine Breadmaking

MAKES 2⅔ CUPS (680 GRAMS) REFRESHED CONTINUOUS WHEAT BARM OR WHEAT BARM SPONGE, AFTER FERMENTATION

1⅓ cups (340 grams) continuous wheat barm (page 430), last refreshed 24 hours ago and kept at 68° F. (20° C.)

1 cup (148 grams) whole-wheat flour including 1 teaspoon (1–2 grams) sprouted-wheat flour

¾ cup (192 grams) water at 68° F. (20° C.)

1–2 teaspoons (28 grams) honey

1. Mix all together to produce a medium thick batter consistency. Stir well.

2. Keep 1⅓ cups (340 grams) in covered container, at 68° F. (20° C.) and allow to ferment for 24 hours as continuous barm ready for next day.

3. Use the remainder (1⅓ cups or 340 grams) to prepare barm sponge: Cover and allow to ferment for 4–8 hours at 86° F. (30° C.) or 8–16 hours at 68° F. (20° C.). Stir well once or twice during fermentation time.

Wheat-Berry Barm Sponge

MAKES 2 CUPS (500 GRAMS) WHEAT-BERRY BARM SPONGE AFTER
FERMENTATION

½ cup (109 grams) whole-wheat berries
⅔ cup (141 grams) water at 68° F. (20° C.)
 1 cup (250 grams) wheat-berry continuous barm (page 431), last refreshed
   24 hours ago and kept at 68° F. (20° C.)
 1 teaspoon (20 grams) honey

1. Mix the whole-wheat berries in amount of water specified in recipe,
and soak for 24 hours.
2. Grind together soaked wheat berries and remaining soaking water,
in a food processor, to form a coarse batter.
3. Mix together ground wheat berries, barm, and honey. Stir well.
Cover and allow to ferment for 4–8 hours at 86° F. (30° C.) or for 8–16
hours at 68° F. (20° C.). Stir well once or twice during the fermentation
time.

Combined Refreshment and Wheat-Berry Barm-Sponge Preparation— Amounts for Daily Breadmaking

MAKES 4 CUPS (1,000 GRAMS) REFRESHED CONTINUOUS WHEAT-
BERRY BARM OR WHEAT-BERRY BARM SPONGE, AFTER
FERMENTATION

 1 cup (218 grams) whole-wheat berries
1⅓ cups (282 grams) water at 68° F. (20° C.)
 2 cups (500 grams) wheat-berry continuous barm (page 431), last
   refreshed 24 hours ago and kept at 68° F. (20° C.)
 1 tablespoon (40 grams) honey

1. Mix whole-wheat berries in amount of water specified in recipe, and soak for 24 hours.

2. Grind together soaked wheat berries and remaining soaking water, in a food processor, to form a coarse batter.

3. Mix together ground wheat berries, barm, and honey. Stir well.

4. Keep 2 cups (500 grams) in covered container, at 68° F. (20° C.) and allow to ferment for 24 hours as continuous barm ready for next day.

5. Use the remainder (2 cups or 500 grams) to prepare barm sponge: Cover and allow to ferment for 4–8 hours at 86° F. (30° C.) or for 8–16 hours at 68° F. (20° C.). Stir well once or twice during the fermentation time.

BARM BREADMAKING AS PART OF YOUR DAILY ROUTINE

The three stages of barm breadmaking are *refreshment, sponge preparation,* and finally *breadmaking.* There is a 24-hour interval between barm refreshment and the making of a sponge and a shorter interval (4–16 hours) between sponge preparation and making the bread. Final breadmaking takes 1½ to 4 hours according to the recipe. If wheat-berry barm is used, then a fourth step, *soaking* the wheat berries, would be introduced at the beginning of the cycle. An extra 24 hours would be needed, for the wheat berries to soak, before they could be used to refresh continuous barm. This may seem daunting until it is realized that wheat-berry soaking, barm refreshment, and barm sponge preparation each require only 5–10 minutes of hands-on time. For daily breadmaking, barm refreshment and barm sponge preparation are performed as a single task. Even the breadmaking stage can be handled with little hands-on time. The only real requirement is to be able to plan and then to stay with the chosen schedule.

A barm breadmaking schedule could begin with the refreshment of continuous barm in the early morning of the first day. The sponge would be made early in the morning of the second day; it would be kept at 86° F. (30° C.) for 4 hours and the bread would be made during the afternoon of the second day.

If evening refreshment of continuous barm in readiness for baking is preferred, then a differently patterned schedule is possible. The process would span three days, but the bread would be made in the morning on baking day: Continuous barm would be refreshed on the evening of the first day. The sponge would be made on the evening of the second day and then kept at only 68° F. (20° C.) overnight for 8–16 hours, in readiness for breadmaking on the morning of the third day.

Another schedule would allow the final bread to be baked in the evening: The barm can be refreshed early in the morning of the first day. The sponge can be made early in the morning of the second day and kept at 68° F. (20° C.) during the day for 8–16 hours, until the evening of the second day, in readiness for the bread baking.

Some examples of barm breadmaking schedules follow:

MORNING BREADMAKING
Occasional Morning Breadmaking:

Day 1: 10 P.M. —Refresh continuous barm.
Day 2: 10 P.M. —Prepare barm sponge. Keep sponge at 68° F. (20° C.) for 8–16 hours.
Day 3: 8 A.M. —Make bread.

Daily Morning Breadmaking:

Day 1: 10 P.M. —Refresh continuous barm.
Day 2: 10 P.M. —Refresh continuous barm / Prepare barm sponge (pages 433 and 434). Keep sponge at 68° F. (20° C.) for 8–16 hours.
Day 3: 8 A.M. —Make bread.
        10 P.M. —Refresh continuous barm / Prepare barm sponge (pages 433 and 434). Keep sponge at 68° F. (20° C.) for 8–16 hours.
Day 4 onward: As for day 3.

Wheat-Berry Barm Breads, Made Occasionally in the Morning:

Day 1: 10 P.M. —Soak wheat berries.
Day 2: 10 P.M. —Refresh continuous barm with soaked wheat berries.
        —Soak wheat berries.
Day 3: 10 P.M. —Prepare wheat-berry barm sponge. Keep sponge at 68° F. (20° C.) for 8–16 hours.
Day 4: 8 A.M. —Make bread.

Daily Morning Wheat-Berry Barm Breadmaking:

Day 1: 10 P.M. —Soak wheat berries (enough for refreshment).

Day 2: 10 P.M.   —Refresh continuous barm with soaked wheat berries.

                    —Soak wheat berries (enough for both sponge and refreshment).

Day 3: 10 P.M.   —Refresh continuous barm. / Prepare barm sponge with soaked wheat berries (page 435). Keep sponge at 68° F. (20° C.) for 8–16 hours.

                    —Soak wheat berries (enough for both sponge and refreshment).

Day 4: 8 A.M.   —Make bread.

       10 P.M.   —Refresh continuous barm. / Prepare barm sponge with soaked wheat berries (page 435). Keep sponge at 68° F. (20° C.) for 8–16 hours.

                    —Soak wheat berries (enough for both sponge and refreshment).

Day 5 onward: As for day 4.

AFTERNOON BREADMAKING
Occasional Afternoon Breadmaking:

Day 1: 8 A.M.   —Refresh continuous barm.

Day 2: 8 A.M.   —Prepare barm sponge. Keep sponge at 86° F. (30° C.) for 4–8 hours.

       1 P.M.   —Make bread.

Daily Afternoon Breadmaking:

Day 1: 8 A.M.   —Refresh continuous barm.

Day 2: 8 A.M.   —Refresh continuous barm. / Prepare barm sponge (pages 433 and 434). Keep sponge at 86° F. (30° C.) for 4–8 hours.

       1 P.M.   —Make bread.

Day 3 onward: As for day 2.

Wheat-Berry Barm Breads, Made Occasionally in the Afternoon:

Day 1: 8 A.M.   —Soak wheat berries.

Day 2: 8 A.M.   —Refresh continuous barm with soaked wheat berries.

                      —Soak wheat berries.

Day 3: 8 A.M.   —Prepare wheat-berry barm sponge. Keep sponge at 86° F. (30° C.) for 4–8 hours.

      1 P.M.   —Make bread.

EVENING BREADMAKING
Occasional Evening Breadmaking:

Day 1: 8 A.M.   —Refresh continuous barm.

Day 2: 8 A.M.   —Prepare barm sponge. Keep sponge at 68° F. (20° C.) for 8–16 hours.

      6 P.M.   —Make bread.

Daily Evening Breadmaking:

Day 1: 8 A.M.   —Refresh continuous barm.

Day 2: 8 A.M.   —Refresh continuous barm. / Prepare barm sponge (pages 433 and 434). Keep sponge at 68° F. (20° C.) for 8–16 hours.

      6 P.M.   —Make bread

Day 3 onward: As for day 2.

Wheat-Berry Barm Breads, Made Occasionally in the Evening:

Day 1: 8 A.M.   —Soak wheat berries.

Day 2: 8 A.M.   —Refresh continuous barm with soaked wheat berries.

                      —Soak wheat berries.

Day 3: 8 A.M.   —Prepare wheat-berry barm sponge. Keep sponge at 68° F. (20° C.) for 8–16 hours.

      6 P.M.   —Make bread.

HARD-WHEAT BARM BREADS

Pocket Bread Buns

*I*nspired by a recipe for Egyptian bread by Claudia Roden, these buns are a thrill to watch baking when they rise up in a matter of seconds on the baking tiles. They are a delicious alternative to hold sandwich fillings or as a dinner bread. Makes 4 cups (1,177 grams, about 2½ pounds) of dough.

FOR SIXTEEN 2-OUNCE (60–65 GRAMS) POCKET BREAD BUNS

3 cups (500 grams) whole hard-wheat flour including 2 teaspoons (5 grams) sprouted wheat flour
1 tablespoon (10 grams) olive oil
2 cups (500 grams) whole hard-wheat barm sponge (page 432)
½ cup (125 grams) water at 86° F. (30° C.)
½ teaspoon (2 grams) salt
1 tablespoon (40 grams) honey

1. Rub flour and oil together in mixing bowl and add barm sponge.
2. Dissolve salt and honey in water; add to mixing bowl. Stir until just completely blended. Dough consistency should be on the firm side. Leave in covered bowl to rise and double in volume (approximately 1 hour).
3. Knead well to develop the dough, 10–20 minutes.
4. Divide dough into 16 pieces (approximately 75 grams per piece) and round each piece. Cover and allow to rest for 20 minutes.
5. On a lightly floured board, press each piece with fingertips or roll out, to a circle of 5 inches (10–15 centimeters) in diameter and a quarter-inch (a half-centimeter) thick. Turn dough piece over two or three times during this process. (Take care to keep the outside edges smooth and unbroken by working always from center toward outside with fingertips or rolling across top surface without rolling off the edges.) Cover and leave to rise for 45 minutes, or until buns appear to be well risen.
6. Position oven tiles beneath broiler so that there will be enough vertical space for the buns to puff freely. Preheat broiler on high setting. Arrange buns (tops uppermost or they might not puff!), on hot oven tiles. Broil until they puff and then turn them over to cook underside.

Broiling time is 1–2 minutes for top and 1 minute for underside. Best texture is achieved by keeping browning to a minimum.

FAT PER BUN: Saturated traces; unsaturated 1.5–2 grams

Breadsticks

*E*njoy these breadsticks served from a tall glass at the dinner table. Makes 4 cups (1,190 grams, about 2½ pounds) of dough.

FOR SIXTY-FOUR ½-BY-10-INCH-LONG BREADSTICKS

> 3 cups (500 grams) whole hard-wheat flour including 2 teaspoons
> (5 grams) sprouted-wheat flour
> 1–2 tablespoons (15 grams) olive oil
> 2 cups (500 grams) whole hard-wheat barm sponge (page 432)
> ½ cup (125 grams) water at 86° F. (30° C.)
> ½ teaspoon (2 grams) salt
> 1 tablespoon (40 grams) honey
> 1 tablespoon (8 grams) barley malt extract powder (nondiastatic)

1. Rub flour and oil together in mixing bowl and add barm sponge.
2. Dissolve salt, honey, and malt in water; add to mixing bowl. Stir until just completely blended. Dough consistency should be on the firm side. Leave in covered bowl to rise and double in volume (approximately 1 hour).
3. Knead well to develop the dough, 10–20 minutes.
4. Divide dough into 16 pieces (approximately 75 grams per piece) and round each piece. Cover and allow to rest for 20 minutes.
5. Form each dough piece into a thin cylindrical shape approximately 10 inches (25 centimeters) long, pinch each piece in half to make 32 pieces, cover, and leave to rest for 10 minutes.
6. Pinch each dough piece in half again to make 64 pieces. Finally, shape breadsticks by rolling and twisting each dough piece between thumb and fingertips of both hands. Work from the middle to the ends of each dough piece, while simultaneously stretching the dough, until the length is approximately 10 inches (25 centimeters). (This method prevents the formation of a hollow center, which can result if the dough is rolled back and forth across a board with the palm of the hand.)

7. Cover the breadsticks and allow to rise for 30 minutes or until they appear to be well rounded and risen.

8. Preheat broiler on high setting and position oven tiles beneath broiler so that there is at least a 4-inch (10-centimeter) gap between the tiles and the heat source. Arrange breadsticks on hot oven tiles. Broil until they puff and then roll them over to cook underside. Broiling time is 1–2 minutes for top and 1 minute for underside. The result at this stage is a soft breadstick with a very thin crust.

9. For crisp breadsticks, allow the soft breadsticks to cool and then store them in an enclosed container for 12–24 hours. (This is to allow the moisture to spread evenly from crumb to crust.)

10. Dry the breadsticks in an oven preheated to 250° F. (120° C.), for 10–20 minutes, or in a food dryer operating to approximately 104° F. (40° C.), for 4–5 hours.

FAT PER **4** BREADSTICKS: Saturated traces; unsaturated 1–2 grams

Cottage Loaf

*T*his is a whole-wheat barm version of an English daily bread, with a dark and crispy crust, remembered from the early 1940s. Makes 4 cups (1,175 grams, about 2½ pounds) of dough.

FOR 1 LARGE LOAF, 2¼ POUNDS (1 KILOGRAM)

3 cups (500 grams) whole hard-wheat flour including 2 teaspoons
   (5 grams) sprouted-wheat flour
2 cups (500 grams) whole hard-wheat barm sponge (page 432)
½ cup (125 grams) water at 86° F. (30° C.)
½ teaspoon (2 grams) salt
1 tablespoon (40 grams) honey
1 tablespoon (8 grams) barley malt extract powder (nondiastatic)

1. Add flour and barm sponge to mixing bowl. Dissolve salt, honey, and malt in water; add to mixing bowl. Stir until just completely blended. Dough consistency should be on the firm side. Leave in covered bowl to rise and double in volume (approximately 1 hour).

2. Knead well to develop the dough, 10–20 minutes.

3. Form one-third of the dough into a ball and the remaining two-thirds of the dough into a second ball. Cover each dough piece and allow to rest on a smooth nonstick surface for 20 minutes.

4. Preheat oven, oven tiles, and cloche at 425° F. (220° C.).

5. Reshape each dough piece into a ball, leave dough balls on a well-floured surface, and again cover for approximately 30 minutes or until they are risen nearly to double.

6. Cut a cross in the center of the larger dough piece and open it so that a fresh surface is exposed. Position the smaller dough piece on top of the cut, floured side up, and with the first finger poke a hole all the way through the loaf. Cover the loaf and allow it to rest for 10 minutes before baking. Transfer to oven on a pele.

7. Bake on preheated, well-seasoned tiles and under preheated cloche for 30 minutes at 425° F. (220° C.). Remove the cloche for the last 5–10 minutes of baking to allow the crust to brown and crisp well.

FAT PER **2** OUNCES: Saturated trace; unsaturated 1–2 grams

Wheat-Berry Bread

A favorite everyday bread that can be enjoyed at every meal. Use this recipe with the best high-protein wheat available and the reward will be a light and deliciously crusted, country-style loaf. With less favorable hard wheats this recipe will still give a delicious loaf, but the texture may be more compact. Makes 4 cups (1,167 grams, about 2½ pounds) of dough.

FOR 1 LARGE LOAF, 2¼ POUNDS (1 KILOGRAM)

3 cups (500 grams) whole hard-wheat flour
2 cups (500 grams) whole hard wheat-berry barm sponge (page 435)
½ teaspoon (2 grams) salt
1 tablespoon (40 grams) honey
½ cup (125 grams) water at 86° F. (30° C)

1. Add flour and barm sponge to mixing bowl. Dissolve salt and honey in water; add to mixing bowl. Stir until just completely blended. Dough consistency should be fairly soft. Leave in covered bowl to rise and double in volume (approximately 1 hour).

2. Knead well to develop bread-dough texture, 10–20 minutes. Form dough into a ball and return to covered bowl, allow to rest for 20 minutes.

3. Reshape dough into ball, put it on parchment paper on a wooden board, and dimple dough all over with fingertips, to prevent bubbles in final crust. Cover with inverted mixing bowl and allow to rise for 45 minutes.

4. Preheat oven, baking tiles, and cloche at 425° F. (220° C.). When ready for baking, make 4 parallel slashes ¼–½ inch (4 millimeters) deep across the loaf in two directions to form a diamond pattern. Use a pele to transfer loaf onto tiles in oven and cover with cloche. Bake for 30 minutes at 425° F. (220° C.). The cloche can be removed for the last 5–10 minutes of baking to allow a crisp crust to develop.

FAT PER 2 OUNCES: Saturated trace; unsaturated 1–2 grams

Suffolk Bread

Suffolk bread is a whole-grain bread baked in a terra cotta loaf pan of a style made in Suffolk, England. The terra cotta allows the bread to brown evenly and imparts a lovely flavor to the crust. Both the Wheat-Berry Barm Bread and the Cottage Loaf doughs can be baked in the Suffolk bread pan.

FOR A 1½-POUND (750-GRAM) LOAF

1. Use two-thirds of the dough in the recipe for either Wheat-Berry Barm Bread or the Cottage Loaf, at the end of the kneading step. Form the dough piece into a ball, cover it, and allow it to rest for 20 minutes.

2. Preheat oven to 425° F. (220° C.).

3. Oil the pan with a mixture of 3 parts olive oil and 1 part liquid lecithin. Using slightly wet hands and a nonstick surface, press and pull the dough into a rectangle that is as wide as the pan is long. Roll up the dough, tuck the ends under, and place seam side down in the pan. Fist the dough evenly into the corners of the pan. Cover the pan and allow the loaf to rise for 45 minutes, or until it has doubled.

4. Slash the length of the loaf. Bake at 425° F. (220° C.) for 30 minutes. Remove loaf from pan and allow to cool on rack.

FAT PER 2 OUNCES: Saturated trace; unsaturated 0.5–1 gram

Machine Bread

*H*igh-protein hard-wheat barm breads can be prepared very successfully in auto-matic bread bakers. Only the highest-protein hard-wheat flours should be used, in order to withstand the vigorous kneading step. Weak gluten flours will produce dense, flat-topped loaves in automatic breadmakers.

FOR 1 LARGE LOAF, 1½ POUNDS (680 GRAMS)

2 cups (340 grams) whole hard-wheat flour including 2 teaspoons
   (4 grams) sprouted-wheat flour
1⅓ cups (340 grams) whole hard-wheat barm sponge (page 433)
⅓ cup (85 grams) water at 86° F. (30° C.)
⅓ teaspoon (1½ grams) finely ground salt
1 tablespoon (28 grams) honey
1 teaspoon (5 grams) barley malt extract powder (nondiastatic)

Follow machine manufacturer's directions, omitting any steps requiring the addition of bakers' yeast.

FAT PER 2 OUNCES: Saturated trace; unsaturated 0.5–1 gram

Raisin Bread

*A*lmost like an English teacake; this raisin bread is good sliced as a snack along with a glass of milk. Delicious toasted for breakfast too. Flavor develops well if it is aged for a few days. Makes 5 cups (1,545 grams, about 3½ pounds) of dough.

FOR TWO 1½-POUND (650-GRAM) LOAVES

2 cups (250 grams) raisins
3 cups (500 grams) whole hard-wheat flour including 2 teaspoons
   (5 grams) sprouted-wheat flour
4 tablespoons (40 grams) almond oil
2 cups (500 grams) whole hard wheat-berry barm sponge (page 435)
½ cup (125 grams) water at 86° F. (30° C.)
½ teaspoon (2 grams) salt

3 tablespoons (120 grams) honey
1 tablespoon (8 grams) dried barley malt extract (nondiastatic)
1 lemon for zest (grated outermost colored peel)

1. Presoak raisins by covering them with freshly boiled water at least ½ hour and preferably 4 hours before using in recipe.
2. Rub flour and oil together in mixing bowl and add barm sponge.
3. Dissolve salt, honey, and malt in water; add to mixing bowl. Add lemon zest. Stir until just completely blended. Dough consistency should be fairly soft. Leave in covered bowl to rise and double in volume (approximately 1 hour).
4. Knead well to develop bread dough texture. Drain raisins and work them gently into dough. Divide dough into two pieces and round them. Allow dough pieces to rest under inverted mixing bowls for 20 minutes.
5. Reshape each dough piece into ball. Dimple the loaf all over with fingertips and leave for final rise on parchment paper on a wooden board. Cover each loaf with an inverted mixing bowl and allow to rise for 45 minutes.
6. Preheat oven, baking tiles, and cloche at 425° F. (220° C.). When ready for baking, cut a cross on the top surface of each loaf. Bake for 30 minutes at 425° F. (220° C.), under cloche. Bake for a few more minutes without cloche, to produce a well-browned firm crust, if necessary.

FAT PER 2 OUNCES: Saturated trace; unsaturated 1.5–2 grams

Soft Spiced Currant Buns

Soft and satisfying, with a warm spicy flavor ideal for winter holidays. The inclu-sion of black pepper was inspired by Elizabeth David's recipe for a sweet spice blend for English cakes and buns. The Romans, according to Apicius, also used pepper in sweet cakes. Steam-cook or bake these buns. Makes 5 cups (1,537 grams, about 3½ pounds) of dough.

SPICE MIXTURE

Use the following spices in approximately equal amounts, enough to produce only sufficient for the recipe, that is, 1–2 teaspoons of spice mixture, so that the flavor is the richest possible.

Whole nutmeg, freshly grated
Black peppercorns or allspice berries
Cinnamon bark
Whole cloves

Using a small mortar and pestle, grind ingredients finely together and discard large pieces that cannot be ground.

DOUGH FOR SOFT SPICED CURRANT BUNS

FOR SIXTEEN 3-OUNCE (80-GRAM) BUNS

2 cups (250 grams) Zante currants
3 cups (500 grams) whole hard-wheat flour including 2 teaspoons
   (5 grams) sprouted-wheat flour
4 tablespoons (40 grams) olive oil
2 cups (500 grams) whole hard-wheat barm sponge (page 432)
½ cup (125 grams) milk freshly boiled and cooled to 86° F. (30° C.)
½ teaspoon (2 grams) salt
3 tablespoons (120 grams) honey
1 level teaspoon (2 grams) spice mixture
1 teaspoon (5 grams) grated fresh ginger root
   Special equipment: Bamboo steamer

1. Presoak currants by covering them with freshly boiled water at least half an hour and preferably 4 hours before using in recipe.
2. Rub flour and oil together in mixing bowl and add barm sponge. Dissolve salt and honey in milk; add to mixing bowl. Add spices and

gingerroot. Stir until just completely blended. Dough consistency should be fairly soft. Leave in covered bowl to rise and double in volume (approximately 1 hour).

3. Knead well to develop bread dough texture. Drain currants and fold gently and evenly into dough. Divide dough into 16 pieces and round them. Cover and allow dough pieces to rest on a nonstick surface for 20 minutes.

4. Reshape buns into rounds and place them on parchment paper circles 4 inches (8–10 centimeters) in diameter on a wooden board. Cover and leave them to rise for 45 minutes.

STEAMED SPICED BUNS

Before cooking the buns, bring water to boil under bamboo steamer and allow to steam for 20 minutes, to clean and equilibrate the steamer.

Arrange buns (on parchment paper) in steamer so that there is plenty of room for the steam to circulate. Cover and steam for 20 minutes. Allow to cool on rack and remove parchment paper as soon as possible.

BAKED SPICED BUNS

Preheat oven, oven tiles, and cloche at 425° F. (220° C.). Bake for 20 minutes at 425° F. (220° C.), under cloche. Allow to cool on rack and remove parchment paper as soon as possible.

FAT PER BUN: Saturated trace; unsaturated 3–5 grams

SOFT-WHEAT BARM BREADS

Plain Scones

*P*erhaps *this is how scones were made before baking powder was invented. These barm scones are undemanding to make. The British would eat them at teatime. Americans would call them biscuits and enjoy them freshly made for breakfast, lunch, or dinner. This dough can also be used to make a piecrust without adding fat; double the amount of honey if it is to be used for a sweet pie and use instead of almond piecrust to make apple pie (page 452). Makes 4 cups (1,167 grams, 2½ pounds) dough.*

FOR SIXTEEN 2-OUNCE (60–65 GRAMS) SCONES

3 cups (500 grams) whole soft white wheat flour including 2 teaspoons
(5 grams) sprouted-wheat flour
2 cups (500 grams) whole soft white wheat barm sponge (page 432)
½ cup (125 grams) water at 86° F. (30° C.)
½ teaspoon (2 grams) salt
1 tablespoon (40 grams) honey

1. Add flour and barm sponge to mixing bowl. Dissolve salt and honey in water and add to mixing bowl. Using as little mixing as possible, completely blend together. Dough consistency should be fairly soft.
2. With slightly wet hands, divide dough into two equal pieces and gently squeeze each into a ball shape. Place each dough piece on parchment paper and, using fingertips, press out into a circle ½ inch (1–2 centimeters) thick. Using a dough cutter, cut through each piece, across the diameter 4 times, to divide it into 8 equal portions, without separating them. Cover the scones with an inverted mixing bowl and allow to rise for 45 minutes.
3. Preheat oven, cloche, and baking tiles at 425° F. (220° C.). Bake under cloche at 425° F. (220° C.) for 20 minutes.

FAT PER SCONE: Saturated trace; unsaturated 2–3 grams

Milk Scones

*U*sing milk and barley malt in these scones makes them just a little more interesting and substantial than plain scones. Makes 4 cups (1,175 grams, about 2½ pounds) of dough.

FOR SIXTEEN 2-OUNCE (60–65 GRAMS) SCONES

3 cups (500 grams) whole soft white wheat flour including 2 teaspoons (5 grams) sprouted-wheat flour

2 cups (500 grams) soft whole white wheat and milk barm sponge (page 432)

½ cup (125 grams) low-fat or nonfat milk, previously boiled and cooled to 86° F. (30° C.)

½ teaspoon (2 grams) finely ground salt

1 tablespoon (40 grams) honey

1 tablespoon (8 grams) barley malt extract powder (nondiastatic)

1. Add flour and barm sponge to mixing bowl. Dissolve salt, honey, and malt in milk and add to mixing bowl. Using as little mixing as possible, completely blend together. Dough consistency should be fairly soft.

2. Divide dough into two equal pieces and round them. Roll out each piece to a thickness of ½ inch (1–2 centimeters) and cut out 8 round scones with a biscuit cutter.

3. Place scones on parchment paper and cover with inverted mixing bowls. Leave to rise for 45 minutes.

4. Preheat oven and baking tiles at 425° F. (220° C.). Brush tops of scones with milk. Transfer scones to oven on parchment paper, using an oven pele. Bake for 20 minutes at 425° F. (220° C.).

FAT PER SCONE (DEPENDS ON MILK USED): Saturated 0.5 grams; unsaturated 2–3 grams

Buttermilk Scone Loaf

*B*uttermilk scone loaf was inspired by Irish soda bread; the soda leavening is replaced with barm. It is quickly made up, flavorful, and wonderful as a breakfast bread. Makes 4 cups (1,200 grams, about 2½ pounds) of dough.

FOR TWO 1-POUND (500 GRAMS) LOAVES

3 cups (500 grams) whole soft white wheat flour including 2 teaspoons (5 grams) sprouted-wheat flour

2 cups (500 grams) whole soft white wheat and buttermilk barm sponge (page 432)

⅔ cup (150 grams) buttermilk or soft yogurt at 68–86° F. (20°–30° C.)

½ teaspoon (2 grams) finely ground salt

1 tablespoon (40 grams) honey

1 tablespoon (8 grams) barley malt extract powder (nondiastatic)

1. Add flour and barm sponge to mixing bowl. Dissolve salt, honey, and malt in buttermilk and add to mixing bowl. Using as little mixing as possible, completely blend together. Dough consistency should be just stiff enough to allow loaves to hold their shape.

2. Divide dough into two equal pieces and gently squeeze into a ball shape. Place each dough piece on parchment paper. Cut a cross on the surface of each loaf. Cover each loaf with an inverted mixing bowl and allow to rise for 45 minutes.

3. Preheat oven, baking tiles, and cloche at 425° F. (220° C.). Bake at 425° F. (220° C.), under cloche, for 20–30 minutes.

FAT PER **3** OUNCES: Saturated 1–3 grams; unsaturated 5–8 grams (depends on buttermilk used)

452 ▲ THE SUPERPYRAMID EATING PROGRAM

Apple Pie with Almond and Wheat Barm Piecrust

A *lmonds enrich the piecrust and apples, honey, and barm combine to give heavenly flavors that you just might never have experienced before. (For an almost nonfat crust, use plain scone dough on page 449.) Makes 5 cups (1,407 grams, about 3 pounds) of dough.*

ALMOND AND WHEAT BARM PIECRUST

FOR TWO 8–9 INCH (20–22 CENTIMETER) DIAMETER PIES

> 3 cups (500 grams) whole soft white wheat flour including 2 teaspoons
> (5 grams) sprouted-wheat flour
> 1½ cups (200 grams) blanched almonds
> 2 cups (500 grams) whole soft white wheat barm sponge (page 432)
> ½ teaspoon (2 grams) salt
> 2 tablespoons (80 grams) honey
> 1 cup (125 grams) water at 86° F. (30° C.)
> Almond oil to coat pie dishes

APPLE PIE FILLING

FOR 1 PIE

> 2–4 cooking apples (250–500 grams peeled and cored apple)
> 2 tablespoons (80 grams) honey
> Spice according to taste

GLAZE

FOR 1 PIE

> 1 tablespoon (40 grams) honey
> 1 tablespoon (15 grams) water

1. Add flour to mixing bowl. Grind almonds finely in a food processor and rub them evenly into the flour. Add barm sponge to mixing bowl. Dissolve salt and honey in water, add to mixing bowl. Using as little mixing as possible, completely blend together. Dough consistency should be just firm enough to roll out easily as pastry.
2. Lightly coat pie dishes with almond oil.
3. Using a lightly floured board and lightly floured hands, divide dough

into two equal pieces and squeeze gently into a ball shape. For each pie, roll out two-thirds of one dough piece to a thickness of ¼ inch (½ centimeter) or less and line pie dish.

4. Peel and core apples. Slice them and arrange evenly on piecrust. Drizzle honey all over the sliced apples. Add desired spices.

5. Roll out remaining part of the dough piece to a thickness of ¼ inch (½ centimeter) or less and cover pie. Trim off excess edging on crust, so that no pastry is left on the pie rim, and gently cut a sand-dollar pattern in the top crust.

6. Cover the pie with an inverted mixing bowl or enclose it in a large plastic bag, and allow it to rise for 45 minutes.

7. Preheat oven and pizza stone at 425° F. (220° C.). Bake at 375° F. (190° C.) for 25–30 minutes. Check that crusts, top and bottom, are well baked. Bake longer if necessary.

8. Soon after removing pie from oven, mix together the honey and water for the glaze. Brush the glaze all over the hot piecrust.

FAT PER SLICE (⅛ OF PIE): Saturated 1 gram; unsaturated 7–9 grams

Pear Pie with Almond Oil and Wheat Barm Piecrust

Pears make delicious pies and the flavor is enhanced with honey and the almond oil and wheat barm crust. (For an almost nonfat crust use Plain Scone dough on page 449.) Makes 4 cups (1,257 grams, about 2¾ pounds) of dough.

ALMOND OIL AND WHEAT BARM PIECRUST

FOR TWO 8-9-INCH (20–22 CENTIMETER) DIAMETER PIES

3 cups (500 grams) whole soft white wheat flour including 2 teaspoons (5 grams) sprouted-wheat flour
5 tablespoons (50 grams) almond oil
2 cups (500 grams) whole soft white wheat barm sponge (page 432)
½ cup (125 grams) water at 86° F. (30° C.)
½ teaspoon (2 grams) salt
2 tablespoons (80 grams) honey
Almond oil to coat pie dishes

PEAR PIE FILLING

FOR 1 PIE

2–4 medium ripe pears (250–500 grams)
  2 tablespoons (80 grams) honey

GLAZE

FOR 1 PIE

1 tablespoon (40 grams) honey
1 tablespoon (15 grams) water

1. Add flour to mixing bowl. Rub oil evenly into the flour. Add barm sponge to mixing bowl. Dissolve salt and honey in water, add to mixing bowl. Using as little mixing as possible, completely blend together. Dough consistency should be just firm enough to roll out easily as pastry.
2. Lightly coat pie dishes with almond oil.
3. Using a lightly floured board and lightly floured hands, divide dough into two equal pieces and squeeze gently into a ball shape. For each pie, roll out two-thirds of one dough piece to a thickness of ¼ inch (½ centimeter) or less and line pie dish.
4. Peel and core pears. Slice them and arrange evenly on piecrust. Drizzle honey all over the sliced pears.
5. Roll out remaining part of the dough piece to a thickness of ¼ inch (½ centimeter) or less and cover pie. Trim off excess edging on crust, so that no pastry is left on the pie rim, and gently cut a pattern of little cutout circles in the top crust, using an apple coring tool or something similar.
6. Cover the pie with an inverted mixing bowl or enclose it in a large plastic bag, and allow it to rise for 45 minutes.
7. Preheat oven and pizza stone at 425° F. (220° C.). Bake at 375° F. (190° C.) for 25–30 minutes. Check that crusts, top and bottom, are well baked. Bake longer if necessary.
8. Soon after removing pie from oven, mix together the honey and water for the glaze. Brush the glaze generously all over the hot piecrust.

FAT PER SLICE (⅛ OF PIE): Saturated 0.5 gram; unsaturated 4–6 grams

Blueberry Muffins

B *lueberry barm muffins are enriched with milk and eggs; serve them at weekend* *and special breakfasts. Makes 4–5 cups (1,392 grams, about 3 pounds) of* *dough.*

FOR EIGHTEEN 2 OUNCE (60–65 GRAMS) MUFFINS

3 tablespoons (25 grams) milk, previously boiled and cooled to 86° F. (30° C.)

½ teaspoon (2 grams) finely ground salt

3 tablespoons (120 grams) honey

2 eggs (95 grams, without shell) at 68° F. (20° C.)

2 cups (500 grams) whole soft white wheat and milk barm sponge (page 432)

250 grams fresh blueberries

400 grams whole soft white wheat flour including 2 teaspoons (4 grams) sprouted-wheat flour

1. In mixing bowl, dissolve salt and honey in milk. Add lightly beaten eggs, followed by barm sponge, and mix well. Add blueberries and stir into mixture. Fold in flour. Mix gently only until uniformly blended. Consistency should be of a thick spoonable batter.

2. Spoon the batter into muffin cups so that they are two-thirds filled. Enclose the muffins in a plastic bag and allow to rise for 45 minutes. Preheat oven and oven tiles at 425° F. (220° C.). Bake at 375° F. (190° C.) for 20 minutes.

FAT PER MUFFIN: Saturated traces; unsaturated 0.5–1 gram

Date-and-Walnut Loaf

*T*he dates and walnuts combine to give an unusual fudgelike texture to this cake. Makes 1,800 grams (about 4 pounds) dough.

FOR TWO 750-GRAM LOAVES

2 cups (250 grams) dates, no pits
2 cups (200 grams) walnuts without shells
½ cup (125 grams) water, freshly boiled
½ teaspoon (2 grams) salt
3 tablespoons (120 grams) honey
1 tablespoon (8 grams) barley malt extract powder (nondiastatic)
2 eggs (95 grams without shell) at 68° F. (20° C.)
2 cups (500 grams) whole soft white wheat barm sponge (page 432)
3 cups (500 grams) whole soft white wheat flour including 2 teaspoons
  (5 grams) sprouted-wheat flour

1. For each loaf, line a square baking pan 7 x 7 x 2 inches (18 x 18 x 4 centimeters) with parchment paper.
2. Separately chop dates and walnuts. In mixing bowl, dissolve salt in freshly boiled water and then add dates. When cooled to 86–104° F. (30–40° C.), mix in honey, malt, and walnuts, followed by lightly beaten eggs and barm sponge. Fold in flour. Gently fold ingredients together until just completely mixed. Consistency should be of a very thick spoonable batter.
3. For each loaf, spoon half the batter into a paper-lined pan to form a thickness of 2 centimeters. Enclose in a plastic bag and allow to rise for 45 minutes.
4. Preheat oven and oven tiles at 425° F. (220° C.). Bake for 30 minutes. Remove from pan and allow to cool on rack. Remove paper when loaf has cooled.

FAT PER 2 OUNCES: Saturated traces; unsaturated 1 gram

Honey-Raisin Rolls

*M*emories of Chelsea buns were the starting point for these honey-raisin rolls. Chelsea buns are usually made with currants rather than raisins, and these rolls can also be made with currants if they are available. Makes 4 cups (1,237 grams, about 2¾ pounds) of dough.

FOR EIGHTEEN 2–3 OUNCE (60–70 GRAM) ROLLS

FRUIT FILLING

2 cups (250 grams) raisins
1 orange for zest (outermost colored peel)
1 tablespoon (40 grams) honey

1. Presoak raisins by covering with freshly boiled water, at least ½ hour and preferably 4 hours before using in recipe.
2. Drain raisins. Grate zest from orange over raisins and add honey. Gently mix together to evenly distribute orange zest and honey.

DOUGH

½ cup (125 grams) water at 86° F. (30° C.)
½ teaspoon (2 grams) salt
2 tablespoons (80 grams) honey
2 cups (500 grams) whole soft white wheat barm sponge (page 432)
3 tablespoons (30 grams) almond oil
3 cups (500 grams) whole soft white wheat flour including 2 teaspoons
   (5 grams) sprouted-wheat flour

HONEY GLAZE

2 tablespoons (80 grams) honey
2 tablespoons (25 grams) water

Dissolve honey in water and use a pastry brush to spread the mixture on tops of rolls.

DOUGH

1. In mixing bowl, dissolve salt and honey in water. Mix in barm sponge. In a separate bowl rub oil into flour and add to mixing bowl. Fold ingredients together until just mixed. Divide dough into two pieces.

2. For each dough piece: Roll out into a rectangle ¼ inch (½ centimeter) thick and evenly cover with half of fruit filling. Form a log shape by rolling up the dough. Pinch seam along length of log shape and place seam down. Cut into 9 equal slices. Arrange slices, cut side up, in a square, on parchment paper, allowing just enough space between to spread and touch when risen. Cover and allow to rise for 45 minutes.
3. Preheat oven, oven tiles, and cloche at 425° F. (220° C.). Bake at 375° F. (190° C.), under cloche, for 40 minutes.
4. Allow to cool a little on rack. Remove paper as soon as possible. Glaze generously, while still hot.

FAT PER ROLL: Saturated traces; unsaturated 0.5–1 gram

Hazelnut Biscotti

*H*azelnut biscotti are a delicious and satisfying snack or dessert cookie. Makes 5 cups (1,530 grams, about 3¼ pounds) of dough.

FOR APPROXIMATELY 32 BISCOTTI (1–2 OUNCES EACH)

½ teaspoon (2 grams) finely ground salt
1 tablespoon (10 grams) water
2 teaspoons (10 milliliters) vanilla extract
3 tablespoons (120 grams) honey
4 eggs (190 grams, without shell) at 68° F. (20° C.), lightly beaten
2 cups (500 grams) whole soft white wheat barm sponge (page 432)
1½ cups (200 grams) hazelnuts, without shells, finely chopped
3 cups (500 grams) whole soft white wheat flour including 2 teaspoons (5 grams) sprouted-wheat flour

1. Use parchment paper to line two baking pans 7 x 7 x 2 inches (18 x 18 x 4 centimeters).
2. In mixing bowl, dissolve salt in water; add vanilla extract, followed by honey, lightly beaten eggs, barm sponge, and finely chopped hazelnuts. Mix well. Fold in the flour and mix only sufficiently to distribute ingredients evenly. The consistency should be of a thick spoonable batter.
3. Divide batter between two baking pans and spread to a thickness of

½–1 inch (2 centimeters). Cover and leave to rise for 45 minutes.

4. Preheat oven and oven tiles at 425° F. (220° C.). Bake at 375° F. (190° C.) for 30 minutes.

5. Remove from pan and cool on rack. Remove paper as soon as possible. When completely cooled, cut each loaf in half and cut 8 slices from each half loaf. Arrange slices separately on a parchment-paper-covered cookie sheet. Allow biscotti to dry by baking them at 325° F. (160° C.) for 15 minutes or more.

FAT PER BISCOTTO: Saturated 0.5 gram; unsaturated 3–7 grams

Raisin-Nutmeg Muffins, Welsh Cakes, and Scones

*T*he flavor combination was inspired by Welsh cakes—small flat griddle cakes full of raisins and emitting a warm spicy aroma as they are cooked on the griddle or bakestone. The same dough can be made up into American-style muffins or in the style of Welsh cakes or scones. Makes 4–5 cups (1,392 grams, about 3 pounds) of dough.

FOR EIGHTEEN 2-OUNCE (60–65 GRAMS) MUFFINS

2 cups (250 grams) raisins or currants

3 tablespoons (25 grams) milk, previously boiled and cooled to 86° F. (30° C.)

½ teaspoon (2 grams) finely ground salt

3 tablespoons (120 grams) honey

2 eggs (95 grams, without shell) at 68° F. (20° C.), lightly beaten

2 cups (500 grams) whole soft white wheat and milk barm sponge (page 432)

2½ cups (400 grams) whole soft white wheat flour including 2 teaspoons (4 grams) sprouted-wheat flour

1 teaspoon (2 grams) nutmeg, freshly grated

1. Soak the raisins ½–4 hours ahead of baking time, in enough boiling water to cover them.

2. In mixing bowl, dissolve salt and honey in milk. Add lightly beaten eggs, followed by barm sponge, and mix well. Drain raisins and stir into mixture. Separately, mix the nutmeg into the flour. Fold the flour into the mixture. Mix gently only until uniformly blended. Consistency should be of a soft spoonable dough.

MUFFINS

1. Spoon the batter into muffin cups so that they are two-thirds filled. Enclose the muffins in a plastic bag and allow to rise for 45 minutes.

2. Preheat oven and oven tiles at 425° F. (220° C.). Bake at 375° F. (190° C.) for 20 minutes.

WELSH CAKES

1. Spoon up egg-sized dough pieces and, using floured hands, gently shape each piece into a flat round cake. Position the cakes on a floured marble slab and press out to a thickness of ¼–½ inch (½–1 centimeter).
2. Cover the cakes and leave them to rise for 45 minutes.
3. Preheat a pizza baking stone at 425° F. (220° C.). Turn oven off. Position hot pizza stone beneath broiler and preheat broiler on a medium-high setting for a few minutes before use. Bake cakes under broiler until well browned on top (1–3 minutes.) Turn cakes over and bake second side until browned (1–2 minutes).

SCONES

1. Use half the dough and squeeze it into a ball. Position the ball of dough in the center of a piece of parchment paper and press it out into a circle half an inch (one centimeter) thick. Divide it into 8 segments using a dough cutter. Cover with an inverted mixing bowl and allow to rise for 45 minutes.
2. Preheat oven and pizza baking stone at 425° F. (220° C.). Bake at 375° F. (190° C.) for 20 minutes.

FAT PER 2-OUNCE MUFFIN, CAKE, OR SCONE: Saturated 0.5–1 (trace without egg yolk); unsaturated 7–9 grams; cholesterol 20–25 milligrams (for whole eggs—none if you substitute egg whites. Use 2 whites for 1 whole egg).

DURUM WHEAT AND KAMUT BARM BREADS

Kamut Pompeii Bread

*T*his bread is designed to be pulled into serving-size pieces, and is based on the pictures of loaves found during excavations of Pompeii. Perhaps these were originally made with durum wheat. Either durum wheat or kamut are suitable for making this loaf. Makes 4 cups (1,167 grams, about 2½ pounds) of dough.

FOR TWO 1-POUND (500-GRAM) LOAVES, 8 2-OUNCE (60–65 GRAMS) SERVINGS PER LOAF

3 cups (500 grams) whole-grain kamut flour including 2 teaspoons
  (5 grams) sprouted-wheat flour
½ cup (125 grams) water at 86° F. (30° C.)
½ teaspoon (2 grams) salt
1 tablespoon (40 grams) honey
500 grams whole kamut barm sponge (page 432)

1. Add flour to mixing bowl. In a separate bowl, dissolve salt and honey in water and add barm sponge to it. Mix together well and add to flour in mixing bowl. Mix until just completely blended. Cover and wait 20 minutes before kneading.

2. Knead briefly to develop dough texture. With slightly wet hands, divide dough into quarters and form each dough piece into a ball. Form a wheel with each dough piece by poking a thumb through the center and enlarging the hole to 1–2 inches (3–5 centimeters). Press the dough on a nonstick surface with fingertips until wheel is a half-centimeter thick and 8–10 inches (20–25 centimeters) in diameter.

3. For each loaf: On parchment paper on a wooden board, arrange 2 wheels, one on top of the other. Lightly press the wheels together with fingertips. Cut through the loaf across diameter, with dough cutter, 4 times to create 8 equal portion marks. Cover and allow to rise for 45 minutes.

4. Preheat oven, oven tiles, and cloche at 425° F. (220° C.). Bake at 425° F. (220° C.) under cloche for 20 minutes.

FAT PER **2** OUNCES: Saturated trace; unsaturated 1–2 grams

Focaccia

This focaccia, flavored with olive oil, makes an ideal lunch bread to eat with soft mozzarella goat cheese, sweet tomatoes in high season, and Greek-style dry olives. Makes 4 cups (1,167 grams, about 2½ pounds) of dough.

FOR TWO 1-POUND (500-GRAM) FOCACCIA

3 cups (500 grams) whole durum wheat flour including 2 teaspoons
(5 grams) sprouted-wheat flour
½ teaspoon (2 grams) salt
1 tablespoon (40 grams) honey
½ cup (125 grams) water at 86° F. (30° C.)
2 cups (500 grams) whole durum wheat barm sponge (page 432)
1–2 tablespoons (7–15 grams) olive oil to flavor crust

1. Add flour to mixing bowl. In a separate bowl, dissolve salt and honey in water and add barm sponge to it. Mix together well and add to flour in mixing bowl. Mix until just completely blended. Cover and wait 20 minutes before kneading.
2. Knead briefly to develop dough texture. Using lightly floured hands and a lightly floured working surface, divide dough in half and form each dough piece into a ball.
3. Position each dough piece on parchment paper on a wooden board. Press dough into a circle by working it with the fingertips until 6–8 inches (15–20 centimeters) in diameter and about ½ inch (1 centimeter) thick. Toward the end of this process dip fingertips in olive oil and so coat the entire upper surface of the bread with olive oil. Cover and leave to rise for 45 minutes or until puffy and nearly doubled in thickness.
4. Preheat oven and pizza stone at 425° F. (220° C.).
5. Gently spread a little more olive oil on the bread using fingertips. Prick a pattern, all over the bread and all the way through, with a cocktail stick or lemon reamer. Transfer to oven on pele.
6. Bake at 425° F. (220° C.) in preheated oven, for 20 minutes.

FAT PER 2 OUNCES (DEPENDING ON AMOUNT OF OLIVE OIL): Saturated trace; unsaturated 2–3 grams

Pizza

*T*his pizza is a decorated version of the focaccia just described. All the accompaniments are baked on top of the dough, which serves as a platter. Pizza properly made and free from high-fat meats and cheeses can be a truly basic Superpyramid food. Makes 4 cups (1,167 grams, about 2½ pounds) of dough.

MAKES FOUR 8-INCH (20-CENTIMETER) DIAMETER PIZZAS

PIZZA DOUGH

3 cups (500 grams) whole durum wheat flour including 2 teaspoons
   (5 grams) sprouted-wheat flour
½ cup (125 grams) water at 86° F. (30° C.)
½ teaspoon (2 grams) salt
1 tablespoon (40 grams) honey
2 cups (500 grams) whole durum wheat barm sponge (page 432)

PIZZA TOPPINGS

FOR FOUR 8-INCH (20-CENTIMETER) PIZZAS

2–3 cups (100 grams) dried tomatoes
1–2 cups (500 grams) soft low-fat mozzarella cheese or regular goat's- or
    cow's-milk mozzarella for an occasional use
  1 cup (48) Greek-style olives
2–3 tablespoons (25 grams) olive oil
   fresh oregano leaves

1. Add flour to mixing bowl. In a separate bowl, dissolve salt and honey in water and add barm sponge to it. Mix together well and add to flour in mixing bowl. Mix until just completely blended. Cover and wait 20 minutes before kneading.
2. Prepare pizza toppings: Soak dried tomatoes in freshly boiled water until softened (5–10 minutes) and then drain them. Slice mozzarella cheese as thinly as possible. Cut olives into halves and remove pits.
3. Knead dough briefly to develop dough texture. Divide dough into quarters and form each dough piece into a ball.
4. Position dough piece on parchment paper on a wooden board. Press each dough piece into a circle by working it with the fingertips until 6–8 inches (15–20 centimeters) in diameter and about ¼ inch (½ centimeter) thick. Toward the end of this process, dip fingertips in olive oil

and so coat the entire upper surface of the dough with olive oil. Keeping a ½-inch (1-centimeter) rim around edge of pizza, spread tomatoes, then cheese and olives, all over pizza. Sprinkle a little olive oil all over and use fingertips to make sure that rim of pizza is well coated with olive oil. Decorate with fresh leaves of oregano. Leave to rise for 45 minutes or until puffy and nearly doubled in thickness.

5. Preheat oven and pizza stone at 425° F. (220° C.).

6. Transfer to oven on pele. Bake at 425° F. (220° C.) in preheated oven, for 15–20 minutes.

FAT PER ¼ PIZZA: With low-fat mozzarella cheese: saturated 4–6; unsaturated 5–7 grams

SPELT BARM BREADS

Spelt Scone Crown

This crown is a variation of the shape of bread found at Pompeii; it is designed to be pulled into small serving pieces. The recipe can also be made up into two plain scone loaves: two round flat dough pieces each divided into 8 or 16 segments, before being set to rise. Makes 4 cups (1,175 grams, about 2½ pounds) of dough.

FOR TWO 1-POUND (500-GRAM) LOAVES, 16 SCONES PER LOAF

3 cups (500 grams) whole-grain spelt flour including 2 teaspoons (5 grams) sprouted-wheat flour
½ teaspoon (2 grams) salt
1 tablespoon (40 grams) honey
1 tablespoon (8 grams) barley malt extract powder (nondiastatic)
½ cup (125 grams) water at 86° F. (30° C.)
2 cups (500 grams) whole spelt barm sponge (page 432)

1. Add flour to mixing bowl. In a separate bowl, dissolve salt, honey, and malt in water. Add this to mixing bowl followed by barm sponge. Mix until just completely blended. Cover and wait for 10 minutes to allow full absorption of liquids.

2. Knead briefly to develop dough texture. Divide dough into 8 equal-sized pieces and round each dough piece. Form a flat wheel from each of 4 dough pieces as follows: With the thumb, pierce through the center of the ball of dough and enlarge the hole to 2 inches (4–5 centimeters)

in diameter. Press the dough, on a marble slab, with fingertips to form a wheel of 6 inches (15 centimeters) in diameter and ¼ inch (½ centimeter) thick.

3. Form each of the remaining 4 dough pieces into a long strip ¼ inch (½ centimeter) thick, 1 inch (2 centimeters) wide, and long enough to surround the wheels.

4. Cover dough pieces and allow them to rest for 10 minutes. For each loaf, on parchment paper, position 2 wheels one on top of the other and then surround the wheels with 2 strips, also one on top of the other. Lightly press the pieces together with fingertips. Divide each loaf into 8 by cutting all the way through the dough with a dough cutter, across the diameter 4 times. Cover and allow to rise 45 minutes before baking.

5. Preheat oven, baking tiles, and cloche at 425° F. (220° C.). Bake under cloche for 20 minutes at 425° F. (220° C.).

6. Serve by breaking loaves into 16 servings.

FAT PER SCONE: Saturated trace; unsaturated 0.5 grams

Spelt Pocket Bread

These spelt pocket bread buns have a delicately different flavor and texture and are easier to make than hard-wheat flour pocket breads. Makes 4 cups (1,190 grams, about 2½ pounds) of dough.

FOR SIXTEEN 2-OUNCE (60–65 GRAMS) POCKET BREADS

  3 cups (500 grams) whole-grain spelt flour including 2 teaspoons
    (5 grams) sprouted-wheat flour
1–2 tablespoons (15 grams) olive oil
  ½ cup (125 grams) water at 86° F. (30° C.)
  ½ teaspoon (2 grams) salt
  1 tablespoon (40 grams) honey
  1 tablespoon (8 grams) barley malt extract powder (nondiastatic)
  2 cups (500 grams) whole spelt barm sponge (page 432)

1. In mixing bowl, rub flour and oil together. Separately dissolve salt, honey, and malt in water. Add solution to mixing bowl followed by barm sponge. Mix until just blended. Consistency should be just stiff enough for breads to hold their shape.

2. Divide dough into 16 equally sized pieces, form each into a ball. Cover and allow to rest for 10 minutes. With lightly floured hands and work surface, use fingertips to press each dough piece out to 4–6 inches (10–15 centimeters) in diameter, and ½ centimeter or less thick. Turn the breads over frequently. Leave the margin of each prepared bread intact by always working from the center of these breads. Arrange breads on a lightly floured board, cover them, and allow them to rise for 45 minutes.

3. Preheat broiler (on high setting) and baking tiles. Allow enough space between broiler and tiles for bread to puff and form pocket. Arrange breads (tops uppermost, or they may not puff!) on hot oven tiles. Broil until they puff and then turn them over to cook underside. Broiling time is 1–2 minutes for top and 1 minute for underside. Best texture is achieved by keeping browning to a minimum.

FAT PER POCKET BREAD: Saturated trace; unsaturated 1–2 gram

References

Books and articles that have been great sources of information while writing the Superpyramid Program

BOOKS
Food, health, history, geography of health and disease

American Heart Association. *Heart and Stroke Facts.* 1991.

Bianchini, F., Corbetta, F., and Pistoia, M. *The Complete Book of Fruits and Vegetables.* New York: Crown, 1973.

Cambell-Pratt, G. *Fermented Foods of the World.* London: Butterworth's, 1987.

Kahn, R. J. *The Staff of Life.* Boston: Little, Brown, 1984.

Keys, A. *Seven Countries.* Cambridge: Harvard University Press, 1980.

Lappe, Frances Moore. *Diet for a Small Planet.* New York: Ballantine, 1982.

Klein, Maggie Blyth. *The Feast of the Olive.* Berkeley: Arts Books, 1983.

National Research Council. *Diet and Cancer.* Washington, D.C.: National Academy Press, 1982

National Research Council. *Diet and Health,* Washington, D.C.: National Academy Press, 1989.

Nieman, David C., Butterworth, Diane E., and Nieman, Catherine N. *Nutrition.* Wm. C. Brown Publishers, 1990.

Paul, A. A., and Southgate, D. A. T. *The Composition of Foods.* London: Her Majesty's Stationery Office, 1978.

Rifkin, Jeremy. *Beyond Beef.* New York: Dutton, 1992.

Senate Select Committee on Nutrition and Human Needs: *Diet Related to Killer Diseases.* Washington, D.C.: U.S. Government Printing Office, 1977.

Simeti, Mary Taylor. *Pomp and Sustenance.* New York: Knopf, 1989.

Spiller, Gene A. *Handbook of Dietary Fiber in Human Nutrition.* Boca Raton, Fla.: CRC Press, 1986.

————. *The Methylxanthine Beverages and Foods.* New York: Alan Liss, 1985.

Spiller, Monica. *The Barm Bakers' Book.* Los Altos, Calif.: HRS Publishing, 1992.

Tannahill, Reay. *Food in History.* New York: Crown, 1988.

Trowell, Hugh C., and Burkitt, Denis P. *Western Diseases.* Cambridge: Harvard University Press, 1981.

Visser, Margaret. *Much Depends on Dinner.* New York: Grove Press, 1986.

Yamuna, Devi. *The Art of Indian Vegetarian Cooking.* New York: Bala Books, 1987.

Exercise, fitness, toxic substances

Cooper, Robert K. *Health and Fitness Excellence.* Boston: Houghton Mifflin, 1989.

Farquhar, John W., and Spiller, Gene A. *The Last Puff.* New York: W. W. Norton, 1991.

Lidell, Lucy. *The Sensual Body.* New York: Simon & Schuster, 1987.

National Research Council. *Alternative Agriculture.* Washington, D.C., National Academy Press, 1989.

ARTICLES AND SCIENTIFIC PAPERS

To avoid a long list of published scientific articles, only key ones are listed. For the reader interested in additional publications on the subject, the articles listed here have long bibliographies for additional reading and study.

Boyle, P., and Zaridze, D. G. "Colorectal Cancer as a Disease of the Environment." *Ecology of Disease,* 1983, 2:241–48.

Braun, Thomas, in *The Mediterranean Diets in Health and Disease* (G. Spiller, ed.), New York: Van Nostrand, 1991.

Burkitt, D. P. "Epidemiology of Cancer of the Colon and Rectum." *Cancer,* 1971, 28:3–13.

Cotton, P. "Data Finally Show Overall Mortality Benefits." *Medical World News,* 1988, 29:45–53.

Banj, H. O., Dyerberg, J., and Nielsen, A. B. "Plasma Lipids and Lipoprotein Pattern in Greenlandic West-Coast Eskimos." *Lancet,* 1971, II:1143–46.

De Boer, J. O., van Ex, A. J. H., et al. "Adaptation of Energy Metabolism to Low Energy Intake." *American Journal of Clinical Nutrition,* 1986, 44:585–95.

De Waard, F. "The Epidemiology of Breast Cancer." *International Journal of Cancer,* 1969, 4:577–86.

Doll, R. "The Geographical Distribution of Cancer." *British Journal of Cancer,* 1969, 23:1–8.

Frazer, G. E., Sabaté, J., et al. "A Possible Protective Effect of Nut Consumption on Risk of Coronary Heart Disease." *Archives of Internal Medicine,* 1991, 152:1416–24.

Grundy, S. M. "Monounsaturated Fatty Acids, Plasma Cholesterol, and Coronary Heart Disease." *American Journal of Clinical Nutrition,* 1987, 45 (5 Suppl):1168–75.

Jenkins, D. J. A., Wong, G. S., et al. "Leguminous Seeds in the Management of Hyperlipidemia." *American Journal of Clinical Nutrition,* 1983, 38:567–73.

Kastellot, H., Da Xien Huang, et al. "Serum Lipids in the People's Republic of China." *Arteriosclerosis,* 1985; 5:427–33.

Knekt, P., Aromaa, A., et al. "Serum Vitamin A and Subsequent Risk of Cancer." *American Journal of Epidemiology,* 1990, 132:857–69.

Lau, B. H. S. "Anticoagulant and Lipid Regulating Effects of Garlic *(Allium sativum),*" in Spiller, G. A., and Scala, J., *New Protective Roles for Selected Nutrients.* New York: Alan Liss, 1989.

Leon, A. S. "Age and Other Predictors of Coronary Heart Disease." *Medicine and Science in Sport and Exercise,* 1987, 19:159–67.

Lissner, L., Odell, P. M., et al. "Variability of Body Weight and Health Outcomes in the Framingham Population." *New England Journal of Medicine,* 1991, 324:1839–44.

Mattson, F. H. "A Changing Role for Dietary Monounsaturated Fatty Acids." *Journal of the American Dietetic Association,* 1989, 89(3):387–91.

McDonald. B. E., Gerrard, J. M., Bruce, V. M., and Corner, E. J. "Comparison of the Effect of Canola Oil and Sunflower Oil on Plasma Lipids and Lipoproteins and on in vivo Thromboxane A_2 and Prostacyclin Production in Healthy Young Men." *American Journal of Clinical Nutrition,* 1989, 50: 1382–88.

McMurray, P. M., Cerquerira, M. T., et al. "Changes in Lipids and Lipoprotein Levels and Body Weight in Tarahumara Indians after Consumption of an Affluent Diet." *New England Journal of Medicine,* 1991, 325:1794–1808.

Mensink, R. P., de Groot, M. J., van den Broeke, L. T., et al. "Effects of Monounsaturated Fatty Acids versus Complex Carbohydrates on Serum Lipoproteins and Apoproteins in Healthy Men and Women." *Metabolism,* 1988, 38 (2):172–78.

Mensink, R. P., and Katan, M. B. "Effect of a Diet Enriched with Monounsaturated or Polyunsaturated Fatty Acids on Levels of Low-density and High-density Lipoprotein Cholesterol in Healthy Women and Men." *New England Journal of Medicine,* 1989, 321(7):436–41.

Muir, C. S., and Parkin, D. M. "The World Cancer Burden: Prevent or Perish." *British Medical Journal,* 1985, 290:5–6.

National Institutes of Health. "Lowering Blood Cholesterol to Prevent Heart Disease." Consensus Development Conference Statement, Vol. 5, no. 7, 1985.

Peto, R., Doll, R., et al. "Can Dietary Beta-carotene Meterially Reduce Human Cancer Rates?" *Nature,* 1981, 290:201–208.

Pisani, P., Berrino, F., et al. "Carrots, Green Vegetables and Lung Cancer." *International Journal of Epidemiology.* 1986, 5:463–68.

Qureshi, A. A., Burger, W. C., et al. "The Structure of an Inhibitor of Cholesterol Biosynthesis Isolated from Barley." *Journal of Biological Chemistry,* 1986, 261:10544–50.

Riccardi, G., and Rosalba, G., in *The Mediterranean Diets in Health and Disease* (G. Spiller, editor). New York: Van Nostrand, 1991.

Salvaggio, A., Periri, K., et al. "Coffee and Cholesterol, an Italian Study." *American Journal of Epidemiology,* 1991, 134:149–56.

Smith, G. D., Shipley, M. J., et al. "Plasma Cholesterol Concentration and Mortality." *Journal of the American Medical Association,* 1992, 267:70–76.

Snowdon, D., Philips, R., and Fraser, G. "Meat Consumption and Fatal Ischemic Heart Disease." *Preventive Medicine,* 1984, 13:490–500.

Spiller, G. A. "Beyond dietary fiber." *American Journal of Clinical Nutrition,* 1991, 54(4):615–17.

———. "Health Effects of Mediterranean Diets and Monounsaturated Fats." *Cereal Foods World,* 1991, 36:812.

Spiller, G. A., Jenkins, D. J. A., Cragen, L. N., et al. "Effect of a Diet High in Monounsaturated Fat from Almonds on Plasma Cholesterol and Lipoproteins." *Journal of the American College of Nutrition,* 1992, 11(2):126–30.

Stehr, P. A., Gloninger, M. F., et al. "Dietary Vitamin A Deficiency and Stomach Cancer." *American Journal of Epidemiology,* 1985, 121:65–70.

Trevisan, M., Krogh, V., Freudenheim J., et al. "Consumption of Olive Oil, Butter, and Vegetable Oils and Coronary Heart Disease Risk Factors." The Research Group ATS-RF2 of the Italian National Research Council. *Journal of the American Medical Association,* 1990, 263(5):688–92.

Watson, R. R., and Leonard, T. K. "Selenium and Vitamins A, E, and C: Nutrients with Cancer Prevention Properties." *Journal of the American Dietetic Association,* 1986, 86:505–510.

Willet, C. W. "The Search for the Causes of Breast and Colon Cancer." *Nature,* 1989, 338:389–94.

Willet, C. W., Stampfer, M. J., et al. "Relation of Meat, Fat, and Fiber Intake to the Risk of Colon Cancer in a Prospective Study Among Women." *New England Journal of Medicine,* 1990, 323:1664–72.

Some Cookbooks Adaptable to The Superpyramid Program

Angel, Gilda. *Sephardic Cooking*. Mount Vernon, N.Y.: Decalogue Books, 1986.

Brody, Jane. *Good Food Book*. New York: Bantam, 1987.

Caggiano, Biba. *Northern Italian Cooking*. Tucson: H.P. Books, 1981.

Connor, Sonja L., and Connor, William E. *The New American Diet*. New York: Simon and Schuster, 1986.

Cunningham, Marion; Laber, Jeri; and Farmer, Fannie Merritt. *The Fannie Farmer Cookbook*. Twelfth Edition. New York: Bantam Books/Alfred Knopf, 1979.

David, Elizabeth. *A Book of Mediterranean Food*. Middlesex, England: Penguin Books, 1965.

———. *English Bread and Yeast Cookery*. American Edition, with notes by Karen Hess. Middlesex, England: Penguin Books, 1980.

———. *Italian Food*. Middlesex, England: Penguin Handbooks, 1977.

Elliot, Rose. *Vegetarian Dishes from around the World*. New York: Pantheon Books, 1981.

Garland, Sarah. *The Complete Book of Herbs and Spices*. New York: The Viking Press, 1979.

Goldbeck, Nikki, and Goldbeck, David. *American Wholefoods Cuisine*. New York: New American Library, 1983.

Greene, Bert. *The Grains Cookbook*. New York: Workman Publishing, 1988.

Gregory, Patricia H. *Bean Banquets*. Santa Barbara: Woodbridge Press, 1984.

Hartley, Dorothy. *Food in England*. London: Macdonald and Jane's, 1954.

Hirsh, David. *The Moosewood Restaurant Kitchen Garden*. New York: Simon and Schuster/Fireside, 1992.

Hoshijo, Kathy. *Kathy Cooks*. New York: Simon and Schuster/Fireside, 1989.

Jaffrey, Madhur. *A Taste of India*. London: Pavillion, 1987.

Katzen, Mollie. *The Enchanted Broccoli Forest*. Berkeley: Ten Speed Press, California, 1982.

Kennedy, Diana. *The Cuisines of Mexico*. New York: Harper & Row, 1972

Klein, Maggie Blyth. *The Feast of the Olive*. Berkeley: Art Books, 1983.

Kluger, Marilyn. *The Wild Flavor*. New York: Henry Holt and Co., 1990.

La Place, Viana. *Verdura: Vegetables Italian Style*. New York: William Morrow, 1991.

La Place, Viana, and Kleiman, Evan. *Cucina Fresca*. New York: William Morrow, 1990.

———. *Cucina Rustica*. New York: William Morrow, 1990.

———. *Pasta Fresca*. New York: William Morrow, 1988.

Lappé, Frances Moore. *Diet for a Small Planet: High Protein Meatless Cooking*. New York: Ballantine Books, 1982.

Lee, Gary. *The Chinese Vegetarian Cook Book*. San Francisco: Nitty Gritty Productions, 1972.

Lo, Kenneth. *Chinese Food*. Middlesex, England: Penguin Books, 1972.

Madison, Deborah. *The Savory Way*. New York: Bantam, 1990.

Madison, Deborah, and Brown, Edward Espe. *The Greens Cookbook*. New York: Bantam Books, 1987.

Main, Jody, and Janello, Nancy. *Sprouts Are Good*. Saratoga, Calif.: Potted Plant Publishing, 1982.

Moosewood Collective. *New Recipes from the Moosewood Restaurant*. New York: Simon and Schuster/Fireside, 1987.

———. *Sunday at the Moosewood Restaurant*. New York: Simon and Schuster/Fireside, 1990.

Ornish, Dean. *Dr. Dean Ornish Program for Reversing Heart Disease*. New York: Random House, 1991. This book has an extensive recipe section.

Philips, Roger. *Wild Foods*. Boston: Little, Brown, 1986.

Raymond, Jennifer. *The Best of Jenny's Kitchen*. Little River, Calif.: SunRay Press, 1980.

Richmond, Sonya. *International Vegetarian Cookery*. New York: Arco Publishing Company, New York, 1974.

Robbins, John. *May All Be Fed: Diet for a New World*. New York: William Morrow, 1992.

Robertson, Laurel; Flinders, Carol; and Godfrey, Bronwen. *The Laurel's Kitchen Bread Book*. New York: Random House, 1984.

Robertson, Laurel; Flinders, Carol; and Ruppenthal, Brian. *The New Laurel's Kitchen*. Berkeley: Ten Speed Press, 1986.

Roden, Claudia. *A Book of Middle Eastern Food*. New York: Vintage Books, 1974.

————. *Mediterranean Cookery*. New York: Alfred A. Knopf, 1987.

Romagnoli, Margaret, and Franco, G. *Carnevale Italiano: The Romagnolis' Meatless Cookbook*. Boston: Little Brown and Company, 1976.

Rombauer, Irma S., and Becker, Marion Rombauer. *Joy of Cooking*. New York: New American Library, 1931.

Saltzman, Joanne. *Amazing Grains*. Tiburon, Calif.: HJ Kramer, 1990.

Sass, Lorna. *Recipes from an Ecological Kitchen*. New York: William Morrow, 1992.

Scott, Jack Denton. *The Complete Book of Pasta: An Italian Cookbook*. New York: Bantam Books, 1970.

Seddon, George, and Burrow, Jackie. *The Natural Food Cookbook*. New York: Exeter Books, 1978.

Shapira, Joel; Shapira, David; and Shapira, Karl. *The Book of Coffee and Tea*. New York, St. Martin's Press, 1975.

Shulman, Martha Rose. *Mediterranean Light*. New York: Bantam, 1989.

Shurtleff, William, and Aoyagi, Akiko. *The Book of Miso*. New York: Ballantine Books, 1982.

————. *The Book of Tempeh*. New York: Ballantine Books, 1982.

————. *The Book of Tofu*. New York: Ballantine Books, 1983.

Simeti, Mary Taylor. *Pomp and Sustenance*. New York: Alfred A. Knopf, 1989.

Singh, Dharamjit. *Indian Cookery*. Middlesex, England: Penguin Books, 1970.

Smith, Jeff. *The Frugal Gourmet*. New York: William Morrow, 1984.

————. *The Frugal Gourmet Cooks Three Ancient Cuisines*. New York: William Morrow, 1989.

Spencer, Colin. *Mediterranean Vegetarian Cooking*. Wellingborough, England: Thorsons Publishing Group, 1986.

Spiller, Monica. *The Barm Bakers' Book*. Los Altos: HRS Press, 1992.

Whyte, Karen Cross. *The Complete Sprouting Cookbook*. San Francisco: Troubadour Press, 1973.

Wolfert, Paula. *Couscous and Other Good Food from Morocco*. New York: Harper & Row, 1973.

Wood, Rebecca. *Quinoa: The Super Grain*. New York: Japan Publications distrib. Harper & Row, 1988.

Yoneda, Soei. *The Heart of Zen Cuisine*. Tokyo and New York: Kodansha International, 1987.

COOKING AND FOODS

Bianchini, Francesco; Corbetta, Francesco; and Pistoia, Marilena. *The Complete Book of Fruits and Vegetables*. New York: Crown Publishers, 1976.

Root, Waverly. *The Food of Italy*. New York: Vintage Books, 1977.

Further Readings and References on Breadmaking

Beard, James. *Beard on Bread.* New York: Knopf, 1973.

Brown, Edward Espe. *The Tassajara Bread Book.* Boulder, Colo.: Shambhala, 1970.

Clayton, Bernard Jr. *The Breads of France.* New York: Bobbs-Merrill, 1978.

David, Elizabeth. *English Bread and Yeast Cookery.* Middlesex, England: Penguin, 1979.

Field, Carol. *The Italian Baker.* New York: Harper & Row, 1985.

Ojakangas, Beatrice. *The Great Scandinavian Baking Book.* Boston and Toronto: Little, Brown, 1988.

Pyler, E. J. *Baking Science & Technology,* Volumes I & II. Merriam, Kansas: Sosland Publishing Company, 1988.

Robertson, Laurel; Flinders, Carol; and Godfrey, Bronwen. *The Laurel's Kitchen Bread Book: A Guide to Whole-Grain Breadmaking.* New York: Random House, 1984.

Romer, Elizabeth. *Italian Pizza and Savory Breads.* London: Grafton Books, 1990.

Spiller, Monica A. "A Mixture of a *Lactobacillus Brevis* and a *Saccharomyces Dairiensis* for Preparing Leavening Barms," U.S. Patent No. 4,666,719; May 1987.

Sources

M ost of the ingredients for a Superpyramid meal can be found in supermarkets, specialty or ethnic stores, and farmers' markets. A few ingredients may not be available in your area and the following sources can either supply them or refer you to a proper outlet.

WHOLE GRAINS AND WHOLE-GRAIN FLOURS

Arrowhead Mills Inc.
110 South Lawton
Hereford, TX 79045
806-364-0730
Whole grains and whole-grain flours

Giusto's Specialty Foods
241 East Harris Avenue
South San Francisco, CA 94080
415-873-6566
Whole grains and whole-grain flours

Kamut Association of
    North America
295 Distribution Street
San Marcos, CA 92069
619-752-5230
Kamut

Maskal Teff
1318 Willow
Caldwell, ID 83605
208-454-3330
Teff

WHOLE GRAINS AND WHOLE-GRAIN FLOURS (continued)

Lundberg Family Farms
P.O. Box 369
Richvale, CA 95974
916-882-4551
Specialty brown rice varieties

Purity Foods
2871 West Jolly Road
Okemos, MI 48864
517-351-9231
Spelt

Walnut Acres
Penn Creek, PA 17862
717-847-0601
Whole grains and whole-grain flours

CULTURES FOR MILK, SOY PRODUCTS, AND BREADMAKING

ASI Inc.
P.O. Box 696
Los Altos, CA 94023
415-941-8288
Dried leavening barm, acidity testing paper, barm cookbooks

GEM Cultures
30301 Sherwood Road
Fort Bragg, CA 95437
707-964-2922
Cultures for sourdough breads; tempeh, miso, and other cultured soy products; kefir and other unusual milk cultures; food culturing cookbooks (and sea vegetables); dried leavening barm

Gold Rush Sourdough
Cal-Gar (Production Plant)
383 Beach Road
Burlingame, CA 94010
201-691-2928
Dry sourdough starter for use with bakers' yeast.

Rosell Institute Inc.
8480 Boulevard St-Laurent
Montréal, Quebec, Canada
H2P 2M6
514-381-5631
Cultures for yogurt, kefir, buttermilk, acidophilus milk; insulated yogurt maker

EDIBLE FLOWER AND HERB SEEDS

Seeds of Change
621 Old Santa Fe Trail #10
Santa Fe, NM 87501
505-983-8956
Both suppliers have a wonderful edible flowers and herb seed collection to help get you started growing safe flowers and fresh herbs.

Shepherd's Garden Seeds
7389 W. Zayante Rd.
Felton, CA 95018

OLIVES AND EXTRA-VIRGIN OLIVE OILS

Peloponnese
2227 Poplar Street
Oakland, CA 94607
510-839-8153
Olive oils and olives from Greece

Santa Barbara Olive Co.
1661 Mission Dr.
Santa Barbara, CA 93463
805-688-9917
Olives and olive oils

Sciabica
P.O. Box 1246
Modesto, CA 95353
209-577-5067
California olive oils

International Olive Oil Council
733 3rd Ave.
New York, NY 10017
212-297-0136
Information on olive oils from different countries

Unusual Vegetable Oils
Specrum Natural
133 Copeland, Street
Petaluma, CA 94952
707-778-8900
A wide variety of vegetable oils

SEA VEGETATION

Mainecoast Sea Vegetables
Shore Road
Franklin, ME 04634
207-565-2907
Edible sea vegetation

Rising Tide Sea Vegetables
P.O. Box 1914
Mendocino, CA 95460
707-937-2109
Edible sea vegetation

KITCHEN EQUIPMENT

Magic Mill
235 West 200 South
Salt Lake City, UT 84101
801-322-1668
High-speed domestic grain mill

Sassafras Enterprises, Inc.
1622 West Carol Avenue
Chicago, IL 60612
312-226-2000
Unglazed ceramic baking tiles, bread cloches (domes), baking pots

Williams-Sonoma
100 North Point Street
San Francisco, CA 94133
415-421-7900
Specialty kitchen equipment

Recipe Index

Acapulco salad, 263
aioli (garlic mayonnaise), 232
almond(s), 208–10, 291–94, 385–86,
    452–54
  and baby sprouted seeds with fruit
    salad, 386
  -broccoli-potato soup, hearty, 291
  eggplant appetizer, 350
  fat content of, 208
  -hazelnut delight, 385
  milk, 239
  oil and wheat barm piecrust, pear pie
    with, 453–54
  Roman ground, and chicken soup or
    stew, 378
  sprouting of, 216
  -vegetable soup, 293–94
  and wheat barm piecrust, apple pie
    with, 452–53
  wild rice salad with lemon vinaigrette
    and, 251–52
  yogurt cheese with honey, fruit, and,
    383
amandine:
  broiled fillet of sole, 375
  lentil-pumpkin soup, 292–93
Angel, Gilda, 311
anise liqueur with melon, 389
antipasto, summer vegetable, 248–49

appetizer, almond eggplant, 350
apple(s):
  pie with almond and wheat barm
    piecrust, 452–53
  Superpyramid scrambled eggs with,
    368
applesauce with kabocha squash, 347
apricots, dried, with quinoa, pistachios,
    and cumin vinaigrette, 254–55
aromatic gravy, roast turkey with, 377
Arte di Mangiar Bene, L' (Artusi), 323*n*
artichoke and carrot stew, spicy, 344–45
Artusi, Pellegrino, 322–25
arugula, whole-wheat spaghetti with,
    317–18
automatic breadmaking, 423–24
avocado(s):
  fat content of, 208
  open-faced sandwich with tomatillo
    salsa, 357
  Superpyramid scrambled eggs with,
    367

baked:
  egg-tofu patties, savory, 371
  red snapper on garlic toasts, 376
Baking Science and Technology (Pyle), 416
bananas, yogurt drink with berries and,
    365

481

salad dressing(s) (cont'd)
  yogurt, pita sandwiches with hummus
    and, 354
  yogurt, with cucumber salad, 247
  yogurt, with lemon and tahini, 225
  zucchini vinaigrette, 265
salmon, poached, 374
salsa:
  fresh garden, 235
  tomatillo, 228
  tomatillo, avocado open-faced
    sandwich with, 357
  verde, 230–31
  verde, summer minestrone with fresh
    tomatoes and, 284–85
salt, 415–16
sandwich(es), 351–55
  avocado open-faced, with tomatillo
    salsa, 357
  falafel, 352
  open-faced, with olive paste and low-
    fat mozzarella cheese, 357
  open-faced, with pesto and tomatoes,
    360
  pita, see pita sandwich(es)
  tempeh, with sprouts, 355
  with yogurt cheese, cucumbers, and
    tomatoes, 360
sauce(s), 218–21, 226–27, 230–35
  fresh tomato, 227
  garlic mayonnaise, 232–33
  garlic mayonnaise without eggs, 233
  Greek garlic, 221
  Lebanese tarator, 226
  miso, 238
  pear, with blue hubbard squash, 348–
    49
  pesto, see pesto
  Tunisian hot pepper, 234
  walnut, with delicata squash, 348
  yogurt, with mint, 364
  see also salsa; vinaigrette
savory:
  baked egg-tofu patties, 371
  chicken, 379
  soybeans, 334
savoy cabbage, buckwheat noodles with,
  319–20
scone(s), 449–51, 460–61
  crown, spelt, 465–66
  loaf, buttermilk, 451
  milk, 450
  plain, 449
scrambled eggs, Superpyramid, 367–
  68

seeds, 219
  baby sprouted, and almonds with fruit
    salad, 386
  fat content of, 208
  sprouting of, 216–17
Sephardic Holiday Cooking (Angel), 311
sesame oil, 208
skordalia (Greek garlic sauce), 221
soft wheat barm breads, see barm breads,
    soft wheat
sole amandine, broiled fillet of, 375
sorrel-potato soup, 272–73
soup(s), 266–96
  almond-vegetable, 293–94
  basic method for making, 266–67
  black bean chili, 280–81
  broths, 267
  buttermilk, with barley and cucumbers,
    278–79
  chicken and Roman ground almond,
    378
  good basic summer vegetable stock,
    270
  good basic winter vegetable stock, 269
  hearty broccoli-potato-almond, 291
  leek, mushroom, and potato, 272
  lentil, with spinach, 274–75
  lentil-pumpkin, amandine, 292–93
  minestrone, 281–89
  miso, 296
  miso broth, 295
  potato-fennel, 273
  potato-leek, 271
  potato-sorrel, 272–73
  southwestern corn, 294
  split-pea, with wild rice, 290
  split-pea, with yogurt, 276–77
  summer minestrone with fresh
    tomatoes and salsa verde, 284–85
  vegetable, with pesto, 281, 288–89
  vegetable stocks for, 267–70
  white bean and pasta, with sage, 281,
    286–87
soupe au pistou (vegetable soup with
    pesto), 281, 288–89
southwestern corn soup, 294
soybeans:
  savory, 334
  see also specific soybean products
spaghetti with arugula, whole-wheat,
    317–18
spelt, 410–12
  barm breads, see barm breads, spelt
spiced, spicy:
  artichoke and carrot stew, 344–45

Subject Index

acidophilus milk, 89–90
addicting substances, 194–95
addition-means-subtraction principle, 29–30
adzuki beans, 75, 77
aerobic exercises, 188–91
  weight control and, 200–201
Africa:
  coffees from, 172
  diet in, 4
age and aging:
  and breast cancer, 25
  and calcium intake, 28, 86–87
  osteoporosis in, 27–28, 86, 158
  and smoking, 195
alcoholic beverages, 176–78, 195
alfalfa sprouts, 115
almonds, 125–26, 131–33, 140–42, 181
  butter of, 133
  milk of, 131
  oil of, 125, 128–29, 132–33, 141
amaranth, 61, 66–67
American Cancer Society, 33, 101
American Heart Association, 33, 127
amino acids, 73
anasazi beans, 76–77
anise, 114
antioxidants, 57, 129–30
  in herbs, 164

in oils, 129
in vegetables and fruits, 99–100, 102, 104
Apicius cookery book, 58
apple cider vinegars, 164
apples, 121
apricots, 121
arabica coffees, 172
arrowroot, 68
artichokes, 114–15
artificial sweeteners, 154
arugula, 107, 164, 181
asparagus, 115
Assam tea leaves, 173
Australia, CHD and colon cancer in, 24
avocados:
  comparisons between olives and, 142–43
  in flat breads, 63
  magnesium in, 98
  oil of, 126, 128, 132–33, 142–43
  on third tier, 40, 122–23, 126, 128, 131–33, 142–43
  weight control and, 201

back pain, bone loss and, 87
bacon, 99, 156, 167
bagels, 64–65
bakers' yeast, 55